family talk

Edited by

Deborah Tannen

Shari Kendall

Cynthia Gordon

family talk

Discourse and Identity in

Four American Families

2007

OXFORD
UNIVERSITY PRESS

Oxford University Press, Inc., publishes works that further
Oxford University's objective of excellence
in research, scholarship, and education.

Oxford   New York
Auckland   Cape Town   Dar es Salaam   Hong Kong   Karachi
Kuala Lumpur   Madrid   Melbourne   Mexico City   Nairobi
New Delhi   Shanghai   Taipei   Toronto

With offices in
Argentina   Austria   Brazil   Chile   Czech Republic   France   Greece
Guatemala   Hungary   Italy   Japan   Poland   Portugal   Singapore
South Korea   Switzerland   Thailand   Turkey   Ukraine   Vietnam

Published by Oxford University Press, Inc.
198 Madison Avenue, New York, New York 10016

www. oup. com

Oxford is a registered trademark of Oxford University Press

Library of Congress Cataloging-in-Publication Data
Family talk : discourse and identity in four American families / edited by Deborah Tannen,
Shari Kendall, Cynthia Gordon.
p. cm.
Includes bibliographical references and index.
ISBN 978-0-19-531388-8; 978-0-19-531389-5 (pbk.)
1. Communication in the family—United States—Case studies.   2. Discourse
analysis—United States   I. Tannen, Deborah.   II. Kendall, Shari, 1965–
III. Gordon, Cynthia, 1975–
HQ536.F37835 2007
306.870973—dc22   2006049548

9 8 7 6 5 4 3 2 1

Printed in the United States of America
on acid-free paper

Acknowledgments

The research project on which these chapters are based was funded by the Alfred P. Sloan Foundation (grant #99-10-7 to Deborah Tannen and Shari Kendall and grant #B2004-40 to Deborah Tannen, Shari Kendall, and Cynthia Gordon); we thank our project officer Kathleen Christensen and the Sloan Foundation for their support. We also are indebted to the research assistants who helped the project come to fruition. Most earnestly, and endlessly, we are deeply grateful to the brave and generous families who made this study possible by opening their lives to us.

Contents

part II Gendered Identities in Dual-Income Families

part III Family Values and Beliefs

About the Contributors

Cynthia Gordon is a postdoctoral fellow at the Center for Myth and Ritual in American Life (MARIAL) at Emory University in Atlanta, Georgia. Her research interests include intertextuality, framing, family interaction, and the discursive construction of identities. Her articles have appeared in *Language in Society, Discourse & Society, Research on Language and Social Interaction, Narrative Inquiry, The Journal of Genetic Counseling,* and *Text & Talk.* <cynthia.gordon@emory.edu>

Alexandra Johnston received her M.A. in East Asian Studies from Stanford University. She was awarded a Fulbright Fellowship to study the education of "returnee" children in Osaka, Japan, and lived there for two years. She received her Ph.D. in Linguistics from Georgetown University. Her dissertation was on how U.S. immigration officers decide to approve or deny visas. She has contributed a chapter to *Discourse and Technology: Multimodal Discourse Analysis.* <johnstam@georgetown.edu>

Shari Kendall is Assistant Professor of Linguistics and Discourse Studies in the Department of English at Texas A&M University. Her research interests include gender and discourse, the discursive construction of identities, work and family discourse, framing and positioning, and interactional sociolinguistics. Her publications include articles in *Discourse & Society*, *Text & Talk*, and *Journal of the Association for Research on Mothering*, and chapters in *The Handbook of Language and Gender* and *Speaking Out: The Female Voice in Public Contexts*. <skendall@tamu.edu>

Philip LeVine worked as a graphic designer and instructor of design at the Academy of Art College in San Francisco. With support from a Regents' Scholarship, he conducted research on French literature and linguistics in Toulouse, France. He received his M.S. in Linguistics from Georgetown University, served as the book review editor of *Visual Communication*, and coedited *Discourse and Technology: Multimodal Discourse Analysis* with Ron Scollon. His early work with text and image inspired his focus on the interrelationship of talk, place, and space. <ps_levine@yahoo.com>

Diana Marinova is a Ph.D. candidate in the Linguistics Department at Georgetown University where she is currently working on her dissertation on neutrality in mediation hearings. Her areas of interest include professional discourse, cross-cultural communication, and applications of linguistics across disciplines. She is the author of a chapter in the 2004 *Proceedings of the Penn Linguistics Colloquium* and coeditor of *Language In Use: Cognitive and Discourse Perspectives on Language and Language Learning*. She also helped compile the 2002 PONS *English-Bulgarian Universal Dictionary*. <dsm7@georgetown.edu>

Aliza Sacknovitz is a Ph.D. candidate in the Department of Linguistics at Georgetown University. Her areas of research include language variation and change, language and identity, and Jewish languages. Her dissertation explores linguistic means of Orthodox Jewish identity construction, focusing on phonological and lexical features and situated discourse. Her publications include biographies of Niklas Luhmann, Henry Lee Smith, Jr., and Donna Jo Napoli for the *Encyclopedia of Language and Linguistics, 2nd edition*, and the coedited *Georgetown University Working Papers in Theoretical Linguistics, volume V*. <ais5@georgetown.edu>

Deborah Tannen is University Professor and Professor of Linguistics at Georgetown University. Her books include *You Just Don't Understand, Talking from 9 to 5, That's Not What I Meant!, I Only Say This Because I Love You*, and *You're Wearing THAT?: Understanding Mothers and Daughters in Conversation.* Her books *Conversational Style: Analyzing Talk Among Friends* and *Talking Voices: Repetition, Dialogue, and Imagery in Conversational Discourse* were recently reissued with new introductions. <www.deborahtannen.com>

Alla V. Tovares is Assistant Professor in the Department of English at Howard University. Her research interests include public/private intertextuality in everyday discourse, family discourse, and Bakhtin's dialogicality in language and interaction. Her articles have appeared in *Text & Talk* and the *Encyclopedia of Communication and Information.* <atovares@howard.edu>

Transcription Conventions

((*words*)) Double parentheses enclose transcriber's comments, in italics.

/words/ Slashes enclose uncertain transcription.

carriage return Each new line represents an intonation unit.

→ An arrow indicates that the intonation unit continues to the next line.

– A dash indicates a truncated intonation unit.

- A hyphen indicates a truncated word or adjustment within an intonation unit, e.g., repeated word, false start.

? A question mark indicates a relatively strong rising intonation.

. A period indicates a falling, final intonation.

, A comma indicates a continuing intonation.

. .	Dots indicate silence (more dots indicate a longer silence).
:	A colon indicates an elongated sound.
CAPS	Capitals indicate emphatic stress.
<laughs>	Angle brackets enclose descriptions of vocal noises, e.g., *laughs, coughs.*
*<manner>*words>	Angle brackets enclose descriptions of the manner in which an utterance is spoken, e.g. *high-pitched, laughing, incredulous.*
words[words] [words]	Square brackets enclose simultaneous talk.

family talk

SHARI KENDALL

one

Introduction: Family Talk

Families are the cradle of language, the original site of everyday discourse, and a touchstone for talk in other contexts.[1] Families are created in part through talk: the daily management of a household, the intimate conversations that forge and maintain relationships, the site for the negotiation of values and beliefs. Yet there has been a greater focus on language in workplaces and other formal institutions than on discourse in this first institution. The chapters in this volume fill this gap in sociolinguistic research by bringing together a variety of linguistic studies based on a single set of data: the naturally occurring, face-to-face interactions of four American families. The studies emerged from a three-year sociolinguistic project carried out at Georgetown University to examine how parents in dual-income families use language to constitute their identities as parents and professionals at home and at work, as well as the interactional and social consequences of these ways of speaking. Since the workplace has received relatively more attention in studies of discourse, this volume focuses on the language the four women and four men use as

---

1. I appreciate Deborah Tannen's and Cynthia Gordon's helpful comments on this chapter.

they interact with one or more family members, with the addition of one father's social talk about family at work.

The volume contributes to the discourse analysis of naturally occurring interaction in general, and of family interaction in particular, while also making significant contributions to theories of framing in interaction and the linguistic creation of identity. Together, the chapters extend our knowledge of family discourse and identify new ways in which family members construct, negotiate, and enact the individual and collective identities that constitute a family. Furthermore, whereas the vast majority of work on family discourse focuses on mothers, several chapters consider the relatively understudied language of fathers. Likewise, a substantial amount of research on family discourse has been based on mealtime interactions recorded in the presence of researchers (Blum-Kulka 1997; Erickson 1982; Ochs & Taylor 1995; Ochs et al. 1992; Pontecorvo & Fasulo 1999; Paugh 2005). In contrast, the studies in this volume are based on interactions that occur in a wide range of settings, which more fully represent these families' experiences. As such, the chapters contribute to the sociolinguistic analysis of face-to-face interaction, some in areas that have been studied primarily through experimental observation, self-report surveys, and interviews. The data set is unique in discourse analysis because the audio recordings span a more extended period of time than previous studies, encompass a wider variety of contexts, and are relatively uncensored, as recordings were made with no researcher present. In addition, we, the researchers, were able to get to know the speakers well enough to place their utterances in context; and we have kept in contact with the families and have thus been able to observe how the families have changed during the seven years since the recordings were made. The volume is also unique in the fact that the same families are considered from multiple perspectives by different authors. This is especially notable in those instances in which different authors examine the same interactions for different purposes.

Three broad themes emerged in the authors' considerations of family discourse in these four families: the underlying dynamics of power and solidarity in the family context in general, and in the interactional framing of individual and shared family identities in particular; the negotiation of gendered identities in conjunction with family identities, especially in relation to the challenges dual-income couples face; and, finally, the complex discursive means through which family members actively assert, negotiate, and confirm their family's beliefs and values when children are present to create individual and shared family identities. These themes are explored further in the next section. In subsequent sections, I describe the genesis of the volume, explain the research methodology, introduce the families, and provide an overview of the chapters and the organization of the volume.

Themes in Family Discourse

Interactional Dynamics: Framing, Power, and Solidarity

The chapters in this volume use an interactional sociolinguistic approach, each drawing on research in one or more areas: linguistic anthropology and the ethnography of communication (e.g., Erickson 1975; Gumperz & Hymes 1972); discourse strategies (e.g., Becker 1995; Gumperz 1982; Tannen 2007 [1989]); dimensions of power and solidarity in interaction (Tannen 1994a); framing theory (e.g., Bateson 1972; Goffman 1981; Tannen 1994b; Tannen & Wallat 1987); and those frameworks similar to framing in their use of stance, alignment, and/or positioning (e.g., Davies & Harré 1990; Ochs 1993; Schiffrin 1996). Two of these frameworks in particular are fundamental to understanding language in interaction in general and family discourse in particular: the frameworks of power and solidarity and framing. In previous work, Tannen (1994a) develops a framework of the ambiguity and polysemy of power and solidarity, arguing that in studying interaction, scholars need to understand that power (or hierarchy, or control) and solidarity (or connection, or intimacy) are not separate, but inextricably intertwined. Tannen (2003) applies the model to family discourse to address the trend to focus exclusively on the power dimension of discourse in families at the expense of the equally influential dimension of intimacy and connection (Blum-Kulka 1997; Ervin-Tripp et al. 1984; Ochs & Taylor 1995; Varenne 1992; Watts 1991). She considers the role of "mother" to illustrate that both family relationships and gender identities within families are negotiated along the dimensions of both power and connection.

In her contribution to this volume (chapter 2), Tannen further demonstrates that family interaction is an ideal site for exploring the complex interrelationship between power and solidarity as relationships among family members are "fundamentally hierarchical" and also "intensely connected." She argues that discourse analysts must consider an utterance's potential for being both a power maneuver and connection maneuver simultaneously. Marinova (chapter 5) uses Tannen's framework to explain the challenges parents (in this case, a father) face in balancing connection and control as children get older. Although it is not the focus of her analysis, Johnston (chapter 7) uses Tannen's framework to reconcile a seeming contradiction between what some parents say and what they do. She suggests that parents may simultaneously serve as gatekeepers in domains such as caregiving and financial management while explicitly expressing egalitarian views for professional and parental role sharing because retaining control of these domains may fulfill family members' co-existing needs for connection and control.

Within interactional sociolinguistics, framing theory is equally crucial for understanding conversational dynamics in family discourse. In the first sociolinguistic volume on framing, Tannen (1993) demonstrates that framing theory is fundamental to linguistic discourse analysis and, conversely, that discourse analysis provides valuable insight into the linguistic means by which frames are actively created. Drawing on Bateson (1972), she explains that "no communication move, verbal or nonverbal, can be understood without reference to a metacommunicative message, or metamessage, about what is going on—that is, what frame of interpretation applies to the move" (Tannen 1993:3). In 1974, Goffman elucidated the levels and types of framing that constitute everyday interaction; and, in his later work (1981), he focused more specifically on language in examining "footings," which he used to capture the subtle shifts in framing and the multiple layers of framing in everyday life. Several chapters in this volume use a framing approach—drawing on the concepts of framing, footing, positioning, and alignment—to show how family members use particular linguistic resources to effect shifts in framing that, among other functions, contribute to family members' negotiations of shared family identities (Tannen, chapter 3), and the individual family identities of "mother" (Gordon, chapter 4) and "father" (Marinova, chapter 5).

Gender, Work, and Family

The second theme in family discourse addressed in this volume is the discursive creation of gendered identities in the family, especially in relation to the links between work and family. Studies of gender in the family are surprisingly rare, given the significance of gender in this domain and the substantial literature on gender and language in other domains. As Kendall suggests elsewhere (2004a), the relative lack of research on gender in family discourse may be a reflex of the women's movement of the 1970s, when the study of gender in linguistics emerged (Lakoff 1975). In a sense, women were demanding choices besides marriage and motherhood, so the focus was on getting women out of the home, not back into it. For this reason, discourse analyses of gender have focused on women's discourse in the workplace (e.g., Ainsworth-Vaughn 1998; Kendall 2004b; Tannen 1994b, c; Kotthoff 1997; McElhinny 1993; West 1990). In addition, although sociologists, anthropologists, and feminists have long recognized the family as a social institution, the study of gender in the family has been excluded from research in this area. For example, Drew & Heritage (1992:59 fn. 1) explicitly exclude family discourse from institutional language: "Notwithstanding the standard sociological usage within which the family is also a social institution, we will avoid using the term to describe activities that would be glossed as family dinners, picnics, and the like."

Gender infiltrates nearly all the chapters in this volume but is forefronted in three chapters that focus on gender as an achieved identity in a social constructivist paradigm. Scholars have found that women and men create gendered identities by using discursive strategies that index sociocultural expectations associated with gender as these individuals use language to accomplish other tasks (e.g., Ochs 1992; Tannen 1994b). Gordon (chapter 4) builds on this research and other work on language and identity to identify the discursive strategies through which one woman creates a gendered parental identity in a common domestic encounter: the babysitting report.

Other chapters bearing on gender contribute to our understanding of how language is used to negotiate, perpetuate, and mitigate challenges faced by dual-career families with children, particularly those families who have made a commitment to sharing childrearing responsibilities. The families participating in the research project represent a growing trend in the United States for both mothers and fathers to be employed outside the home (Clark 2002; Coontz 2000; Waite & Nielsen 2001). This change in the structuring of families raises the question of whether and how this shift influences families' daily lives and the gendered identities that mothers and fathers create both at home and in the workplace. These sociocultural factors provide the backdrop for the chapters by Kendall (chapter 6), Johnston (chapter 7), and Gordon, Tannen, and Sacknovitz (chapter 8). The chapters by Kendall and Johnston examine the interactions between spouses to consider how these women and men negotiate caregiving roles (Johnston) and caregiving and breadwinning roles (Kendall). Gordon et al. approach this question from the perspective of the workplace, examining how one man talks about family at work and relating the patterns to past findings on gender and social talk at work.

Family Values, Beliefs, and Shared Identities

The third theme of family discourse in this volume is the linguistic negotiation of family values, beliefs, and identities. In linguistics and linguistic anthropology, the study of family discourse has appeared primarily in the work of researchers in child language acquisition, such as Shoshana Blum-Kulka (1997) and Elinor Ochs and her colleagues and students (e.g., Ochs & Taylor 1995). These and other scholars have considered how parents socialize children to embrace family values: points of view and beliefs that characterize a family (Liebes & Ribak 1991, 1992; Liebes et al. 1991; Ochs 1992, 1993; Ochs, Smith & Taylor 1996; Pontecorvo & Fasulo 1997, 1999; Ribak 1997; Tulviste et al. 2002). Research on family discourse has focused on the socialization of interactional patterns that vary by culture, such as narrative practices (e.g., Blum-Kulka 1997); and it has been based primarily on mealtime interaction (e.g., Ochs, Smith & Taylor 1996; Pontecorvo & Fasulo 1999; Paugh 2005). Three chapters in this volume contribute to the extensive work addressing the socialization of family values and beliefs. However, these chapters do not focus on the child's language but instead widen the lens to identify new ways in which family members jointly assert, negotiate, and confirm their family's beliefs and values when children are present: through multiple, intertextual discourse strategies in the creation of a family's shared political identity (Gordon, chapter 9); by creating "common ground" in discussions about physical space (LeVine, chapter 10); and through dialogic interaction with the television (Tovares, chapter 11). Gordon demonstrates that a family political identity can be a fundamental component of family identity. She demonstrates how family members "work moment by moment to produce, negotiate, and socialize one another into the political aspect" of this identity. LeVine demonstrates that family values may be created, shared, and confirmed through talk about place as one father and son discuss who lives in the houses surrounding them. Tovares uses a Bakhtinian dialogic approach to demonstrate how families socialize children in interactions prompted by television programs.

Description of the Study

All the chapters examine a single body of data based on a research project supported by a grant from the Alfred P. Sloan Foundation to Shari Kendall and Deborah Tannen. Four dual-income families with children participated in this project. This section describes the events leading to this research project, then introduces the families and how they became involved in the study, and lastly explains how the data were collected.

Genesis of the Project

Although this volume is about family discourse, it first emerged for me as an interest in gender and language in the workplace, an interest further enhanced by a seminar Deborah Tannen was teaching on language in the workplace at Georgetown University in 1992, and by Tannen's (1994c) publication reporting her sociolinguistic study of talk in several large corporations. A central focus of Tannen's book, and of my own work, was exploring the linguistic means through which women and men express and constitute authority in the workplace (see Kendall & Tannen 1997; Kendall 2004b). However, one suggestion made by Tannen (1994c) continued to intrigue me: the possibility that women in positions of authority draw on images of mothers, or ways of speaking used by or associated with mothers, to constitute their institutional authority. To address this question, I employed the methodology used by Tannen (1994c) in her analysis of talk at work but extended the research design to include the workplace and the home as well. I arranged for one woman to tape-record herself both at work and at home to consider how she constituted her authority when speaking as a mother with her daughter and as a manager with her subordinates. This study was the basis for my dissertation, *The Interpenetration of Gendered Spheres* (Kendall 1999), which served as a pilot study for the project on which the present volume is based (see also Kendall 2003).

Meanwhile, Tannen shifted her focus to the relatively unstudied discourse in the family domain (see Tannen 2001, 2003a, b), which continues her focus on the language of everyday conversation in general and of interpersonal relationships in particular (Tannen 1984, 1986, 2007 [1989]). In 2000, Tannen and Kendall received funding for the research project on which this volume is based, from the Alfred P. Sloan Foundation. Tannen's contributions to this volume (chapters 2 and 3) reflect her focus on family discourse, while my contribution (chapter 6) reflects my focus on the intersection of work and family. Our co-editor, Cynthia Gordon, was a research team member on the original grant and coprincipal investigator on a follow-up grant.

Locating Families

The first task that Deborah Tannen and Shari Kendall faced when the research project began was to locate four families willing to tape themselves at work and at home. Tannen accepted several invitations to give lectures in the D.C. area and mentioned the project and our interest in finding participants at the end of her lectures. After each lecture, several attendees expressed an interest in volunteering. She also contacted the director of a women's center in Virginia, who offered to post flyers and include notices in their organizational newsletter. Kendall prepared notices and flyers to be posted at this and other locations, and she and several helpers posted flyers in key locations, such as video stores, cafes, and dry cleaners, within their respective residential areas. Finally, Tannen was a guest on *The Diane Rehm Show* (a radio talk show on NPR), discussing the topic of balancing work and family. During the broadcast, she mentioned the project and our interest in finding participants. Our requirements were that both parents work outside the home. Numerous potential volunteers contacted either Tannen or Kendall. Interestingly, many couples were willing to tape at home, but taping at work turned out to be an obstacle in many cases. In the end, we recruited the first four families who were willing, and got permission, to tape at work as well as home. Two families had one child between two and three, one had a four-year-old child, and the fourth had grown children, the youngest being in high school.

Taping

Once a couple had committed to participating, Tannen and Kendall met with them in their homes to describe the project and their terms of participation. Each parent tape-recorded themselves using Sony DATs (digital audio tape-recorders) and lavaliere microphones, which they carried with them. The DATs record continuously for four hours on one side of the tape without needing to be turned over, so they require only minimal attention; they are relatively small (about 3 by 5 inches); and they produce CD quality sound. Kendall met with each couple a few days before they began taping to provide them with the equipment and teach them how to use it. They were given a step-by-step instruction sheet prepared by Kendall for easy reference and were asked to tape-record for seven days from morning until night. After taping was completed, adult participants were shadowed by a research team member, who spent one or more days with them to become familiar with the family, the work situation, and their coworkers. Tannen and Kendall also arranged gatherings for each family so that all the research team members could meet the families. The tapes were then logged for content by, in most cases, the research team member who had shadowed that participant; and, finally, the tape recordings were transcribed by team members and other students at Georgetown University under the direction of Kendall.

Family Profiles

The four families who participated in the research project live in the greater Washington, D.C., area. All families are dual-income and middle-class (in accordance with the mandate of the Sloan Foundation); all families are also white. Parents in the participating families are highly educated, all but one having at least a bachelor's degree (and that one did attend college). All names are pseudonyms but reflect the parents' use of the same, different, or hyphenated surnames.

Janet & Steve Neeley-Mason

Janet and Steve Neeley-Mason and their daughter Natalie (2 years 11 months) lived in a quiet suburban housing development on the outskirts of the D.C. metro area in Virginia. The couple's last name, Neeley-Mason, is a hyphenated version of Janet and Steve's given last names (Neeley and Mason, respectively). The couple volunteered after Janet saw a flyer posted at one of her places of employment. At the time of recording, they were 33 years old and had been married for 6 years. Janet was about 7 months pregnant. Both grew up in Northern Virginia. Janet worked approximately 8 to 10 hours a week as a therapist in three locations to acquire internship hours toward her master's degree in psychotherapy. She had a bachelor's degree in theater. Steve worked full-time as a video producer and part-time as a waiter at two different restaurants. He also had a bachelor's degree in theater. Their daughter, Natalie, did not attend a daycare center because Janet and Steve arranged for one parent to be home while the other was at work when possible, and Janet's mother regularly assisted with childcare. Natalie did, however, attend preschool three days a week (from 8:30–12). Janet and Steve appear in the chapters by Tannen (chapter 2), Gordon (chapter 4), Kendall (chapter 6), and Tovares (chapter 11).

Kathy Peterson & Sam Foley

Kathy Peterson, Sam Foley, and their daughter Kira (2 years 1 month) lived on a busy street in the Virginia suburbs just outside the border of the District of Columbia. Kathy heard about the study when a professor in a course she was taking told her about Tannen's call for volunteers on the radio. Kathy and Sam were both 37 years old and had been married for 5½ years. Kathy was about 8 months pregnant at the time of recording. She grew up in Baltimore, Maryland. Sam grew up in the city in which they currently lived. Kathy worked as an advertising sales agent in a professional organization. Before Kira was born, she worked full-time (40 hours per week), and then reduced her hours to 30 hours per week, which was the situation at the time of recording. She supervised one (female) assistant. There were five people in her section at work, all women. She was taking courses one day a week in Baltimore toward a master's degree in psychology. Sam worked full-time as a physicist in a government organization. His section consisted of eight people, all men. He was taking courses toward a doctorate in astrophysics. Both Kathy and Sam worked 4 days a week so they could spend one weekday at home with Kira. The federal government makes the full-time, four-day schedule an option for most of its employees, so Sam was able to remain full-time. For the three weekdays neither parent was home, Kira was in daycare at Kathy's workplace. Kathy and Sam appear in the chapters by Tannen (chapters 2 and 3), Kendall (chapter 6), Johnston (chapter 7), and Tovares (chapter 11).

Clara Shepherd & Neil Sylvan

Clara Shepherd, Neil Sylvan, son Jason (4 years 10 months), and their two dogs, Tater and Rickie, lived on a quiet suburban street in Virginia at the outer edge of the D.C. metro area. The couple volunteered to participate in the project following a lecture Tannen gave at the organization where

Clara worked. Clara and Neil were 43 years old and had been together as a couple for 16 years. Clara, who was raised in Pennsylvania, was Assistant Director in a government organization. She had a master's degree in Public Administration and was taking courses to earn a master's degree in marriage and family therapy. Neil, whose father was in the military, had lived in Massachusetts, Virginia, Florida, and abroad. He was Vice President for Finance and Administration at a non-profit agency. He had a master's degree in business administration and was a Certified Public Accountant. Their son Jason attended preschool full-time. Clara and/or Neil appear in the chapters by Tannen (chapter 3), Gordon et al. (chapter 8), Gordon (chapter 9), LeVine (chapter 10), and Tovares (chapter 11).

Nora Marsh & Greg Bradley

The fourth family is Nora Marsh, Greg Bradley, and their three children: John (22), Susan (20), and Jeremy (17). The parents and youngest child lived on a quiet residential street in Maryland, just outside the D.C. metro area. They have a cat and a dog, a golden retriever. At the time of taping, the youngest child was in high school, the middle child was in college, and the oldest was a professional musician who was living with his parents temporarily before moving to San Francisco. This family first heard about the project when Nora attended a talk by Tannen about work-family issues. The parents were both 46 years old. Nora, originally from Boston, was the Assistant Head of a private school in Virginia. She was taking classes part-time to earn her master's degree in educational administration. Greg, who was originally from Connecticut, was an educational entertainer who performed a one-man show for children in public schools and theatrical venues. At the time of recording, Susan was visiting from college, so all three children were home. Nora and/or Greg appear in the chapters by Tannen (chapter 3), Marinova (chapter 5), and Tovares (chapter 11).

The Data

A total of 460 hours were recorded and transcribed. Janet and Steve tape-recorded 165 hours over the course of seven consecutive days beginning February 23, 2000. They were shadowed by Cynthia Gordon and Shari Kendall, respectively. Kathy and Sam tape-recorded 134 hours over the course of 14 consecutive days beginning February 18, 2000. One reason they tape-recorded longer than 7 days was due to technical difficulties with one of their tape-recorders. They were shadowed by Sigrid Norris and Alexandra Johnston. Clara and Neil recorded 89 hours over 7 days beginning November 6, 2000 (although for one day they taped only 2 hours). They were shadowed by Cynthia Gordon and Philip LeVine. Nora and Greg recorded 75 hours over 9 days beginning June 19, 2000. Nora recorded for 6 days and Greg recorded for 7 days. They were shadowed by Shari Kendall and Alexandra Johnston.

Chapter Overview

All chapters address in some way how identities are constructed, negotiated, and enacted moment by moment in the discourse of these families. The volume is divided into three parts reflecting the themes that emerged from the analyses, as described above. Chapters are placed with those other chapters that most share a single focus, although there are similarities that cross-cut these categories. I identify some of these similarities following the chapter summaries.

Part I, comprising chapters 2 through 5, focuses on the dynamics underlying family discourse, particularly framing and the dimensions of power and solidarity. The chapters show how analyses of these dynamics contribute to our understanding of how women and men discursively negotiate identities for themselves as mothers and fathers, and as members of a family. The volume begins with the two chapters by Deborah Tannen, which lay the foundation for subsequent chapters. In chapter 2, "Power Maneuvers and Connection Maneuvers in Family Interaction," Tannen outlines her framework of the ambiguity and polysemy of the dimensions of power and solidarity in conversational interaction as well as the importance of these dimensions in family discourse. She examines excerpts from two of the families (Janet & Steve, Kathy & Sam) to demonstrate that it is not possible to gain a full understanding of the dynamics of family interaction by focusing exclusively on the power dimension, as has been the tendency in studies of family discourse. Rather, speakers' utterances are complex interplays of both "power maneuvers" and "connection maneuvers": speakers struggle for the power to determine their own actions and influence the actions of others, and simultaneously seek connection, the desire to "reinforce and not undermine the intimate connections that constitute their involvement with each other as members of a family." Tannen concludes that discourse analysts must consider both dimensions when attempting to explain interactional patterns in family discourse.

In chapter 3, "Talking the Dog: Framing Pets as Interactional Resources in Family Discourse," Deborah Tannen introduces the discursive strategy of "ventriloquizing" to explain how family members use their pet dogs as a resource for managing interpersonal interactions and thus engage in "exhibiting, reinforcing, and creating their identity as a family." By examining the interaction in the two families that had pet dogs (Clara & Neil, Nora & Greg), she demonstrates that when a family member speaks as the dog or speaks to the dog in the presence of another family member, the speaker introduces a note of humor into the interaction, which shifts the framing and footing of the participants. The chapter further advances an understanding of framing in interaction, including the relevance of Bakhtin's notion of polyvocality for conversational discourse, in the sense that talking through pets allows speakers to distance themselves figuratively from their own utterances. It also introduces an enlightening discursive resource through which family members create and maintain a shared family identity.

In chapter 4, "I just feel horribly embarrassed when she does that": Constituting a Mother's Identity," Cynthia Gordon explores how one woman (Janet) linguistically creates a gendered parental identity while talking with her husband and her brother, who babysat their daughter. As her brother describes their daughter's misbehavior, the mother uses several interactional strategies in her responses that simultaneously work in concert toward constructing a coherent identity. Gordon demonstrates that when these verbal practices are interpreted within the sociocultural context, some of them are "sex-class linked" (Goffman 1977; Tannen 1994b) and others are linked to what it means to be a parent; together, they produce the identity "mother." Gordon's study contributes to research on the linguistic creation of identity in everyday interaction in general, and more specifically in family interaction, by demonstrating how gendered and parental identities are intertwined within family discourse.

In chapter 5, "Finding the Right Balance between Connection and Control: A Father's Identity Construction in Conversations with His College-Age Daughter," Diana Marinova draws on the frameworks of framing and power and solidarity to explore how one father (Greg) constructs his identity as a father in conversations with his twenty-year-old daughter.

She demonstrates, drawing on Tannen (2001), that the father engages in a complex balancing of a caretaking frame (forefronting hierarchy) and a sociable frame (forefronting connection) as he attempts to motivate his daughter to prepare for her upcoming study-abroad semester. She also demonstrates that he creates a parental identity with others (his wife, a travel agent, secretary, and neighbor) with whom he discusses the difficulties he is having in encouraging his daughter to take more responsibility. Marinova's analysis contributes to the linguistic creation of identity by considering how parental identities emerge through the language a parent uses to simultaneously reprimand his daughter and maintain an egalitarian father-daughter relationship. Accomplishing these disparate goals requires the father to engage in a complex negotiation of identities. The chapter also provides a rare glimpse into the discourse of fathers, and particularly into the conversational dynamics of a father and his grown daughter.

Chapters 6 through 8 in Part II consider the creation of family identities in relation to issues faced by dual-income couples. In chapter 6, "Father as Breadwinner, Mother as Worker: Gendered Positions in Feminist and Traditional Discourses of Work and Family," Shari Kendall demonstrates that when the women in two families (Janet, Kathy) talk about conflicts between work and family in a range of contexts, they are not merely concerned with who does what in the household but are engaged in a personal struggle between their parental and professional identities as they attempt to reconcile competing discourses of gender relations. When these women talk about work and family, they negotiate the forms and meanings of their parental and work-related identities through the positions they take up themselves and make available to their husbands in relation to traditional and feminist discourses about work and family. Using framing and positioning theory, Kendall demonstrates that these women articulate an ideology of egalitarian role sharing but linguistically position their husbands, though not themselves, as breadwinners. Kendall's chapter provides insights into how modern dual-income couples with children negotiate work-family issues by identifying complex relationships among language, sociocultural ideologies, discourses, and everyday practices. In addition, the analysis contributes to the discourse of face-to-face verbal interaction by considering strategies previously used to analyze representations of mothers and fathers in written texts and the media (Lazar 2000; Sunderland 2000).

In chapter 7, "Gatekeeping in the Family: How Family Members Position One Another as Decision Makers," Alexandra Johnston explores gatekeeping in the family context, where "gatekeeping" refers to "any situation in which an institutional member is empowered to make decisions affecting others" (Scollon 1981:4). Although the couple in one family (Kathy & Sam) espouses the discourse of "egalitarian coparenting," both spouses collaboratively position the mother as gatekeeper in the care of their child, and the father as gatekeeper in managing their finances. She suggests that the apparent discrepancy between this couple's ideology and behavior may result from their need to fulfill the co-existing but contradictory needs for connection and control (Tannen 2001; this volume, chapter 2). By using sociolinguistic methods, Johnston contributes to the study of maternal gatekeeping in social psychology, which tends to rely on self-report surveys and statistical correlations. She also contributes to the substantial literature on gatekeeping in sociolinguistics by identifying the linguistic means by which the identity of "gatekeeper" is (co-)constructed. Finally, Johnston's chapter is a groundbreaking application of gatekeeping to the family realm.

In chapter 8, "A Working Father: One Man's Talk about Parenting at Work," Cynthia Gordon, Deborah Tannen, and Aliza Sacknovitz examine how one father (Neil) talks about family at work. Specifically, the authors consider how this father interactionally creates and draws upon his identity as a father at work in conversations with his coworkers, and how being a parent interpenetrates the work sphere. The extent to which the father talks about his family in personal terms and the kinds of interactional rituals he engages in with his coworkers (e.g., troubles talk) contrast with prior observations about how men and fathers talk at work. The authors find that the father's identity as a parent serves as a resource for sociability with his coworkers and for providing support for colleagues who are also parents; that his parental responsibilities at times interfere with his work-related responsibilities; and that, through his talk about family at work, he positions himself as one half of a parenting team and also as a parenting expert. These findings provide insight into what it means to be a working father, while also providing a rare glimpse into the workplace discourse of a working father who does a significant amount of caregiving.

Chapters 9 through 11 in Part III focus on the discursive means through which family members negotiate and confirm their family's beliefs and values when children are present; and how, through this negotiation, family members create shared family identities. In chapter 9, "'Al Gore's our guy': Linguistically Constructing a Family Political Identity," Cynthia Gordon considers how members of one family, Clara, Neil, and their son Jason, who tape-recorded during the week of the 2000 U.S. Presidential Election, construct a family identity based on their support of Democratic Party candidate Al Gore. The chapter illustrates how family members use linguistic strategies to create a group, rather than individual, identity and how political socialization is multidirectional in the family context, where all family members play a role in constructing the family identity. It also contributes to research in political socialization, wherein researchers have previously claimed that the family is of great importance in this process but have relied on interviews and surveys.

In chapter 10, "Sharing Common Ground: The Role of Place Reference in Parent-Child Conversation," Philip LeVine considers the relationship between place and language in interactions in which a father (Neil) and his four-year-old son talk about their neighborhood surroundings. LeVine focuses on those instances in which awareness of surroundings surfaces as a topic of talk and explores how place reference contributes to the creation of a family identity. The father orients his son to a new physical condition in his environment (an unknown person working in the neighborhood) and helps him gain a better understanding of the social landscape of the neighborhood by talking about who lives where, with whom, and how these people and places differ from their own family and home. LeVine demonstrates that place serves as a resource for talk, that place and talk stand in a mutually constitutive relationship, and that family members may use such talk to strengthen interpersonal bonds and confirm matching perceptions and meanings connected to place, including shared family beliefs. By using sociolinguistic methods, LeVine contributes to the research area of cultural or humanistic geography, meeting a call for explorations of the ways in which language transforms "space" into a sense of "place." The chapter also contributes to the research area of language and identity by providing descriptions of means whereby individuals may create identities through oppositions and similarities to others.

In chapter 11, "Family Members Interacting While Watching TV," Alla V. Tovares investigates the relationship between the public and the private in family discourse by examining how family members in all four families linguistically engage with each other as they watch television. She demonstrates that family members negotiate and maintain their family's values, beliefs, and identities by repeating words and phrases from television programs. By uniting Tannen's (2007 [1989]) work on repetition as a discourse feature with Bakhtin's "dialogicality" and Kristeva's "intertextuality," Tovares argues that the public and private interpenetrate within interactions in which family members repeat television texts. She demonstrates that family members do not passively repeat words and phrases from television texts but create a "dialogic unity": a complex combination of public and private that is saturated with previous and new meanings. This talk both reflects and transforms the lives of the viewers and "links family members with the world that lies outside their circle of family and friends." Tovares contributes to our understanding of Bakhtin's relevance to the analysis of verbal interaction, and she provides a glimpse into a prevalent type of talk in which all the participants in this research project participated: watching and talking about television programs.

In addition to the themes represented in the three parts of the volume, the chapters share other theoretical, methodological, and topical aspects as well, including analyses of fathers' discourse in father-child interaction (LeVine, chapter 10; Marinova, chapter 5) and a father talking about family at work (Gordon et al., chapter 8); a focus on the linguistic creation of identities (Kendall, chapter 6; Gordon, chapter 4; Marinova, chapter 5); the extension of Bakhtin's notions of polyvocality (Tannen, chapter 3) and dialogicality and answerability (Tovares, chapter 11); intertextuality in language use across interactions involving some or all of the same interlocutors (Gordon, chapter 9; LeVine, chapter 10; Tovares, chapter 11); and the distinction between "us" and "them" in the creation of a shared family identity (Gordon, chapter 9; LeVine, chapter 10). In addition, the chapters are roughly divided between those focusing on how individuals use language to construct their identities within the family (chapters 3 through 8) and those that consider families as groups of individuals who together negotiate shared family identities (chapter 2, chapters 9 through 11). Finally, the chapters focus on different combinations of participants: parent-child interaction with a young child (LeVine, chapter 10); parent-child interaction with a grown child (Marinova, chapter 5); adult interaction (Gordon, chapter 4; Kendall, chapter 6; Gordon et al., chapter 8); family interaction involving children and both parents (Gordon, chapter 9); or a combination of these types (Tannen, chapters 2, 3; Johnston, chapter 7; Tovares, chapter 11).

Conclusion

The chapters of this volume together explore the themes of identity construction and how families accomplish "familyness" in their own unique ways. It contributes to work exploring how identities are constructed in discourse, the interactional dynamics underlying family discourse and how families create their sense of family in interaction. At the same time, it contributes to a frames-theoretic approach to the analysis of discourse in general and to the literature on family discourse in particular. It adds to work that has examined family discourse on the micro-level, focusing on specific linguistic features for analysis. The research design—providing relatively uncensored recordings of everything each family said for a week at home and at work—makes this a unique study that explores how families communicate across a range of contexts. In this, it provides a groundbreaking view of how dual-career, white, middle-class American families conduct their daily lives.

References

Ainsworth-Vaughn, Nancy. 1998. Claiming power in doctor-patient talk. Oxford: Oxford University Press.

Bateson, Gregory. 1972. Steps to an ecology of mind. New York: Ballantine.

Becker, A. L. 1995. Beyond translation: Essays toward a modern philology. Ann Arbor: University of Michigan Press.

Blum-Kulka, Shoshana. 1997. Dinner talk: Cultural patterns of sociability and socialization in family discourse. Mahwah, N.J.: Erlbaum.

Clark, Kim. 25 November 2002. Mommy's home: More parents choose to quit work to raise their kids. U.S. News & World Report, 32–33, 36, 38.

Coontz, Stephanie. 2000. The way we never were: American families and the nostalgia trap. New York: Basic Books.

Davies, Bronwyn, and Rom Harré. 1990. Positioning: Conversation and the production of selves. Journal for the Theory of Social Behavior 20(1).43–63.

Drew, Paul, and John Heritage, eds. 1992. Talk at work: Interaction in institutional settings. Cambridge: Cambridge University Press.

Erickson, Frederick. 1975. Gatekeeping and the melting pot: Interaction in counseling encounters. Harvard Educational Review 45(1).44–70.

Erickson, Frederick. 1982. Money tree, lasagna bush, salt and pepper: Social construction of topical cohesion in a conversation among Italian-Americans. Analyzing discourse: Text and talk. Georgetown University Round Table on Languages and Linguistics 1981, ed. Deborah Tannen, 43–70. Washington, D.C.: Georgetown University Press.

Ervin-Tripp, Susan, Mary Catherine O'Connor, and Jarrett Rosenberg. 1984.

Language and power in the family. Language and power, ed. Cheris Kramarae, Muriel Schultz, and William M. O'Barr, 116–135. New York: Sage.

Goffman, Erving. 1974. Frame analysis: An essay on the organization of experience. Boston: Northeastern University Press.

Goffman, Erving. 1977. The arrangement between the sexes. Theory and Society 4(3).301–331.

Goffman, Erving. 1981. Footings. Forms of talk, 124–159. Philadelphia: University of Pennsylvania Press.

Gumperz, John J. 1982. Discourse strategies. Cambridge: Cambridge University Press.

Gumperz, John J., and Dell Hymes. 1972. Directions in sociolinguistics: The ethnography of communication. New York: Holt, Rinehart & Winston.

Kendall, Shari. 1999. The interpenetration of (gendered) spheres: An interactional sociolinguistic analysis of a mother at work and at home. Washington, D.C.: Georgetown University dissertation.

Kendall, Shari. 2003. Creating gendered identities through directives at work and home. Handbook of language and gender, ed. Janet Holmes and Miriam Meyerhoff, 600–623. Malden, Mass., and Oxford: Blackwell.

Kendall, Shari. 2004a. Mother's place in Language and Woman's Place. Language and woman's place: Text and commentaries, revised and expanded edition, original text by Robin Tolmach Lakoff, ed. Mary Bucholtz, 202–208. New York: Oxford University Press.

Kendall, Shari. 2004b. Framing authority: Gender, face, and mitigation at a radio network. Discourse & Society 15(1).55–79.

Kendall, Shari, and Deborah Tannen. 1997. Gender and language in the workplace. Gender and discourse, ed. Ruth Wodak, 81–105. London: Sage.

Kotthoff, Helga. 1997. The interactional achievement of expert status: Creating asymmetries by "teaching conversational lecture" in TV discussions. Communicating gender in context, ed. Helga Kotthoff and Ruth Wodak, 139–178. Amsterdam: Benjamins.

Lakoff, Robin. 1975. Language and woman's place. New York: Harper and Row.

Lazar, Michelle M. 2000. Gender, discourse and semiotics: The politics of parenthood representations. Discourse & Society 11(3).373–400.

Liebes, Tamar, and Rivka Ribak. 1991. A mother's battle against TV news: A case study of political socialization. Discourse & Society 2(2).203–222.

Liebes, Tamar, and Rivka Ribak. 1992. The contribution of family culture to political participation, political outlook, and its reproduction. Communication Research 19(5).618–641.

Liebes, Tamar, Elihu Katz, and Rivka Ribak. 1991. Ideological reproduction. Political Behavior 13(3).237–252.

McElhinny, Bonnie S. 1992. "I don't smile much anymore": Affect, gender, and the discourse of Pittsburgh police officers. Locating power: Proceedings of the second Berkeley women and language conference, ed. Kira Hall, Mary Bucholtz, and Birch Moonwomon, 386–403. Berkeley, Calif.: Berkeley Women and Language Group.

Ochs, Elinor. 1992. Indexing gender. Rethinking context: Language as an interactive phenomenon, ed. Alessandro Duranti and Charles Goodwin, 335–358. Cambridge: Cambridge University Press.

Ochs, Elinor. 1993. Constructing social identity: A language socialization perspective. Research on Language and Social Interaction 26(3).287–306.

Ochs, Elinor, Ruth Smith, and Carolyn Taylor. 1996. Detective stories at dinnertime: Problem-solving through co-narration. The matrix of language: Contemporary linguistic anthropology, ed. Donald Brenneis and Ronald K. S. Macaulay, 39–55. Boulder, Colo.: Westview Press, Inc.

Ochs, Elinor, and Carolyn Taylor. 1995. The "Father knows best" dynamic in family dinner narratives. Gender articulated: Language and the socially constructed self, ed. Kira Hall and Mary Bucholtz, 97–121. New York and London: Routledge.

Ochs, Elinor, Carolyn Taylor, Dina Rudolph, and Ruth Smith. 1992. Storytelling as a theory-building activity. Discourse Processes 15(1).37–72.

Paugh, Amy L. 2005. Learning about work at dinnertime: Language socialization in dual-earner American families. Discourse & Society 16(1).55–78.

Pontecorvo, Clotilde, and Alessandra Fasulo. 1997. Learning to argue in family shared discourse: The reconstruction of past events. Discourse, tools, and reasoning: Essays on situated cognition, ed. Lauren B. Resnick, Roger Säljö, Clotilde Pontecorvo, and Barbara Burge, 406–442. Berlin: Springer.

Pontecorvo, Clotilde, and Alessandro Fasulo. 1999. Planning a typical Italian meal: A family reflection on culture. Culture and Psychology 5(3).313–335.

Ribak, Rivka. 1997. Socialization as and through conversation: Political discourse in Israeli families. Comparative Education Review 41(1).71–96.

Schiffrin, Deborah. 1996. Narrative as self-portrait: Sociolinguistic constructions of identity. Language in Society 25(2).167–203.

Scollon, Ron. 1981. Human knowledge and the institution's knowledge. Final report on National Institute of Education Grant No. G-80-0185: Communication patterns and retention in a public university, 1–26. Fairbanks, Alaska: Center for Cross-Cultural Studies, University of Alaska.

Sunderland, Jane. 2000. Baby entertainer, bumbling assistant and line manager: Discourses of fatherhood in parentcraft texts. Discourse & Society 11(2).249–274.

Tannen, Deborah. 1984. Conversational style: Analyzing talk among friends. Norwood, N.J.: Ablex. Rpt. Oxford University Press 2005.

Tannen, Deborah. 1986. That's not what I meant!: How conversational style makes or breaks relationships. New York: Ballantine.

Tannen, Deborah, ed. 1993. Framing in discourse. Oxford and New York: Oxford University Press.

Tannen, Deborah. 1994a. The relativity of linguistic strategies: Rethinking power and solidarity in gender and dominance. Gender and discourse, 19–52. Oxford and New York: Oxford University Press.

Tannen, Deborah. 1994b. The sex-class linked framing of talk at work. Gender and discourse, 95–221. New York: Oxford University Press.

Tannen, Deborah. 1994c. Talking from 9 to 5: Women and men at work. New York: HarperCollins.

Tannen, Deborah. 2001. "I only say this because I love you": Talking to your parents, partner, sibs, and kids when you're all adults. New York: Ballantine Books.

Tannen, Deborah. 2003a. Gender and family interaction. Handbook of language and gender, ed. Janet Holmes and Miriam Meyerhoff, 179–201. Malden, Mass., and Oxford: Blackwell.

Tannen, Deborah. 2003b. Power maneuvers or connection maneuvers? Ventriloquizing in family interaction. Linguistics, language, and the real world: Discourse and beyond. Georgetown University Round Table on Languages and Linguistics 2001, ed. Deborah Tannen and James E. Alatis, 50–62. Washington, D.C.: Georgetown University Press.

Tannen, Deborah. 2007 (1989). Talking voices: Repetition, dialogue, and imagery in conversational discourse. Cambridge: Cambridge University Press.

Tannen, Deborah, and Cynthia Wallat. 1987. Interactive frames and knowledge schemas in interaction: Examples from a medical examination/interview. Social Psychology Quarterly 50(2).205–216. Reprinted in Deborah Tannen, ed. 1993. Framing in discourse, 57–76. New York and Oxford: Oxford University Press.

Tulviste, Tiia, Luule Mizera, Boel de Geer, and Marja-Terttu Tryggvason. 2002. Regulatory comments as tools of family socialization: A comparison of Estonian, Swedish and Finnish mealtime interaction. Language in Society 31(5).655–678.

Varenne, Hervé. 1992. Ambiguous harmony: Family talk in America. Norwood, N.J.: Ablex.

Waite, Linda J., and Mark Nielsen. 2001. The rise of the dual-earner family: 1963–1997. Working families: The transformation of the American home, ed. Rosanna Hertz and Nancy L. Marshall, 23–41. Berkeley: University of California Press.

Watts, Richard J. 1991. Power in family discourse. Berlin: Mouton de Gruyter.

West, Candace. 1990. Not just doctor's orders: Directive-response sequences in patients' visits to women and men physicians. Discourse & Society 1(1).85–112.

part I

Interactional Dynamics: Power and Solidarity

DEBORAH TANNEN

two

Power Maneuvers and Connection Maneuvers

in Family Interaction

amily interaction[1] has long been the object of study by scholars in a
wide range of fields, but their ranks have been joined by linguists and
linguistic anthropologists relatively recently. Prominent among these
have been researchers concerned with understanding children's acquisition of language, such as Shoshana Blum-Kulka (1997) and Elinor Ochs
and her colleagues and students (Ochs et al. 1996; Ochs & Taylor 1992a,
1992b, 1995; Ochs et al. 1992). My own interest in family interaction
(Tannen 2001, 2003b) has developed out of my continuing focus on the
language of everyday conversation in general and of interpersonal relationships in particular (Tannen 1984, 1986, 2007 [1989]). In extending
my analysis of conversational discourse to the domain of family dis-

1. The power connection grid was first presented in Tannen (1994) and is reproduced
here with permission from Oxford University Press. The theoretical background on power
and solidarity as it applies to mothers is based on sections previously included in Tannen
(2003b). The introductory sections and parts of the analysis of the "homecoming" example
also appear in Tannen (2003a). The rest of this chapter is appearing here for the first time. I
would like to thank the generous and open-hearted families who participated in the project;
the research assistants who shadowed the families, transcribed the tapes, and directed me to
examples that matched my interests; and Shari Kendall, who ran the project and without whom
I would never have undertaken it in the first place.

course, I draw upon and contribute to two theoretical frameworks I have been developing for a number of years: first, the ambiguity and polysemy of power and solidarity (Tannen 1994), and second, the linguistic framing of verbal interaction (Tannen & Wallat 1993 [1987], Tannen 1996). I have been developing these frameworks both as a continuation of my overriding goal of understanding what drives interactional discourse and also as a corrective to the widespread tendency to focus on power in discourse. I have argued that in studying interaction, we need to understand power (or hierarchy, or control) not as separate from or opposite to solidarity (or connection, or intimacy) but as inseparable from and intertwined with it. Because relationships among family members are fundamentally hierarchical and also intensely connected, family interaction is an ideal site for exploring the complex interrelationship between power and solidarity.

In the present chapter, I begin by briefly recapping my theoretical framework of power and solidarity. Those who have encountered this discussion elsewhere are encouraged to skip to the next section, wherein I explore the intertwined nature of power and solidarity in the context of the crucial family role of mother. I then examine excerpts from three extended tape-recorded conversations that took place among two of the families in the Work and Family Project in order to demonstrate how exploring the interplay of power and connection adds to our understanding of the linguistic strategies found in family interaction. In each case, I demonstrate that the conversational strategies used by the mother and father are simultaneously, and inextricably, both "power maneuvers" and "connection maneuvers." My analysis and discussion thus add to our understanding of the discourse analysis of interaction in general and to the specific understanding of family discourse.

The Ambiguity and Polysemy of Power and Solidarity

Many researchers have analyzed interaction, in the family as elsewhere, as a struggle for power. For example, Watts (1991:145), in a book entitled *Power in Family Discourse*, defines power as "the ability of an individual to achieve her/his desired goals." Similarly, in a book about family conversation, Varenne (1992:76) explains, "The power we are interested in here is the power of the catalyst who, with a minimal amount of its own energy, gets other entities to spend large amounts of their own."[2] Millar et al. (1984) write of "control maneuvers" and note that in family therapy, "Conflict takes place within the power dimension of relationships." My claim is that family interaction (including conflict) also takes place within the intimacy dimension, and we can also speak of—indeed, need to speak of—"connection maneuvers."

Elsewhere (Tannen 1994), I explore and argue for what I call the ambiguity and polysemy of power and solidarity—or, in different terms, of status or hierarchy on one hand and of connection or intimacy on the other. By "ambiguity" I mean that any utterance can reflect and create either power or solidarity. By "polysemy" I mean that any utterance can reflect or create both at once. Here I briefly recap this analysis.

In conventional wisdom, as well as in research tracing back to Brown & Gilman's (1960) classic study of power and solidarity, Americans have tended to conceptualize the relationship between hierarchy (or power) and connection (or solidarity) as unidimensional and mutually exclusive.[3] (See figure 2.1.) In other words, the assumption is that particular utterances reflect relationships governed either by power or by solidarity.

Family relationships are at the heart of this conception. For example, Americans frequently use the terms "sisters" and "brothers" to indicate "close and equal." So if a woman says of her friend, "We are like sisters,"

power	solidarity
asymmetry	symmetry
hierarchy	equality
distance	closeness

Figure 2.1. Unidimensional view of power and connection

2. Blum-Kulka (1997), whose book *Dinner Talk* compares American, Israeli, and American-Israeli families, discusses parents' dual and sometimes conflicting needs both to socialize their children in the sense of teaching them what they need to know and at the same time to socialize with them in the sense of enjoying their company. This perspective indirectly addresses the interrelationship of power and connection in the family.

3. I have struggled, through many papers, with the best way to acknowledge Brown & Gilman's original conception of power and solidarity without misrepresenting it, especially given my objections (Tannen 1998, 2002) to the academic convention of obligatorily posing one's work in opposition to work that came before. On one hand, Brown & Gilman acknowledge that relationships can be both equal and solidary, or unequal and solidary, yet they also claim that power governs asymmetrical relationships where one is subordinate to another, whereas solidarity governs symmetrical relationships characterized by social equality and similarity.

the implication is, "We are as close as siblings; there are no status games, no one-upping between us." In contrast, hierarchical relationships are assumed to preclude closeness. Thus, in military and workplace contexts, most Americans regard it as self-evident that friendships across levels of rank are problematic and discouraged if not explicitly prohibited.

I suggest that in reality the relationship between power (or hierarchy) and solidarity (or connection) is not a single dimension but a multidimensional grid. (See figure 2.2.)

This grid represents the dimensions of hierarchy and of connection as two intersecting axes. One axis (I represent it as a vertical one) stretches between hierarchy and equality, while the other (which I represent as a horizontal axis) stretches between closeness and distance. A single linguistic strategy can operate on either axis to create power, connection, or both. For example, in conversation, if one person begins speaking while another is speaking, the resulting overlap of voices is ambiguous in that it can be an interruption (an attempt to display or create power or status over the other speaker) or a cooperative expression of enthusiastic listenership (an attempt to display or create solidarity or connection). It is also polysemous in that it can be both, as when speakers share a conversational style by which an aggressive mutual struggle for the floor is enjoyed as friendly

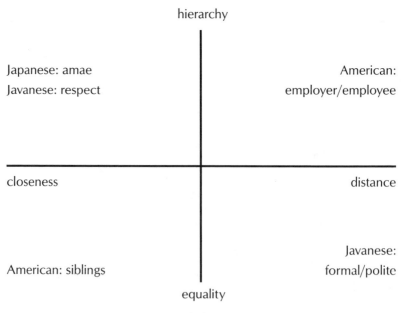

hierarchy

| Japanese: amae | American: |
| Javanese: respect | employer/employee |

closeness   distance

| | Javanese: |
| American: siblings | formal/polite |

equality

Figure 2.2. Multidimensional model

competition. To the extent that two speakers enjoy such competitive conversations, power entails solidarity.

In the context of family interaction, imagine an interchange in which one person announces, "I'm going to take a walk," and a second replies, "Wait, I'll go with you. I just have to make a phone call first." This request could be intended (or experienced) as a power maneuver: the second person is making the first wait before taking a walk. (The tendency to experience being made to wait as a power play is captured in the expression, "Just a dime waiting on a dollar.")[4] But the request could also be intended (or perceived) as a connection maneuver: a bid to take a walk together, to express and reinforce the closeness of the relationship. Thus it is ambiguous with regard to power and solidarity. It is also polysemous, because it is an inextricable combination of both. The motive of walking together, a bid for closeness, constitutes a limit on the other's freedom of movement. Indeed, living with another person in a close relationship inevitably requires accommodations that limit freedom. Thus solidarity entails power.

Mother: A Paradigm Case of the Ambiguity and Polysemy of Power and Connection

If the family is a key locus for understanding the complex and inextricable relationship between power (negotiations along the hierarchy-equality axis) and connection (negotiations along the closeness-distance axis), nowhere does this relationship become clearer than in the role of a key family member, mother. It surfaces both in the language spoken to mothers and the language spoken by mothers. For example, Hildred Geertz (1989 [1961]:20), writing about *The Javanese Family*, notes that there are, in Javanese, "two major levels of language, respect and familiarity." (I would point out that, in light of the grid presented above, these are two different dimensions: respect is situated on the hierarchy-equality axis, whereas familiarity is a function of the closeness-distance axis.) Geertz observes that Javanese children use the familiar register when speaking with their parents and siblings until about age ten or twelve, when they gradu-

---

4. I heard this expression from Dave Quady, a manager at a company at which I was doing research on workplace interaction; he told me that a colleague of his had used the expression to capture their frustration when they found themselves waiting to see a higher ranking colleague.

ally shift to the respect register in adulthood. However, Geertz adds, "Most people continue to speak to the mother in the same way as they did as children; a few shift to respect in adulthood" (22). This leaves open the question whether mothers are addressed in the familiar rather than the respect register because they receive less respect than fathers, or because their children feel closer to them. I suspect it is both at once, and that each entails the other: feeling closer to Mother entails feeling less intimidated by her and therefore less respectful; feeling less need to demonstrate respect paves the way for greater closeness.

Although the lexical distinction between respect and familiar registers is not found in the English language, nonetheless there are linguistic phenomena in English that parallel those described by Geertz in Javanese. Ervin-Tripp et al. (1984) looked at the forms of "control acts" in American family discourse in order to gauge power in that context. They found that "effective power and esteem were related to age" (134). Again, however, "the mothers in our sample were an important exception to the pattern . . ." (135). The authors note that mothers in their caregiving role "received nondeferent orders, suggesting that the children expected compliance and believed their desires to be justification enough." As with Javanese, one could ask whether American children use more bald imperatives when speaking to their mothers because they have less respect for them, or because they feel closer to them, or (as seems most likely) both. In other words, American children's use of nondeferent orders to their mothers, like Javanese children's use of the familiar register with their mothers, is both ambiguous and polysemous with regard to power and solidarity.

Power Lines—or Connection Lines—in Telling Your Day

Both Blum-Kulka (1997) and Ochs & Taylor (1992a, 1992b, 1995) identify a conversational ritual that typifies talk at dinner in many American families: a ritual that Blum-Kulka dubs "telling your day." When the family includes a mother and father (as the families recorded in both these studies did), American mothers typically encourage children to tell their fathers about events experienced during the day.

Ochs & Taylor give the examples of a mother who urges a child, "Tell Dad what you thought about gymnastics and what you did," and another who prompts, "Chuck did you tell Daddy what happened at karate when you came in your new uniform? What did Daisy do for you?" (1992b:310). Ochs & Taylor note that in a majority of the instances recorded in their study, fathers responded to the resultant stories by passing judgment, assessing the rightness of their children's actions and feelings, and thereby setting up a constellation the researchers call "Father knows best." The family power structure, Ochs & Taylor observe, is established in these story-telling dynamics. Just as Mother typically prompted a child to tell Daddy what happened, older siblings were much more likely to urge younger ones to tell about something that happened than the other way around. Children were most often "problematizees"—the ones whose behavior was judged by others. Rarely were they "problematizers"—the ones who questioned others' behavior as problematic. This situates children firmly at the bottom of the hierarchy. Fathers were situated at the top of the family hierarchy, as they were the most frequent problematizers and rarely were problematizees. In keeping with the findings of Ervin-Tripp et al., mothers found themselves in the position of problematizees (the ones whose behavior was held up for judgment) as often as they were problematizers (the ones who were judging others).

In this revealing study, Ochs & Taylor identify a crucial dynamic in middle-class American families by which the family exhibits a power structure with the father at the top and the mother somewhere above the children but below the father. They further show that mothers play a crucial role in setting up this dynamic: "Father as problematizer," they argue, is "facilitated . . . by the active role of mothers who sometimes (perhaps inadvertently) set fathers up as potential problematizers—by introducing the stories and reports of children and mothers in the first place and orienting them towards fathers as primary recipients" (1992b:329). For me, the word "inadvertently" is key. I argue that the "Father knows best" dynamic results from gender differences in assumptions about the place of talk in a relationship, and that it reflects the inextricable relationship between power and connection. In this view, the mother who initiates a "telling your day" routine is trying to create closeness and involvement by exchanging details of daily life, a verbal ritual frequently observed to characterize women's friendships, as I explain elsewhere (Tannen 1990). For her it is a connection maneuver. Thus when she encourages her children to tell their day to their father, she is trying to involve the father with the children in much the way she herself creates involvement.

A father, however, who does not routinely ask, "How was your day?" is not necessarily evincing lack of interest in being close to his children.

Rather, he likely does not assume that closeness is created by the verbal ritual of telling the details of one's day. So fathers, looking elsewhere for reasons that their wives are urging their children to report their activities, may well conclude that they are being asked to evaluate and judge the children's behavior. Thus it is not the mothers' initiation of the "telling your day" routine in itself that sets fathers up as family judge. Instead, the "Father knows best" dynamic is created by the interaction of divergent gender-related patterns.[5] A linguistic strategy intended as a connection maneuver functions simultaneously as a power maneuver—one, however, that compromises rather than enhances the mother's power, or status, in the interaction and in the family. This outcome results from the ambiguity and polysemy of power and solidarity.

All the examples that follow illustrate the complex interweaving of power maneuvers and connection maneuvers in family interaction. I argue that understanding the interplay of these dynamics adds to our understanding of the linguistic strategies that characterize family interaction, many of which are examined and analyzed in succeeding chapters in this volume.

Power and Connection in Giving Directions

The first example comes from the family composed of Janet, Steve, and their three-year-old daughter Natalie. (The excerpt was transcribed and identified for analysis by Philip LeVine.) In the interchange, Janet is trying to get Steve to do something—a chore needed for the good of the family. Insofar as she is trying to influence Steve's actions, she may be seen as exercising a power maneuver. Insofar as the action is not for her personal benefit but for the good of the family, she may be seen as carrying out a connection maneuver. Moreover, the way in which she goes about trying to influence Steve's behavior mixes connection with power.

5. Among the many scenarios of male/female interaction that I describe in my book *You Just Don't Understand*, one of the most frequently cited and widely recognized (by readers) is an interchange in which a woman tries to initiate a "how was your day" routine and is met with advice rather than matching experiences. I attribute this to the ritual nature of the routine for many women, and their assumption that the routine expresses and creates closeness. Not recognizing or sharing the routine, many men hear the recitation of daily problems as a request for advice. This may well be the pattern evinced in the examples Ochs & Taylor report. Moreover, unlike many mothers, a father may not regard closeness as the most important barometer of his relationship with his children. See Henwood (1993) for evidence that women tend to judge the mother-daughter relationship by how close it is. There is no parallel evidence that men regard closeness in the same way.

The couple is planning to apply for a credit card. Janet has filled out the application, but she feels it should be copied before it is mailed. Since Steve has access to a copy machine at work, she asks him to take the materials with him to work the next day, copy the application, attach a voided check as required, and mail it. However, the way in which she asks Steve to do this offends him, and his protest in turn offends her. This is how the exchange goes:

(1) Janet: Okay, so you'll have to attach the voided check here,
            after you make the Xerox copy. Okay?
            ((*Steve takes the papers*))
            Okay just- Please get that out tomorrow.
            I'm counting on you, bubbles.
            I'm counting on you, cuddles.
     Steve: Oh, for Pete's sake.
     Janet: What do you mean by that?
     Steve: What do YOU mean by that?
     Janet: Oh, honey, I just mean I'm COUNTING on you.
     Steve: Yes but you say it in a way
            that suggests I can't be counted on.
     Janet: I never said that.
     Steve: I'm talking about your TONE.

When Steve protests (*Oh, for Pete's sake*) the way Janet reinforced her request (*I'm counting on you, bubbles. I'm counting on you, cuddles.*), he explains that he hears his wife as implying that he is unreliable (*you say it in a way that suggests I can't be counted on*). Janet protests against his protest: *I never said that.* Elsewhere (Tannen 2001) I have characterized this verbal maneuver as "crying literal meaning": Janet claims responsibility only for the message of her utterance—the literal meaning of the words spoken—and denies (*I never said that*) the "metamessage," that is, the many meanings implied by the way she said those words, which Steve refers to generally as her "tone."

   This interchange is a complex web of power maneuvers and connection maneuvers. The detailed instructions Janet gives Steve (*you'll have to attach the voided check here, after you make the Xerox copy*) reinforce the power-maneuver aspect of her giving him an assignment. They suggest a parent giving directions to a child who hasn't enough life experience to know exactly how to carry out an assigned task. (Bear in mind that the power dynamic inherently reflects the hierarchical nature of parent/child relations.) When she repeats the request (*Please get that out tomorrow*) and follows up with the reminder, *I'm counting on you*, then repeats that reminder, she further reinforces the hierarchical dynamic. When Steve protests, he makes clear that he is experiencing the way in which Janet frames her request as a power maneuver.

Janet's discourse, however, also includes terms of endearment ("bubbles," "cuddles") that signal the couple's closeness and the affection she feels for Steve. Indeed, the frequent use of these and other highly stylized expressions of affection is part of this couple's "familylect," as Cynthia Gordon (2003) has observed, and using elements of their familylect metaphorically signals the couple's closeness. Indeed, I surmise that Janet's use of the connection-maneuver terms of endearment are intended to override the power-maneuver aspect of her giving and repeatedly reinforcing directions to Steve. (For readers who may react negatively, as Steve did, to Janet's mixing of power and connection in this way, I note that in the end Steve did forget to copy and mail the credit card application.)

The Ambiguity and Polysemy of Power and Connection in a Homecoming Encounter

Kendall (2006) has identified homecomings as a frequent site of conflict in the discourse recorded by families in our study. Although at first glance a parent's return home might seem to be occasion for unmitigated celebration, in reality Kendall found that the change in participants and circumstances constitutes potential stress, which is aggravated when family members differ in their moods and expectations. The next example took place among Kathy, Sam, and their daughter, Kira. The development of the tension and the way that Kathy and Sam manage it are a fascinating blend of connection maneuvers and power maneuvers.

The exchange (which was transcribed and identified for analysis by Alexandra Johnston, the research team member who shadowed Sam) takes place in the family's home at the end of the day, immediately before and after Sam's return from work. Earlier, Kathy picked Kira up from day care, arrived home with her, and gave her dinner. Now Kathy has heard the arrival of Sam's car and prepares their two-year-old (but largely preverbal) daughter for her father's arrival. When Sam enters the house and sits down to eat a snack, Kira tries to climb onto his lap. Sam, however, is tired and hungry and reacts with annoyance, which makes Kira cry. Sam immediately modifies his way of talking to Kira in order to mollify her, but the effect of his initial rejection is not so easy to repair. Kathy then mediates the interaction between father and daughter. (In the transcript, Kathy's reference to "pop" is to a "juice pop"—frozen juice on a stick.)

(2) Kathy: Daddy's home.
    Kira: Da da .
    Kathy: Daddy's going to be home in a minute.
    Kira: Da da pop.
           Da da pop.
           Da da pop.
    Kathy: You gonna give Da da a pop?
    Kira: Yes.
           Shoes. Shoes. ahh.
    Kathy: You gonna tell Daddy to take his shoes off?
           ((*Father comes home, 5 minutes' intervening talk*))
           ((*Kira tries to climb onto her father*))
    Sam: I'm eating! ((*very irritated*))
           Daddy eats. ((*more apologetic*))
           ((*Kira begins to cry*))
           Da da eats.
           ((*Kira cries*))
           You wanna come up?
    Kira: Oo ee yeah ((*cries*))
           . . .
    Kathy: She got her feelings hurt.
    Sam: How come Ki-Ki gets to eat
           and Daddy doesn't get to eat?
           . . .
    Kathy: I think she just wanted
           some Daddy's attention.
           ((*Kira cries*))
           You were missing Daddy today, weren't you?
           ((*Kira cries*))
           You were missing Daddy, weren't you?
           ((*Kira cries*))
           Can you say,

"I was just missing you Daddy,
that was all?"
Kira: <*crying*> Nnnooo.>
Kathy: "And I don't really feel too good."
Kira: <*crying*> Nnnooo.>
Kathy: No, she doesn't feel too good either.
. . . ((*intervening talk; logistics*))
Kathy: Why are you so edgy?
Sam: 'Cause I haven't eaten yet.
Kathy: Why didn't you get a SNACK
on the way home or something?
Save your family a little stress.
Kira: Mm mm
Kathy: Yeah give us a break, Daddy.
We just miss you.
We try to get your attention
and then you come home
and you go →
ROW ROW ROW ROW. ((*rhymes with "how"*))
Kira: Row! Row!

Among the many aspects of this interchange that are of interest, I will focus on the interplay of power and solidarity, or control and connection, in both Kathy's and Sam's utterances.

Consider first Sam's exchanges with Kira. The way in which Sam's rejection of Kira's bid to climb onto his lap (*I'm eating!*) sparks Kira's ongoing and not easily mollified crying illustrates Varenne's (1992:76) definition of power (which I cited at the outset) as the influence "of the catalyst who, with a minimal amount of its own energy, gets other entities to spend large amounts of their own." Sam immediately attempts to repair the damage first by explaining his reaction (*Daddy eats*) and then by inviting Kira to sit on his lap after all (*You wanna come up?*). These attempts to soothe his daughter's feelings are progressively more slanted toward connection, in both form and content. In content, Sam's utterances go from rejecting Kira's physical approach (*I'm eating!*) to inviting it (*You wanna come up?*). At the same time, the paralinguistic features of his utterances—the tone in which he speaks—go from the snappish annoyance of his first reaction (described by the transcriber as "very irritated") to a more modulated tone ("more apologetic") to a highly modulated invitation to do just what he was rebuffing. In this way, the tone in which Sam speaks also progresses from the power-laden rebuff to a solidarity-focused invitation.

Perhaps most intriguing is the progressively closer connection to his daughter that is constituted by the indexicality of the lexical realizations by which Sam refers to himself. In his first utterance (*I'm eating!*), Sam uses the first person singular pronoun to represent himself from his own point of view just as his rejection of Kira's attempt to climb onto his lap reflects his own feelings of hunger and fatigue. In his next utterance (*Daddy eats*), he refers to himself as "Daddy," a noun that reflects his daughter's, not his own, perspective. (To himself, he is "I." To her, he is "Daddy.") Just as he is beginning to take into account her feelings, his point of view is shifting to reflect her point of view linguistically as well. Finally, Sam's perspective moves closer to Kira's—indeed, merges with hers—as he refers to himself in the baby-talk register that she herself uses to refer to him (*Da da eats*). Thus each succeeding utterance linguistically creates a progressively closer connection to his daughter, even as his authority to determine whether or not she climbs onto his lap reflects the power he holds over her. In this way, Sam's utterances constitute connection maneuvers as well as power maneuvers.

In the succeeding section of this interchange, Kathy steps in to mediate the interaction between Sam and Kira. Here, too, the form of Kathy's utterances reflects progressively closer alignments with her daughter, even as the stance she takes up as mediator between her husband and daughter positions her as the expert on Kira's emotions and how they should be managed—in other words, a position of power. (See Johnston this volume and Kendall this volume for discussions of how Kathy often comments on Sam's caretaking of Kira, thus constituting herself as chief caregiver, although they share primary caregiving responsibilities.)

As we saw with Sam, Kathy's repeated explanations of why Kira is crying move progressively closer to Kira's point of view. In the first line (*She got her feelings hurt*), Kathy speaks about Kira to Sam; in this utterance, mother and daughter are linguistically distinct. She next addresses Kira directly (*You were missing Daddy, weren't you?*), bringing herself into direct alignment with the child. She then models for Kira what she might say to articulate her own feelings (*Can you say, "I was just missing you, Daddy, that was all?"*). Here she animates Kira's feelings, but linguistically marks the fact that she is doing so by beginning "Can you say?" This introducer separates her point of view from her child's, even as she is articulating the child's perspective.

Kathy's next line (*"And I don't really feel too good"*) continues to merge Kathy with Kira linguistically, as Kathy is speaking but says "I," meaning Kira. This may be interpreted either as still modified by "Can you say?" or as a new, "ventriloquized" utterance, in which Kathy is not just suggesting to Kira what she might say but is actually speaking *as* Kira. In any case, Kathy is expressing Kira's point of view using the first person pronoun. Finally, she mitigates her alignment with Kira and re-orients to Sam by addressing him and referring to Kira rather than animating her (*No, she doesn't feel too good either*). Kathy thus moves progressively closer to Kira, discursively, by gradually shifting from referring to Kira in the third person to ventriloquizing her—that is, merging her persona with Kira's by animating Kira's voice. Moreover, by communicating to both Kira and Sam in the same utterances, Kathy is connecting the three of them as a family.

Kathy's explanation of why Kira is crying (*She got her feelings hurt*) is an indirect criticism of Sam because it entails the assumption that a father should not hurt his daughter's feelings. After a short spate of intervening talk, Kathy makes this injunction more explicit.

Although the "we" in *"We just miss you"* could conceivably indicate that Kathy and Kira both miss Sam, the continuation (*We try to get your attention . . .*) makes clear that Kathy is speaking for (and as) Kira. Then, still speaking as Kira, she mimics how Sam comes across from Kira's point of view: *you go ROW ROW ROW ROW*. In this utterance, Kathy is animating Kira animating Sam. So the linguistic strategy by which Kathy tells Sam that he should alter his behavior (a control maneuver) also linguistically merges the three of them (a connection maneuver).

By speaking as, to, and through Kira, Kathy creates connection between Kira and her father, explains Kira's feelings both to Sam and to Kira herself, explains to Sam why he's been unfair to Kira, and aligns herself with her daughter as a team. (She could have aligned with Sam by telling their daughter to let Daddy eat, as another mother in our study did in the same situation.) At the same time, she exercises power by positioning herself as the authority on Kira's emotions, as well as how Sam should relate to Kira. Finally, by speaking for Kira, who cannot yet speak, she enters into the alignment between Sam and Kira and thus frames the three of them as a single unit, a family. Thus both Kathy's and Sam's participation in this exchange can be understood as subtle and complex blends of power maneuvers and solidarity maneuvers.

Power Maneuvers and Solidarity Maneuvers in an Argument

The next and final example comes from the same family as the preceding one. (It too was transcribed and identified for analysis by Alexandra Johnston.) On the surface, the interchange is a power struggle over who will control the making of popcorn. Yet even this unmistakable series of power maneuvers is shot through with connection maneuvers.

The interchange begins one evening when Kathy is in the kitchen, and Sam is in another room watching their daughter Kira. Sam calls out to Kathy:

> (3a) Sam: Kathy! Kath! Let's switch.
> You take care of her.
> I'll do whatever you're doing.

With this, Sam makes a bid to switch places with Kathy. Insofar as he is seeking to influence her actions—both to stop her doing what she is doing and to get her to take over what he has been doing—Sam's utterance is a power maneuver. It is impossible to know his motives, but it seems likely that he wishes to turn over the caretaking of Kira to Kathy. Kathy resists Sam's suggestion, explaining her resistance with reference not to the caretaking of Kira but rather to the task she is performing in the kitchen. Moreover, the reason she gives for resisting Sam's bid to trade places rests on his incompetence at popcorn making:

> (3b) Kathy: I'm making popcorn.
> You always burn it.
> Sam: No I don't!
> I never burn it.
> I make it perfect.
> ((*He joins Kathy in the kitchen*))
> You making popcorn?
> In the big pot?
> Kathy: Yes, but you're going to ruin it.
> Sam: No I won't.
> I'll get it just right.

To the extent that Kathy deflects Sam's request to influence her actions, as well as the extent to which she impugns his competence, Kathy's moves are power maneuvers. However, to the extent that she rests her case on the chances for a successful batch of popcorn for everyone to eat, she frames her refusal as a connection maneuver: it will redound to the good of the family if Kathy makes the popcorn rather than Sam. (In contrast, had she resisted Sam's request by saying, "I don't want to watch Kira; I like making popcorn and want to keep doing it," her utterance would have been more uniformly a power maneuver: wanting to control her own actions for her own good.)

In the interchange that follows, Kathy uses their daughter Kira as a resource in her communication with Sam. (Elsewhere I examine the use of nonverbal children [Tannen 2003a] and pets [this volume] as resources in communication between adults.) Kathy proposes a compromise between her preference and Sam's by suggesting that she can take care of Kira and also make the popcorn at the same time. By proposing a compromise, Kathy performs a power maneuver (resisting Sam's request to relinquish popcorn making to him) mixed with a connection maneuver (both acceding to Sam's request and also establishing a direct alignment with Kira.) Rather than addressing this proposal directly to Sam, she frames it as a suggestion to Kira, within earshot of Sam:

(3c) Kathy: You wanna help Mommy make popcorn?
     Kira: Okay.
     Kathy: Let's not let Daddy do it.
     Kira: Okay.
     Kathy: Okay, come on.

By framing her resistance to Sam's proposal as an invitation directed to Kira, Kathy avoids direct confrontation with Sam and establishes a direct connection to Kira. This is another sense in which her utterance is not only a power maneuver (resisting his bid to control her actions) but also a connection maneuver (establishing connection with Kira and avoiding direct confrontation with Sam).

Sam, however, does not accept this compromise. Furthermore, his ensuing conversational moves focus more and more on Kathy's accusation that he habitually burns popcorn when he prepares it:

(3d) Sam: I know how to make popcorn!
     Kathy: Let's hurry up so Daddy doesn't . . .
     Sam: I can make popcorn better than you can!

In this and succeeding moves, Sam ups the ante from "I know how" to "I can do it better than you" to "You are an incompetent popcorn maker," with the result that the interchange begins to take on the character of an argument:

(3e) Sam: I cook every kernel!
    Kathy: No you won't.
      Sam: I will too!
           I don't!
           It's never burned!
           It always burns when you do it!
    Kathy: Don't make excuses!
      Sam: There's a trick to it.
    Kathy: I know the trick!
      Sam: No you don't, 'cause you always burn it.
    Kathy: I DO NOT! What are you, crazy?

From the conversation alone, it is impossible to know whose claims are accurate: whether it is Kathy or Sam who has a history of success at making popcorn. Evidence accrues in the interchange, however, that Kathy is right about Sam's tendency to burn the popcorn:

(3f) Kathy: Just heat it! Heat it! No, I don't want you. . .
      Sam: It's going, it's going. Hear it?
    Kathy: It's too slow.
           It's all soaking in.
           You hear that little. . .
      Sam: It's not soaking in, it's fine.
    Kathy: It's just a few kernels.
      Sam: All the popcorn is being popped!

Kathy's injunctions to Sam to *Just heat it! Heat it!* are power maneuvers insofar as she is trying to get him to alter his actions. They are also connection maneuvers to the extent that she is trying to ensure an outcome that will benefit the entire family (edible popcorn rather than burned unpopped kernels of corn in the pot). Sam, however, resists her suggestions for how to adjust his popcorn making and denies her claims about the ominous nature of the sounds emanating from the pot.

Given Sam's resistance to following her suggestions, Kathy again tries to wrest control of the popcorn making in an indirect way. She reminds Sam of another task he is obligated to perform:

(3g) Kathy: You gotta take the trash outside.
    Sam: I can't, I'm doing the popcorn.
    Kathy: I'll DO it,
           I'll watch it.
           You take the trash out
           and come back in a few minutes and—
    Sam: Well, because it'll burn!

One might describe this move on Kathy's part as a power maneuver masquerading as a connection maneuver. Were Sam to initiate the performance of another obligation, Kathy's offer to watch the popcorn while he's taking out the trash would be a connection maneuver. However, given the history of this interaction, Sam does not perceive it that way.

It isn't long before Kathy gets to say, "See, what'd I tell you?" Her contention that it is Sam, not she, who habitually burns popcorn is supported by the outcome: burned popcorn. But Sam doesn't see this result as a reason to admit fault:

(3h) Sam: Well, I never USE this pot.
          I use the other pot.
    Kathy: It's not the pot! It's you!
    Sam: It's the pot.
         It doesn't heat up properly.
         If it did, then it would get hot.
    Kathy: Just throw it all away.
    Sam: You should have let me do it from the start.
    Kathy: You DID it from the start!
    Sam: No, I didn't.
         You chose this pan.
         I would've chosen a different pan.

The way this interchange ends seems unremittingly a power maneuver: although he did indeed burn the popcorn, Sam assigns fault to the pot and to Kathy for having chosen the pot. Where, one might ask, is a connection maneuver detectable here? Intriguingly, the burning of popcorn and the relative blame assigned to people and pots becomes a reference point for family solidarity.

The "popcorn fight" entered this family's lore because I described and analyzed it in a book (Tannen 2001) that Sam and Kathy had occasion to read.[6] Four years after this conversation took place, I was visiting the family again in order to follow up our original study and to interview Kathy in connection with another study.[7] As Kathy and I were talking in the living room of their home, Sam appeared with a mischievous grin on his face and said, "Did you hear we settled the popcorn argument? It was the pot." Kathy responded with puzzlement: "What?" Sam reminded her of a recent occasion when the popcorn had burned because of the pot. "That was a different pot," Kathy replied. We all laughed at the reminder of the mundane argument that had entered not only family lore but the public domain. It was a way for the couple to signal connection not only to each other, but also to me: the popcorn fight was a reference point not only to an experience that Kathy and Sam had shared, but one that linked me to the family as well. In this sense, Sam's reference to the popcorn fight was a connection maneuver. But to the extent that he was still (though somewhat playfully) claiming his innocence despite the fact that he had burned the popcorn, Sam's remark was also a power maneuver.

Conclusion

In this chapter, I have examined three extended interchanges that took place among two of the families that participated in our study of family interaction. In each case, I have demonstrated that the utterances of both speakers can be understood as complex and subtle combinations of power maneuvers and connection maneuvers. Whereas there is ample prior research examining family interaction as apparent or subtle struggles for power—understood as each speaker's desire to determine her or his own actions and influence the actions of the other—I have argued here that a less examined but equally pervasive and important pattern is the struggle for connection, which may be understood as each speaker's desire to

6. In keeping with my standard practice, I showed the analysis to Sam and Kathy before I included it in my book in order to make sure that I got it right and that they felt comfortable with my using their words in this way.

7. The book for which I interviewed Kathy is on mother-daughter conversations.

reinforce and not undermine the intimate connections that constitute their involvement with each other as members of a family. Being in hierarchical relation to each other does not preclude being close, and being closely connected does not preclude being involved in struggles for power. Quite the contrary, being members of a family entails both struggles for power and struggles for connection.

The creation of both power relations and solidarity relations in a single interchange could be seen as evidence for the ambiguity of power and solidarity. In other words, a given utterance could be intended or perceived as establishing either power or solidarity. In this regard, recall that in the first example, Janet is giving Steve detailed and repeated instructions about how to prepare and mail a credit card application; in the second example, Kathy is indirectly criticizing Sam for making their daughter cry; and in the third example, Kathy is trying first to retain control of the activity of making popcorn and then to influence Sam's execution of the same activity. To the extent that Janet and Kathy are trying to alter their spouses' behavior, they are engaging in power maneuvers. However, insofar as they are trying to achieve results that will benefit the family as a whole rather than themselves as individuals, their moves can be understood as connection maneuvers.

Janet's and Kathy's utterances are ambiguous with respect to power and solidarity to the extent that they can be understood either as creating and expressing power relations or as creating and expressing solidarity relations. However, in most of the cases I discussed, speakers' utterances could be seen as creating and expressing both power and solidarity at the same time. Thus, when Janet tried to get Steve to follow her instructions in mailing the credit card application, she was both exercising power and exercising connection. The connection aspect was reinforced by her use of terms of endearment ("bubbles," "cuddles"). And when Kathy tried to explain to Kira as well as to Sam why he made her cry, and how Kira might better manage and express her emotions, Kathy was both creating and expressing her authority as chief childcare provider and also creating and expressing solidarity among the three as a family. Finally, when Kathy exerted efforts to involve Kira in making popcorn, she was acceding to Sam's suggestion that she take over watching Kira at the same time that she was trying to maintain control of popcorn making.

I am suggesting, then, that whenever researchers examine interaction for evidence of power negotiations, they ask themselves how the utterances examined also create and express solidarity relations. I am suggesting, moreover, that considering both power and solidarity provides for a deeper and more accurate understanding of family interaction, and that family interaction is an ideal site for exploring and better understanding the ambiguity and polysemy of power and solidarity. When we find ourselves identifying power maneuvers, our understanding of the interaction will be more accurate if we also seek to identify connection maneuvers and to understand how the two types of maneuvers relate to each other and intertwine.

References

Blum-Kulka, Shoshana. 1997. Dinner talk: Cultural patterns of sociability and socialization in family discourse. Mahwah, N.J.: Erlbaum.

Brown, Roger, and Albert Gilman. 1960. The pronouns of power and solidarity. Style in language, ed. Thomas Sebeok, 253–276. Cambridge, Mass.: M.I.T. Press.

Ervin-Tripp, Susan, Mary Catherine O'Connor, and Jarrett Rosenberg. 1984. Language and power in the family. Language and power, ed. Cheris Kramarae, Muriel Schultz, and William M. O'Barr, 116–135. New York: Sage.

Geertz, Hildred. 1989[1961]. The Javanese family: A study of kinship and socialization. Prospect Heights, Ill.: Waveland Press.

Gordon, Cynthia. 2003. Intertextuality in family discourse: Shared prior text as a resource for framing. Washington, D.C.: Georgetown University dissertation.

Henwood, Karen L. 1993. Women and later life: The discursive construction of identities within family relationships. Journal of Aging Studies 7(3).303–319.

Kendall, Shari. 2006. "Honey, I'm home!": Framing in family dinnertime homecomings. Text & Talk 26(4/5).411–441.

Millar, Frank E., L. Edna Rogers, and Janet Beavin Bavelas. 1984. Identifying patterns of verbal conflict in interpersonal dynamics. The Western Journal of Speech Communication 48.231–246.

Ochs, Elinor, and Carolyn Taylor. 1992a. Mothers' role in the everday reconstruction of "Father knows best." Locating power: Proceedings of the Second Berkeley Women and Language Conference, ed. Kira Hall, Mary Bucholtz, and Birch Moonwomon, 447–463. Berkeley: Berkeley Women and Language Group.

Ochs, Elinor, and Carolyn Taylor. 1992b. Family narrative as political activity. Discourse & Society 3(3).301–340.

Ochs, Elinor, and Carolyn Taylor. 1996. The "Father knows best" dynamic in family dinner narratives. Gender articulated: Language and the socially constructed self, ed. Kira Hall and Mary Bucholtz, 97–121. New York and London: Routledge.

Ochs, Elinor, Clotilde Pontecorvo, and Alessandra Fasulo. 1996. Socializing taste. Ethnos 61(1–2).7–46.

Ochs, Elinor, Carolyn Taylor, Dina Rudolph, and Ruth Smith. 1992. Storytelling as a theory-building activity. Discourse Processes 15.37–72.

Tannen, Deborah. 1986. That's not what I meant!: How conversational style makes or breaks relationships. New York: Ballantine.

Tannen, Deborah. 1990. You just don't understand: Women and men in conversation. New York: Quill.

Tannen, Deborah. 1994. The relativity of linguistic strategies: Rethinking power and solidarity in gender and dominance. Gender and discourse, 19–52. Oxford and New York: Oxford University Press.

Tannen, Deborah. 1996. The sex-class linked framing of talk at work. Gender and discourse, paperback edition, 195–221. Oxford and New York: Oxford University Press.

Tannen, Deborah. 1998. The argument culture: Stopping America's war of words. New York: Ballantine.

Tannen, Deborah. 2001. I only say this because I love you: Talking to your parents, partner, sibs, and kids when you're all adults. New York: Ballantine.

Tannen, Deborah. 2002. Agonism in academic discourse. Journal of Pragmatics 34(10–11).1651–1669.

Tannen, Deborah. 2003a. Power maneuvers or connection maneuvers? Ventriloquizing in family interaction. Linguistics, language, and the real world: Discourse and beyond. Georgetown University Round Table on Languages and Linguistics 2001, ed. Deborah Tannen and James E. Alatis, 50–62. Washington, D.C.: Georgetown University Press.

Tannen, Deborah. 2003b. Gender and family interaction. Handbook of language and gender, ed. Janet Holmes and Miriam Meyerhoff, 179–201. Malden, Mass., and Oxford, UK: Blackwell.

Tannen, Deborah. 2007 [1989]. Talking voices: Repetition, dialogue, and imagery in conversational discourse. Cambridge: Cambridge University Press.

Tannen, Deborah, and Cynthia Wallat. 1987. Interactive frames and knowledge schemas in interaction: Examples from a medical examination/interview. Social Psychology Quarterly 50(2).205–216. Reprinted in Framing in discourse, ed. Deborah Tannen, 57–76. New York and Oxford: Oxford University Press, 1993.

Varenne, Hervé. 1992. Ambiguous harmony: Family talk in America. Norwood, N.J.: Ablex.

Watts, Richard J. 1991. Power in family discourse. Berlin: Mouton de Gruyter.

DEBORAH TANNEN

three

Talking the Dog: Framing Pets as Interactional

Resources in Family Discourse

A couple who live together are having an argument.[1] The man suddenly turns to their pet dog and says in a high-pitched baby-talk register, "Mommy's so mean tonight. You better sit over here and protect me." This makes the woman laugh—especially because she is a petite 5'2"; her boyfriend is 6'4" and weighs 285 pounds; and the dog is a ten-pound Chihuahua mix.

A young woman, the only child of a single mother, is visiting home from college. At one point her mother tells her, "Pay lots of attention to the cat; she misses you so much."

1. I am grateful to my co-PI, Shari Kendall; to the generous families who participated in the project; to "Clara," who read a pre-publication draft and offered her perspective, and to the research assistants who worked on the project. I am particularly grateful to Cynthia Gordon, who shadowed Clara, transcribed her tapes, and led me to the examples I cite from her discourse. Versions of this paper were delivered at the Georgetown University Round Table on Languages and Linguistics 2002, Washington, D.C., March 7, 2002, and at the annual meeting of the American Association of Applied Linguistics, Arlington, Va., March 24, 2003. Cynthia Gordon provided helpful comments on an earlier draft, as did two anonymous reviewers. This article (in only slightly different form) was originally published in *Research on Language and Social Interaction* 37:4 (2004).

These two anecdotal examples illustrate a phenomenon I have been examining in depth: a discursive strategy by which the speakers, in communicating with each other, use as a resource nonverbal third parties —preverbal children or pets. Elsewhere (Tannen 2003) I examine the phenomenon more generally. The present study focuses exclusively on examples in which the nonverbal third parties are pet dogs.

The term "resource," as I am using it, has much in common with what Scollon (2001:4) following Wertsch (1998) calls "mediational means": "material objects in the world (including the materiality of the social actors . . .)" through which "mediated action is carried out" (where "mediated action" is the unit of analysis rather than a text or discourse). In other words, in the examples I will examine, one family member mediates interaction with a second family member by speaking as, to, or about a pet dog who is present. The analysis of ways in which family members speak through pets extends our understanding of what Gumperz (1982) calls "contextualization cues": that is, how "paralinguistic and prosodic features" and other aspects of linguistic realization function to frame utterances and position speakers in interaction.

Arluke & Sanders (1996), in their analysis of interactions in a veterinary clinic, observe numerous instances in which pet owners speak for their pets. Bilger (2003:48) notes that "according to a recent survey by the American Animal Hospital Association, sixty-three per cent of pet owners say 'I love you' to their pets every day." In these instances of speaking for and speaking to animals, the animal is arguably (to use Goffman's [1981] framework) the principal. In contrast, the phenomenon I address in the present study is the discursive practice by which speakers talk to and through their pets in order to communicate to human family members. In the examples I present, dogs are not the principals in the interaction. Rather, they are resources for communication among humans.[2]

---

2. This is not to argue that the speakers might not also be communicating to the pet. As an anonymous reviewer pointed out, a human who interrupts a family argument to speak to a pet might after all be trying to reassure the pet that all is well. This possibility is not denied by my focus on the way in which the speaker is using the pet as a resource for negotiating the argument with the other person, i.e., by re-keying the interchange as humorous. Focusing on one aspect of an utterance—the way in which it is used to mediate human interaction—does not imply that the utterance might not be doing other interactional work as well. Quite the contrary, we can assume that any utterance is doing multiple interactional work. In terms I have developed elsewhere (Tannen 1994, this volume), every utterance is ambiguous (it can be intended or interpreted to have one meaning or another) and polysemous (it can be intended or interpreted to have more than one meaning at once).

The two anecdotal examples presented at the outset illustrate ways in which pets can become resources for communication between humans. In the first example, when the 285-pound boyfriend uses baby-talk register while speaking in the second person to address the couple's pet dog, he uses the dog as a resource to (1) mediate a conflict with his girlfriend; (2) effect a frame shift from conflict to humor; and (3) frame the couple as a family. This last function is particularly interesting from the point of view of family discourse. Whereas the playful key in itself provides an indirect means to end the couple's argument, positioning their pet as their baby goes a long way toward redressing the threat to their unity and intimacy posed by the argument. This positioning is accomplished by at least two related linguistic strategies: first, the baby-talk register, and, second, referring to his girlfriend as "Mommy." (This usage places the man in the mainstream of pet owners. Arluke & Sanders report that "veterinary clients . . . routinely referred to themselves as 'Mommy' or 'Dad'" [p. 68]; according to Bilger, "Eighty-three per cent [of pet owners] refer to themselves as their pet's mom or dad" [p. 48].)

In the other example described at the outset, the mother who tells her daughter, home from college, to pay lots of attention to the cat who missed her very much doesn't address the cat directly but nonetheless uses the cat as a resource for communicating to her daughter. The daughter reported that she understood her mother to be indicating that she herself missed her daughter. By directing the daughter's attention to the cat rather than herself, however, the mother avoided potential conflict with her daughter, who might well have protested a demand from her mother to "Pay lots of attention to me." I would argue, perhaps a bit more tenuously, that by speaking for the cat, the mother constituted the dyadic pair (mother-daughter) as a triadic unit (mother-daughter-cat), perhaps thereby more closely approximating the popular conception of family.

In what follows, I present six examples taken from the tape-recorded conversations of two families in order to illustrate how family members use pet dogs as resources in their interactions. Specifically, the pets become resources by which speakers buffer criticism, effect frame shifts, mediate or avoid conflict, and both reflect and constitute the participants' family identities. Before turning to these examples, I briefly sketch the theoretical background against which prior research has addressed phenomena related to those illustrated by the examples analyzed in the present study.

Theoretical Background: Speaking through Third Parties

Ventriloquizing

In three of the six examples that follow, family members use pets as resources in their interactions by speaking as their pets. I use the term "ventriloquizing" to describe the discursive strategy by which a participant speaks in the voice of a nonverbal third party in the presence of that party. This strategy is situated at the intersection of two linguistic phenomena I have been examining for many years: on one hand, constructed dialogue (Tannen 2007 [1989]); on the other, framing in discourse (Tannen 1993). "Constructed dialogue" is my term for what has been called (misleadingly, I argue) "reported speech," that is, animating speech in another's voice. Ventriloquizing is a special case of constructed dialogue in that a ventriloquizing speaker animates another's voice in the presence of that other. It is also a kind of frame-shifting insofar as a speaker who utters dialogue as if it were spoken in the voice of another is assuming a new and different footing vis-à-vis the participants and the subject of discourse, where "footing" is defined, following Goffman (1981:128), as "the alignment we take up to ourselves and the others present as expressed in the way we manage the production or reception of an utterance." In other words, through realizations of pitch, amplitude, intonational contours, voice quality, pronoun choice, and other linguistic markers of point of view, speakers verbally position themselves *as* their pets. Put another way, talking through dogs is a kind of frame-shifting insofar as a speaker who utters dialogue as if it were spoken in the voice of another is assuming a new and different footing vis-à-vis the participants and the subject of discourse.

To illustrate how I am using the term "ventriloquizing," I will briefly recap an example discussed in more detail elsewhere (Tannen 2003; chapter 2, this volume). This example comes from a third family who participated in our study: Kathy, Sam, and their daughter Kira, who, at the age of two years one month, was only minimally verbal.[3] In the following interchange, Kathy was at home with Kira when Sam returned from work,

---

3. Alexandra Johnston is the research assistant who shadowed the father in this family, transcribed the interchange from which this example comes, and brought this example to my attention.

tired and hungry, and quickly began eating a snack. Kira, who had eaten dinner earlier with her mother, tried to climb onto her father's lap. Sam snapped, "I'm eating!" and Kira began to cry. Speaking in a high-pitched, sing-song baby-talk register, Kathy addressed Kira:

> Can you say,
> → I was just trying to get some Daddy's attention,
> → and I don't really feel too good, either.

Kathy introduced this utterance by addressing Kira and asking "Can you say?" But by using a baby-talk register, and the first person singular "I" (at other times she animated the child using the second person singular "we"), she spoke *as* the child in order to accomplish a variety of communicative tasks at once. She (1) indirectly criticized Sam for snapping at their daughter and making her cry, (2) explained Kira's point of view to Sam, and (3) provided a lesson to Kira that she might one day convey her emotions and needs more effectively with words rather than with tears. (Elsewhere Kathy states this lesson directly by saying to Kira, "Use your words" —an injunction that is common to the point of formulaic among preschool teachers and parents.) The lines indicated by arrows, spoken in the first person and in baby-talk register, are those I would characterize as ventriloquizing because Kathy framed her words as Kira's. She spoke *as* her daughter.

A number of discourse analysts address phenomena like what I refer to as ventriloquizing, with or without using this term or related ones. Schiffrin (1993) investigates the discourse strategy she calls "speaking for another," by which, for example, a woman says on behalf of her guest, "She's on a diet," when the guest declines candy offered by the woman's husband. Scollon (2001), whose interest is "mediated discourse," notes a wide range of types and uses of a baby-talk register in interaction. One such type is what he calls "through baby talk," in which "two participants are speaking to each other with the presence of the infant to mediate what might otherwise be impossible or difficult utterances" (93). Scollon illustrates "through baby talk" with an example exchange in which he was carrying his two-month-old baby daughter while making a purchase in a store. The cashier, after telling her customer the amount he owed, turned to address the infant in his arms by saying in baby talk, "Where's Mommy?" Scollon replied, also in baby talk, "Mommy's at home." He notes that both he and the cashier spoke *through* the infant in order to exchange information and concerns that would have been difficult to articulate directly. He paraphrases the cashier's "hidden dialogue" as "Where is this child's mother; who are you and why are you caring for the child?" and his own as "I'm the father; her mother's at home. And everything is O.K. with this relationship."

Bakhtin (1981) is frequently cited as the source of the concept and term "ventriloquate." Bubnova & Malcuzynski (2001) explain that the term "ventriloquate" is actually the innovation of translators Caryl Emerson and Michael Holquist and that the concept that has come to be associated with this term is not found in Bakhtin's own writing.[4] Bubnova & Malcuzynski present the passage from "Discourse and the Novel" in which this term appears, as translated into English by Emerson and Holquist. At this point in his essay, Bakhtin is discussing the use of language in prose literature:

> The author does not speak in a given language (from which he distances himself to a greater or lesser degree), but he speaks, as it were, *through* a language that has somehow more or less materialized, become objectivized, that he merely ventriloquates. (299)

Bubnova & Malcuzynski note that the passage says, more literally:

> the language through which the author speaks is more densified, objectified, as if it would appear to be at a certain distance from his lips.

They observe, further, that there is a Russian word for "ventriloquism," but neither the term nor any notion related to it appears anywhere in Bakhtin's works.

It is easy to see how the verb "ventriloquate" would seem an appropriate English word to convey the sense of using language in a way that appears to be "at a certain distance from" the speaker's lips. Bubnova & Malcuzynski emphasize, however, that Bakhtin's point in this passage is that an author of prose fiction finds the "language" of the novel given in the conventions of literary discourse. An author must speak *through* those conventions. This is therefore quite a different context from that of conversational discourse. Although Bakhtin apparently did not use the term

---

4. I would like to acknowledge the path by which I traced this paper in order to thank those who played a part. Cynthia Gordon posted an Internet query, to which Jill Brody replied in a message that directed our attention to the Bubnova and Malcuzynski paper and to Pierrette Malcuzynski herself.

and was concerned with literary discourse, one of the effects of what I am calling ventriloquizing in conversational discourse is precisely to make the words spoken "appear to be at a certain distance" from the speaker's lips, in the sense of distancing the speaker from responsibility for the utterance.[5] Thus, although the term "ventriloquize" does not trace, after all, to Bakhtin, Bakhtin's notion of polyvocality, by which an author's words appear "at a certain distance" from the speaker's lips, does nonetheless capture an aspect of interaction that is crucial for our understanding of how speakers use pets as a resource in communicating with each other. The term "ventriloquize," following Bakhtin in spirit if not in terminology, captures the sense in which family members, by voicing their dogs, distance themselves (figuratively, of course) from their own utterances.

Speaking through Intermediaries: A Cross-Cultural View

Speaking through an intermediary is a phenomenon well documented in the anthropological literature. Many such examples come from societies in which it is taboo for individuals in certain kin relations to address each other directly; others simply illustrate the use of children and pets as intermediaries in conversational interactions. For example, Schottman (1993) reports a complex indirect discursive strategy among the Baatombu of northern Benin by which speakers communicate grievances by assigning a proverb as a dog's name; they can then invoke the proverb to express their grievance simply by calling or addressing the dog. Haviland (1986) examines a multi-party interaction in a small Tzotzil-speaking Mexican village to support his claim that conversational mechanisms are designed around multi-party rather than dialogic interaction. At one point in the interaction, a man teases an eleven-year-old boy by playfully offering his daughter as a prospective wife for the boy, adding, "But you must first test her to see if she is any good" (266). The embarrassed boy does not respond, but his father provides a response for him: "'Am I just a baby that I'll take orders from your daughter?' you should say that" (268). Haviland observes that the father is teaching his son not to "let such joking remarks pass" but may also be indirectly communicating that he himself is not to be taken for a fool (279).

---

5. This is particularly pleasing to me, as it is in keeping with my claim (Tannen 2007[1989]) that the discourse strategies we consider quintessentially literary are pervasive and automatic in conversational discourse.

Another anthropological example comes from Schieffelin's (1990) study of Kaluli language development in interaction. Kaluli mothers, Schieffelin demonstrates, use the word "elema" to model for children what to say.[6] In the following example (92) a nine-month-old baby boy has taken Bambi's (the author's) net bag. His mother instructs the boy's two-year-old sister Meli to chastise her baby brother by saying to Meli, "Don't take—elema." In response, Meli tells her baby brother, "Don't take!" The mother adds, "This is Bambi's!—elema. Is it yours?!—elema," and Meli repeats, "Is it yours?!" The mother then gently takes the bag away from the baby.

Americans might, in a similar situation, expect a mother to speak directly to her baby, instructing him not to take what is not his. The Kaluli mother is accomplishing the same result (indeed, she herself physically returns the bag to its owner), but she does so in a way that involves her other child. Thus, as Schieffelin shows, the Kaluli mother (1) teaches Meli a lesson in values, (2) encourages Meli's language development, and (3) socializes Meli into the older-sister role toward her brother—a role that, according to Schieffelin, is fundamental to Kaluli society.

Another aspect of Kaluli discourse is reminiscent of ventriloquizing. Schieffelin notes:

> Kaluli mothers tend to face their babies outward so that they can
> be seen by and see others who are part of the social group. Older
> children greet and address infants, and in response to this moth-
> ers hold their infants face outward and while moving them, speak
> in a special high-pitched, nasalized register (similar to one that
> Kaluli use when speaking to dogs). These infants look as if they
> are talking to someone while their mothers speak for them. (71)

This is similar to our examples in intriguing ways. First, Schieffelin notes that mothers face their babies outward to involve children in social interaction from the very start of their lives, and to teach them not only how to speak but also how to behave, how to regard others, what to value, and so on. Also of interest is Schieffelin's observation that the voice quality used to animate the infant's speech, that is to "ventriloquize" the infant, is akin to the "special high-pitched, nasalized register" that the Kaluli use when speaking to dogs. This reinforces the claim that there is an organic rela-

6. Schieffelin uses the phonetic symbol /ɛ/ for the vowel sound that I am representing with alphabetic "e" in "elema" and "Meli." She notes (p. 254) that this sound is pronounced like the "e" in English "bet."

tionship between the framing of speech as the voicing of infants, on one hand, and as addressed to animals on the other.

The finding that adults often address pets in registers similar to those used in addressing infants has also been documented for English speakers (Burnham, Kitamura & Vollmer-Conna 2002; Hirsh-Pasek & Treiman 1982; see Mitchell 2001 for a comprehensive overview). Roberts (2002), examining videotaped interactions that took place in veterinary clinics, observed that veterinary personnel regularly use baby-talk register to address pets and to "voice" pets in order to reassure pet owners as well as communicate to them face-threatening information such as criticism or disagreement. These findings are similar to the functions of talking to, as, and through pets that I describe in family discourse. My purpose, however, in addition to examining how pets are incorporated as participants in interactions, is to understand how family members use pets as resources in their interactions with each other. This understanding, moreover, serves my larger purpose of illuminating the subtle shifts in framing and footing that characterize discourse among family members as well as the function of such frame shifts in constituting the family's shared identity.

The Families

The examples analyzed in the present study are taken from the transcriptions and tape recordings of two of the families who audio-taped their own interactions for a week each as part of their participation in the Work and Family Project. Of the four families who participated in the project, two had pet dogs. These are the two families whose transcribed interactions provide the data from which the examples examined are drawn.

Talking the Dog in Family Discourse

In what follows, I present six examples to illustrate ways in which dogs become resources in interaction among human family members. Among the interactional goals that are served by speaking through, for, and to the dogs are: effecting a frame shift to a humorous key, buffering criticism, delivering praise, teaching values, resolving potential conflict, and creating a family identity that includes the dogs as family members.

The first three examples come from a family consisting of Clara, Neil, and their son Jason, who was four years, ten months at the time of taping.[7] (All names, of persons and pets, are pseudonyms.) The family has two small dogs, pugs named Tater and Rickie, whom Clara herself, in an email reply to a query, referred to as "my favorite family members."

Example 1: Buffering Criticism

The first example illustrates how a mother uses the resource of voicing the dogs in order to chastise her son and to encourage him to improve his behavior.

At the time of this example, Clara has been home with Jason and is frustrated because he has refused to pick up and put away his toys. She indirectly chastises Jason for his recalcitrance by ventriloquizing the dogs. I use the term "ventriloquizing" because in this example (and in the next two as well), Clara speaks *as* the dogs, animating their voices. By voicing the dogs, Clara frames her criticism in a humorous rather than an acrimonious key:

(1)   Clara: ((*to dog*)) What (do) you have.
                <high pitched> Come again?
                Tater and Rickie! You guys, say,>
→   *<extra high pitch>* "We're naughty,
→   but we're not as naughty as Jason,
→   he's naughtiest.
→   We- we just know it!">
                Okay, careful there Jason,
                remember?

By using an extremely high-pitched baby-talk register, and by speaking in the first person plural ("we"), Clara frames her utterance as the dogs' discourse. In animating the dogs, she does not specify an addressee, but it is clear that Jason is the intended recipient of the communication. The markedness of Clara's high-pitched animation of the dogs stands out not only in its own right but also because it contrasts noticeably with the lower pitched, more

7. Cynthia Gordon is the research team member who shadowed Clara at home and at work, transcribed these interactions, and brought these examples to my attention.

unmarked voice quality in which she addresses her son. When she addresses Jason directly (*Okay, careful there Jason*), she speaks at a far less marked pitch level, more as one would address an adult than as one would address a baby.

Clara's conversational move is, on one level, face-threatening and op-positional: she is chastising her son for failing to pick up his toys, and she is trying to get him to do so. Yet by ventriloquizing the dogs, she funda-mentally alters the nature of her communication. For one thing, ventrilo-quizing introduces a note of humor, since the dogs obviously can neither speak nor understand the words she is figuratively putting in their mouths. At a deeper level, we can observe that ventriloquizing is a form of teasing, a frame-bending speech move. In the terms Bateson (1972) used when presenting his theory of framing, teasing conveys affection on the meta-message level while the words are hostile or adversarial on the message level. Moreover, by using indirectness, teasing, and humor, Clara buffers the criticism and deflects the confrontation constituted by that criticism. Her ventriloquizing lightens the mood and indicates that she is not deeply angry at Jason for failing to pick up his toys. She has found, moreover, that he is more likely to comply with her request if it is presented in this light-hearted manner than he would if she introduced a tone of serious anger.[8]

Example 2: Ventriloquizing Praise, Constituting Family

In Example 2, Clara again ventriloquizes the dogs, but in this case the in-teractive goal is to compliment Jason rather than to criticize him. This example shows, moreover, how animating the dogs also serves to integrate the dogs as family members. The behavior at issue is the same as it was in Example 1: picking up and putting away toys.

It is late Friday morning. Clara is not working on this day, and Jason has stayed home from school because he has been sick, so mother and son are going to go out for breakfast. In preparation for the outing, she again focuses on putting away toys, but this time Jason is cooperating rather than

---

8. An email query confirmed my hypothesis that Clara had learned by experience that her son was more likely to comply with her requests when she framed them in this way. Clara replied to my query in an email dated March 1, 2004, "My style was to indirectly get the point across to Jason in a way that did not raise his defensiveness or encourage him to assert his independence through refusal. The dogs, cats, and others came in very handy. In the situa-tion you reported, I feel sure from his reactions that Jason typically knew what I was doing, but he found the whole thing so comical that he went along."

resisting. Indeed, he is not only putting away his own toys but offering to do the same with the toys "belonging" to one of the dogs, Tater. In response, Clara speaks first *to* the dog and then *as* the dog responding to Jason:

(2)   Jason: I'm gonna put some of Tater's toys in there.
        Clara: <exhales>
        Jason: Where's Tater's [toys?]
        Clara: [Put] your shoesies on.
                ((short pause))
                Good job!
        Jason: /I'm putting his—/
        Clara: <high-pitched> Tater,
→   he's even puttin' your toys away!
→   Tater says,
→   <funny voice> "Yes, I never put them away!
→   I consider my family to be a sl- a slew of maids,
→   servants.">>

In the first part of her discursive move, Clara addresses the dog (*Tater, he's even puttin' your toys away!*) in order to praise her son. In the second part, she ventriloquizes the dog as if to provide a required response, an acknowledgment of the favor. But rather than the expected "thank you," which would represent the dog expressing human-like gratitude, Clara animates the dog's indifference to Jason's good deed and further interprets that indifference as arrogance, which such ingratitude would be if Tater were a person rather than an animal.

By ventriloquizing the dog, Clara first and foremost introduces a note of humor. It is funny to represent a dog as an ungrateful family member. The key of humor is reinforced not only by the stance Clara creates for the dog—a persona so grand that he regards the other family members as his "maids" and "servants"—but also by the baby-talk register created by the voice quality, high pitch, and intonation pattern in which she animates the dog. It is funny for a full-grown adult to speak in a marked high-pitch baby-talk register. Clara also signals and creates a casual key by the deletion of the final "-ng" so that "putting" becomes "puttin'" (*he's even puttin' your toys away*). It seems that Clara uses this humor partly to amuse herself. At the same time, her discursive moves accomplish a number of other types of conversational work. For one thing, she teaches Jason a lesson in values: family members should not expect other family members to pick up after them. The mechanism of this lesson is amusingly subtle. Whereas Jason's failure to put away his toys is faultable, a dog cannot seriously be faulted for the same lapse. Framing Tater as one who faultably expects others to function as maids or servants is a humorous way to convey this lesson to Jason.

I would argue that ventriloquizing the dog in this context serves another interactive purpose as well: linguistically constituting the interactants as a family. Clara and Neil have had one of the dogs, Rickie, longer—eight years longer—than they have had Jason. On one level, Clara and Neil enhanced their joint identity as a family with the "adoption" (Clara's term) of this first dog.[9] In this example, by voicing the dog, Clara integrates the dog into the interaction, thus constituting herself, her child, and their dogs as an intertwined unit—a family. Moreover, as Arluke & Sanders (1996:67) point out, the very act of speaking for an animal constitutes a claim and demonstration of an intimate relationship with that animal. In this example, then, Clara is demonstrating the intimacy of her relationship with the dog, an intimacy that reinforces the family-member identity that she is creating for him.

In sum, this example shows that by ventriloquizing the dog Tater, Clara integrates the dog into the family, expresses her affection for and intimacy with the dog, and creates an identity for him as a family member, at the same time that she uses the dog as a resource for praising her son, teaching him a lesson in values, and reinforcing the identity of the human-and-animal grouping as a family.

Example 3: Framing the Dog as a Conversational Participant

Example 3 is a continuation of the same interaction between Clara and Jason. This segment involves the other family dog, Rickie. Here Clara draws on the discursive resource of Rickie's growling and then barking in order

---

9. In answer to a question emailed by Cynthia Gordon asking how long Clara and Neil had had the dogs, Clara replied, "Rickie was born on 2/2/88, and we adopted him when he was about 6 months old. Tater was born on 12/8/98, but we adopted him from Pug Rescue in July of 99, so he was about 6 1/2 months when we adopted him." Although using the verb "adopt" to represent the acquisition of pets is commonplace and therefore arguably formulaic, I believe it also functions to indicate a level of commitment to the acquired animal and perhaps to "family-ize" the unit created by the addition of a pet to a household.

first, to incorporate the dog's vocalization as a conversational contribution, and second, to create an amusing imaginary scenario in which the small dog is reframed as a watchdog, and the sound of machinery outside the house is reframed as a threat to the family's safety:

(3)   Jason: I'm gonna need to put this box away.
               ((*short pause*))
               There's another box
               that has the little aliens in it, ((*dog growls*))
               and you [have to /???/]
→ Clara: [<*high-pitched*> Rickie, you wild] little dog!>
      Jason: I have a game that has aliens in it,
               it's in the box.
      Clara: Oh, okay. ((*short pause, dog barks*))
→   <*high-pitched*> Oh Rickie, you're so tough!
→   He says, ["I'm hearin' things."]
      Jason: [/???/]
→ Clara: "Yep, and there are those big machines out there,
→   and I'm gonna be defendin' this house
→   'til I- 'til I . pass out!">

The sound of the dog Rickie first growling and then barking provides a resource for Clara to introduce humor by applying a watchdog schema to a dog who is obviously unsuited to this task. Though double the weight of the ten-pound Chihuahua mix in the anecdote presented at the beginning of this paper, Rickie is quite small and very old. At twelve, he is suffering from back paralysis and is missing most of his teeth. The watchdog schema is therefore a ready source of humor; it is obviously funny to refer to the small, ailing Rickie as "wild" and "tough."

In addition to using them as a resource for humor, Clara simultaneously uses the growling and barking as a resource for framing Rickie as a family member. She ratifies the dog's vocalizations as conversational contributions by providing an account of their "meaning." According to the Website pugs.com, "Behind a closed door, the pugs' deeper bark (than other small breeds) often sounds like a much larger dog than they are." This description explains in part why Clara might respond to Rickie's growl and bark by playfully exaggerating their import (*Rickie, you wild little dog!*, *Oh Rickie, you're so tough!*).

As in the preceding example, immediately after speaking *to* the dog, Clara speaks *as* the dog. By voicing Rickie's reply to her utterance, she frames the dog as a participant who both receives and contributes conversational turns. By ventriloquizing the dog, Clara interprets the cause of his growls and barks (*big machines out there*) and reframes the dog's responses to outside noise as motivated in terms of human interaction (*defendin' this house*). As in the lines discussed earlier, Clara drops the -ng endings of her verbs, thereby creating a casual, playful key for her utterances ("*I'm hearin' things,*" "*I'm gonna be defendin' this house*"). Thus Clara draws on the dog's growls and barks not only as a resource for humor but also in order to frame the dog as a family member participating in the interaction. Moreover, I would argue that the interchange reinforces solidarity between Clara and Jason as they share not only the humor of talking the dog but also the knowledge structure schema (Tannen & Wallat 1993 [1987]) that makes the humor comprehensible—the shared nature of a "watchdog script."

Example 4: Human Interaction as a Resource for Talking to Pets

The next example shows Clara using a dog as a resource in interaction with Neil. Here Clara again uses the watchdog schema to introduce a humorous key, this time to criticize Neil for a small lapse. This interchange takes place during the evening. Clara is at home, and Neil returns from a brief trip to the local convenience store. After a few shared observations about a topic of relevance to current events, the following exchange occurs:

(4)   Clara: You leave the door open for any reason?
                   ((*short pause, sound of door shutting*))
→   <baby talk> Rickie,
→   he's helpin' burglars come in,
→   and you have to defend us Rick.>

Here Clara speaks *to* rather than *as* the dog, yet she uses the same high-pitched, baby-talk register that she uses when she ventriloquizes the dogs. Rickie can no more understand her discourse than utter it—or than defend her and Neil against burglars.

Clara's initial question to Neil (*You leave the door open for any reason?*) is in itself an indirect linguistic strategy. Rather than tell him directly to close the door, she frames her complaint as a question about his motives. That Neil doesn't answer the question is not surprising since the question is most likely not a literal request for information but an indirect request for action—which Neil apparently provides by closing the door. (It is not possible to know for sure from the audiotape who closed the door.) Since the door is heard to be shut before Clara goes on to address the dog, one may well ask what purpose is served by Clara's utterances to the dog. On one level, I suspect Clara simply used the dog as a sounding board for her own inner dialogue. The watchdog schema provides a resource for verbalizing what would otherwise be unstated, though obvious: the reason that it's important to keep the door to the house closed.

I suggest, however, another possible explanation for Clara's utterance to the dog in this instance. The exchange regarding the door provides a resource for Clara to talk to the dog, much as one talks nonsense to a baby: the subject of the talk is not significant, but the sound of the talk, with all its paralinguistic and prosodic richness, provides an occasion to express the positive emotion—fondness, attachment—that the speaker feels toward the child, or, in this case, the dog. At the same time, it does the important work of including the nonverbal family member in conversational interaction, ratifying, as it were, the child (or the dog) as a family member. In the previous examples we could say that the dog provided a resource for managing interpersonal interaction; that level is present in this example as well. But this example also illustrates yet another function of ventriloquizing: a sense in which the interaction among humans provides a resource for a pet owner to express affection and attachment to the dog and to thereby enact the integration of the pet into the family. Just as humans reinforce their interpersonal connections through talk, whether or not there is anything important to talk about at a given moment, humans similarly reinforce their connections to pets through talk, whether or not there is anything to be communicated to the pet. Talking to the pet about something that just happened with a human, therefore, provides material for such talk.

Example 5: Buffering a Complaint

The last two examples come from another family. Nora and Greg have three children. At the time of taping, the youngest was in high school, the next was in college, and the oldest was working as a professional musician. In a book examining family interaction (Tannen 2001), I used examples from Nora and Greg's interactions in order to illustrate how a couple successfully avoided or defused conflict by using humor and apologies. (The fact that their children were teenagers or older, and therefore required less labor-intensive care, may well have played a role here.) In Example 5, Greg has been inconvenienced because Nora neglected to tell him that she had taken the dog for a walk earlier in the day. Instead of lodging a complaint against Nora, however, Greg addresses his complaint to the dog, thus buffering (while still communicating) the criticism.

It is evening following a long day's work. Greg is about to take the family dog out for his daily run when he passes Nora, who informs him that she has already done that. The interchange proceeds as follows.

(5)	Greg:	I'm going to take him out.
	Nora:	He's been out once.
	Greg:	Oh, he has?
	Nora:	We had a long walk this morning.
	Greg:	Oh, I didn't know that.
	Nora:	Sorry.
		I meant to tell you.
		I kept forgetting to tell—<*laughs*>
→	Greg:	((*to dog*)) Well why didn't YOU tell us?
→		We'll do a short one then, okay?

Greg has reason to be annoyed at Nora. Her having forgotten to tell him she'd taken the dog for a walk has inconvenienced him. (He says, as we will see below, that he would have continued working longer had he known.) Greg could well have directly registered a complaint as an accusation, "You should have told me," or a challenge, "Why didn't you tell me?" Instead he made a statement about his own ignorance (*Oh, I didn't know that*). As with the preceding examples, addressing himself to the dog rather than his wife introduces a note of humor. In this case, addressing the dog also provides a way for Greg to avoid directly blaming Nora when he asks the dog, *Well why didn't YOU tell us?* Since it is obvious that the dog could not have done so, this utterance does indirectly address the complaint to Nora. But its being indirect rather than direct, mediated by a humorous discursive move, takes the sting out of the complaint. The dog provides a resource for accomplishing this mediation.

Also interesting is Greg's use of the plural "us" rather than "me." It seems clear that when he asks the dog, *Why didn't you tell us?* the plural "us" refers to one person, himself. This usage strikes me as akin to the use of first person plural in expressions such as "Give us a hug." It is a form of speech reminiscent of adults speaking to children (Wills 1977), or perhaps to other adults, toward whom they feel affection. In this sense, Greg, like Clara in the preceding examples, creates a family-like atmosphere of affection and inclusion in the way he addresses the dog, as well as in the fact that he speaks to the dog at all.

Example 6: Occasioning an Apology

The last example shows how talking to a dog becomes the means by which a potential conflict is deflected and then resolved. In other words, the dog becomes the resource for resolving a conflict.

Example 6 is a continuation of the interchange presented in the preceding example. Greg lets Nora know that he's been inconvenienced:

(6)   Greg: I would've stayed and worked if I'd known.
  →   ((*to dog*)) Now I got you all excited.
       Nora: Sorry.
       Greg: Well I probably should've asked you.

Greg's expression of frustration is in two parts. The first part is the fact that he stopped work earlier than he otherwise would have in order to take the dog for a walk (*I would've stayed and worked if I'd known*). The second part is his explanation of why he cannot simply undo this effect by abandoning his plan to take the dog for a walk and returning to work. (Greg's office is in his home.) The reason he cannot do this is provided in an utterance addressed to the dog (*Now I got you all excited*). His compromise is to take the dog for a walk, but a shorter one than he had intended.

The potential for conflict between Nora and Greg is buffered by the way both produce their succeeding utterances. Nora apologizes for her lapse and its consequences (*Sorry*), and Greg responds by assuming part of the blame (*Well I probably should've asked you*). This brief exchange illustrates the two-part nature of a canonical apology routine in which each party takes responsibility for some degree of fault, so neither is left in the compromising position of taking all the blame. This couple often offered and accepted apologies; I have identified this as an element in their apparently harmonious household (Tannen 2001). Example 6 shows that talking the dog provides a resource by which apologies are freely exchanged. One could argue that Greg set the scene for Nora's apology by downplaying the gravity of her offense, and this he did in part by addressing his complaint to the dog rather than to her. Talking to the dog introduced a note of humor and deflected the confrontation through a third party. Nora's apology then set the scene for Greg's balancing admission that he too was guilty of a lapse in assuming, without asking, that the dog needed to be taken for a walk.

This example shows, then, the complex negotiation of complaint, explanation, apology, and redress by which a potential conflict was resolved. In accomplishing this negotiation, Greg used the dog as a resource by which to mediate the resolution.

Conclusion

The six examples I have presented illustrate how family members who tape-recorded their conversations over the course of a week used their pet dogs as resources in mediating their interactions with each other. I have demonstrated in these examples that talking the dog accomplishes multiple intertwined and overlaid interactive feats. Among the interactive goals that family members accomplished by using dogs as resources are: occasioning a switch out of an argument frame, rekeying the interaction as humorous, buffering criticism, reinforcing solidarity among family members, delivering praise, teaching values to a child, providing the occasion to talk as a way of enacting affection for pets, reinforcing a couple's bond by positioning them as "Mommy" and "Daddy" to their dog, resolving a conflict by conveying and triggering an apology, framing pets as family members, and reinforcing bonds among individuals who live together by exhibiting, reinforcing, and creating their identity as a family.

My purpose has been to examine and explore the linguistic strategies by which family members use dogs as resources in their interactions with each other. Examples of family members talking as, to, or about their dogs, in the dogs' presence, constitute instances of the continuous, seamless shifts in framing and footing that characterize conversational discourse in general and family discourse in particular. By talking through dogs, family members enlist their pets as resources by which to manage and enact communication among themselves. Examining the use of pets as interactional resources thus adds to our understanding of framing in discourse. The analysis also enriches our understanding of Bakhtin's notion of polyvocality and its relevance to conversational discourse, in the sense that talking through pets allows speakers to distance themselves, figuratively, from their own utterances. The analysis also contributes to our understanding of family discourse by allowing us to see how pets are framed, through talk, as family members. Understanding these processes helps us understand how talking the dog is a resource by which speakers accomplish interaction while reflecting and constituting their family identity.

References

Arluke, Arnold, and Clinton R. Sanders. 1996. Regarding animals. Philadelphia: Temple University Press.

Bakhtin, M. M. 1981 [1975]. The dialogic imagination. Austin: The University of Texas Press.

Bilger, Burkhard. 2003. The last meow. The New Yorker, September 8, 2003. 46–53.

Bubnova, Tatiana, and M.-Pierette Malcuzynski. 2001. The invention of Bakhtin (or the art of ventriloquism and other alien [counter]feits). Paper presented at the Tenth International Conference on Bakhtin, Gdansk, Poland, July 2001.

Burnham, Denis, Christine Kitamura, and Ute Vollmer-Conna. 2002. What's new pussycat? On talking to babies and animals. Science 296, May 24, 2002, 1435.

Goffman, Erving. 1981. Forms of talk. Philadelphia: University of Pennsylvania Press.

Gumperz, John J. 1982. Discourse strategies. Cambridge: Cambridge University Press.

Haviland, John. 1986. "Con buenos chiles": Talk, targets and teasing in Zinacantan. Text 6(3).249–282.

Hirsh-Pasek, Kathy, and Rebecca Treiman. 1982. Doggerel: Motherese in a new context. Journal of Child Language 9.229–237.

Mitchell, Robert W. 2001. Americans' talk to dogs: Similarities and differences with talk to infants. Research on Language and Social Interaction 34(2).183–210.

Roberts, Felicia. 2002. "You bite?": Functionality of animal directed utterances in veterinary clinic visits. Paper presented at National Communication Association, New Orleans, La., November 22, 2002.

Schieffelin, Bambi B. 1990. The give and take of everyday life: Language socialization of Kaluli children. Cambridge: Cambridge University Press.

Schiffrin, Deborah. 1993. "Speaking for another" in sociolinguistic interviews: Alignments, identities, and frames. Framing in discourse, ed. Deborah Tannen, 231–263. New York and Oxford: Oxford University Press.

Schottman, Wendy. 1993. Proverbial dog names of the Baatombu: A strategic alternative to silence. Language in Society 22(4).539–554.

Scollon, Ron. 2001. On the ontogenesis of a social actor: From object to agency in baby talk. Mediated discourse: The nexus of practice, 86–112. London: Routledge.

Tannen, Deborah, ed. 1993. Framing in discourse. Oxford and New York: Oxford University Press.

Tannen, Deborah. 1994. The relativity of linguistic strategies: Rethinking power and solidarity in gender and dominance. Gender and discourse, 19–52. Oxford and New York: Oxford University Press.

Tannen, Deborah. 2001. I only say this because I love you: Talking to your parents, partner, sibs, and kids when you're all adults. New York: Ballantine.

Tannen, Deborah. 2003. Power maneuvers or connection maneuvers? Ventriloquizing in family interaction. Linguistics, language, and the real world: Discourse and beyond. Georgetown University Round Table on Languages and Linguistics 2001, ed. Deborah Tannen and James E. Alatis, 50–62. Washington, D.C.: Georgetown University Press.

Tannen, Deborah. 2007 [1989]. Talking voices: Repetition, dialogue, and imagery in conversational discourse. Cambridge: Cambridge University Press.

Tannen, Deborah, and Cynthia Wallat. 1993 [1987]. Interactive frames and knowledge schemas in interaction: Examples from a medical examination/ interview. Social Psychology Quarterly 50(2).205–216. Reprinted in Framing in discourse, ed. Deborah Tannen, 57–76. New York and Oxford: Oxford University Press, 1993.

Wertsch, James V. 1998. Mind as action. New York: Oxford University Press.

Wills, Dorothy David. 1977. Participant deixis in English and baby talk. Talking to children: Language input and acquisition, ed. Catherine E. Snow and Charles A. Ferguson, 271–295. Cambridge: Cambridge University Press.

CYNTHIA GORDON

four

"I just feel horribly embarrassed when she does that": Constituting a Mother's Identity

Numerous researchers have suggested that individuals use language, and in particular narrative language, to construct identities.[1] For example, Polkinghorne (1988:150) argues, "we achieve our personal identities and self-concept through the use of narrative configuration." Riessman (1992:232) suggests that "narrative allows us to create who we are," while Gergen (1987) proposes that the self is constructed through virtually all discourse. Ochs (1993:296) argues that "at any given actual moment," interactants are "actively constructing their social identities rather than passively living out some cultural prescription of social identity." Speakers thus continually construct identities in all types of discourse. Recent sociolinguistic inquiry into personal and social identity has incorporated such constructivist views. For example, Schiffrin (1996) shows how two women use narrative to create what she calls "self-portraits" of themselves as mothers in sociolinguistic interviews. Schiffrin's (2000, 2002) analyses of one Holocaust survivor's oral life history show that—and in what ways —the narrator draws on specific linguistic resources in discursively

1. I thank the Sloan Foundation for funding this study and Janet and Steve and their family for their participation. I am grateful to Deborah Tannen and Shari Kendall for their extensive comments on earlier versions of this paper.

representing her relationship with her mother and her friends. In a related vein, Adelswärd & Nilholm (2000) illustrate how one mother uses language to construct her maternal identity in a parent-teacher-pupil conference.

This analysis builds on past work by considering identity construction in verbal interaction from an interactional sociolinguistic perspective. Like Schiffrin and Adelswärd & Nilholm, I consider the construction of the identity of "mother." However, whereas they examine identity construction in the contexts of interviews and parent-teacher-pupil conferences respectively, I analyze how one mother's maternal identity is constructed in one everyday family conversation. Toward this end, I analyze a naturally occurring interaction between the mother (Janet), father (Steve), and uncle (Kevin) of a two-year-eleven-month-old child (Natalie).

In this interaction, Kevin, Janet's younger brother, tells Janet and Steve how their daughter (mis)behaved while he babysat her that day. Following Ochs (1993:288), who suggests that "speakers attempt to construct the social identities of themselves and others through verbally performing certain social *acts* and verbally displaying certain *stances*," I argue that Janet constructs her identity or "paints a portrait" of herself as a mother through performing social acts and taking up stances toward the topic of talk, particularly her daughter's and brother's story world behaviors, as well as toward her interlocutors. In this way, I illustrate how sociocultural expectations about what it means to be a mother are indexed through talk to create that identity.

Specifically, I demonstrate how Janet performs social acts and takes up affective stances that are socioculturally linked to the identities of "parent," "woman," and particularly "mother." I show that through (1) *requesting details* about her brother's day with her daughter, (2) *providing details* of her child's life in response to her brother's report, (3) *providing assessments* of her daughter's and her brother's story world behaviors, and (4) *accounting for* her daughter's misbehavior, Janet takes up alignments that construct her identity as a mother because these acts and the affective stances she builds into them are linked to cultural perceptions of parents, women, and mothers.

In what follows, I first review past work on alignment and identity construction and describe how prior work on these topics has made reference to cultural perceptions of gender and parental identities. Second, I introduce Janet and her conversational partners in more detail. Third, I present two short conversations between Janet and her husband that serve to contextualize the longer conversation that is the focus of this analysis. I then turn to that conversation, demonstrating how, through the social acts she performs and the affective stances she takes up, Janet constructs both a gendered and parental identity. Throughout, I contrast Janet's verbal behavior with her husband's. Finally, I consider how Janet's taking up parental and gendered alignments works toward her overall identity construction as a mother.

Alignment and Identity Construction

Creating Identities in Interaction: Acts, Stances, and Sociocultural Knowledge

In articulating footing, Goffman suggests that a "participant's alignment, or set, or stance, or posture, or projected self is somehow at issue" (1981:128). Work in sociolinguistics considering identity from a social constructivist perspective identifies *alignment, footing, stance,* or *position* as integral to locating identity construction in interaction. For example, Schiffrin (1996) identifies several aspects of alignment that make what she refers to as "identity displays." She examines how individuals construct maternal identities in narrative by analyzing two stories told by women in sociolinguistic interviews. Both narrators verbalize experiences wherein they represent relationships between themselves and younger women in their families who depart from norms of the family. In narrating these experiences, these women construct their identities by creating positions between themselves as story world figures and other figures in the story, and between themselves as tellers and their audience. For example, one mother creates a story world in which her daughter is portrayed as taking responsibility for her own actions (going on an interfaith date), allowing the mother to portray herself as neutral (rather than critical) and permissive (rather than controlling). Through such strategies, the mother is able to construct "a position of mother/daughter solidarity and closeness" (180).

Schiffrin shows that identity can be displayed through linguistic strategies on several levels of discourse that create alignments, including, but not limited to, syntax, speech acts, repetition, and "constructed dialogue" (Tannen 2007 [1989]). She thus identifies some aspects of language that are potentially useful in constructivist examinations of identity and specifically identifies these aspects because they create alignments or positions. Schiffrin's (2000, 2002) subsequent research on an oral life history interview of one Holocaust survivor likewise explores the identity of "mother," this time examining how it is borne out in linguistic representations of the mother-daughter relationship. For instance, Schiffrin (2000) considers what the narrator, Ilse, says about her mother and, importantly, how she says it. For example, when Ilse describes how her mother left her behind in Germany before the Holocaust while she herself immigrated with her new husband to America, she lessens her mother's responsibility for this action through the patterned use of referring terms (using first the full noun phrase "my mother" and continuing with "zero" pronoun). Zero pronouns used in this manner, Schiffrin argues, "background and de-emphasize the mother's role in actions, and hence, her agency" (14).

Similar to Schiffrin, Wortham (2000) considers one narrative told by a woman in her late fifties in an interview setting to explore how she represents herself as a particular sort of person through the positions she takes up toward her audience and the positions she creates between herself and other story world characters. Thus Wortham focuses on "how the self *represented* in an autobiographical narrative and the self *enacted* in the same narrative can interrelate so as to partly construct the self" (158). He shows that the narrator simultaneously constructs positions of passivity (for herself as a seven-year-old story world character) and agentivity (as a narrator), arguing that in creating this duality of positions, the narrator indexes that her current self-identity as an agentive individual needs to be continuously maintained.

Unlike Schiffrin and Wortham, Adelswärd & Nilholm (2000) consider identity work in non-narrative discourse. They also focus on a different context, analyzing identities, including the identity of "mother," as they are constructed during the course of a parent-teacher-pupil conference. Like Schiffrin (1996, 2000, 2002), they consider the mother's identity as it is tied to the identity of "child." In their data, the child, Cindy, has Down syndrome and is present in the parent-teacher-pupil interaction. They find that the mother uses a host of linguistic strategies to help her daughter present herself as a competent interlocutor. For example, she elaborates on and interprets Cindy's turns. Adelswärd & Nilholm (2000:545) argue that, "To help one's daughter present her identity in a favorable way is to simultaneously display the identity of a good mother."

Adelswärd & Nilholm identify Goffman's notions of *alignment* and *footing* as critical to identity construction; likewise, Ochs (1993) calls attention to *stances* and *social acts*. For Ochs, a "social act" is "any socially recognized, goal-directed behavior, such as making a request, contradicting another person, or interrupting someone" (288). A "stance" is a "display of a socially recognized view or attitude," including epistemic and affective attitudes (288). Ochs suggests that both acts and stances create identities in interaction because they create alignments between participants and/or between participants and topics of talk.

Ochs (1993) notes that the relation of language to social identity is "mediated by the interlocutors' understandings of conventions for doing particular social acts and stances and the interlocutors' understandings of how acts and stances are resources for structuring particular social identities (Brown & Levinson 1979)" (289). She thus emphasizes the complexity of the language-identity link, noting that

> particular acts and particular stances have local conventional links that bind them together to form particular social identities. Social identity is a complex social meaning that can be distilled into the act and stance meanings that bring it into being. From this point of view, social identity is not usually explicitly encoded by language but rather is a social meaning that one usually *infers* on the basis of one's sense of the act and stance meanings encoded by linguistic constructions. (289)

Ochs thus stresses that the link between language use, on the one hand, and identity, on the other, depends on joint understanding of conventional sociocultural meanings. Similarly, Schiffrin (1996) argues that sociocultural knowledge plays an important part in stories that make identity claims. She makes use of "sociolinguistic knowledge about the performance of social actions through the use of words, as well as social and cultural knowledge about families and family roles" in locating identity construction in the discourse she analyzes (172). She notes that stories are situated *locally*, or in a here-and-now interaction, as well as *globally*, meaning their interpretation depends on shared cultural knowledge.

In sum, a number of researchers have suggested that participants claim or construct identities through creating positions, stances, or alignments in conversation. Alignments can be created between figures in a story world, or by linguistically performing acts and taking up stances to topics of talk or to other interactants in both narrative and non-narrative discourse. Significantly, both Schiffrin and Ochs stress that sociocultural knowledge plays a key role for analysts (and for interactants) in linking specific conversational acts, stances, or positions with particular identities. Ochs describes this as follows:

> Whether or not a particular social identity does indeed take hold in social interaction depends minimally on (a) whether a speaker and other interlocutors share cultural and linguistic conventions for

constructing particular acts and stances; (b) whether the speaker and other interlocutors share economic, political, or social histories and conventions that associate those acts and stances with the particular identity a speaker is trying to project; and (c) whether other interlocutors are able and willing or are otherwise constrained to ratify the speaker's claim to that identity. (290)

Alignments and Gendered Identities

The creation of alignments and stances has been linked to the linguistic construction of socioculturally meaningful identities of all types, including both gender and parental identities. Tannen (1996:196), using terminology introduced by Goffman (1977), suggests that "ways of talking that pattern by gender" can be referred to as "sex-class linked," meaning that they are "linked to the *class* of women or men rather than necessarily to individual members of these classes." Tannen thus links gendered behavior directly to work on alignments, stating:

> The most fruitful approaches to examining gender and language, then, do not try to link behavior directly to individuals of one sex or the other but rather begin by asking how interaction is framed—in Goffman's terms, what *alignments* speakers are taking up. Davies and Harré (1990), in a similar spirit, ask how speakers are *positioning* themselves with respect to the situation—and then ask where women and men tend to fall in this pattern. (199–200)

This is much like Ochs's (1992) argument that individuals assume stances that are associated in a given cultural context with being female or male and her (1993) claim that all alignments take on identity-significant meanings only in a cultural context. Similarly, this view is congruent with Schiffrin's (1996) suggestion that the construction of positions, including positions that are gendered, is dependent on sociocultural knowledge.

Sociocultural Knowledge, Women, and Mothers

There are many sociocultural expectations for women in general and mothers in particular that can be indexed through talk to work toward creating those identities. For example, mothers are often thought of as being responsible for their children's every shortcoming in American culture. The tendency for society to blame mothers for everything has been noted by various authors, recently by Tannen (2001). In his study of how people save face in interaction, Schlenker (1980) gives a number of examples where parents, particularly mothers, feel the need to engage in "impression management" (Goffman 1959) in the form of an account or an apology because they are (or imagine themselves to be) perceived as responsible for their children's failures. For example, Schlenker offers, "a mother is mortified when her small daughter asks why their hostess is so fat" (126). An account, or "a statement made by a social actor to explain unanticipated or untoward behavior" (Scott & Lyman 1968:46) can be used to attempt to do impression management, including to explain a child's transgression. As Scott & Lyman point out, "Every account is a manifestation of the underlying negotiation of identities" that occurs in interaction (59).

Schlenker notes that indirect linkages between parents and the behaviors of their children are not only informally enacted in everyday conversation, they are also formally sanctioned by law. For example, parents can be held legally responsible if their child damages the property of another. Schlenker remarks, "the parents, presumably, are charged with the task of bringing up their children 'properly'; if they fail, they are responsible. (This presumed failure of parents partially explains why parents are so easily embarrassed, and defensive, when their children misbehave in public)" (139). Because parents, and especially mothers, are perceived in some way as responsible for their children's misbehavior, they may account for their behavior or apologize for it in order to save face. Thus doing "impression management" for one's child's behaviors has links to both parents in general and mothers in particular.

Sociocultural knowledge also links the sharing and soliciting of details with the discourse of women and of mothers. Tannen (2007 [1989], 1990) finds that women often share and solicit details as a way of building involvement between interlocutors, where "involvement" refers to "an internal, even emotional connection individuals feel which binds them to other people as well as to places, things, activities, ideas, memories, and words" (1989:12). Thus it is typically women more than men who want to know and share all those "relatively insignificant details about daily life" (1989:12). In her words, "The noticing of details shows caring and involvement. Men, however, often find women's involvement in details irritating. . . . Conversely, many women complain that men don't tell enough details" (1990:115).

Personal details are more commonly a feature linked to women's talk rather than to men's, as they create intimacy and connection, often a primary conversational goal of women. To incorporate Ochs's (1993) terminology, the social acts of providing and soliciting details are conventionally linked to connection and the discourse of women. In Tannen's (1996) terms, the social acts of gathering and giving of details can be seen as "sex-class linked."

The solicitation and sharing of details has also been linked specifically to the discourse of mothers. Ochs & Taylor (1992a, 1992b, 1995) identify what they call the "Father knows best" phenomenon in family dinnertime conversation. They summarize "Father knows best" as follows:

> (a) mothers introduce narratives (about themselves and their children) that set up fathers as primary recipients (and implicitly sanction them as evaluators of others' actions, thoughts, conditions and feelings); (b) fathers turn such opportunity spaces into forums for problematizing, with mothers themselves as their chief targets, very often on the grounds of incompetence; and (c) mothers respond in defense of themselves and their children via counter-problematizing of fathers' evaluative comments. (1992a:461)

Ochs & Taylor identify mothers' introducing of narratives as "setting up" fathers to judge story world behaviors of both mothers and children. However, Tannen (2001, 2003, this volume) suggests that another way of looking at this interactional pattern is in terms of detail and involvement: perhaps the mothers in Ochs & Taylor's study wanted to create intimacy and involvement between members of the family, including between fathers and children, and they attempted to do this by prompting their children to share details about what was happening in their daily lives.

Anecdotal evidence suggests not only that mothers encourage the sharing of details in the family context in pursuit of intimacy but additionally that knowing the details of family members' lives, particularly the lives of their daughters, is typically perceived as part of the role of being a mother. Henwood (1993), through her analysis of interviews with sixty women, has shown that mothers judge their relationships with their daughters by how close they are and that exchanging details of daily life is typically seen as a sign of closeness.

One mother quoted in *The New Our Bodies, Ourselves* (1992:169) remarks that part of her identity of being a mother is knowing details of her
children's lives:

> After fifteen years of being a full-time homemaker, I decided to go
> to school. My husband and I divided up all the jobs and responsi-
> bilities so I could finish school and work at a fairly demanding job
> full-time. *Everything was working out fine, I thought, until one day
> Jim made some passing remark about one of our daughters and some
> problem she was having with her boyfriend. I was shocked to realize
> that something was going on I knew nothing about. I was no longer
> the "nerve center" of the family. That was a loss, because for many
> years knowing all those details had been my source of power within
> the family.* Yet on balance the change has been good for all of us.
> Being the nerve center was holding me back from developing
> other parts of myself, and as I moved out into the world, Jim grew
> a great deal closer to the kids. (italics added)

This mother reflects a sense of initial shock and loss upon realizing that her
husband knew a detail of their daughter's life that she, a mother recently
returning to the working world, did not. She realizes that all information is
no longer flowing through her and that her identity as a mother is fundamentally changed because of it. Similarly, Henwood remarks that mother-
daughter relationships are socioculturally, at least in the ideal, characterized
as close and that details play a role in this characterization. Both support
Tannen's (1990) discussion of the role of intimacy in women's relationships
and the role of details in creating intimacy. So details are culturally linked
to the talk of both women and mothers; eliciting and providing details could
be considered a sex-class linked interactional behavior and a behavior linked
specifically to mothers.

"Assessment" as a Social Act

As "accounting for child misbehavior" and "sharing/gathering details" can
be seen as social acts, so too can assessing, or "evaluating in some fashion
persons and events being described" (Goodwin & Goodwin 1992:154).
Prior work on assessments by Pomerantz (1984), Goodwin & Goodwin
(1992), and Holt (2000) illustrates that assessment is a highly interactive
phenomenon and not just the product of a single speaker. Pomerantz

(1984) suggests that assessment occurs collaboratively in her exploration of how first assessments shape second assessments. Goodwin & Goodwin (1992:15), in their investigation of how assessments construct context, suggest that assessment often occurs as part of an "assessment activity" where individuals not only make their own assessments but also "monitor the assessment-relevant actions of others." Such an activity, Goodwin & Goodwin suggest, often results in participants coordinating assessments to make congruent understanding visible in conversation. In a related vein, Holt (2000) demonstrates how story tellers use "direct reported speech" (or what Tannen [2007 (1989)] calls "constructed dialogue") to occasion recipients to directly assess the purported words of others, at which point the teller then collaborates in the recipient's assessment. This sequence, Holt argues, results in highly collaborative forms of participation and a realignment of participants.

Though prior work on assessments suggests that they are created by and creators of the sequential unfolding of interaction and acknowledges that participants can "realign" via the production of assessments, there has been little exploration of the role of assessments in creating relationships or identities in talk. Taken in the context of Ochs's (1993) work, however, assessments can be linked to identity construction—performing the social act of assessment, which entails taking an evaluative stance toward something or someone, creates alignments that can work to construct identities in interaction. My analysis extends the view of assessments as sequentially occasioned to show that they are social acts that index appreciation, rapport, and sympathy and, in so doing, can contribute to identity construction in conversations among family members. Before turning to the analysis of how Janet uses a range of linguistic strategies (including assessing) to create her identity as a mother, I first give some background information on the participants and the conversations I examine.

The Family

To consider how a maternal identity is interactionally constructed in family discourse, I focus on an interaction between one mother (Janet), her husband Steve, and her younger brother Kevin. In addition, I consider two other tape-recorded interactions between Janet and Steve that occurred prior to the interaction with Kevin and serve to contextualize Janet and Steve's interactional behaviors. All of these interactions are drawn from the Work and Family Project for which the mother and father each carried a digital tape recorder for a week. I was the research team member who shadowed Janet, listened to the entirety of her tapes, and transcribed many of them.

The examples that I analyze relate to the fact that at the time of taping, Janet and Steve's two-year-eleven-month-old daughter Natalie was regularly throwing temper tantrums. One afternoon/evening while Janet and Steve took Janet and Kevin's mother to the emergency room (she was dehydrated due to an ongoing illness), Kevin agreed to babysit Natalie and had to deal with her tantrums. Kevin, several years younger than Janet, lived nearby but did not normally babysit Natalie. At the time of taping he was not married and had no children of his own. I focus on the interaction in which Kevin reports to Janet and Steve how Natalie misbehaved while he babysat her. However, due to the extended taping period of the larger study, this analysis is also able to consider other conversations relevant to the interpretation of this interaction and to how Janet uses it to construct her identity as a mother. I begin by considering two conversations between Janet and Steve.

Analysis: Creating a Mother's Identity

Gendered Alignments in Conversations between Spouses

In this section, I analyze two short conversations between Janet and Steve that highlight sociocultural patterns linked to the discourse of women and men and serve to contextualize Janet and Steve's interactional behaviors in the conversation they have with Kevin. The first conversation deals with the topic of child misbehavior, while in the second Janet and Steve discuss the topic of "details." Recall that in American culture, mothers more than fathers tend to be seen (or see themselves) as responsible for their children's shortcomings, while the giving and collecting of personal details is sex-class linked with women.

Listening to interactions captured on Janet and Steve's tapes throughout the week of taping, I realized that each takes a different stance toward Natalie's misbehavior, which is important to how Janet constructs her identity as a mother in the later interaction where Natalie's misbehavior is a primary topic of talk. Excerpt 1 shows one segment of conversation that is relevant to the interaction with Kevin, as in it Janet and Steve talk about their daughter's tantrums and reveal the different stances they take toward them. The interaction occurred the night before Kevin babysat Natalie. Janet and Steve talk while tidying up the kitchen; Natalie is already in bed. In this interaction, Janet brings up the fact that earlier that day, Natalie had screamed at Aunt Sylvia (Steve's sister). (Boldface is used to call attention to analytically important lines.)

(1) 1 Janet: Ugh!
     2   Weren't you just so humiliated →
     3   when she started screaming at Aunt Sylvia.
     4   <laughs slightly>
     5   ((short pause))
     6 Steve: No.
     7 Janet: I just feel—
     8 Steve: I don't take that personally.
     9 Janet: **I just feel horribly embarrassed →**
    10   **when she goes off- when she does that.**
    11 Steve: [/I don't ?/]
    12 Janet: [Like it's] **some reflection of our bad parenting.**
    13 Steve: **I don't think we are bad parents,**
    14   **I think we're good parents.**
    15   ((short pause))
    16 Janet: <sighs>
    17 Steve: **I think we're good parents →**
    18   **and I think she's very two.**
    19 Janet: Yeah,
    20   that's for sure.
    21   ((short pause))
    22   I just want to know why she's more two now—
    23 Steve: [/Well,/]
    24 Janet: [<laughing> I want] to know why →
    25   she's more two now that she's almost three!>
    26 Steve: Well,
    27   my impression is that three →
    28   is not much better than two.
    29 Janet: <laughing> Really?>
    30 Steve: Yeah.

This interaction shows that for Janet, the mother, Natalie's screaming is *humiliating* and could be construed as a reflection of *bad parenting*. For

Steve, the father, the screaming is simply age-appropriate behavior. The fact that Janet expresses concern about parental responsibility for her child's bad behavior (whereas Steve does not) fits into the larger pattern articulated by Schlenker (1980) and Tannen (2001) wherein mothers, more than fathers, tend to be seen as (or feel) responsible for their children's shortcomings. It also serves as background to why, in the conversation Janet and Steve have with Kevin the next day, Janet accounts for Natalie's misbehavior, while Steve does not.

One other conversation serves to contextualize Janet and Steve's linguistic behaviors in their interaction with Kevin while also revealing sociocultural knowledge about sex-class linked ways of speaking. This is a conversation Janet and Steve had while at the hospital waiting for Janet's mother to be released. Steve had just called Kevin, who was then at home with Natalie. He returns to where Janet is waiting, and the conversation in excerpt 2 ensues between Janet and Steve.

(2)   1   Janet: Did you reach him?
      2   Steve: Yep.
      3   Janet: How's he making out.
      4   Steve: They're doing okay.
      5   Janet: Was he on the phone or?
      6   Steve: I didn't ask.
      7   Janet: Oh.
      8   So he picked up?
      9   Steve: Yeah.
     10   Janet: /?? eat?/
     11   Steve: I just said were you able to get yourself something, ((*to eat*))
     12   he said yes.
     13   **Guys don't go into detail.**
     14   [<*chuckles*>]
     15   Janet: [I know,]
     16   **guys don't get any details.**
     17   Steve: **You get the critical information out there,**
     18   **and then say . [g—]**
     19   Janet: [Did] you tell him about bedtime?
     20   Steve: Yeah,
     21   he's gonna start putting her down now.
     22   Janet: Oh,
     23   all right.

This conversation is significant because it links to, and in some ways explains, an interactional pattern Janet exhibits in the later interaction she and Steve have with Kevin (requesting and providing details). This conversation shows that Janet's and Steve's gender ideologies echo broader cultural ideologies about gender that link "going into details" with the discourse of women (or, at the very least, that they are aware of these ideologies). Note also that Janet's interruption of Steve (line 19) underlines the importance of her agenda: she is interested in gathering details, rather than talking about the activity of detail-gathering.[2]

Janet's request for and use of details in the conversation she has with Steve and Kevin help construct her identity as a mother in that conversation, which is the focus of this analysis. I turn to this interaction now.

Gendered and Parental Alignments in a Report of Child Misbehavior

When Janet and Steve return from the emergency room and talk to Kevin, they first report on how the trip went; then Janet asks Kevin about his day. Talking about Kevin's day begins as shown in excerpt 3, which is transcribed in columns. Each participant's conversational contributions appear in his or her own column, and words appearing in different columns but on the same line are overlapping. Empty lines indicate pauses.

(3)

	Kevin	Janet	Steve
1		How was your day.	
2			
3			
4	Challenging.		
5		Uh oh.	
6			Oh boy.
7		<laughing slightly> What	
8		happened.>	
9	There were a few meltdowns.		
10		Oh no,	Oh no:.
11		really?	
12		What happened.	
13	Well right after you guys left,		
14		Yeah.	
15	she spilled— we were doing		
16	the um finger-paint,		
17	and she spilled water all over		
18	her . dress,		

As the interaction unfolds, Kevin continues his description of his day with Natalie, including how Natalie threw a temper tantrum and screamed when he wanted her to change her dress, and how she also had a temper

2. I thank Elizabeth Keating for calling this to my attention.

tantrum later when she did not want to go to bed. Through most of this interaction, Kevin is thus sharing information with Janet and Steve about how their daughter behaved (and particularly how she misbehaved) while he babysat her, while Janet and Steve respond to this information.

Although each participant has a different relationship to Natalie (mother, father, and uncle) and to one another (sister, brother, brother-in-law, husband, wife), and each uses the interaction to present these identities to some extent, the three adults are also united through this interaction. Through exhibiting their mutual appreciation for Natalie's verbal precociousness, sharing laughter about how cute and entertaining (though at times difficult) she is, and recognizing the burden of the shared task of dealing with the challenges she presents, the adults are in many ways a bonded unit. However, each participant also differentiates him or herself in the interaction through his or her verbal participation. Janet in particular uses this interaction to construct her identity as a mother, and this is the focus of the analysis that follows, where I argue that Janet accomplishes this through four different forms of conversational contributions: (1) requesting details, (2) providing details, (3) making assessments, and (4) accounting for her daughter's misbehavior.

(1) Requesting details

The first way Janet takes up a gendered, "maternal" alignment in this interaction is by requesting details. As evidenced previously in excerpt 3, it is Janet who opens the frame wherein Kevin, in the role of "babysitter," needs to provide information to Janet and Steve. She does this through requesting information from Kevin (line 1: *How was your day.* lines 7–8 and 12: *What happened.*). As Kevin gives his description of his day with Natalie, Janet continues to ask questions seeking more information and details. For example, in excerpt 4 Janet asks Kevin what he did when Natalie was screaming. Note too that by laughing, Janet mitigates the severity of Natalie's transgression. (Lines of particular analytical importance appear in bold.)

(4)

	Kevin	Janet	Steve
89		So what did you	
90		<*laughing slightly*> do when>	
91		she was screaming.	
92			
93		<*laughs slightly*>	
94	Just ignored it.		

In excerpt 5, Janet asks if Kevin took Natalie outside to play.

(5)

	Kevin	Janet	Steve
265		Did you get outside at all?	
266	Yeah we went to the—		
267	We went to BOTH		
268	playgrounds actually,		

In excerpt 6, Janet asks for information about Natalie's bedtime.

(6)

	Kevin	Janet	Steve
286		So what time- about what	
287		time would you say	
288		she went to sleep.	
289	I took her up there at like eight,		

Excerpts 4–6 show that only Janet intersperses the interaction with Kevin with questions seeking details about his day with Natalie. This is consonant with Steve's earlier comment to Janet while they were at the hospital that *Guys don't go into details.* Through this sociocultural lens, Janet's solicitation of details can be seen as a sex-class linked behavior, following Tannen (1996).

(2) Providing details

Related to Janet's pattern of requesting details, she also provides details about her daughter's life, punctuating the interaction with images of mother-daughter closeness. When Kevin confirms that Natalie screamed at him and recounts how this came about, Janet offers details that reveal her "nerve center" status in the family, or the fact that she knows intimate details of her daughter's life. In excerpt 7, Janet asks Kevin what he did when Natalie was screaming, and Kevin responds with a play-by-play of their conversation using constructed dialogue. In the boldfaced utterance in this excerpt, Janet responds to Kevin's account, positioning herself as someone who knows that Natalie is an extremely verbal child through providing a detail.

(7)

	Kevin	Janet	Steve
89		So what did you	
90		<laughing slightly> do when>	
91		she was screaming.	
92			
93		<laughing slightly>	
94	Just ignored it.		
95		That's good.	
96	She asked me if I was happy,		

97	and I said no,		
98		<laughs>	
99	"Why are you not happy,"		
100	I said it- "when you cry		
101	it makes me sad,"		
102	so then the rest of the night,		
103	"why /was/ you sad		
104	when I cried."		
105		<laughs>	
106		Right.	
107			<laughing> Oh Go:d.>
108		Yeah then you have to	
109		talk about it for three hours.	
110	Mhm.		
111		Yeah.	
112			<laughing> Oh no.>

Janet responds to Kevin's account of Natalie wanting to talk about the fact that he was upset in a way that reveals her familiarity with Natalie's behavioral patterns, specifically her desire to talk about conflict. Mentioning this detail begins to paint a picture of mother-child intimacy between Janet and Natalie. This picture continues to come into focus as the conversation goes on, specifically when Janet asks a question that correctly predicts how Natalie acted when Kevin told Natalie he was upset with her. This is shown in excerpt 8, which is continuous with excerpt 7.

(8)

	Kevin	Janet	Steve
113		Yeah, yeah did she keep	
114		asking you if you were	
115		happy NOW.	
116	((nonverbally indicates yes?))	<laughs>	
117			<laughs>
118		Yeah that's the only blessing.	

In this excerpt, Janet further constructs a position of intimacy with her daughter: they are so intimate that Janet not only knows the details of Natalie's behavioral patterns, but she can actually predict how Natalie behaved before Kevin tells about it.

In excerpt 9, which is continuous with excerpt 8, Janet again mentions a detail of Natalie's life. After Kevin (apparently) indicates that Natalie did keep asking if he was happy, Janet explains that Natalie does not like when people are upset with her.

(9)

	Kevin	Janet	Steve
119		She doesn't like- she doesn't	
120		like that part of it.	
121		She doesn't like	
122		when you're unhappy with her.	

Through this comment, Janet continues to display intimacy between mother and daughter. In addition, as the mothers in Ochs & Taylor's

(1992a, 1992b, 1995) study could be seen as seeking to create involvement with the fathers by having the children tell stories about their days (see Tannen 2001, 2003, this volume), here Janet could be seen as creating involvement with Kevin by telling details about Natalie.

The most prominent example of Janet providing details about Natalie's life is shown in excerpt 10. Kevin has just finished explaining that Natalie would not stop talking at bedtime and that he finally got her to go to sleep simply by asking her to close her eyes.

(10)

	Kevin	Janet	Steve
328		That child will just	
329		talk and talk .	
330	Oh she talked.	and talk.	
331			
332		She's Miss Conversation.	
333	Mhm.		
334		That's her new thing	
335		at naptime,	
336		I say, "okay it's time to close	
337		our eyes, and settle down.	
338		And be QUIET,"	
339		and all of a sudden she's	
340		having this little .	
341		one-woman . show,	
342		talking to herself,	
343		talking to . the clock,	
344			
345		it's like she doesn't even	
346		get it that she's not	
347		being quiet.	
348	<laughs slightly>		<laughs slightly>

This description of Natalie's naptime behavior invokes a scene populated by two people—Janet and Natalie. It indexes the time they spend together and allows Janet to position herself as an insider to the details of Natalie's life. It also allows Janet to share details of her typical day with Natalie with Kevin, perhaps seeking to create involvement with him. And this, in addition to requesting details, could be seen as a sex-class linked behavior and a social act that is linked to the discourse of mothers.

(3) Making assessments

(a) *Natalie's behavior*

Up to this point, I have addressed only linguistic patterns that Janet and Steve do not share: requesting and providing details. However, Janet and Steve do participate similarly in this interaction in one respect: they both evaluate Natalie's behavior and Kevin's babysitting behavior. In doing so, following Ochs & Taylor (1992a, 1992b, 1995), they could be seen as enacting a "panopticon-like role" (following Bentham [1791] in Foucault [1979]) in judging their child's behavior. Excerpt 11 shows how the "assessment activity" (Goodwin & Goodwin 1992) begins. (This excerpt was also shown as part of excerpt 3. Janet and Steve's assessments appear in bold.)

(11)

	Kevin	Janet	Steve
1		How was your day.	
2			
3			
4	Challenging.		
5		Uh oh.	
6			Oh boy
7		<laughing slightly> What	
8		happened.>	
9	There were a few meltdowns.		
10		Oh no,	Oh no:.
11		really?	

The assessment activity begins when Janet responds to Kevin's description of his day as *Challenging* with *Uh oh*. The lines drawn in the excerpt highlight the progression of the assessments. They show that Janet is first to respond to Kevin: she offers the first recipient assessment, while Steve responds with a second assessment that matches Janet's first. Both Janet and Steve assess Natalie's behavior as problematic, matching Kevin's initial evaluation.

Excerpt 12 shows how the assessment activity continues to play out as the interaction unfolds.

(12)

	Kevin	Janet	Steve
20	so I told her if we were		
21	going to go out		
22	we should change her,		
23		Right.	
24	she didn't want to change,		
25		Oh God.	
26	so the full- .		
27		<sighing> U:h.>	
28	the full issue,		
29	and,		<slightly laughing> Oh God.>
30		Oh no.	
31	/there's-/	Screaming?	
32	Oh yeah.		
33		Oh God,	
34	She- every time she'd		
35	/howl tonight/,		
36	she'd gotten to the point where		
37	she was kind of choking		
38	herself.		
39		Oh God.	
40	I'm sure you've seen that.		Oh God. Oh God. .

The lines in the excerpt highlight repetition of the evaluative response *Oh God*. Janet first offers this recipient assessment, while Steve responds with a second assessment that matches Janet's first.

This pattern of Janet responding first and Steve echoing continues throughout the interaction. Both parents take on the role of judge vis-à-vis Natalie's misbehavior, but it is Janet who leads the assessment activity and is most active in exhibiting congruent understanding with Kevin concerning her daughter's misbehavior. Thus in providing first recipient assessments to Steve's seconds, she is taking up a stance wherein she leads the way both judging (a parental stance) and in creating rapport with Kevin through her matching recipient assessments (a sex-class linked conversational pattern that may also relate to her being his sister).

Similarly, Janet leads the way in matching assessments with Kevin where he evaluates Natalie's behaviors as cute or humorous. In excerpt 13, Kevin describes how he got Natalie to go to sleep, and Janet and Steve agree that his description is humorous.

(13)

	Kevin	Janet	Steve
298	Well she kept talking,		
299	and I finally said,		
300	"Can you do me a favor?		
301	Can you close your eyes		
302	for a minute?"		
303	And then that was it,	*<laughs>*	
304	she went out.		
305		*<laughing>* Oh is that right.	*<laughs heartily>*
306		"Oh my God, it's a miracle!">	*<laughs heartily>*
307	Yeah.		
308		*<laughing>* That's very funny.>	
309		*<laughs>*	*<laughing>* "Do you think—"
310		*<laughing>* "Shut your yap	
311		and close your eyes!">	
312	I just said, "Can you-		
313	can we close our eyes for		
314	a few seconds?"		
315	And she didn't say yes,		
316	she just ((*demonstrates*))		
317		*<laughs heartily>*	*<laughs heartily>*
318	And after like five seconds,		
319	I thought to myself,		
320	"Do I dare . look up?"		
321	And then I heard the snoring.	*<laughing>* "Do I dare try	
322		to leave?">	
323	Then I heard the snore.		
324			*<laughing>* Then you heard
325			the snore!>
326		Oh that's funny.	
327			Oh Kevin.

In this excerpt, constructed dialogue, laughter, repetition, and explicit evaluation all serve to assess the content of Kevin's talk as humorous and thereby create alignments between Janet and Steve and Natalie's behavior and between Janet and Steve and Kevin. As Kevin tells his story, he implicitly assesses Natalie's behavior as amusing. Janet and Steve both evaluate Kevin's story as funny through laughter. Janet also does so explicitly by saying, *That's very funny.*

The constructed dialogue offered by Janet and Steve also serves an evaluative function. In line 306, Janet contributes a line of dialogue, *"Oh my God, it's a miracle,"* to Kevin's story, presumably from his perspective. Then Steve begins to add a line of dialogue, *"Do you think—"* also from Kevin's perspective, but self-interrupts as Janet herself offers another line to the story, *"Shut your yap [mouth] and close your eyes,"* again speaking as if she were Kevin in the story world. In performing this act, which Tannen (2003, this volume) refers to as "ventriloquizing," Janet claims or constructs rapport with Kevin and involvement in his story.

Repetition also plays a role in creating involvement in this excerpt, again following the work of Tannen (2007 [1989]), who suggests that repetition can create conversational involvement. In excerpt 14, I re-present lines that are repeated.

(14)

	Kevin	Janet	Steve
318	And after like five seconds,		
319	I thought to myself,		
320	"do I dare . look up?"		
321	And then I heard the snoring.	<*laughing*> "Do I dare try	
322		to leave?">	
323	Then I heard the snore.		
324			<*laughing*> Then you heard
325			the snore!>
326		Oh that's funny.	
327			Oh Kevin.

Here, repetition is connected with lines in the transcript. First, Janet repeats, with a bit of variation, Kevin's constructed dialogue in the story (Kevin: *"do I dare . look up?"*/Janet: *"Do I dare try to leave?"*). Then, a conversational moment later, Steve repeats Kevin's utterance, *Then I heard the snore*, only replacing "I" with "you." This is another example of Janet exhibiting a form of assessment and Steve a moment later exhibiting that same form. Because these assessments show involvement with Kevin's story and with Kevin, they do relationship work; and because Janet assesses first and Steve does second, she leads the way in this activity.

(b) *Kevin's behavior*

In the previous section, I showed that Janet and Steve both assess Natalie's behavior, enacting the roles of parents vis-à-vis Kevin's role of babysitter and Natalie's position of child and topic of discussion. Based on the sequential placement of their assessments, specifically the fact that Janet takes the lead in issuing assessments that address Kevin's *positive face* (Brown

& Levinson 1987), I suggested that she is taking the lead performing relationship work, that is, building rapport. In this section, a similar pattern emerges, but this time Janet and Steve assess Kevin's performance as a babysitter.

In excerpt 15, Kevin "confesses" one of his shortcomings as a babysitter —that he allowed Natalie to eat cookies. Janet assesses Kevin's behavior as being acceptable, and Steve supports and echoes her assessment. (Note that the mention of *the Jill method of feeding a child* in the excerpt refers to a friend of Janet and Steve who freely gives Natalie sweets.)

(15)

	Kevin	Janet	Steve
129	So she ate her fair share of		
130	cookies and stuff tonight,		
131	I have to take		
132	full responsibility for .		
133		<*laughs*>	
134		For the- for the Jill method	
135		of feeding . a child?	
136		Oh well,	
137		whatever gets you	
138		through the night.	
139			That's right.
140	Well I made some (pastina),		
141	and she kind of liked that so,		
142		Oh she did,	
143	We- we ate some of that	yeah.	
144	together.		
145		Oh yeah.	
146	So I'm—		
147		Well that's fine.	
148		Don't- don't give THAT	
149		a thought.	
150		If it helped you get through,	Yeah.
151		<*laughing*> that's fine.>	
152			Whatever it takes.

In this excerpt, Kevin tells Janet and Steve that he allowed Natalie to have *cookies and stuff*. In lines 136–138, Janet evaluates Kevin's babysitting behavior with, *Oh well, whatever gets you through the night*, showing support for Kevin. Steve supports this utterance by uttering, *That's right*. Then, in lines 147–151, Janet again reassures Kevin that he need not worry about giving Natalie treats by uttering, *Well that's fine. Don't give THAT a thought*. Again, Steve supports her in taking this alignment toward Kevin's babysitting behavior and toward Kevin, this time by uttering *Yeah*, and then, *Whatever it takes*, an echo of Janet's *whatever gets you through the night*.

In excerpt 16, Janet and Steve assess Kevin's babysitting behavior as commendable. In this example, Janet provides a positive assessment of the fact that Kevin took Natalie to both of the playgrounds near their house with *O::h!* Then, she and Steve produce simultaneous assessments evaluating his taking Natalie to the playgrounds as *good*.

(16)

	Kevin	Janet	Steve
265		Did you get outside at all?	
266	Yeah we went to the—		
267	We went to BOTH		
268	playgrounds actually,		
269		O::h!	
270	had lots of fun.		
271		Oh that's good.	That's good.
272		I'm sure she loved that.	
273	She did!		
274		Oh that was good,	
275		I'm glad she got outside.	
276	Yeah I know, we were out		
277	there for a while actually.		
278		Good.	
279		Good.	
280	Got some good slides in,		
281	some good swinging,		
282		Well that's good,	
283		that's good.	

Janet and Steve simultaneously introduce *good* as the assessing adjective. Janet repeats assessments including the word *good* over and over, and Kevin also joins in on this assessment activity, describing their *slides* and *swinging* at the playground as *good* in lines 280–281.

Good resurfaces as an assessing adjective of choice, as shown in excerpt 17. Here Kevin tells Janet and Steve what time Natalie went to bed, and they respond with assessments including the word *good*.

(17)

	Kevin	Janet	Steve
286		So what time- about what time	
287		would you say	
288		she went to sleep.	
289			
290	I took her up there at like eight,		
291	and she finally fell asleep	Yeah.	
292	around eight-thirty.		
293			That's good.
294		Oh that was good.	
295			Yeah that's really good.
296		Very impressive Kevin.	
297		That's . not easy.	

In this assessment sequence, it is Steve who begins the assessment of this portion of Kevin's report, recycling the term *good*, first uttered by Janet earlier in the interaction. Although Steve first introduces the term *good* in this particular sequence, Janet still takes a very active role in showing approval for Kevin. When Steve says, *That's good*, Janet exhibits a similar affective stance with *Oh that was good*. When Steve upgrades to *Yeah that's really good*, Janet upgrades her assessment to *Very impressive Kevin. That's not easy*. Thus, even when Janet does not provide the first recipient assessment in this interaction, her verbal contributions still work to build rapport among the participants.

There are also examples in which Kevin talks about his actions as a babysitter and only Janet explicitly assesses them, again taking the lead in performing the verbal relationship work with Kevin. In excerpt 18, Kevin confesses that he forgot to brush Natalie's teeth.

(18)

	Kevin	Janet	Steve
180	Well, I finally got her in bed,		
181	and um,	<laughs>	<laughs>
182	once she was in there	<laughs>	
183	I realized I forgot		
184	to brush her teeth,		
185	but I . wrote that off too.		
186			Yeah.
187		Yeah, <laughing> don't	
188		worry about that.>	

In excerpt 18, Janet is the sole parental assessor of Kevin's behavior, as she assesses his actions as not worthy of worry. This is the same case as in excerpt 19, when Kevin tells Janet and Steve how he dealt with Natalie's screaming.

(19)

	Kevin	Janet	Steve
89		So what did you	
90		<laughing slightly> do when>	
91		she was screaming.	
92			
93		<laughing slightly>	
94	Just ignored it.		
95		That's good.	

In this excerpt, only Janet positively evaluates Kevin's babysitting behavior through verbal contributions; Steve remains silent. Again, Janet's lone assessment shows approval of Kevin.

In sum, in this section I have shown that both Janet and Steve assess Kevin's babysitting behavior, either reassuring him that his less-than-ideal behaviors (e.g., forgetting to brush Natalie's teeth, giving her cookies) are acceptable or commending him for his good behaviors (e.g., taking Natalie to two playgrounds). There are two major patterns of assessment of Kevin's behavior: (1) Janet offers an assessment and Steve repeats it, (2) only Janet assesses his behavior. There is one example each of Steve offering the first assessment and of them simultaneously assessing. However, the main pattern is that Steve provides second assessments to Janet's primary recipient assessments, and her assessments punctuate the interaction more consistently and more often than Steve's. Janet thus steadily verbally shows involvement with Kevin, building rapport through showing approval of him as a babysitter.

Considering the assessments of both Natalie's behavior and Kevin's behavior, Janet leads the enactment of the "parental panopticon" and performs the majority of the relationship work in this interaction across the excerpts. She takes the lead in assessing her child's behavior negatively (simultaneously matching Kevin's evaluations, creating a supportive stance), in showing appreciation for Kevin's narration of Natalie's amusing behaviors, and in reassuring and showing approval of Kevin as a babysitter. In this way, Janet leads the way in taking a parental stance (judging her child and the babysitter) and a gendered or sex-class linked stance (doing relationship work and building rapport with her brother).

(4) Providing an account

The last interactional pattern is one only Janet exhibits: accounting for her daughter's misbehavior. How this comes about appears in excerpt 20.

(20)

	Kevin	Janet	Steve
59		Did she scream?	
60	Oh yeah.		
61		I d- we don't know what this	
62		screaming is.	
63		She just started doing it.	
64		I don't—	
65		I would expect it when she	
66		was just turning two,	
67		but . going on three,	
68			
69		everythingI read says . it's	
70		supposed to start settling down.	
71	Hm.		
72			<*yawning*> Maybe it's her
73			last hurrah.>
74		Yeah maybe.	

Here Janet moves toward her account of her daughter's screaming. In excerpt 21, which is continuous with excerpt 20, Janet provides an account for Natalie's behavior.

(21)

	Kevin	Janet	Steve
75		Well, I think she- I think she's	
76		y'know, partially . picks up on .	
77		She's pretty perceptive,	
78		y'know, and I think she knows	
79		Mom's not been well,	
80		and . picks up on the tension	
81		about that.	
82	Hm.		
83		I don't know if that fully	
84		explains it but,	
85		<*laughs slightly*>	
86			
87			

In this excerpt, Janet is doing "impression management," even though her daughter's behavior, not her own, is at issue. This suggests that Janet is worried that she will be perceived as responsible for Natalie's misbehavior. Steve provides no such account. Janet's account in this interaction harks back to the conversation (shown in excerpt 1) where she says to Steve she feels like Natalie's screaming could be construed as *some reflection of our bad parenting* and is *humiliating*. She is thus taking up a maternal stance in the interaction by providing this account, as this account is embedded in a culture in which mothers are typically blamed for their children's shortcomings.

Conclusion

This analysis has focused on exploring one naturally occurring interaction between family members, illustrating how non-narrative behavior, specifically what might be thought of as "recipient behavior," can be the locus of identity construction in family interaction. I argue that by performing certain acts and taking up particular stances toward Kevin's report of his day babysitting Natalie and toward her co-interlocutors, Janet paints a portrait of herself—it is, in this interaction, primarily the portrait of a mother.

The portrait of Janet as a mother is created principally through the acts she performs in the interaction, acts that are socioculturally linked to the identities of "woman" and "parent"—in short, they are linked to the class "mother." These acts set up alignments between Janet and the content of Kevin's talk, specifically his babysitting behavior and Natalie's behavior, as well as between Janet and Kevin as interactional partners. Implicit in my analysis has been the fact that Janet constructs her identity on two different *discourse planes*, as defined by Schiffrin (1987). One is by way of the *ideational structure* through her alignments to the topic of talk, specifically Kevin's and Natalie's story world behaviors; the other is on the level of *participation frameworks* (Goffman 1981) by taking up alignments vis-à-vis other interactants. In Schiffrin's (1996:198) words, "social identity is locally situated: who we are is, at least partially, a product of where we are and who we are with, both in interactional and story worlds." Although Janet does not technically tell any narratives (save one brief habitual narrative about naptime) and is not a figure in a story world in this interaction, she takes up alignments vis-à-vis those who are—Kevin and Natalie—as well as toward her interactional partners, particularly Kevin.

This analysis has demonstrated that in creating these alignments, Janet constructs her identity in this interaction. I suggested that Janet performs four social acts in this interaction to construct her identity as a mother. I argued that, first, by *making requests for details* about her child's day with the babysitter and, second, by *providing details* about her daughter's life, Janet takes up gendered and parental stances. Interest in details in interaction is linked to involvement, intimacy, and the talk of women, following the work of Tannen (2007 [1989], 1990). Taking up the stance as an interlocutor interested in the details of children's lives is related to the identity of "mother." Thus, by requesting and providing details about Natalie's life, Janet indexes the relationship she has with her daughter as intimate, or as congruent with the socioculturally ideal mother-daughter bond. This works to construct Janet's identity as a mother. Details also work to create intimacy in the interaction with Kevin, doing relationship work, which is primarily seen as "women's work." Third, by *providing assessments* of her daughter's and the babysitter's behaviors, she enacts what Ochs & Taylor (1992a, 1992b, 1995) refer to as "the parental panopticon," or parents' right to monitor and judge the behaviors of their children (and, I would suggest, their children's babysitters). I showed that Janet's assessments exhibit congruent understanding with Kevin about Natalie's behavior and show her approval of Kevin. This creates a supportive stance vis-à-vis Kevin. Janet's active participation and the fact that she takes a leadership role in this activity positions her as a parent and as a woman who is using assessments to build rapport with her co-interactants. Fourth, in *accounting for* her daughter's misbehavior, Janet links herself to discourse in which a mother is held responsible (or feels responsible) for her child's every shortcoming. By exhibiting the need to engage in impression management due to her daughter's misbehavior, Janet positions herself as potentially being held responsible for it. In a cultural climate in which mothers are explicitly or implicitly blamed for their children's shortcomings, Janet constructs her identity as a mother by indexing the guilt associated with this blame in the social act of accounting.

Taken together, I suggest that these social acts related to details, assessments, and accounts create alignments that are at once gendered and parental. In other words, by performing social acts that have certain sociocultural meanings, Janet takes up alignments in interaction and thereby constructs one salient aspect of her identity: she "paints a portrait" of herself as a mother.

This analysis has drawn on past work from several main topic areas and contributes to each of them. First, I have considered assessments from an interactional sociolinguistic perspective, adding to past work, such as by Pomerantz (1984), Goodwin & Goodwin (1992), and Holt (2000), that considers assessments from a sequential, but not from an interpersonal, perspective. I have demonstrated that assessments create interpersonal alignments in interaction that are meaningful on multiple levels. I showed that assessments can index appreciation, rapport, and sympathy. I argued that in order to understand the meaning of certain types of assessments, the understanding of sociocultural patterns is necessary. For example, in order to understand Janet and Steve's "Oh Gods," it is necessary to understand what it means to be a middle-class parent in the United States and have a child who misbehaves. Taking this analytical perspective, I have shown that assessments are jointly created in interaction not only in terms of sequence but also in terms of people working together to create interpersonal relationships and identities.

Second, this chapter contributes to our understanding of what it means to be a mother and what it means to construct a mother identity in interaction. Drawing on sociocultural information about mothers, gender, parents, and interaction patterns, I have linked social acts, alignments, sociocultural expectations, and interactional behavior. These data provide evidence that in the day-to-day interactions of parents, interactional behaviors both construct identities and point to the sociocultural underpinnings of those identities. They also indicate that identities are multifaceted and can be created by indexing more than one identity in a single discourse. I showed that to be a mother is to be, for example, a woman, a parent, a confidant, a detail-gatherer, an interactional partner, and an active narrative recipient.

Finally and perhaps most importantly, this research contributes to a research goal in contemporary sociolinguistics: to explore identity from a social constructivist perspective and link specific linguistic features of text to identity construction. Toward that end, I have built on the work of Schiffrin (1996, 2000, 2002) and Adelswärd & Nilholm (2000), in particular, who identify linguistic devices and conversational moves by which a maternal identity and a mother-child relationship are created. By applying Ochs's (1993) argument that social acts and stances construct identities in interaction, I identified detail giving and gathering, assessing, and accounting as linguistic moves that may work toward creating a maternal identity in family conversation.

Schiffrin (1996:197) writes, "who we are is sustained by our ongoing interactions with others, and the way we position ourselves to those others." Perhaps nowhere is this more apparent than in the context of family. I have shown in this analysis that narrative recipients can position themselves simultaneously vis-à-vis familial story world characters and vis-à-vis their familial interlocutors through their interactional behavior. In doing so, I have demonstrated that social acts and affective stances exhibited in conversation are relevant to maternal identity construction; linked these acts and stances to sociocultural and sociolinguistic information about women, parents, and mothers; and thereby revealed how the portrait of a mother emerges in interaction.

References

Adelswärd, Viveka, and Claes Nilholm. 2000. Who is Cindy? Aspects of identity work in a teacher-parent-pupil talk at a special school. Text 20(4).545–568.

Bentham, Jeremy. 1791. Panopticon. London: T. Payne.

Brown, Penelope, and Steven C. Levinson. 1979. Social structure, groups, and interaction. Social markers in speech, ed. K. Scherer and Howard Giles, 291–341. Cambridge: Cambridge University Press.

Brown, Penelope, and Steven C. Levinson. 1987. Politeness. Cambridge: Cambridge University Press.

Davies, Bronwyn, and Rom Harré. 1990. Positioning: Conversation and the production of selves. Journal for the Theory of Social Behavior 20.43–63.

Foucault, Michel. 1979. Discipline and punish: The birth of the prison, trans. Alan Sheridan. New York: Random House.

Gergen, Kenneth. 1987. Towards self as relationship. Self and identity: Psychosocial perspectives, ed. Krysia Yardley and Terry Honess, 53–63. New York: Wiley.

Goffman, Erving. 1981. Footing. Forms of talk, 124–159. Philadelphia: University of Pennsylvania Press.

Goffman, Erving. 1977. The arrangement between the sexes. Theory and Society 4(3).301–331.

Goffman, Erving. 1959. The presentation of self in everyday life. Garden City, N.Y.: Doubleday.

Goodwin, Charles, and Marjorie Harness Goodwin. 1992. Assessments and the construction of context. Rethinking context: Language as an interactive phenomenon, ed. Alessandro Duranti and Charles Goodwin, 147–189. Cambridge: Cambridge University Press.

Henwood, Karen L. 1993. Women and later life: The discursive construction of identities within family relationships. Journal of Aging Studies 7(3).303–319.

Holt, Elizabeth. 2000. Reporting and reacting: Concurrent responses to reported speech. Research on Language and Social Interaction 33(4).425–454.

The New Our Bodies, Ourselves. 1992. By The Boston Women's Health Book Collective. New York: Touchstone.

Ochs, Elinor. 1992. Indexing gender. Rethinking context: Language as an interactive phenomenon, ed. Alessandro Duranti and Charles Goodwin, 335–358. Cambridge: Cambridge University Press.

Ochs, Elinor. 1993. Constructing social identity: A language socialization perspective. Research on Language and Social Interaction 26(3).287–306.

Ochs, Elinor, and Carolyn Taylor. 1992a. Mothers' role in the everyday reconstruction of "Father knows best." Locating power: Proceedings of the Second Berkeley Women and Language Conference, April 4 and 5, 1992, ed. Kira Hall, Mary Bucholtz, and Birch Moonwomon, 447–462. Berkeley: Berkeley Women and Language Group, University of California.

Ochs, Elinor, and Carolyn Taylor. 1992b. Family narrative as political activity. Discourse & Society 3(3).301–340.

Ochs, Elinor, and Carolyn Taylor. 1995. The "Father knows best" dynamic in family dinner narratives. Gender articulated: Language and the socially constructed self, ed. Kira Hall and Mary Bucholtz, 97–121. New York and London: Routledge.

Polkinghorne, Donald. 1988. Narrative knowing and the human sciences. Albany: SUNY Press.

Pomerantz, Anita. 1984. Agreeing and disagreeing with assessments: Some features of preferred/dispreferred turn shapes. Structures of social action: Studies in conversation analysis, ed. J. Maxwell Atkinson and John Heritage, 57–101. Cambridge: Cambridge University Press.

Riessman, Catherine Kohler. 1992. Making sense of marital violence: One woman's narrative. Storied lives: The cultural politics of self-understanding, ed. George C. Rosenwald and Richard L. Ochberg, 231–249. New Haven and London: Yale University Press.

Schiffrin, Deborah. 1987. Discourse markers. Cambridge: Cambridge University Press.

Schiffrin, Deborah. 1996. Narrative as self-portrait: Sociolinguistic constructions of identity. Language in Society 25.167–203.

Schiffrin, Deborah. 2000. Mother/daughter discourse in a Holocaust oral history: "Because then you admit that you're guilty." Narrative Inquiry 10(1).1–44.

Schiffrin, Deborah. 2002. Mother and friends in a Holocaust life story. Language in Society 31.309–353.

Schlenker, Barry R. 1980. Impression management: The self-concept, social identity, and interpersonal relations. Monterey, Calif.: Brooks/Cole Publishing Co.

Scott, Marvin B., and Stanford M. Lyman. 1968. Accounts. American Sociological Review 33(1).46–62.

Tannen, Deborah. 1990. You just don't understand: Women and men in conversation. New York: Ballantine Books.

Tannen, Deborah. 1996. The sex-class linked framing of talk at work. Gender and discourse, 195–331. New York: Oxford University Press.

Tannen, Deborah. 2001. I only say this because I love you: How the way we talk can make or break family relationships throughout our lives. New York: Random House.

Tannen, Deborah. 2003. Power maneuvers or connection maneuvers? Ventriloquizing in family interaction. Linguistics, language and the real world: Discourse and beyond. Georgetown University Round Table on Languages and Linguistics, 2001, ed. Deborah Tannen and James E. Alatis, 50–62. Washington, D.C.: Georgetown University Press.

Tannen, Deborah. 2007 [1989]. Talking voices: Repetition, dialogue, and imagery in conversational discourse. Cambridge: Cambridge University Press.

Wortham, Stanton. 2000. Interactional positioning and narrative self-construction. Narrative Inquiry 10(1).157–184.

DIANA MARINOVA

five

Finding the Right Balance between Connection and Control: A Father's Identity Construction in Conversations with His College-Age Daughter

Identity construction as an ongoing process has been of considerable interest to linguistic inquiry in recent years.[1] It has been examined across a wide range of interactional contexts and from different perspectives. Most current research views identity construction as a dynamic process emerging from one's interactions with others, while at the same time utilizing preconceived notions about the self in specific social circumstances. For example, Schiffrin (1996) analyzes how mothers create "self-portraits" of themselves as mothers through the narratives they tell during sociolinguistic interviews. Looking again at family roles, but from an anthropological perspective and drawing on narratives in conversational data, Ochs & Taylor (1995) examine the negotiation and transformation of identities among family members engaged in the activity of dinner-table story-telling. Blum-Kulka (1997), too, examines interactions recorded at dinnertime. Adopting a cross-cultural perspective, she discusses how parents try to be sociable with children (chat for enjoyment) while at the

1. I would like to thank Deborah Tannen and Shari Kendall for allowing me access to the data. I would also like to thank Deborah Tannen for her detailed and helpful comments on earlier versions of the chapter.

same time socializing them (teaching them values, cultural rules regarding interaction, etc.).

Like Ochs & Taylor and Blum-Kulka, I investigate naturally occurring family discourse and analyze interactions among family members to examine the discursive nature of identity construction. I focus, however, on the interplay of caretaking and socializing frames (Tannen 2001) as evident in the conversational contributions of a father concerning his college-age daughter. More specifically, I explore how the father constructs and displays his identity as a concerned parent through discourse with his twenty-year-old daughter regarding her lack of action in preparing for an upcoming study-abroad semester in Spain. I also draw upon interactions between the father and non-family members that position him as a concerned parent. As part of their participation in the larger research project, both parents carried digital tape recorders, taping nearly every interaction they had over the course of about a week. In contrast to past studies that examine family discourse drawing upon data from isolated interactions, I base my analysis on real-life, naturally occurring data that took place over an extended period of time.

Following Ochs's (1993) approach to identity construction as an ongoing process (see also Gordon this volume), I suggest that the father takes the stance of a concerned parent vis-à-vis his daughter by (1) expressing concern and assessing his daughter's lack of action; (2) giving directives to get his daughter to be more organized; (3) providing reasons for a particular action and warning his daughter of possible consequences due to her lack of action; and (4) asking for further details about the study-abroad semester and giving advice. By analyzing examples of these social acts, I demonstrate how the father, through his insistence that the daughter take a more proactive stance, creates an alignment between himself and his interlocutors that serves to construct his parental identity.

I first review recent work on identity construction and framing in family discourse. Second, I briefly introduce the participants whose discourse I analyze. Third, drawing upon past research on identity as well as upon research on framing in family discourse, I analyze specific examples of conversational contributions and the social acts through which the father constructs his identity as a parent. This is followed by a brief discussion of the progression of the strategies the father uses over the course of about a week to get his daughter to be more organized. I conclude by summarizing my findings about parental identity construction and discuss how they advance our understanding of interaction in general.

Identity Construction and Framing in Family Discourse

Adopting the perspective of interactional sociolinguistics, Gordon (this volume) considers how one woman's maternal identity is constructed in everyday conversation. Following Ochs (1993), she argues that the mother constructs her identity through performing social acts and taking affective stances that construct at once a gendered and parental identity. Gordon illustrates how the mother through providing and requesting details, making assessments, and accounting for her daughter's misbehavior takes up alignments in interaction and thereby constructs her identity not simply as a woman or as a parent, but as a mother. By investigating linguistic devices and conversational moves through which a maternal identity and a mother-child relationship are created, Gordon's study sheds further light on gender-related patterns of interaction in family discourse.

In keeping with her ongoing interest in the forces that drive interactional discourse, Tannen (2001) discusses the dynamics that underlie family interaction from a sociolinguistic perspective. She introduces the concepts of control and connection and their intersection as two axes of a grid to show that family relations are fundamentally hierarchical as well as deeply connected (see also Tannen this volume). In her own words (2001:11), "Both connection and control are at the heart of family." Furthermore, she argues that hierarchy is not inherently unsavory. On the contrary, it can be a source of comfort and protection, for example, in a parent-child relationship. Connection, at the same time, can be stifling, especially as children enter their teenage years. It is then that parents' striving for closeness is often perceived as overwhelming.

Borrowing Bateson's (1972) concept of frame to refer to the participants' interpretation of the ongoing interaction, Tannen suggests that the clash between a caretaking frame (instructing and taking care of the children) and a socializing frame (enjoying their company) is often the key to understanding parent-child discourse. As children get older, family relations undergo a transformation and the hierarchical parent-child system is replaced by an egalitarian peer-peer system. In this stage of familial relations, conflicts often arise, as Tannen points out, because it becomes more difficult to find the right balance between connection and control.

Tannen's observation that parents strive for egalitarian (sociable) conversations as children approach adulthood yet still engage in the caretaking frame seems to be related to Blum-Kulka's (1997) discussion of sociability/

socializing frames at dinner.[2] Comparing patterns of dinner-table interactions of American, Israeli, and American-Israeli families, Blum-Kulka points out that when family dinners are shared both physically and conversationally with children, they allow parents to engage verbally with children for enjoyment (that is, to be sociable with children), while at the same time dinners may serve as a context in which children are socialized to the local belief systems and discourse practices. Thus, exploring further parents' needs to both socialize and socialize with their children seems to be crucial in order to gain a better understanding of parent-child interaction.

To summarize, recent research on identity construction and framing in family discourse has focused on language as a means through which family members negotiate their relationships. Following Ochs (1993), Gordon (this volume) demonstrates how the identity of "mother" is constructed in conversation and shows the key role sociocultural knowledge plays in linking specific interactional strategies with this identity. Both Tannen (2001) and Blum-Kulka (1997) discuss the dual and sometimes conflicting needs (or desires) on the part of parents to place their relationship with their children in the egalitarian peer-peer system yet still teach them what they need to know. Drawing upon the above-mentioned studies, I look into how one father constructs his parental identity through his conversational discourse and how he strives to find the right balance between connection and control.

Data and Participants

Data for the study come from the week of audio-taped conversations among the members of one family: Greg and Nora, in their late forties, and their daughter Susan (20), who is a sophomore at a local college. Susan has two siblings, Jeremy (17) and John (22). As part of their participation in the larger research project, both parents carried digital tape recorders, taping nearly every interaction they had over the course of a week in the summer of 2000. The father is a self-employed performer whose work is done partly on the road and partly at home. When he is not setting up performances onsite, he is working on future projects in his office in the basement of the house. The mother is Assistant Head of a private school. Additionally, she takes night classes toward her master's degree once a week. As a result, it is the father who tends to spend more time at home during the weekdays.

2. Thanks to Cynthia Gordon for pointing this out.

An issue of concern that comes up frequently in the family interactions that were captured on tape over the course of the week is the lack of action on the part of the daughter as her study-abroad semester in Seville, Spain, draws nearer. The excerpts that I analyze here come from two conversations between Greg and his daughter. The first conversation, which includes excerpts 4, 5, 7, 8, occurs on a Monday morning before Susan goes on a beach trip, whereas the second conversation (excerpts 9, 10, 11) occurs five days later on a Saturday morning. After his first conversation with Susan, Greg calls up his wife, who is at work, to discuss how to better approach the situation. In addition to discussing the upcoming trip with family members, the father shares his concern regarding the trip in interactions with non-family members, such as his secretary (Martha), a travel agent, and his friend (Lloyd). The interactions with non-family members, too, position him as a concerned parent.

In my analysis of how the father constructs his identity as a parent in dealing with his daughter's upcoming study-abroad semester, I draw upon his interactions with three groups of people: non-family members, his spouse, and his daughter. I suggest that the father takes up the stance of a concerned parent vis-à-vis the issue at hand by (1) expressing concern and assessing his daughter's lack of action when speaking with non-family members, his spouse, and his daughter; (2) giving directives to get his daughter to be more organized; (3) providing reasons and warning his daughter of possible adverse consequences; and (4) asking his daughter for information about the study-abroad semester and giving her advice. In what follows, I analyze examples of the above-mentioned social acts and examine how they convey the father's concern and create an alignment between him and his interlocutors that serves to construct his parental identity. Through his insistence that his daughter take a more proactive stance toward the study-abroad semester, the father constructs his identity as a responsible parent who guides his daughter through the organization process and tries to ultimately make sure she is well prepared for the trip.

Expressing Concern and Assessing His Daughter's Lack of Action

In this section, I show how the father displays his identity as a parent by expressing concern and assessing his daughter's lack of action in interactions with both family and non-family members. In my analysis of the excerpts, I draw upon Tannen's (2001) concept of a caretaking frame (instructing and taking care of the children) versus a socializing frame (enjoying their company). Tannen notes that as children get older, they want to be perceived as equals in a socializing frame, whereas their parents sometimes put them in a caretaking frame, and the two clashing frames might lead to conflictual situations.

The following excerpt takes place on a Monday. Greg is downstairs in his office and is talking to his secretary, Martha, when the issue of the upcoming study-abroad semester comes up:

(1) 1   Greg: Susan is the point of concern these days.
     2   Martha: /??/ I don't believe it.
     3   Greg: What's that?
     4   Martha: I said I can't believe it.
     5   Greg: Well,
     6   she's just not doing anything about this trip you know,
     7   and we're getting concerned.
     8   It is kind of a big deal.
     9   Martha: I didn't think it was considered a trip.
     10 Greg: Well, it's her semester, that's right,
     11   so it's a- it is kind of a big deal- kind of a big deal.
     12 Martha: Well what is it that she's supposed to be doing?
     13 Greg: Ah passport
     14   flights.
     15   A lot of stuff,
     16   that kind of stuff.

Right at the outset of the conversation, Greg positions himself as an involved parent by sharing his concerns about his daughter: *Susan is the point of concern these days* (line 1). In addition to acting as a prompting device, Martha's comment, *I don't believe it*, in line 2 implies that Susan is usually not a problem. In providing details about the exact nature of the concern, Greg looks at the upcoming trip from the caretaking frame and presents Susan's lack of action as a cause for concern in the family: *she's just not doing anything about this trip you know, and we're getting concerned* (lines 6–7). By repeatedly assessing the study-abroad semester as *kind of a big deal* (lines 8 and 11), Greg conveys the importance he attributes to the event.

Another example of the caretaking frame in which Greg positions his relationship with his daughter Susan occurs later that day when he calls up a travel agent to check the airfare to Spain:

(2) 8 Greg: My daughter is gonna be spending a semester in Seville, Spain.
     9   So I'm looking to get um, prices for a round trip ticket,
     10   and uh, this is actually—
     11   I wanna put a fire under her behind, really.
     12   Right.

Greg's explanation in line 11, *I wanna put a fire under her behind, really*, evaluates his daughter's lack of action and is at the same time an expression of concern. By calling up a travel agent to check the airfare for his daughter, Greg signals his concern that Susan is not as advanced in preparing for the trip abroad as she should be at this point in time, and he is doing some of the preparation for her.

The interconnectedness between the caretaking frame and the "assessment activity" (Goodwin & Goodwin 1992) is also evident in Greg's interactions with his friend Lloyd, which takes place over the phone a couple of days after his conversations with Martha and the travel agent. In response to Lloyd's question about his daughter, Greg says:

(3) 1 Greg: Susan is doing well,
     2   but she's REALLY, you know,
     3   lazing about the summer.
     4   She's driving us a little bit nuts
     5   because she's planning to go to SEVILLE
     6   for the fall semester,
     7   uh, Seville, Spain,
     8   and uh .. so we have,
     9   you know, a lot of organizing there,
     10   and uh—..

Through his emphasis on the intensifier "really" (line 2) and his use of the predicate "lazing" (line 3), the father reveals his dissatisfaction with the current state of affairs, which he views as the result of his daughter's lack of action. In the next line (4), Greg positions both himself and his wife as concerned parents who worry about the upcoming event: *She's driving us a little bit nuts*. He creates a caretaking frame in lines 8–9 by using the first person plural pronoun "we" in *and uh .. so we have, you know, a lot of organizing there*, which signals that he perceives himself as being actively involved in the preparations for the upcoming trip and ultimately responsible for its going well.

In addition to expressing his concern about the upcoming trip and assessing his daughter's lack of action in interactions with non-family members, Greg discusses the matter with Susan as well. The following excerpts come from a conversation that takes place as Susan is getting ready to go to the beach for a two-day vacation with her friends. She is reading a magazine in the living room, and Greg brings up the question of travel arrangements:

(4) 20   Greg: Do you have any idea of the different options of—
     21   is it a six weeks to two month window
     22   on doing the passport?
     23   Susan: Yeah, I guess so.
     24   Greg: <*chuckles*> You might not have to—
     25   you might have to like,
     26   you know, spend a lot of extra money
     27   if you let it go past,
     28   I think, six weeks to two months is the <*sighs*> window.
     29   You're getting close to that window.
     30   Susan: /??/
     31   Greg: Okay you are—we're going to have a meeting on this are [you]
     32   Susan: [I know]
     33   Greg: It seems like you've been ducking this thing pretty big,
     34   you don't want to talk about this.
     35   Susan: I was WORKING on Saturday.
     36   Greg: I know I know but basically you have a re—
     37   an avoidance kind of thing going on, you know,
     38   it's "don't talk to me now— about it"
     39   and you know obviously we're getting real concerned.

The father's assumption is that the daughter should be more active in preparing for the trip. Greg starts out by reminding Susan of the deadlines she has to keep in order to get her passport ready on time and to avoid paying extra money. To convey his concern and dissatisfaction with the situation, he employs the same strategy as the one he uses in his telephone conversation with Lloyd (excerpt 3). Through his choice of the lexical items *ducking* (line 33) and *avoidance kind of thing going on* (line 37), both of which denote ways of evading unpleasant tasks, Greg reveals that he perceives Susan's attitude as immature since ultimately it is her trip and she should be more actively involved in the organizational chores. By expressing his dissatisfaction with the progress his daughter has made so far (or lack thereof), Greg evokes the caretaking frame and places Susan in the one-down position of the recipient of criticism. Because of his growing concern, the father suggests having a family meeting to deal with the problem.

The next excerpt comes from the same conversation and gives details about the family meeting:

(5) 83   Greg: That's your primary goal on Wednesday evening
    84   is to get all this straightened out, get a list,
    85   see your parents,
    86   we're going to be paying for a lot of this,
    87   we want to understand what's going on,
    88   right now we don't understand what's going on.
    89 Susan: <softly> Right.>
    90   Greg: And we're getting nervous that it's going to cost a lot more money,
    91   and that the ultimate worry is that you—
    92   that it's not going to happen,
    93   and that you're not going to be able to go
    94   and because of just lack of
    95   uh
    96 Susan: Motivation.
    97   Greg: We:ll, organization,
    98   not motivation,
    99   organization.

Here, Greg again expresses his concern and provides reasons: *we're going to be paying for a lot of this* (line 86), *we're getting nervous that it's going to cost a lot more money* (line 90), and *the ultimate worry is that you—that it's not going to happen* (lines 91–92). Although money does seem to be a major concern for Greg, he is even more concerned that the study-abroad semester will fail to happen due to his daughter's *lack of organization*. Through his conversational contributions the father portrays Susan as somebody who is not active enough and who needs to be taken care of. Added to this is his warning of possible consequences due to lack of action: *you're not going to be able to go and because of just lack of [. . .] organization* (lines 93–99). The last couple of lines from excerpt 5 are interesting in terms of the alignment Susan takes. Note that when Greg pauses in *and that you're not going to be able to go and because of just lack of uh* (lines 93–95) to search for a word to describe his daughter's point of weakness, Susan volunteers that word herself, *Motivation* (line 96). By offering a word critical of herself, she aligns with her father.[3]

Later on that day, Greg relates the conversation with his daughter to his wife, Nora, over the phone. In relating the conversation and planning the family meeting to get the daughter to be more organized, the father explicitly positions himself and his wife in the caretaking role (note that the recorder only captured Greg's side of the call):

(6) 1 Greg: No she's- no, she's not.
     2   I told her we have to,
     3   I said the most important thing Wednesday night is that we meet.
     4   She said, "Well can we— let's have an early meeting."
     5   I said, "We're not going to do that,
     6   the most—
     7   your NUMBER ONE thing is having a meeting with us,
     8   and then AFTER that's all done,
     9   the SECONDary thing is your social schedule."
    10   So I told her the— y'know, that's it.
    11   That's the first thing is- is uh,
    12   so for Wednesday, we should be doing more than asking questions,
    13   we should be actually writing an outline WITH her.

In addition to setting his daughter's priorities, *your NUMBER ONE thing is having a meeting with us* (line 7) and *the SECONDary thing is your social schedule* (line 9), Greg also suggests that both he and his wife become more engaged in the travel arrangements: *so for Wednesday, we should be doing more than asking questions, we should be actually writing an outline WITH her* (lines 12–13). Because of his growing concern, the father feels the need to take a firmer grip on the organization for the study-abroad semester.

Giving Directives

In this section, I show how the father's use of directives reveals a shift from an egalitarian frame to a caregiving frame in two interactions with his daughter. The first two excerpts (7, 8) come from the Monday conversa-

3. Thanks to Deborah Tannen for pointing this out.

tion Greg has with Susan. The next excerpt (9) comes from an interaction that occurs five days later.

Ervin-Tripp (1976) shows that directives include a wide range of utterances from explicit imperatives to utterances that are formally identical to questions. She suggests that directives contain the component of a desired act and that interlocutors learn to interpret the selection of the form of a directive based on interpersonal relations. Citing a model proposed by Sinclair & Coulthard (1974:33), Ervin-Tripp interprets hints and questions as directives if (1) the agent is "we," "someone," or there is no agent; (2) they refer to action or activity within the obligation of the addressee; and (3) in case "we" is used, it is directed to a subordinate. This model is also effective in describing family interactions.

The next two excerpts come from the same Monday conversation as excerpts 4 and 5. The conversation begins when Greg walks into the room and, seeing that his daughter is reading a magazine, suggests that she go find her birth certificate so that she can apply for a passport. At first, he tries approaching the subject of travel arrangements indirectly by embedding the directive in a question (line 8):

(7) 8   Greg: Why don't you just do yo- your passport thing now?
     9   Get that over.
    10   Susan: I was just gonna hop in the shower.
    11   Greg: It's it's not a big deal right?
    12   It's just you've got to fill out a form?

A couple of lines later, however, when Susan does not respond to the subject of the passport, he switches to a direct imperative:

(8) 41 Greg: Here you're reading this and → ((*re: a magazine*))
     42   that's not dealing with your— now the passport's →
     43   something you could deal with pretty quickly or →
     44   just go look for the birth certificate.
     45   You've got fifteen minutes,
     46   you should go look for it for fifteen minutes,
     47   if that's what's stopping you.
     48   That's the one thing you could just go do right now
     49   which would be moving you to:wards…
     50   It makes me just think you're really ambivalent about going.
     51 Susan: No I'm not ambivalent about going.

The switch from an embedded directive to an on-record imperative in the course of one conversation is indicative of a change in the father's perception of how he should approach the problem.

Greg first phrases the directive as a question, *Why don't you just do yo-your passport thing now? Get that over* (lines 8–9), signaling through the indirect form of the directive that he treats his daughter as a person of equal status who can take care of the travel arrangements. Later on, however, by switching to a direct imperative, *just go look for the birth certificate* (line 44), he evokes the caretaking frame and places their relationship in the parent-child hierarchy. In an attempt to urge his daughter to take some action, Greg repeats his directive from line 44 again in line 46: *you should go look for it.* The irritation that he feels, because of his daughter's laid-back attitude, is further displayed by repeating the time *fifteen minutes* in lines 45 to 46 as the time it would take to accomplish some travel-related task.

The father also issues directives regarding money matters. It is a Saturday morning, and both father and daughter are at the house. Susan, who has a part-time job as a waitress, had to cancel work because she burned her hand with an iron. The topic of conversation shifts from advice on how to handle the burned hand to advice on how to handle work situations. Prior to the following excerpt, Greg tells Susan that she can work for him over the summer and save up money for Seville:

(9) 5 Greg: Once again,
     6   you gotta figure out
     7   how much you wanna make.
     8   You gotta get your mark.
     9   So you say
    10   "This is how many hours I can work for you Dad
    11   because I wanna make this much money."
    12   'Cause if you don't do that,
    13   for some reason,
    14   it will slide by
    15   and you end up with no money for Seville.

In addition to giving his daughter directives about how to get financially prepared for the study-abroad semester (lines 6–8), the father also warns her that if she does not do what she is told to do, she will not have any pocket money in Seville. Greg places their interaction in the caretaking frame by suggesting his daughter work for him over the summer, by giving her instructions on how to handle money matters, and by warning her of possible consequences—which I will discuss in more detail in the next section.

Providing Reasons and Issuing Warnings

As described above, Tannen (2001) views the parent-child relationship as gradually shifting from a caretaking frame to a socializing frame as children get older. This shift often results in the parents facing the challenge of finding the right balance between connection and control. The third strategy Greg employs in trying to get his daughter to be more involved in the arrangements for her study-abroad semester (giving reasons and issuing warnings) provides a good example of his juggling the caretaking with the socializing frame, though in the end it is the caretaking frame that dominates the conversation.

The following excerpt comes from the same conversation as excerpt 9. Here again Greg brings up the topic of money matters in his interaction with Susan:

(10) 1   Greg: It's up to YOU: . .
        2   BUT right now you've GOT to write down what you want to go →
        3   to Seville with.
        4   Susan: 'Kay.
        5   Greg: How would you wanna spend this summer.
        6   You've just gotta have a simple <*chuckling*> budget.>
        7   Susan: Yeah.
        8   Greg: If you don't do it,
        9   it won't happen,
       10   and you're gonna be in Seville,
       11   and you'll . have no money.
       12 Susan: I'll write it out today.
       13 Greg: Yeah just write down—
       14   I'm- I'm going to write down today, what I want. .
       15   Um to start,
       16   what I want YOU to do this summer,
       17   what I want JEREMY to do this summer, ((*Jeremy=youngest son*))
       18   what I want John to do this summer, for my business,
                    ((*John=oldest son*))
       19   What I hope to, you know, get <*clears throat*>

20   from you guys.
21 Susan: Okay.
22   Greg: A:nd um . try to take it from there.

The conversation starts with Greg giving a directive about what Susan should do: *BUT right now you've GOT to write down what you want to go to Seville with* (lines 2–3), which places her in a one-down position. The care-taking frame continues to dominate the conversation in the next few lines (8–11), in which the father warns the daughter of possible consequences (she won't have money) if she does not write down her budget and start saving money for Seville. Greg gives a personal example of what he himself is going to do as a way of urging Susan to follow suit: *I'm going to write down today, what I want* (line 14). Note, however, that the father does not suggest that he and his daughter get together to write down the list (which might put them on a more equal footing). Instead he states that he himself will make a list of what he wants his daughter to do (line 16), thus placing her in a position of someone who still needs to be told what to do.

Asking for Further Details and Offering Advice

Asking for further details and giving advice are yet other acts through which the father displays his stance vis-à-vis the arrangements for the study-abroad semester and creates an alignment between himself and his daughter that serves to construct his parental identity.

Prior to the following excerpt, Greg informs Susan that he is getting her a laptop and tells her she should check which Internet connection she will have in her residence hall in Seville. In line 34, the topic shifts to language issues the daughter might run into during her study-abroad semester:

(11) 34   Greg: You're taught in English?
     35 Susan: Mhm.
     36   Greg: Oh:.
     37 Susan: I quit my language classes.
     38   My Spanish is good enough so.
     39   /I can understand/ the history of Spain in Spanish .
     40   except the Seville accent,
     41   I don't understand that.
     42   Greg: Have you heard the Seville accent?

((*lines 43–56 omitted: Susan talks about someone who spoke Spanish but could not understand the Sevillian accent*))

57 Greg: Uh-oh, you better—
58   You know, what you might wanna do is um .
59   see if you can get anything recorded.
60   [Like going—]
61 Susan: [/Yeah, like/ some] movies or something.
62 Greg: Call up the um . Spanish embassy .
63   and say, you know,
64 Susan: That's a good idea.
65 Greg: Yeah, say "I'm going to Seville,
66   and I've heard it's an unusual accent,
67   my Spanish is basically- it's American taught,
68   <*inbreath*> is there anything I can get on prerecorded tape →
69   that can sort of,
70   you know,
71   get me going in the right direction, like a movie."
72   /Maybe a Spanish [movie]/ where they speak with a Seville accent or,
73 Susan: [Yeah.]
74   That's a really good idea.
75 Greg: Especially if it's a movie with- with SUBtitles.

Greg's questions *You're taught in English?* (line 34) and *Have you heard the Seville accent?* (line 42) can be viewed from both the caretaking and the socializing frames. If viewed from the caretaking frame, the questions imply that the daughter still needs someone to watch out for her and to alert her of possible difficulties. On the other hand, if viewed from the socializing frame, the questions can be perceived as creating a sense of connectedness and involvement between the father and his daughter. Even though questions might imply inability to deal with things on one's own, they are also a sign of caring. The same double meaning, as Tannen (2001) points out, is present in giving advice.

In excerpt 11, Greg also offers advice to Susan on how to make sure she will be able to communicate with Spanish speakers who have a Sevillian accent. Not only does he suggest that she should call up the Spanish Embassy, but he also tells her exactly what to say. Note also that by switching to a first person singular pronoun, he enacts a hypothetical phone call between his daughter and an employee at the Embassy in lines 65 to 71 in which Susan asks for tapes of people speaking in the Sevillian accent.

Tannen's (2007 [1989]) concept of "constructed dialogue" provides an apt description of the function of the enactment of the hypothetical phone call. Tannen points out that "the construction of the dialogue . . . expresses the relationship not between the quoted party and the topic of talk but rather [the relationship] between the quoting party and the audience to whom the quotation is delivered" (109). By offering unsolicited advice on how exactly to handle the situation, the father puts Susan in a one-down position. However, in her replies—*That's a good idea* (line 64) and *That's a really good idea* (line 74)—she seems to appreciate and accept the advice.

Discussion

In the previous section, I analyzed instances of discourse through which Greg constructs his parental identity in conversations with both family and non-family members where the topic is his daughter's study-abroad semester. Drawing upon a data set of a full week of taped interaction, I was able to trace how the issue progressed over the course of a week and to note patterns in the strategies Greg used to get Susan to be more organized and proactive. During the first day of taping, Greg expressed his concern about the upcoming trip in talking to his secretary, Martha, and later called up a travel agent to check the airfare to Seville, Spain. In addition to that, he also talked to Susan before she left for a two-day vacation. During that conversation, Greg warned his daughter of possible consequences due to her lack of action and issued directives to get her to be more organized. Following Greg's suggestion, they agreed upon holding a family meeting after Susan got back from her vacation to talk about organizational issues about the trip. Later, Greg related the conversation to his wife, Nora, and the two of them discussed what things to cover at that meeting.[4]

As the week progressed, Greg continued asking Susan for further details about the study-abroad semester (e.g., availability of computer connections at the dorm, familiarity with the Sevillian accent, money matters) and provided her with advice on how to get better prepared for the trip, thus further constructing his identity as a concerned and responsible father. Toward the end of the period of taping, Greg talked on the phone with his friend

---

4. There is no tape recording of a family meeting during the week in question. Furthermore, there are no references to it in subsequent conversations. This leads me to believe that the family meeting did not take place as planned.

Lloyd. In that conversation, he again expressed his dissatisfaction with the organization of the trip so far and positioned both his wife and himself as concerned parents who worried about the upcoming event.

In sum, a detailed analysis of Greg's conversational contributions throughout the week of taping reveals that even though his daughter is twenty years of age, and ostensibly an adult, he still puts their relationship in the caretaking frame, at least in some situations. The stance of a concerned parent that Greg takes vis-à-vis the study-abroad semester conveys his need to still protect and provide guidance for his daughter and serves to construct his identity as a parent. In response to a recent e-mail inquiry, Susan's mother explained that despite all odds, Susan did go to Seville for her study-abroad semester and the trip went well. In fact, Susan took another trip abroad the following year and, they reported, she was much better prepared this time.[5]

Conclusion

In this chapter, I analyzed tape-recorded, naturally occurring conversations among members of one family, as well as their interactions with non-family members, with the purpose of exploring how the father constructs his identity as a parent through conversational contributions regarding his twenty-year-old daughter's lack of action as her study-abroad semester draws nearer. Drawing upon Tannen's (2001) observation of the complex interplay of caretaking and socializing frames in family discourse, I argued that the father by evoking and maintaining the caretaking frame over the course of the week shapes his parental identity as a concerned and responsible father.

In my analysis of spontaneous interactions as they occurred among family members in the routine of their own home, I suggested that the father portrays himself as a concerned parent through performing the following social acts: expressing concern, giving directives, providing reasons and giving warnings, asking for information, and giving advice. I demonstrated how the father, through his insistence that his daughter take a more proactive attitude, creates an alignment between himself and his interlocutors that serves to construct his parental identity as a responsible

---

5. Personal communication with Deborah Tannen, who followed up with the family after taping.

father who will guide his daughter through the organization process and ultimately make sure she is well prepared for her trip. As previous research has suggested, investigating verbal strategies and conversational moves deepens our understanding of interactional patterns and moment-by-moment identity construction. It is hoped that this analysis through its focus on one father's use of the caretaking frame in interactions with his college-age daughter contributes further to a better understanding of family discourse.

References

Bateson, Gregory. 1972. Steps to an ecology of mind. New York: Ballantine.

Blum-Kulka, Shoshana. 1997. Dinner talk: Cultural patterns of sociability and socialization in family discourse. Mahwah, N.J.: Erlbaum.

Ervin-Tripp, Susan. 1976. Is Sybil there? The structure of some American English directives. Language in Society 5.25–66.

Goodwin, Charles, and Marjorie Harness Goodwin. 1992. Assessments and the construction of context. Rethinking context: Language as an interactive phenomenon, ed. Alessandro Duranti and Charles Goodwin, 147–189. Cambridge: Cambridge University Press.

Ochs, Elinor. 1993. Constructing social identity: A language socialization perspective. Research on Language and Social Interaction 26(3).287–306.

Ochs, Elinor, and Carolyn Taylor. 1995. The "Father knows best" dynamic in dinnertime narratives. Gender articulated: Language and the socially constructed self, ed. Kira Hall and Mary Bucholtz, 97–120. New York and London: Routledge.

Schiffrin, Deborah. 1996. Narrative as self-portrait: Sociolinguistic constructions of identity. Language in society 25(2).167–203.

Sinclair, John, and Malcolm Coulthard. 1974. Toward an analysis of discourse. London: Oxford University Press.

Tannen, Deborah. 2001. I only say this because I love you: How the way we talk can make or break family relationships throughout our lives. New York: Random House.

Tannen, Deborah. 2007 [1989]. Talking voices: Repetition, dialogue, and imagery in conversational discourse. Cambridge: Cambridge University Press.

part II

Gendered Identities in Dual-Income Families

SHARI KENDALL

six

Father as Breadwinner, Mother as Worker:

Gendered Positions in Feminist and Traditional

Discourses of Work and Family

The rise of the dual-income family is the "most dramatic, far-reaching change affecting women, men, and families" in the latter half of the twentieth century (Waite & Nielsen 2001:35), particularly in regard to the "dramatic influx" of women with young children into the workforce (Coontz 2000:167).[1] Whereas one-quarter of children in two-parent families had a mother who worked full-time in the early 1960s, about half did by 1997 (Waite & Nielsen 2001). For children age six and over, this figure reached 69% by 2002 (Clark 2002). In conjunction with these changes, many couples have attempted to share work and family roles more equally. The couples who participated in the Work and Family Project each expressed this goal, identifying it as one reason they were interested in participating. However, like many other dual-earner couples, it became clear

1. I am grateful to Deborah Tannen for her support throughout the Work and Family Project and to both her and Cynthia Gordon for their helpful comments on several drafts of this chapter. I am also grateful to the Sloan Foundation for supporting this project, and, finally, I am especially grateful to these families who allowed us to enter their lives. Earlier versions of parts of this chapter were given at the Georgetown University Round Table on Languages and Linguistics, Washington, D.C., March 9, 2001; the Annual Meeting of the Anthropological Association, Washington, D.C., November 28, 2001; and the American Association of Applied Linguistics, Portland, Oregon, May 2, 2004. Any errors or omissions are my own.

that a range of external pressures were continuing to channel the women and men into caregiving and breadwinning roles, respectively. These pressures emerged during the week(s) the couples tape-recorded in the form of arguments about work and family, and as a frequent topic between spouses and between participants and their colleagues, friends, siblings, parents, and professional contacts (e.g., educational advisors, financial planners).

In this chapter, I focus on two women (Kathy and Janet) from two families to demonstrate that interactions involving work and family do not concern merely who does what but entail a personal struggle in the individuals' identities as they attempt to reconcile competing discourses of gender relations.[2] The women negotiate the forms and meanings of their parental and work-related identities through the positions they discursively take up themselves and make available to their husbands in relation to traditional and feminist discourses of work and family.

A traditional discourse of work and family is based on gendered positions with women positioned as primary caregivers and fathers as breadwinners. A feminist discourse of work and family is based on egalitarian role sharing, with both women and men positioned as primary caregivers and breadwinners. However, the two women in the study do not position themselves and their husbands within one of these discourses alone. By attending to the women's constructions of both parental and work-related identities, it is possible to see that their positionings create a hybrid discourse of work and family: a contemporary discourse of role sharing that is constituted by gendered positions as in a traditional discourse and role sharing as in a feminist discourse. I demonstrate that the women constitute their own and their husbands' identities as caregivers asymmetrically, positioning themselves as primary caregivers and their husbands as secondary caregivers (see also Johnston this volume). In addition, I argue that the women constitute themselves as primary caregivers by indexing a contemporary ideology of appropriate caregiving practices: the "ideology of intensive mothering" (Hays 1996). I then demonstrate that there is a parallel, asymmetrical discrepancy in the women's constructions of work-

2. In discourse analysis, there are two meanings of "discourse": as a stretch of language in use and as social languages or ways of "behaving, interacting, valuing, thinking, believing, speaking, and often reading and writing that are accepted as instantiations of particular roles" (Gee 1999b:viii–ix). Gee differentiates these two meanings by referring to the former as little-d discourse and the latter as big-D discourse.

related identities: although the women discursively construct work identities by taking up the position of "worker," they position their husbands, but not themselves, as "breadwinners" (Potuchek 1997). The contemporary discourse of role sharing represents a compromise between traditional and feminist discourses, enabling the women to simultaneously maintain their work identities within a feminist discourse and to sustain their identities as "good mothers."

In what follows, I first address how individuals create identities through positioning within discourses and then introduce discourses of work and family. I then present examples from the two families to illustrate how the women create gendered parental and professional identities through the dynamic allocation of discursive positions in relation to dominant discourses of work and family. In the conclusion, I discuss how a contemporary discourse of role sharing constitutes an uneasy compromise between traditional and feminist discourses.

Positioning, Discourse and Identity

Discourses and Identities

Davies & Harré (1990:47) describe positioning as the interactional process through which individuals produce "a diversity of selves." At each moment in an encounter, participants take up, resist, and assign positions by locating self and other in relation to values or characteristics (e.g., definitive or tentative); types of people in "social category formations" (e.g., father/daughter); and *discourses*: ways of speaking and behavior that occur at "the disciplinary, the political, the cultural and the small group level," and/or "develop around a specific topic, such as gender or class." Participants locate self and other within positions that are made available by discourses; for example, a discourse of paternalism has the associated positions of "independent powerful man" and "dependent helpless woman" (van Langenhove & Harré 1999:45). Individuals create identities by discursively taking up, contesting, or countering the positions that discourses make available. Moreover, speakers create identities by selecting from a range of discourses that have developed around a sphere of social practice— such as the discourses about gender and work-family issues discussed in this chapter. Discourses are ideologically invested ways of "signifying a particular domain of social practice from a particular perspective"

(Fairclough 1995:14). Consequently, as Gee (1999a:18) explains, discourses are always defined in relationships of "complicity and contestation" with other discourses; they can compete with each other or "create distinct and incompatible versions of reality."

Individuals position self and other within multiple, and often conflicting, discourses as they interact with others (Baxter 2002). At times, individuals may experience "ideological dilemmas": tensions between conflicting cultural ideals or perspectives (Billig et al. 1988). Such dilemmas may lead to transformations in the identities of individuals over time. In his analysis of Ingo Hasselbach's autobiography in which Hasselbach explains why he embraced and then repudiated the neo-Nazi movement in East Germany in the 1980s and 90s, Tappan (2000:101) argues that the development of "moral identity" (i.e., an ideologically mediated identity) entails a process of "ideological becoming" (Bakhtin 1981), through which individuals engage in an "ongoing dialogue with the words of others." Drawing on Bakhtin (1981), Tappan explains that an individual encounters "externally authoritative" discourses in actual dialogues with others and in written texts. These discourses become "internally persuasive" when the individual selectively assimilates their words and other forms of language; these discourses then enter into struggles with other internally persuasive forms of discourse. In this view, the development of identity consists of recurring shifts as individuals reject and reconcile conflicting discourses.

Discourses and Gendered Identities

Current conceptualizations of the relationship between language and gendered identities are theoretically consonant with a discourse approach. Davies & Harré's (1990) conception of discourse stems from Foucault's (1972:49) description as "practices that systematically form the objects of which they speak." Butler (1990, 1993, 1999) elaborates Foucault's concept in her performative theory of gender: individuals' practices bring gender into being, forming the "objects of which they speak," that is, gendered women and men, "through the repetition or citation of a prior, authoritative set of practices" (Butler 1993:223). Similarly, Goffman (1976) explains that the gendered self is accomplished through ritualized display: exhibiting ways of talking and behaving that are conventionally associated with gender. In language research, this relationship between identity and verbal and nonverbal practices is known as "indexing" (Hanks 1992, 2000). Kroskrity (2000:111) explains, "Identities may be linguistically constructed through the use of communicative practices (e.g., greeting formulae, maintenance of mutual gaze, regulation of participation) that are indexed, through members' normative use, to their group."

Ochs (1992) introduced indexing to gender and language research, arguing that the relationship between gender and language is indirect and indexically mediated: linguistic features directly communicate acts in certain contexts (e.g., the imperative mode indexes the act of ordering) and simultaneously constitute stances (e.g., uncertainty). The performance of these acts and stances may help constitute the user's gendered identity by being socioculturally associated with (i.e., indexing) sociocultural expectations and beliefs about women and men. Tannen (1994), using Goffman's (1977) term, argues that individuals create gendered identities by using language that is "sex-class linked" (class in the sense of logical types): ways of speaking are associated with the class of women or the class of men. The thread that binds these theoretical approaches is the idea that individuals create gendered identities through concrete verbal and nonverbal actions that index bodies of socially and historically constructed beliefs about gender. These bodies of beliefs are discourses of gender: ways of understanding and talking about gender that have developed over time through social and historical processes. In this chapter, I argue that one process through which women and men create gendered selves is through the dynamic allocation—or framing (Goffman 1974, 1981; Tannen 1994) —of positions that index sociocultural discourses of gender.[3]

3. Davies & Harré (1990) present positioning theory as an alternative to Goffman's framing. However, Davies & Harré's concept of the "story line" is essentially a frame; it shares the defining characteristic of the frame as an individual's cognitive understanding of what is taking place, which provides essential contexts of interpretation for social acts: "The story line in which the person takes themselves to be embedded is a critical element in the process of establishing the meaning of the utterance in question" (51). However, Davies & Harré also use "story line" and "narrative" metaphorically to relate the individual's discursively constructed self within a current interaction to other selves they have created over time: "every conversation is a discussion of a topic and the telling of, whether explicitly or implicitly, one or more personal stories" (48). The story line thus serves two analytic purposes: the participant's understanding of what is taking place in an interaction and the ongoing discursive construction of identity. I reserve framing theory for the former. Within an interactional sociolinguistic approach, positioning alone cannot account for the complex dynamics of interaction. Conversely, a framing approach benefits from positioning theory based on the elaboration of social indexicals (e.g., social category formations). Current theories of gender and discourse hold that women and men create gendered identities by indexing verbal and nonverbal behaviors associated with women and men. Positioning elaborates this perspective by identifying some of the constructs that are so indexed, discourses being one of them.

The analysis of the two women's discourse I examine in this study suggests that these women face an ideological dilemma as evidenced by the competing discourses of gender relations that emerge in their talk. They create their parental and professional identities in relation to these discourses by claiming and rejecting positions in traditional and feminist discourses, ultimately transforming these discourses into a contemporary discourse of gender relations.

Traditional and Feminist Discourses of Work and Family

The feminist discourse used by the two women in this study is shaped by "second wave" feminism that emerged in the post–WWII era and extended into the 1990s, but was defined primarily in the 1960s and 1970s by pioneers such as Gloria Steinem (1983), Betty Friedan (1963), Simone de Beauvoir (1952), Kate Millett (1970), and others (see Thornham 2000; Lotz 2003).[4] This form of feminism is characterized by an emphasis on integrating women into the public sphere without delay, bringing them "into full participation in the mainstream of American society now, assuming all the privilege and responsibilities thereof in truly equal partnership with men" (Thornham 2000:30). Thus, early in the movement, feminist discourses revolved around women's right to work outside the home. However, many women with dependents encountered difficulties when they entered the workplace because they found a culture of work that is based on the lives of those without primary responsibility for children—the vast majority of whom are men. The workplace expects and rewards an "ideal worker" who works full-time and overtime, takes little or no time off for

---

4. Although there are many strains of feminism in different times and places, contemporary feminist writers generally recognize three waves. The first was defined by the suffragist movement and ended with the passage of the Nineteenth Amendment in 1920. The second wave gained momentum in the 1960s and 1970s. The third wave can be said to have begun with the release of Roiphe (1993), in which she rejects what she perceives as feminism "celebrating women's victimization" (Shugart 2001:132), and two edited collections (Walker 1995; Findien 1995), which contain "autobiographical accounts of young women struggling with feminism in the context of the world as they know it" (Shugart 2001:132). These accounts "construct third-wave feminism rhetorically as informal, grassroots, individualistic, aggressive, diverse, and characterized by a penchant for contradictions and inconsistencies." Post-feminism is often conflated with third-wave feminism (Brooks 1997; Phoca & Wright 1999); however, the former is generally used to characterize a group of conservative feminists who "explicitly define themselves against and criticize feminists of the second wave" (Heywood & Drake 1997:1). See also Orr (1997), Shugart et al. (2001), and Lotz (2003).

childbearing or child rearing, and is supported by "a flow of family work most men enjoy [receive] but most women do not" (Williams 2001:24).

Likewise, working mothers faced difficulties in the home, and a corollary issue soon emerged: the need for men to do their fair share of domestic work. Feminists argued for "communal child-care centers, accessible abortion, the dissemination of birth control information, and *the sharing of housework* to free women from the confines of domesticity" (Echols 1990:44, emphasis added). The latter concern was fueled by Hochschild's (1989) influential book in which she argued that although women had acquired additional responsibilities outside the home, they still performed a greater portion of work in the home, working roughly fifteen hours longer each week than men—an extra month of twenty-four-hour days a year. She concluded, "Just as there is a wage gap between men and women in the workplace, there is a 'leisure gap' between them at home. Most women work one shift at the office or factory and a 'second shift' at home" (4).

The emphasis on whether or not fathers give equal time to equal tasks in domestic work and childcare has dominated feminist discourses concerning women and domestic work from the 1960s to the present, with the consensus that fathers need to do more in order to do their fair share. Phoenix & Woollett (1991:35) identified the dramatic increase in the number of "expert discourses" on parenting during the 1960s and 1970s, including "[f]eminist writings [that] pointed out how little fathers did for and with their children." Richardson (1993:51) observed that by the mid-1980s, "[m]ost authors of childrearing advice books encouraged fathers to become more involved in the care of their children." Hochschild's work on "the second shift" was no exception; she concluded that "[m]ost working mothers are already doing all they can, doing that extra month a year. It is men who can do more" (235).

In a later study of dual-income families with children, Hochschild (1997:20) addressed the question of whether women's and men's actual practices had achieved the egalitarian goal of role sharing during the eight years after *The Second Shift* was published. She found that what had changed was that many couples maintained an egalitarian ideology of coparenting—believing that they were sharing—even though the women continued to do more domestic work and childcare, thus undermining egalitarian ideologies through traditional practices. More recent studies confirm that the sex-based division of labor at home today is similar to that described by Hochschild in 1989: women still do at least twice as much housework and childcare as their partners—even when both parents work full-time (Bianchi et al. 2000; Buunk et al. 2000; Coltrane 2000; Lee & Waite 2005; Robinson & Godbey 1999).

The traditional discourse rejected by the two women whose discourse I examine emerged in the 1950s and 1960s and is personified by television characters like June Cleaver and Margaret Anderson in *Leave It to Beaver* and *Father Knows Best*, two of the television sitcoms of that time period "in which moms were moms, kids were kids, and fathers knew best" (Kassel 1997). In this family model, fathers are breadwinners, who do not engage in housework or childcare, and mothers are caregivers and homemakers who selflessly attend to the needs of their children while vacuuming in high heels and pearls.

Although, as Coontz (2000) argues, this "traditional family" never actually existed, it continues to serve as a touchstone against which other—traditional and non-traditional—ideologies of family are measured.[5] Himsel & Goldberg (2003:863) find that the image of the "traditional family" explains why some men, who ostensibly believe in sharing housework, report that their division of labor is fair even though their wives do more: instead of comparing themselves with their wives, they compare themselves with an image of the "generalized" father of the past "whose meager contributions to family work" positively enhance these men's relatively greater involvement. Similarly, I find, the construct of the traditional mother who stays home full-time and devotes herself exclusively to her children and husband serves as a nemesis for women with egalitarian, feminist views.

Language, Gender, Work, and Family

Research on language, gender, and work-family issues focuses on the feminist topics described above. One strand addresses the question of whether mothers and fathers are represented as equal partners in parenting. Sunderland (2000) examines parenting materials (booklets, brochures, magazines, and manuals) to determine whether they have achieved egalitarian repre-

5. The endurance of these shows in our collective memory was demonstrated by Reep & Dambrot (1994), who asked college students to name the first television parents to come to mind. Over 75% of the students named the same seven mothers and eight fathers, including the parents in these shows, which had been absent from prime-time television for over twenty years: *Father Knows Best* (1954–1963), *Leave It to Beaver* (1957–1963), and *The Donna Reed Show* (1958–1966). (Others were *The Brady Bunch*, *The Cosby Show*, *Family Ties*, *Growing Pains*, and *Happy Days*.)

sentations of fathers' involvement in childcare. She finds that multiple discourses "thread their way through the texts, positioning fathers and mothers differently" and suggesting "a particular representation of gender identities and relations" (254). For example, there are two discourses of fatherhood: "father as baby entertainer" and "father as mother's bumbling assistant." In the former, fathers are disproportionately represented as engaging children in "fun" and "play," whereas mothers are represented as performing basic caregiving tasks. In the latter, mothers are told to "follow your instincts," whereas fathers are represented as feeling "less confident" and as "keen to be involved, but . . . not sure how to go about it" (263). Together, these discourses support an overarching traditional discourse of "part-time father and mother as main parent" (249). For example, fathers are encouraged to "help" mothers in the care of children and are represented as "stepping in" when mothers need them (258). Sunderland concludes that, although these parenting materials encourage men to take a greater role in childcare, women are still endorsed as primary caregivers.

Patterson (2004) examines discourses of gender, parenting, and sexuality in postings to the on-line bulletin board, "you and your partner," at Parentcenter.com. She identifies Sunderland's overarching discourse of "part-time father, mother as main parent." For example, one poster expresses appreciation that her husband "helps with a lot of the housework and is good about helping with the kids" (31). However, Patterson also identifies an intriguing relationship between this discourse and discourses of sexuality regarding the participants' spouses. She observes that in the messages, the posters agree that, "Simply put, if the father can fulfill his role as part-time helper, then the mother can fulfill her role as sexually desiring subject within the relationship" (34). In other words, women who participate on this Website counsel other women to reward their husbands sexually as a means for getting them to "help" mothers with the children. In one discussion about how women can shift from being a mother with one's children to being a sexual being with one's partner, one poster counsels another to "Tell [your husband] what you're wanting [sex] and watch how quick he offers to take over bedtime duty!" (34).

A second strand of research on language, gender, and work-family issues identifies competing discourses that represent and construct different conceptualizations of gender relations. In each case, egalitarian, feminist discourses and positions are undercut by conflicting conservative discourses. Edley & Wetherell (1997:203) interviewed seventeen- and eighteen-year-old boys in "a UK-based, single-sex independent school" to examine the discursive positions taken up by groups of dominant and non-dominant boys in the school. They identify competing positions of masculinity that are based primarily on fathers' involvement at home, which they describe as reflecting types of masculinity that Rutherford (1988) found in popular culture. Edley & Wetherell (1997:215) describe them as the "retributive man," a more traditional form of masculine identity in which men are "the (major) breadwinner of the family and the principal source of authority within the home," and the "new man" who is a "softer, more sensitive and caring individual, who also avoids sexist language, changes nappies [diapers] and loves to shop all day for his own clothes."

Edley & Wetherell find that the non-dominant group of boys in this school use the alternative "new man" discourse of masculinity to distinguish themselves from the dominant boys in the school. However, they most often transform the traditional "retributive man" discourse by claiming strength, the quality most prized by the dominant boys and most central to traditional masculinity as well: non-dominant boys present themselves "as *capable* of physical aggression," but as having the strength to "control such outbursts" (212, emphasis in original). Edley & Wetherell conclude that this marginalized group of non-dominant boys challenges the hegemonic group by using alternative discourses but ultimately creates identities "in dialogue with the identities which were to be challenged and superseded" (215). Thus, these boys transform dominant discourses of conventional masculinity by adapting them in ways that will include them.

Lazar (2000) examines representations of women and men in a Singaporean national advertising campaign, which was launched by the government to encourage couples to have children in order to stem the steadily decreasing birthrate. She found that representations of women and men were embedded in two contending discourses: a discourse of egalitarian gender relations, characterized by symmetry in gender roles and expectations, and a discourse of conservative gender relations, characterized by asymmetry. In the advertisements, the egalitarian discourse is realized by, for example, discursive devices that cast women and men as joint participants in parenting, using the gender-neutral term "parent" rather than gender-specific terms such as "mother" and "father." The conservative discourse appears in advertisements that state or imply that balancing family and career is problematic for mothers but not for fathers. For example, an advertisement directed at women asks, "How will you divide your time between the kids, housework, and the office?" (391). In contrast, advertisements that show men's career commitments competing with family cast this as expected and understandable: "even though my work takes me away, when it comes to joy and dreams, my children are the key" (386).

In the egalitarian discourse, Lazar (2000:380) also finds a construct they dub the "New Man": a "caring, sensitive and nurturing" father who is involved in the domestic sphere as well as the workplace. However, these men are encouraged to have children for their own happiness and career success: one ad directed at men asks, "Why build your career alone? It [family] also provides stability, encouragement and support. Isn't that what you need for a successful career?" (386). Moreover, this "new man" is countered by what Lazar refers to as "other-centered motherhood": "women's acute consciousness (or consideration) of their husbands and their children in the enactment of their motherhood identity" (388). For example, women are encouraged to have a second child for the benefit of a first child: one ad directed at women states, "But there's one precious gift, which only you can give—a brother or sister" (390). Therefore, women are encouraged to consider the needs of their children out of a sense of maternal duty, regardless of how they themselves might feel, while men are encouraged to pursue their own self-interests. Lazar concludes that although asymmetry is not as blatant as it was previously, discourses of egalitarian and conservative gender relations co-exist in the same ad or set of ads and work together to maintain "a largely unchallenged conservative gender order" (373).

In summary, some studies of gendered discourses of work and family identify two opposing discourses: an asymmetrical traditional discourse and a symmetrical egalitarian discourse (Edley & Wetherell 1997; Lazar 2000). This egalitarian discourse remains an ideal because fathers fail to perform their fair share of domestic work (Patterson 2004; Sunderland 2000), or because the egalitarian discourse interacts with traditional discourses to reproduce a more traditional gender order, specifically one in which mothers are expected to put the needs of their children before their own (Lazar 2000). Finally, women continue to be represented as primary caregivers and fathers as secondary caregivers in the form of the "new man," who shares primary caregiving, and the "traditional man," who does not (Edley & Wetherell 1997); the father whose career justifiably intrudes into family life, but the mother whose career must not (Lazar 2000); and the overarching "part-time father" and "mother as main parent" (Patterson 2004; Sunderland 2000).

Studies identifying discrepancies between a feminist ideal of role sharing and actual practices in the home are a crucial component of research on gender, language, and family. For couples seeking a more egalitarian division of domestic labor, the redefinition of men as caregivers is a necessary step. However, discussions of work and family have tended to overlook a comparable redefinition of women's roles. In this chapter, I suggest that although women with children have entered the workforce in increasing numbers, many of these women and their partners have not redefined women as breadwinners. Thus, paralleling Sunderland's overarching discourse of "part-time father and mother as main parent," I propose a complementary discourse of the work sphere: father as breadwinner and mother as worker.

A Model of Gendered Discourses

Breadwinners and Intensive Mothers

The two women in the present chapter take up positions within a contemporary discourse that has evolved from a traditional discourse characterized by asymmetrical roles and a feminist discourse characterized by symmetrical role sharing to simultaneously maintain their work identities and a prevailing ideology of intensive mothering. Potuchek (1997:4) explains that breadwinning is not the same as employment: it "involves not only paid employment, but also the day-to-day obligation to earn money for the financial support of a family. The breadwinner has a duty to work, and leaving the labor force (even temporarily) is not an option." Potuchek identified the distinction between breadwinning and employment based on several studies of women's and men's attitudes about work. Male and female respondents reported that they would expect men to continue working if the female partner could support the family; but if the man supported the family, it would be the woman's choice to continue working or not. In other words, men, but not women, are obligated to work, regardless of the circumstances.

The women whose discourse I examine in this study distance themselves from the image of a traditional housewife. Instead, they articulate an "ideology of intensive mothering," a contemporary model of socially appropriate caregiving that Hays (1996) identifies based on analyses of childrearing practices since the Middle Ages, in-depth interviews with mothers, and contemporary childrearing manuals. This ideology is characterized by the following beliefs: (1) mothers should be the primary care-givers; (2) the child's needs, rather than the mother's needs, should guide proper childcare; (3) parenting should be labor-intensive and emotion-ally absorbing so that parents must spend the maximum amount of time with children; (4) caregiving should be financially expensive due to the enhancements of family life required by intensive mothering; and (5) caregiving should be expert-guided through parenting manuals, etc.

The contemporary discourse of role sharing represents an attempt to reconcile feminist and traditional discourse but is fraught with tensions of its own. Hays (1996) argues that current tensions about work and fam-ily are exacerbated by contemporary models of socially appropriate moth-ering. She contrasts the ideology of intensive mothering with an ideology of the workplace based on the "rational calculation of self-interest" (4) and argues that a logic of unselfish nurturing is contradictory in a society in which over half of all mothers with young children work outside the home and in which the logic of "self-interested gain" guides behavior in other spheres. She calls these "two puzzling phenomena" the "cultural contra-dictions of contemporary motherhood" (x).

The two women I discuss in this chapter face the contradictory demands of these two ideologies on a personal level. Consequently, they position them-selves as workers and their husbands as breadwinners to simultaneously maintain a feminist perspective and construct work identities consistent with an incompatible, prevailing "ideology of intensive mothering" within a tra-ditional discourse. In the following section, I outline the model of gendered discourses and positions that I apply in the analysis.

Contemporary Discourse of Role Sharing

Discourses of gender, work, and family are constituted, in part, by different parental and professional positions. A traditional discourse is characterized by asymmetry in gender roles and expectations: women are positioned as intensive mothers and men are positioned as breadwinners who are obligated to provide the family with essential financial support. In contrast, the femi-nist discourse is characterized by symmetry in gender roles and expectations: women and men are both positioned as primary caregivers and breadwinners. A third discourse, the contemporary discourse of role sharing, draws from the other two discourses in particular ways. As in feminist discourses, both women and men participate in childcare and paid employment; however,

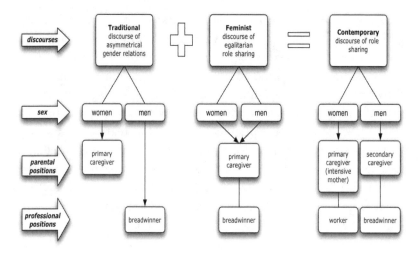

Figure 6.1. Gendered discourses of role sharing

as within traditional discourses, women and men are positioned asymmetrically within these spheres. In the domestic sphere, women are positioned as intensive mothers and fathers as secondary caregivers. In the employment sphere, women are positioned as workers and men as breadwinners.

Figure 6.1 displays the traditional, feminist, and contemporary discourses along with the parental and professional positions that are associated with them. In addition, it illustrates how the traditional and feminist discourses combine to create the contemporary discourse of role sharing. In a traditional discourse, women and men are dominant in different positions. In a feminist discourse, women and men share positions. In a contemporary discourse of role sharing, women and men share positions but are predominant in traditional positions.

After introducing the families in the remainder of this section, I demonstrate how the two mothers take up positions within a contemporary discourse of role sharing, which entails characteristics of traditional and feminist discourses.

Two Families

The analysis is based on the two families who have one daughter between two and three years of age and are expecting their second child within a few months. The first family is Kathy, Sam, and their daughter Kira, who is 2 years and 1 month old. Kathy works reduced hours and both parents have adjusted their work schedules to spend time with their daughter. Sam takes Mondays off work, and Kathy takes Fridays off. Kira is in daycare the remaining 3 days of the work week. The second family is Janet, Steve, and their daughter Natalie, who is 2 years and 11 months. Janet works approximately 8 hours a week as a psychotherapist in two different jobs to acquire clinical experience while working toward her degree in psychotherapy. Steve works full-time at a small video production company and part-time as a waiter in two different restaurants. In addition, both Janet and Steve perform in a children's theater on Saturdays.

Kathy and Sam taped themselves over the course of two weeks, yielding 135 recorded hours. Although Janet and Steve taped only 7 days, they taped for longer periods of time each day, yielding 165 hours. The analysis is based on all the interactions in which work and family become a topic of conversation in some way within the 300 hours of naturally occurring talk produced by these couples. By examining these stretches of talk, I found that both couples were experiencing specific conflicts between work and family during the recording period—and it was in these instances that the women's and men's identities as parents and workers became most salient. Therefore, I begin each analysis with a description of these conflicts. I explain how Kathy and then Janet position themselves and their husbands in caregiving positions, followed by a section describing how they position themselves and their husbands in work-related positions.

Positioning within Discourses of Work and Family

Parental Positions: Kathy & Sam

For Kathy and Sam, the primary work-family conflict that emerges during the taping period is the high cost of daycare that will be required when their second child is born. This topic surfaces throughout the taping period because both partners view the increased cost as pressure for Kathy to quit her job. In the first example, Kathy engages in a contemporary discourse of role sharing by positioning herself and her husband within feminist and traditional discourses.

The excerpt occurs in a meeting Kathy arranged with a (female) financial advisor, in which the discussion revolves around whether it is economically viable for Kathy to continue working. Throughout the meeting, Kathy expresses her ideology of work and family as she explains the situation. In excerpt 1, Kathy explains that she and Sam have arranged their work schedules so that both of them can be primary caregivers. She highlights how important it is to her that she and her husband share in the care of their daughter and expresses the concern that if she did not work, Sam would not be involved in *primary caretaking* (line 17):

(1) *Financial meeting, Monday: Kathy, Sam, Financial Advisor*

1	Kathy:	Well, right now we feel like we have such great balance,
2		because she's at a daycare on-site at my work,
3		she's only there three days a week.
4		He takes off Mondays,
5		I take off Fridays, . .
6		um, he's home with her in the mornings,
7		I'm home with her in the evenings.
8		So we really have a nice balance
9		where he's spending just as much time with her as I am.
10	Advisor:	Mmm.
11	Kathy:	And: u::m we— it's important to ME,
12		'cause I know that if I were to stay home,
13		I would be the, y'know,
14		I'd have all the- the time with her,
15		which is- is fine for me,
16		but it's important for both of us
17		to be part of her primary caretaking.

Kathy engages in a discourse of intensive mothering by explaining that she and Sam have arranged their work schedules to spend as much time with their daughter as possible. However, she also positions herself and Sam as equal caregivers in a feminist discourse of egalitarian role sharing by emphasizing the symmetry in their work and caregiving arrangements, verbalizing this symmetry through parallel syntactic structures: *He takes off Mondays, I take off Fridays; he's home with her in the mornings, I'm home with her in the evenings* (lines 4–7). Also, in a feminist discourse, she expresses concern about the father's involvement in caregiving: *So we really have a nice balance where he's spending just as much time with her as I am* (lines 8–9) and *it's important for both of us to be part of her primary caretaking* (lines 16–17). Kathy indexes her knowledge of feminist discourses by referring to *primary caretaking* (line 17), not just caretaking. However, although Kathy positions herself and Sam as equal caregivers, she subtly undercuts Sam's positioning as a primary caregiver by implicitly claiming a feminist position for herself alone through a false start and repair. She begins to say *we*, but then shifts to *me*, emphasizing the distinction by emphasizing the repair (line 11): *And: u::m we— it's important to ME*. In this way, she suggests that she and her husband are not equal proponents of their caregiving arrangements.[6]

Although Kathy positions herself and her husband as primary caregivers in the meeting with the financial advisor, she positions Sam as a secondary caregiver within actual caregiving situations. For example, in excerpt 2, Kathy attempts to get Kira, who is sick, to spit out a cough drop Sam has given her so that she can take a chewable medicine tablet:[7]

(2) *Getting ready for the day, Friday morning: Kathy, Sam, Kira*

  1 Kathy: Chew! .
  2   Eat your chewies.
  3 Kira: *<whimpers>*
  4 Kathy: They make you feel better. .
  5 Kira: *<whimpers>*
  6 Kathy: Eat your chewies, please . . .
  7 Kira: [m-—]
  8 Kathy: [Oh,] you have your cough drop. You gotta take that out first. .
  9   Yuck!
10 Kira: Whas' that?
11 Kathy: It's a cough drop. You don't want that anyway.
12 Kira: Wassat.
13 Sam: I don't know. She just wanted it. .
14 Kathy: *<sighs>*
15   . .
16 Sam: It CAN'T hurt her.
17 Kathy: Well, it can choke her.
18 Kira: *<coughs>*
19 Sam: We:ll, it's not anything—*<chuckles>*
20   *<chuckling>* It's not anything we haven't done before. >

---

6. In a review of more than 200 scholarly articles and books on household labor published between 1989 and 1999, Coltrane (2000:1221) concludes that egalitarian ideologies influence the sharing of household labor and that the "fit between spouses' attitudes" has an additional effect: If both spouses share similar egalitarian views, they are more likely to put those ideals into practice.

7. Thanks to Cynthia Gordon for pointing out this example to me.

Kathy first tells Kira to take the chewable medicine tablet and then sees that Kira is sucking on a cough drop. Rather than waiting for Kira to finish the cough drop, Kathy tells her to take it out of her mouth (line 8): *Oh, you have your cough drop. You gotta take that out first.* This seems merely practical until Kathy passes judgment on the cough drop by following up with *Yuck!*, an expression suggesting disgust (line 9). Kathy's expression gets Kira's attention; she asks *Whas' that?* (line 10). Kathy responds in a way that again passes judgment on the cough drop: *It's a cough drop. You don't want that anyway* (line 11). Sam then defends giving Kira the cough drop by stating that Kira did, in fact, *want* the cough drop (line 13): *I don't know. She just wanted it.*

When Kathy sighs in line 14, Sam takes this as further recrimination. He defends himself by saying that *It CAN'T hurt her* (line 16). Kathy counters by telling him that it can (line 17): *Well, it can choke her.* Sam then reminds her that they have given Kira cough drops before (line 20): *<chuckling> It's not anything we haven't done before>.* By saying this in a light-hearted manner, he diffuses any potential tension over the matter. Although Kathy directs her negative evaluation of the cough drop to Kira, Sam responds to the criticism and defends his caregiving decision. By judging his actions, especially in the presence of the child, Kathy establishes herself as the ultimate authority on childcare and, thus, positions herself and Sam asymmetrically as primary and secondary caregivers.

Parental Positions: Janet & Steve

For Janet and Steve, conflicts about work and family occur when circumstances cast them into traditional roles: Steve's work intruding into family life and family life intruding into Janet's work—a common gender-related pattern in work-family conflict (Fu & Shaffer 2001). Janet, like Kathy, subscribes to a feminist ideology of egalitarian role sharing. Although Steve works substantially more hours in paid employment, they both arrange their time so that Steve can act as a primary caregiver on a regular basis. In addition, even though Janet is the primary caregiver based on fewer hours of paid employment, she expresses her dissatisfaction about family life interfering with her work and work interfering with Steve's family responsibilities.

In excerpt 3, Janet expresses her frustration that Steve's work intrudes into his family time. The exchange occurs on Friday evening during an argument. Earlier that morning, Steve had forgotten his commitment to accompany

Janet to an obstetrician appointment. On being reminded, he had to phone his coworker and explain that he would be late. Then the doctor kept them waiting, and Steve left before Janet saw the doctor. In the argument that ensues that evening, Janet expresses her resentment that his commitments at work relieve him of responsibilities at home: she is the one who is forced to be flexible by canceling her work-related obligations to stay at home when the situation requires it. Immediately before the excerpt, Steve reminds Janet that he did ultimately come to the doctor's office. Janet responds:

(3) *Friday evening argument: Janet & Steve*
1 Janet: But you left!
2   Didn't you? .
3   I don't get that luxury,
4   I don't get to leave,
5   I have to stay there.
6   I don't get the luxury of being able to work,
7   and- and not be unaffected by things.
8   I have to pick up Natalie early,
9   I have to miss a- a- you know, a part of a meeting that I was going to.
10   <*choked*> If a babysitter doesn't show up,
11   I'm the one who has to stay home. >

Janet outlines a number of situations in which she recently had to miss work-related activities (e.g., *part of a meeting* in line 9) due to external circumstances, then contrasts this with the fact that Steve does not have to make these kinds of sacrifices (lines 6–7): *I don't get the luxury of being able to work, and- and not be unaffected by things.* Janet indexes a feminist discourse by expressing her frustration with their current situation, which does not afford them egalitarian roles.

Janet also articulates a feminist discourse by making it clear that she expects Steve to participate in child-related activities—even for the child who is not yet born. Excerpt 4 occurs Wednesday night when they are sitting in bed reading. She chastises him for not writing in the birth journal (in which expectant parents record their experiences and thoughts about the impending birth) or reading parenting manuals (*books* in the excerpt) in preparation for the birth of their second child:

(4) *Reading in bed Wednesday night: Janet & Steve*
1 Janet: You haven't written one entry. .

2	When you say you have nothing to do, you could write an entry.
3	You don't read your books,
4	<chuckling> you don't do your entries.>
5	You did a lot of entries last time.
6	What will your SON think when he looks at that?
7	He'll say, "What's up Da:d?
8	What about my- when I: was coming into the world."
9	And you'll have to say, "Son, I couldn't be bothered."

In lines 7–9, Janet attempts to persuade Steve to write in the birth journal by discursively speaking for the child through the use of constructed dialogue (Tannen 2007 [1989], this volume). Referring to the expected baby as *he*, Janet says, *He'll say, "What's up Da:d? / What about my– when I: was coming into the world"* (lines 7–8). By making it clear that Steve needs to fulfill his child-related obligations, Janet positions him as a caregiver. In this exchange, she also articulates a discourse of intensive mothering by focusing her criticism on Steve's failure to put the child's needs first, by expecting labor-intensive parenting in the form of writing in a birth journal, and by demonstrating that she is attuned to what the experts say: *You don't read your books* (line 3).

In caregiving situations, Janet positions Steve as secondary caregiver, and herself as primary caregiver, by judging his performance as a father (as Kathy does Sam in excerpt 2 above). Janet is the one who monitors Steve's caregiving activities, not the reverse. In excerpt 5, Janet corrects Steve's actions as he attempts to get Natalie to use the portable *potty*. Steve and Natalie have been playing Go Fish, a card game, while Janet has been talking on the phone. At one point, Natalie indicates that she needs to use the toilet but wants to continue playing instead. Janet, no longer on the telephone, comes into the room with Steve and Natalie while Steve is trying to convince Natalie to use the *potty*. Janet intervenes at line 16:

(5) *Playing Sunday morning: Steve, Natalie (and Janet)*

1	Steve:	Here, why don't– let's bring your potty around so you can sit on the potty.
2		. . . .
3	Steve:	OOPS.
4	Natalie:	I don't want . .
5		I'm- . . I am dry. I am dry Daddy.
6		. . . .

7	Natalie:	I wanna play Go Fish.
8		I wanna play Go Fish Daddy.
9	Steve:	Okay. Well we can't play Go Fish.
10	Natalie:	Why?
11	Steve:	Let's sit on the potty, and play Go Fish.
12	Natalie:	No I wanna play Go Fish standing up.
13	Steve:	Sweetheart I'm-I am nervous, you- you did not make your tinkles.
14		We can do it both at the same time.
15	Natalie:	No, I don't wanna do it all . at the same time, I wa-
16	Janet:	Daddy don't <spelling> P U S H. >
17	Natalie:	[I—]
18	Steve:	[Okay.]
19	Natalie:	I wanna dress up.
20	Steve:	You wanna dress up?
21	Natalie:	Yes.
22	Steve:	Okay let's dress up. Yes.

Janet positions Steve as secondary caregiver and herself as primary care-giver by judging his performance when dealing with Natalie. Her admo-nition to not be too forceful about getting Natalie to use the toilet, *Daddy don't P U S H* ("push" spelled out) in line 16, stems from the fact that both parents are attempting to toilet-train Natalie and to deal with her current tendency to have temper tantrums when crossed. Thus, Janet informs Steve that he is not handling the situation appropriately and per-haps gains unchallenged compliance due to their shared goal. In his sub-sequent turn (line 18), Steve accepts Janet's assessment by agreeing, *Okay*, and by discontinuing his efforts to get Natalie to use the toilet. Then, when Natalie says she wants to play *dress up*, he agrees (line 22): *Okay let's dress up. Yes.*

Both Kathy and Janet position their husbands as secondary caregivers and themselves as intensive mothers within primary caregiver positions. Together these positionings are not compatible with traditional or femi-nist discourses of gender relations. In a traditional discourse, fathers are not positioned as caregivers, and in a feminist discourse, women and men are positioned symmetrically, not as primary and secondary caregivers. Instead, Kathy and Janet constitute gendered orientations to caregiving in a contemporary discourse of role sharing. The women and men share the caregiving role, as in a feminist arrangement, and the women main-tain the position of primary caregiver as in a traditional arrangement.

The remainder of this section focuses on the work-related positions in the discourses of traditional, feminist, and contemporary gender relations. As in the previous section on caregiving, I demonstrate, first, that both Kathy and Janet embrace an ideology of feminist role sharing by positioning themselves as workers; and, second, that although Kathy and Janet do not index a traditional discourse, they do not index a feminist discourse either. Instead, they engage in a contemporary discourse of role sharing by positioning themselves as workers and their husbands as breadwinners.

Kathy articulates a contemporary discourse of gender relations by simultaneously positioning herself within feminist and traditional discourses. In excerpt 6, which takes place in Kathy and Sam's meeting with a financial advisor, Kathy positions herself within a feminist discourse by claiming a professional identity. However, she positions herself within a traditional discourse by not claiming the characteristics of a breadwinner: as having an obligation to work for the essential support of the family. In the excerpt, Kathy states that it makes *financial sense* for her to quit working because paying for a second child in daycare would require all her income, but she also informs the advisor that she is going to continue working for a year to see if they can manage financially:

(6) *Financial meeting, Monday: Kathy, Sam, Financial Advisor*

1	Kathy:	And it does make financial sense for me to quit working,
2		\<*inhales*\> with the cost of daycare, that I'm using .
3		Um: . I don't wanna give up my career.
4	Advisor:	Mm [hm,]
5	Kathy:	[So,] . we're gonna be—,
6		I'm gonna be working,
7		at pretty much a break-even point,
8		and it's a decision I'm making, just—
9		We're gonna do it for a year,
10		and then see what happens.

Kathy positions herself within an egalitarian discourse by presenting herself as a professional through the use of the word "career" instead of "job" (line 3): *I don't wanna give up my career.* A "career" is something to be pursued and worked for, whereas a "job" does not convey equal value. She also claims this identity by expressing her plans to continue working regardless of her income and expenses.

However, she does not take up the position of breadwinner because she does not claim the two defining characteristics of the breadwinner. First, rather than assuming that she will continue to work based on the breadwinner's obligation—and right—to work, she characterizes her career as being dependent on other factors, namely, the cost of daycare. Second, rather than viewing their incomes as one sum from which they pay their expenses, Kathy talks about Sam's income as paying for essential expenses and hers as paying for supplemental expenses. In the excerpt, she frames daycare as being an expense that she incurs through her paid employment. In line 2, she uses the first person singular 'I' to say, *the cost of daycare, that I'm using,* rather than *the cost of daycare that "we're" using;* and, when she explains that she is going to continue working for a year, she begins with a false start using the plural pronoun 'we', *we're gonna be,* but then shifts to the singular 'I', *I'm gonna be working, at pretty much a break-even point* (lines 6–7).

In excerpt 7, Kathy positions her husband as a breadwinner by classifying his salary as paying for essential expenses, but she does not claim a breadwinning identity for herself. This exchange takes place in their meeting with the financial advisor. The advisor has just exhorted them to keep careful track of their spending for a month to identify areas in which they spend too much. Sam asks Kathy how she keeps track of her spending, and Kathy responds (the *condo* in line 3 is a beach house that they own and rent out):

(7) *Financial meeting, Monday: Kathy, Sam, Financial Advisor*
1 Sam: How do you . do your money,
2   do you write- have you been writing checks or do cash-out, or,
3 Kathy: All of my money has been going to the condo expenses,
4 Sam: Okay,
5 Kathy: and then, you've been giving me a hundred dollars a month in cash- a hundred dollars a week in cash to, spend on groceries,

Although Kathy and Sam attempt to share the labor of childcare, their *salaries* have a division of labor. They view Kathy's salary as paying for the enhancements of life, in this case, a second home (the *condo*, line 3). Sam, in contrast, pays for food, an essential family expense; and even though Kathy is employed, she expresses their arrangement as Sam *giving* her this money: *you've been giving me a hundred dollars a month in cash– a hundred dollars a week in cash to, spend on groceries* (line 5).

Since breadwinners must provide for essential expenses, the issue of whether individuals who are considered breadwinners earn enough income to do so arises. (In excerpt 6 above, Kathy questioned whether her income would cover childcare expenses alone.) The following examples also take place in Kathy and Sam's meeting with the financial advisor. The advisor states that, although Kathy's income is relatively low, she benefits from greater flexibility. Kathy responds by pointing out that Sam does not have a high income, but he also benefits by having greater flexibility:

(8) *Financial meeting, Monday: Kathy, Sam, Financial Advisor*
```
1  Advisor:  And uh, you know, and- and that is sometimes a trade off for-
2            for those current expenses,
3  Kathy:    and it's the same with him too,
4            he doesn't—
5            Uh ye- I- probably, this is, you know,
6            to say this about a man—
7            He- his–he doesn't make a real high income either,
8            but the trade off with him also is the flexibility,
```

If Kathy had explained that both she and Sam earned less because they valued greater flexibility, she would have maintained a feminist discourse. Instead, she differentiates their incomes based on gender (line 6): *to say this about a man.* This gendered asymmetry is emphasized by her manner of delivery. She speaks disfluently when telling the advisor that Sam has a relatively low salary: she speaks in a lower volume and at a slower rate, hesitates and has false starts, and uses the hedge *probably* (lines 5–6): *Uh ye- I— probably, this is, you know, to say this about a man.* Her mode of delivery frames her statement as a delicate issue due to the extra verbiage, pauses, and disfluencies that delay the introduction of the main point and thus reduce the "perceptual or cognitive salience" of a sensitive topic (Linell & Bredmar 1996:355). In doing so, her mode of delivery functions as a face-saving device for Sam, thus preserving their connection as spouses. Yet it also brings attention to the discrepancy in how she views the roles of her own and her husband's incomes.

In the discussion of excerpt 6 above, I explained that a defining characteristic of breadwinning is that a breadwinner's work is not optional and therefore not contingent on external factors. In that example, Kathy frames her work as optional by talking about her employment as being contingent on the cost of daycare. In the next two excerpts, I demonstrate that Kathy frames her employment as optional by providing non-financial motivations for working outside the home.

During the taping period, she mentions several reasons for working in a number of interactions, including the meeting with the financial advisor and an after-dinner chat with Sam. Excerpt 9 is from the meeting with the financial advisor. Kathy says, somewhat facetiously, that her work keeps her from spending too much money:

(9) *Financial meeting, Monday: Kathy, Sam, Financial Advisor*
1   Kathy: Okay that's- and that's another thing,
2   just being at work,
3   Advisor: Uh huh.
4   Kathy: keeps me out of the stores,

Although this reason is tongue-in-cheek, it would be unlikely that Sam would make a similar statement, and it frames Kathy's work as optional.

Kathy also frames her work as optional by providing reasons for working. In excerpt 10, Kathy and Sam are discussing their financial situation after dinner one Sunday evening. Kathy mentions how she personally benefits from working:

(10) *Sunday evening after dinner: Kathy & Sam*
1   Kathy: I guess I would be MORE stressed if you worked full time—
2   if you worked five days, and I worked five days,
3   I'd feel like we had no balance.
4   I guess, really, work for me right now is a . diversion,
5   gives my life balance.
6   Plus it gives me independence .
7   a little.
8   And that's what I don't want to lose.
9   I don't like the idea of- of really leaving the work force.
10   Not that I really think you're gonna leave me high and dry, but.
11   I just don't want to leave.
12 Sam: Now would you do a nanny at all?
13 Kathy: No, I don't want a nanny, because . .
14   defeats the purpose really,
15   of why I want them to be in daycare.

16 Sam: Yeah.

17 Kathy: I guess if we had three, we wouldn't have to resort to something
            like that.

Kathy simultaneously indexes feminist and traditional discourses as she talks with Sam about work. She describes her work as a *diversion*, which casts her employment as contingent and positions herself within a traditional discourse of gender relations in which women's work and other activities outside the home are seen as supplements to their more serious work in the home. She indexes feminist and traditional discourses when she mentions that her work gives her life *balance* and *independence*, a goal of feminism, while casting her work as optional rather than obligatory.

As Kathy and Sam's conversation continues, Kathy assumes the position of intensive mother (lines 12–17). In line 12, Sam asks whether she would consider hiring a nanny instead of putting the second child in daycare. In response to Sam's question, Kathy reveals that one reason she wants their children in daycare is to socialize with other children. She explains that having a nanny *defeats the purpose* for having the children in daycare. The meaning of this statement is clarified a moment later when she says that if they had three children, they would not need to *resort to* daycare (line 17). In other words, the children would be able to socialize with each other. By observing that daycare is beneficial to her children, Kathy simultaneously supports her right to work and suggests that she is a good mother because she is considering her children's needs before her own, even when she is not with them. In this way, she constitutes herself as a paid employee in a way that is consistent with an identity as intensive mother but is not consistent with an identity as breadwinner.

Employment Positions: Janet & Steve

Janet has already cut back her work hours to the extent that, if she cut them any further, she would no longer be working outside the home. Nevertheless, she defends her work identity by rejecting the label associated with this final step. Throughout the week of recording, she reiterates to friends, her work supervisor, and her educational counselor that she is not a "stay-at-home mom." In these interactions, she recounts a recent experience in which she had to cancel all her work-related engagements for two days because of a snowstorm and other factors such as her own mother's ongoing illness and, therefore, had to stay at home with her daughter (the circumstances she referred to in the argument with her husband in excerpt 3 above). She rejects the position of a traditional mother in the "evaluation" within these stories—that component of personal experience narratives in which narrators express the significance of the story and their attitudes toward the events (Labov & Waletzky 1967).

For example, in a telephone conversation between Janet and her friend Ted, Janet emphasizes her work identity by distancing herself from mothers who do stay at home:

(11) *Telephone call, Sunday morning: Janet & Ted*
    1 Janet: there were a couple- there were a couple of days I had to miss work
                    in the past month,
    2   because- well because of my mom one week,
    3   and then because of the ice-storm the- the other day,
    4   and it was like all in one week,
    5   and I was like,
    6   I am NOT a full-time <*chuckling*> stay-at-home mom.>
    7   That's what I've learned.
    8   Because it's just like BRUTAL,
    9   it's just- I- I don't know how they do it.

Janet sets up an opposition between herself and mothers who are not employed outside the home by referring to them in the third person, as *they* in *I don't know how they do it* (line 9), and thus disassociating herself from those mothers. As Johnstone (1996:186) observes, one way people create identities through talk is by "how they are identified by others with social groups and how they identify themselves, or refuse to identify themselves, with social groups."

Although Janet disassociates herself from women who do not work outside the home, she does not position herself as a breadwinner. However, she does position Steve in this way by identifying him as the only possible source of the essential financial support required of breadwinners. For example, she does so during a dinner party that she is giving at her house on Saturday evening while Steve is working at a restaurant. The guests are three women who attended graduate school with Janet and now get together once a month. One of the women is married, one is contemplating getting engaged, and one is single. Janet is the only one who has a child. As the friends are catching up on each other's lives, Janet talks about Steve's work situation:

(12) *Saturday evening dinner party: Janet & Friends*

    1 Janet: And his boss is . y'know his boss is a workaholic,

    2   whose idea is that, y'know, Steve should be there as much as he is.

    3   And it's like- and I said to Steve,

    4   I said, "Honey if he- if he wants to give you a third of the company,

    5   and a third of potential profits,

    6   that's one thing," I said.

    7   "But right now, you're an employee,

    8   and you're not making enough to make ends meet.

    9   They can't y'know—

    10   You've got to work TWO OTHER JOBS,

    11   for us to survive.

    12   There's only so much you can do," y'know.

In this stretch of talk, Janet makes it clear that Steve must provide the essential financial support. Through constructed dialogue, she addresses Steve, telling him that "*you're not making enough to make ends meet*" (line 8) and "*you've got to work TWO OTHER JOBS, for us to survive*" (lines 10–11).

In addition, Janet, like Kathy, avoids positioning herself as a breadwinner by giving reasons other than financial support for why she works. One recurring motivation given by Janet and others for mothers working outside the home is the concept of "stimulation." In excerpt 13, Janet is talking on the phone with her friend Ted in the same conversation that appeared in excerpt 11 above. After she tells him why she had to stay home with her daughter, Ted implies that Janet works because they need the money—which they actually do. However, Janet denies that this is the reason and, instead, names other benefits for working:

(13) *Telephone call, Sunday morning: Janet & Ted*

    1 Ted: We have a lot of that in my neighborhood,

    2   I'll tell you that right now,

    3 Janet: What,

    4   stay-at-home moms?

    5 Ted: Yes.

    6 Janet: U:h.

    7 Ted: Because of their rich husbands,

    8   you know,

    9   [and they're like-] they're just like / ? -/

10 Janet: [Well sure.]

11 Ted: they're just like— I don't know,

12   I just think it's weird.

13 Janet: See,

14   you know what,

15   I- for me it's- it's not—

16   Of course you know these days it's not really about money
      because—

17   Well my one job,

18   but my other job it's so unpredictable,

19 Ted: Sure.

20 Janet: u- if people are coming or not,

21   that it's not like money we count on,

22   but just to get out,

23   and be stimulated.

Janet linguistically negotiates her position in relation to traditional and contemporary discourses of work and family as she and Ted frame the conversation. Within a traditional discourse, a woman works only if the family needs a supplementary income, whereas, in a feminist discourse of egalitarian role sharing, a mother would work even if the family did not require two incomes. Ted positions the "stay-at-home moms" in his neighborhood within a traditional discourse by implying that they don't work because they don't need the money (line 7): *Because of their rich husbands.* At this point in the conversation, if Janet acknowledged that she works because she does need the money, she would take up the position Ted makes available to her and, thus, frame herself as a traditional mother. Instead, Janet states that she works *just to get out, and be stimulated* (lines 23–24). By providing a reason other than income for working, she rejects the positioning within the traditional framework on the one hand but rejects the position of breadwinner within a feminist discourse on the other. Instead, she positions herself within a contemporary discourse of role sharing in which men are breadwinners and women are workers who are not obligated to work.

Working outside the home as a means of stimulation is raised on other occasions as well. For example, during Janet's dinner party with her friends (which also appears in excerpt 12), Janet and her friends co-construct reasons that Janet should not be a "full-time stay-at-home mom." The topic begins when Janet tells her friends about the two days she had to cancel her work engagements and stay home with her daughter (which she also described to her friend Ted in excerpt 11 above):

(14) *Saturday evening dinner party: Janet & friends*

```
 1  Janet:  I tell ya,
 2          it's just a . a TRAPPED feeling you know,
 3          you're just saying <shaky voice>"Oh my God,
 4          [get me] out of here.">
 5  ???:    [Mm.]
 6  Janet:  I don't know how people do it,
 7          I- I don't know how—
 8          I don't know how mothers do it,
 9          fathers,
10          anybody sits at home full-time. .
11          But it's not for me.
12  ???:    Mhm.
13  All:    [<laugh>]
14  Vicki:  [/It's all right,/] at least you recognize [that.]
15  Pam:                                    [Yeah that's g-]—
16  Vicki:  I mean God you could be forcing yourself to BE here,
17  Janet:  No,
18  Vicki:  and then taking all that frustration out on her,
19  Janet:  Right,
20          no,
21          I'm- I'm-
22  Pam:    Mhm.
23  Janet:  I'm just so much happier when . you know you can get out and
            get- [feel] →
24  Becky:       [Yeah.]
25  Janet:  stimulated,
26  Pam:    Mhm.
27  Janet:  and you know,
28  Vicki:  Carry on a conversation.
29  Janet:  Right.
30  Becky:  Yeah.
```

After Janet explains that she does not want to be a mother who stays home with the children full-time, one of her friends points out that if a mother does not have outside stimulation, this may negatively impact a child (line 18): *and then taking all that frustration out on her* [the child]. The friend's statement makes Janet's participation in the workforce consistent with the ideology of intensive mothering because, according to this ideology, the child's needs, and not the mother's, should guide proper childcare. Within this perspective, if mother's working outside the home benefits the child, then the work is justified.

In her response, Janet rejects the position her friend makes available to her, that of an intensive mother who would work only for the benefit of the child. Although she first agrees with her friend's assessment of the benefits of working, *Right*, in line 19, she immediately rejects her friend's reasoning within the same turn in line 20, *no*, and she reframes the friend's statement by changing the reason to one that benefits herself and not necessarily her child (lines 23 and 25): *I'm- I'm- I'm just so much happier when . you know, you can get out and get- feel stimulated.* In this way, she resists being positioned within a traditional parental discourse, as she does when talking with her friend Ted on the telephone (excerpt 13 above). However, she also rejects the position of breadwinner by framing her work as optional.

Both Kathy and Janet position their husbands as breadwinners and themselves as workers. Like the parental positions they create, these positionings are not compatible with traditional or feminist discourses of gender relations. In a traditional discourse, mothers are not positioned as workers, and in a feminist discourse, women and men are positioned symmetrically as breadwinners, not as breadwinners and workers. Instead, Kathy and Janet constitute gendered orientations to paid employment in a contemporary discourse of role sharing. The women and men participate in paid employment, as in a feminist arrangement, and the men maintain the position of breadwinner, as in a traditional arrangement.

Discussion

This chapter contributes to the linguistic study of identity in naturally occurring interactions by considering how individuals negotiate the meanings of their social identities through positioning in relation to conflicting, ideologically invested discourses. The analysis shows the complexities of these positionings and their importance to these women's sense of themselves. The women in these two couples linguistically position themselves and their husbands in ways that reflect current understandings of work and family balance. An overt assumption of work-family balance is egalitarian role sharing. Thus, the women position themselves and their husbands in non-traditional roles: they position themselves as workers, and they position their husbands as caregivers. However, both women attach different meanings to their own and their husband's employment. Although they actively display work identities, they construct these identities in ways consistent with an ideology of "intensive mothering" by positioning their husbands, but not themselves, as breadwinners.

Previous research in linguistics and sociology suggests that couples in which women retain control over caregiving fall short of an egalitarian ideal of role sharing. However, considering how the women constitute their work identities in addition to their caregiving identities yields a different perspective: these women construct their caregiving and work identities within a contemporary discourse of role sharing that has evolved from traditional and feminist discourses. In this contemporary discourse, men participate in caregiving as secondary caregivers (as opposed to primary caregivers), and women participate in the workplace as workers, that is, secondary breadwinners (as opposed to primary breadwinners). This arrangement preserves the role sharing of feminist discourses and the asymmetry of traditional discourses.

A contemporary discourse of role sharing constitutes an uneasy compromise between traditional and feminist discourses. Viewing mothers as workers rather than breadwinners endangers their paid employment within individual families: if a woman's employment is viewed as contingent and supplemental, it is more likely to be reconsidered. It is for this reason that Kathy's employment comes under scrutiny when the couple considers the cost of the new baby. Although other factors come into play, such as breastfeeding and the relative income of the parents, if both members of the couple perceived themselves as breadwinners whose careers do not require justification, this option might not have been seriously considered. For couples seeking egalitarian role sharing, the recognition of breadwinning is crucial. Women's employment outside the home and the father's participation in the home are not sufficient. There must be an accompanying change in how the women and men perceive and constitute their identities in these domains.

Some women are not seeking egalitarian role sharing in the workplace; others are seeking this arrangement but are not able to attain it based on the conditions of their lives. The difficulty for analysts is identifying the difference. As one measure, it is necessary to analyze the discourse of choice. The U.S. Census Bureau (2002) reports that "[f]or the first time in 25 years, a growing number of women are *choosing* to take time out of the workforce to care for their children" (in Rowe-Finkbeiner 2003, emphasis added). The proportion of working mothers with infants declined from a record high of 59% in 1998 to 55% in 2000, which Downs & Smith (2001) describe as "the first significant decline since the Census Bureau began publishing this statistic in 1976" (in Rowe-Finkbeiner 2003). Media coverage has sensationalized a particular demographic of highly educated, professional women who, they claim, choose to take time out of the workforce to care for their children. The cover of *The New York Times Magazine* posed the question and response, "Why don't more women get to the top? . . . The answer, according to many professional women turned moms, is: 'They choose not to'" (Douglas 2003).

Do these women "choose," or are there no alternatives? Williams (2004:6) points out, "If you ask a stay-at-home mom if she is happy with her choice, most will say yes." However, if you ask whether she would have "preferred to have *both parents* work reasonable hours and stay on (slower-but-steady) career tracks, many will say 'That's what I *really* want: better choices'" (emphasis in original). For women who want or need to remain employed, institutional options must be available. Organizations addressing these issues call for high quality national daycare, paid maternity and paternity leaves, reduced work schedules, and options providing greater flexibility (Douglas 2003).

Although statistics indicate that more mothers are staying home, this applies only to women with children under 5 years old. The percentage of dual-earner families with older kids, ages 6 through 17, has remained stable for nearly a decade at 69% (Clark 2002). These statistics indicate that many women stay home until the child is 6, then return to the workplace when their children reach school age. This employment pattern is part of an overarching trend of "sequencing," a term coined by Cardozo (1986) to describe women who move in and out of professional careers for caregiving purposes. As she expresses it: "Yes, they have it all . . . but not all at the same time" (in Kaufman & Quigley 2000:1). Garbi (2004:2) notes that mothers currently in their 20s and 30s ("Generation X") have different expectations than did working mothers of the 1980s and '90s: "They expect options like flextime or part-time hours, telecommuting—and the freedom to leave the workplace entirely if they can afford it." According to Carol Evans, CEO and President of Working Mother Media, which tracks the 100 best firms for working mothers, "[f]lexibility is the most important factor for employees today." She continues, "Generation X moms may want to work only one day a week, but they still think of themselves as career women" (Garbi 2004:1). Kaufman & Quigley (2000:1) acknowledge that women who are staying home are, in one sense, "traditional wives and mothers"; but based on interviews they held with women nationwide, they argue that they are also "very nontraditional": "we found a surprising number of savvy, educated, take-charge women who have courageously carved out a unique role that is part traditional, part feminist."

The ability to "sequence" is a significant gain for working mothers; however, many of these women are not aware of the financial implications of taking time away from paid employment. Waldfogel (1998) finds that women who take time out to stay at home incur serious penalties that impact future career advancement. Financial disadvantages include lost wages, lost contributions to Social Security (reducing retirement income), lost salary increases based on advancement, and unequal pay when re-entering the workforce. Together, these factors produce a "mommy wage gap" at specific points in time as well as in lifetime earnings. According to Waldfogel, mothers re-entering the paid workforce earn 10% less than women with similar educational backgrounds and experience. Currently, a 30-year-old woman without dependents earns nearly 95% of men's pay compared to 70% in the 1980s. In contrast, for working mothers, that figure rose from a low 60% to 75%. Lundberg & Rose (2000), focusing on several years surrounding the birth of the first child, estimated that mothers' wages fall by 5% on average after the first birth; mothers who are continuously employed, however, face no penalty at all. In regard to lifetime earnings, for every year out of the labor force, a parent reduces his or her total earnings by at least 2 percent (Clark 2002). Though the wage gap between men and women has fallen in recent decades, the family gap between the wages of mothers and other adults has actually *increased* (Waldfogel 1997). Williams concludes that this "mommy wage gap" is "so clear and deep" that it has created "an economy of mothers and others" (in Cummins 2003).

In order to stay in the workforce, many mothers shift to part-time employment after childbirth. Of the 72% of mothers with children younger than 18 who remain in the labor force, nearly one-third work fewer than 40 hours a week (Pleticha 2004). However, these part-time jobs are generally lower in status and have less pay and fewer career opportunities (Barnett et al. 2000). Also, they do not have parity in pay and benefits to full-time positions. Most professional women do not opt for reduced-hours options because, like other work-life programs, the economic costs in the form of forgone wages and career advancement are perceived to be too great (Judiesch & Lyness 1999; Tausig & Fenwick 2001).

In *Unbending Gender*, Williams (2001:16) notes, "If two-thirds of mothers of childbearing age do not perform as ideal workers" (a worker willing and able to work for 40 years straight, taking no time off for childbearing or childrearing), "we need to know how they come to that decision." Although the analysis of women's language is by no means capable of answering this question, it does provide a glimpse of how this process occurs on a day-by-day basis as women talk with family, friends, and others about the issues they are facing and the oftentimes painful shifts in identity they are undergoing as they make their decisions. Through language, these women position and reposition themselves among competing ideologies of gender relations within the sociocultural and economic constraints in which they must forge their identities as women, workers, wives, and mothers.

Postscript

When I first presented this analysis in 2001, I made some predictions about the possible outcomes of Kathy's and Janet's "ideological becomings" based on the positionings they took up and rejected within traditional and feminist discourses. Although Janet was working few hours when we tape-recorded, she consistently rejected the positioning of a stay-at-home mother and the positioning as breadwinner. In this way, she clearly articulated the contemporary discourse of role sharing in which women and men share roles, but asymmetrically. At the time of taping, Janet was completing her education to become a psychotherapist. Shortly thereafter she started her own practice.

At the time of recording, Kathy was working nearly full-time, but her career was "on probation" as they planned for the birth of their second child. She told the financial advisor that she was going to continue working for a year *and then see what happens* (excerpt 6, line 10). Throughout the recording period, she was ambivalent about remaining in the workforce: she wanted to continue working but did not believe it was practical, especially in terms of finances. In this conclusion, she would not be alone. The cost of childcare has a significant effect on the employment of women with pre-school-aged children (Han & Waldfogel 2001). As a result of these external pressures to leave the workforce, Kathy focused on reasons that she should and should not continue to work. However, by considering reasons at all, she did not construct her identity as a breadwinner. Furthermore, unlike Janet, she did not reject the possibility of staying home with her children. Kathy's ideological becoming, therefore, seemed to be a painful shift in identity from being a member of the paid workforce to being a stay-at-home mother. This is not an easy task for a woman who expresses an ideology of egalitarian role sharing and otherwise demonstrates that she is knowledgeable about, and supports, the tenets of second-wave feminism. What the discursive analysis accomplishes is to show the difficult evolution of identity many women may experience when they leave the workforce—as Kathy eventually does.

A few months after tape-recording, Kathy's second child was born and, after extended maternity leave, she cut her work to three days a week and worked until her workplace found a replacement. Sam continued to work four days a week so he could spend time with the children. Kathy then worked approximately seven hours a week at home as a freelance writer. About two and a half years after taping, she quit her freelance job to be with her children at home and to finish her degree, which she received about half a year later. Thus, she left paid employment less than three years after taping was completed. Half a year after that, she had their third child. Four and a half years after taping, Kathy home-schooled the two oldest children two days a week, Sam did one day, and the children attended a private school half a day for the two remaining days of the week. Kathy volunteered two hours a week at home for an organization helping women, which is a career she intends to pursue sometime later when the children are in school full-time. At the time of writing, Kathy reports to us that she and Sam are happier and less stressed because, she says, they are now doing only two jobs (taking care of home/family and Sam's career) instead of three (the addition of her own career). As she did several years ago when we conducted the study, she simultaneously positions herself within a traditional discourse by staying at home with children and a feminist discourse by asserting that taking care of home and family IS work.

References

Barnett, Rosalind Chait, and Karen C. Gareis. 2000. Reduced-hours employment: The relationship between difficulty of trade-offs and quality of life. Work and Occupations 27(2).168–187.
Bakhtin, M. M. 1981. The dialogic imagination: Four essays, trans. Carl Emerson and Michael Holquist, ed. Michael Holquist. Austin: University of Texas Press.

Baxter, Judith. 2002. Competing discourses in the classroom: A post-structuralist discourse analysis of girls' and boys' speech in public contexts. Discourse & Society 13(6).827–842.

Bianchi, Suzanne M., Melissa A. Milkie, Liana C. Sayer, and John P. Robinson. 2000. Is anyone doing the housework?: Trends in the gender division of household labor. Social Forces 79(1).191–228.

Billig, Michael, Susan Condor, Derek Edwards, Mike Gane, David Middleton, and Alan Radley. 1988. Ideological dilemmas: A social psychology of everyday thinking. Thousand Oaks, Calif.: Sage.

Brooks, Ann. 1997. Postfeminisms: Feminism, cultural theory, and cultural forms. New York: Routledge.

Butler, Judith. 1990. Performative acts and gender constitution: An essay in phenomenology and feminist theory. Performing feminisms: Feminist critical theory and theatre, ed. Sue-Ellen Case, 270–82. Baltimore: Johns Hopkins University Press.

Butler, Judith. 1993. Bodies that matter: On the discursive limits of "sex." New York: Routledge.

Butler, Judith. 1999. Gender trouble, tenth edition. New York and London: Routledge.

Buunk, Bram P., Esther S. Kluwer, Mieks K. Schuurman, and Frans W. Siero. 2000. The division of labor among egalitarian and traditional women: Differences in discontent, social comparison, and false consensus. Journal of Applied Social Psychology 30(4).759–779.

Cardozo, Arlene Rossen. 1986. Sequencing: A new solution for women who want marriage, career, and family. New York: Collier Books.

Clark, Kim. 25 November 2002. Mommy's home: More parents choose to quit work to raise their kids. U.S. News & World Report, 32–33, 36, 38.

Coltrane, Scott. 2000. Research on household labor: Modeling and measuring the social embeddedness of routine family work. Journal of Marriage and the Family 62(4).1208–1233.

Coontz, Stephanie. 2000. The way we never were: American families and the nostalgia trap. New York: Basic Books.

Cummins, H. J. 17 June 2003. Opinions divided about fairness of "mommy wage gap." Bradenton.com. http://www.bradenton.com/mld/bradentonherald/business/6104381.htm. (23 August 2004).

Davies, Bronwyn, and Rom Harré. 1990. Positioning: Conversation and the production of selves. Journal for the Theory of Social Behavior 20(1).43–63.

De Beauvoir, Simone. 1952. The second sex. New York: Knopf.

Downs, Barbara, and Kristin Smith, U.S. Census Bureau. 2001. Maternity leave among first-time mothers. Paper presented at the annual meeting of the Population Association of America, Washington, D.C., March 29–31, 2001.

Douglas, Susan J. 2003. Mommas in the marketplace. In These Times. Posted November 17, 2003. http://www.alternet.org/story/17200.

Echols, Alice. 1990. Daring to be bad: Radical feminism in America, 1967–1975. Minneapolis: University of Minnesota Press.

Edley, Nigel, and Margaret Wetherell. 1997. Jockeying for position: The construction of masculine identities. Discourse & Society 8(2).203–217.

Fairclough, Norman. 1995. Critical discourse analysis. London and New York: Longman.

Findien, Barbara, ed. 1995. Listen up: Voices from the next feminist generation. Seattle: Seal Press.

Foucault, Michel. 1972. The archaeology of knowledge. London: Tavistock.

Friedan, Betty. 1963. The feminine mystique. New York: Norton.

Fu, Carmen K., and Margaret A. Shaffer. 2001. The tug of work and family: Direct and indirect domain-specific determinants of work-family conflict. Personnel Review 30(5).502–522.

Garbi, Jill. 1 Feb 2004. Mothering readers. Folio First Day. http://www.findarticles.com/p/ articles/mi_m3065/is_2_33/ai_112683528/ (7 October 2006).

Gee, James Paul. 1999a. Discourses and social languages. Discourse analysis: Theory and method, 11–39. New York: Routledge.

Gee, James Paul. 1999b. Social linguistics and literacies: Ideology in discourse, second edition. London: Taylor and Francis.

Goffman, Erving. 1974. Frame analysis: An essay on the organization of experience. Boston: Northeastern University Press.

Goffman, Erving. 1976. Gender advertisements. Cambridge: Harvard University Press.

Goffman, Erving. 1977. The arrangement between the sexes. Theory and Society 4(3).301–331.

Goffman, Erving. 1981. Footings. Forms of talk, 124–159. Philadelphia: University of Pennsylvania Press.

Han, Wenjui, and Jane Waldfogel. 2001. Child care costs and women's employment: A comparison of single and married mothers with pre-school-aged children. Social Science Quarterly 82(3).552–568.

Hanks, William F. 1992. The indexical ground of deictic reference. Rethinking context: Language as an interactive phenomenon, ed. Alessandro Duranti and Charles Goodwin, 43–77. Cambridge: Cambridge University Press.

Hanks, William F. 2000. Indexicality. Journal of Linguistic Anthropology 9(1–2).124–126.

Hays, Sharon. 1996. The cultural contradictions of motherhood. New Haven and London: Yale University Press.

Heywood, Leslie, and Jennifer Drake. 1997. Third wave agenda: Being feminist, doing feminism. Minneapolis: University of Minnesota Press.

Himsel, Amy J., and Wendy A. Goldberg. 2003. Social comparisons and satisfaction with the division of housework: Implications for men's and women's role strain. Journal of Family Issues 24(7).843–866.

Hochschild, Arlie, with Anne Machung. 1989. The second shift: Working parents and the revolution at home. New York: Avon Books.

Hochschild, Arlie. 1997. The time bind: When work becomes home and home becomes work. New York: Metropolitan Books.

Johnstone, Barbara. 1996. The linguistic individual: Self-expression in language and linguistics. New York: Oxford University Press.

Judiesch, Michael K., and Karen S. Lyness. 1999. Left behind?: The impact of leaves of absence on managers' career success. Academy of Management Journal 42(6).641–651.

Kassel, Michael B. 1997. Father knows best: U.S. domestic comedy. Museum of broadcast communications encyclopedia of television, ed. Horace Newcomb, Cary O'Dell, and Noelle Watson. Chicago: Fitzroy Dearborn Publishers. http://www.museum.tv/archives/etv/F/htmlF/fatherknows/fatherknows.htm (7 October 2006).

Kaufman, Loretta E., and Mary W. Quigley. 2000. And what do you do?: When women choose to stay home. Berkeley: Wild Cat Canyon Press.

Kroskrity, Paul V. 2000. Identity. Journal of Linguistic Anthropology 9(1–2):111–114.

Labov, William, and Joshua Waletzky. 1967. Narrative analysis. Essays on the verbal and visual arts, ed. June Helm, 12–44. Seattle: University of Washington Press.

Lazar, Michelle M. 2000. Gender, discourse and semiotics: The politics of parenthood representations. Discourse & Society 11(3).373–400.

Lee, Yun-Suk, and Linda J. Waite. 2005. Husbands' and wives' time spent on housework: A comparison of measures. Journal of Marriage and Family 67(22).328–336.

Linell, Per, and Margareta Bredmar. 1996. Reconstructing topical sensitivity: Aspects of facework in talks between midwives and expectant mothers. Research on Language and Social Interaction 29(4).347–379.

Lotz, Amanda D. 2003. Communicating third-wave feminism and new social movements: Challenges for the next century of feminist endeavor. Women and Language 26(1).2–9.

Lundberg, Shelly, and Elaina Rose. 2000. Parenthood and the earnings of married men and women. Labour Economics 7(6).689–710.

Millett, Kate. 1970. Sexual politics. Garden City, N.Y.: Doubleday.

Ochs, Elinor. 1992. Indexing gender. Rethinking context: Language as an interactive phenomenon, ed. Charles Goodwin and Alessandro Duranti, 335–358. Cambridge: Cambridge University Press.

Orr, Catherine M. 1997. Charting the currents of the third wave. Hypatia 12(3).29–45.

Patterson, Susan. Unpublished manuscript. The sexual mom: Motherhood, identity, and discourse in online bulletin boards. Paper written for seminar on discourse analysis, taught by Shari Kendall, Texas A & M University, May 12, 2004.

Phoca, Sophia, and Rebecca Wright. 1999. Introducing postfeminism. New York: Totem Books.

Phoenix, Ann, and Anne Woollett. 1991. Motherhood: Social constructions, politics, and psychology. Motherhood: Meanings, practices and ideologies, ed. Ann Phoenix, Anne Woollett, and Eva Lloyd, 13–27. London: Sage.

Pleticha, Kim. 2004. The mommy wars: The case for a cease fire. The mother's movement online. http://www.mothersmovement.org/features/cease_fire/cease_fire_p1.htm (7 October 2006).

Potuchek, Jean L. 1997. Who supports the family?: Gender and breadwinning in dual-earner marriages. Stanford: Stanford University Press.

Reep, Diana C., and Faye H. Dambrot. 1994. TV parents: Fathers (and now mothers) know best. Journal of Popular Culture 28(2).13–23.

Richardson, Diane. 1993. Women, motherhood, and childrearing. New York: Palgrave.

Robinson, John P., and Geoffrey Godbey. 1999. Time for life: The surprising ways Americans use their time. University Park, Pa.: The Pennsylvania State University Press.

Roiphe, Katie. 1993. The morning after: Sex, fear and feminism on campus. Boston: Back Bay Books.

Rowe-Finkbeiner, Kristin. March/April 2003. Juggling career and home: Albright, O'Connor, and you. Mothering Magazine 117 March/April. http://www.mothering.com/growing_child/family_society/juggling_career.html (7 October 2006).

Rutherford, Jonathan. 1988. Who's that man? Male order: Unwrapping masculinity, ed. Rowena Chapman and Jonathan Rutherford, 21–67. London: Lawrence and Wishart.

Shugart, Helene A. 2001. Isn't it ironic: The intersection of third-wave feminism and generation X. Women's Studies in Communication 24(2).131–168.

Shugart, Helene A., Catherine Egley Waggoner, and D. Lynn O'Brien Hallstein. 2001. Mediating third-wave feminism: Appropriation as postmodern media practice. Critical Studies in Media Communication 18(2).194–210.

Steinem, Gloria. 1983. Outrageous acts and everyday rebellions. New York: New American Library.

Sunderland, Jane. 2000. Baby entertainer, bumbling assistant and line manager: Discourses of fatherhood in parentcraft texts. Discourse & Society 11(2).249–274.

Tannen, Deborah. 2007 [1989]. Talking voices: Repetition, dialogue, and imagery in conversational discourse. Cambridge: Cambridge University Press.

Tannen, Deborah. 1994. The sex-class linked framing of talk at work. Gender and Discourse, 195–221. New York and Oxford: Oxford University Press.

Tappan, Mark B. 2000. Autobiography, mediated action, and the development of moral identity. Narrative Inquiry 10(1).81–109.

Tausig, Mark, and Rudy Fenwick. 2001. Unbinding time: Alternate work schedules and work-life balance. Journal of Family and Economic Issues 22(2).101–119.

Thornham, Sue. 2000. Second-wave feminism. The Routledge critical dictionary of feminism and postfeminism, ed. Sarah Gamble, 29–42. New York and London: Routledge.

van Langenhove, Luk, and Rom Harré. 1999. Introducing positioning theory. Positioning theory, ed. Rom Harré and Luk van Langenhove, 14–31. Oxford: Blackwell.

Waite, Linda J., and Mark R. Nielsen. 2001. The rise of the dual career family: 1963–1997. Working families: The transformation of the American home, ed. Rosanna Hertz and Nancy L. Marshall, 23–41. Berkeley: University of California Press.

Waldfogel, Jane. 1997. The effects of children on women's wages. American Sociological Review 62(2).209–217.

Waldfogel, Jane. 1998. Understanding the "family gap" in pay for women with children. Journal of Economic Perspectives 12(1).137–156.

Walker, Rebecca, ed. 1995. To be real: Telling the truth and changing the face of feminism. New York: Doubleday.

Williams, Joan. 2001. Unbending gender: Why family and work conflict and what to do about it. New York and Oxford: Oxford University Press.

Williams, Joan. 11 May 2004. Do women "opt out" because they have different values?: The maternal wall. Program on Work Life Law, American University, Washington College of Law. http://www.bcfwp.org/Powerpoints/Williams04.pdf (7 October 2006).

ALEXANDRA JOHNSTON

seven

Gatekeeping in the Family: How Family Members Position One Another as Decision Makers

Interactional sociolinguistics has a rich literature on institutional gatekeeping but has not yet applied the metaphor of gatekeeping to the family domain.[1] Social psychology has a growing body of research focused on "maternal gatekeeping" but has not employed discourse analytic methods to study the verbal interactions between spouses that underlie the phenomenon. This chapter aims to bridge the gap between those literatures. I introduce the term "parental gatekeeping" to capture how members of one couple who participated in the Work and Family Project, Kathy and Sam, position Kathy as gatekeeper of caregiving, the primary decision maker in caring for their daughter Kira (2 years and 1 month), despite the fact that both parents participate in the discourse of egalitarian coparenting by expressing the importance of both parents acting as primary caregivers. Similarly, both parents position Sam as financial gatekeeper, the primary decision maker in managing their money. Through discourse analysis of Kathy and Sam's interactions, I find that, contrary to previous studies of maternal

1. I would like to thank the Sloan Foundation for supporting this project, the families who generously participated in it, and Dr. Deborah Tannen for her feedback on earlier versions of this chapter and her abundant support and encouragement throughout.

gatekeeping, discourse and actions consistent with the principles of egalitarian coparenting co-occur with instances of gatekeeping.

First, I consider how the gatekeeping metaphor has come to be used in studies of institutional gatekeeping in the field of interactional sociolinguistics. Next I survey results of research on maternal gatekeeping in social psychology. I consider the nuances that the term "gatekeeping" has accrued from its various uses and how it needs to be carefully considered when applied to the family domain in order to avoid unnecessary attributions of blame. Then I turn to examples drawn from the conversations of Kathy and Sam as they negotiate common family issues of childcare and household finances. I show how each partner contributes to positioning the other as the primary decision maker in these two domains: Kathy in childcare, and Sam in budgeting. Finally, I conclude that co-existing patterns of egalitarian coparenting and gatekeeping do not necessarily constitute an unworkable paradox but, on the contrary, may serve to fulfill different and complementary needs.

The Gatekeeping Metaphor in Interactional Sociolinguistics

The use of the term "gatekeeping" within academic research has a literary antecedent in a 1914 short story by Franz Kafka. In "Before the Law," Kafka (1993) exaggerates the literal images evoked by the gatekeeping metaphor to create a parable about social relationships and individual experience. A country man approaches the door to the Law and asks for admission from a stern, arrogant "doorkeeper," who denies him. The man tries every means to persuade the doorkeeper to admit him: argument, bribery, pleading, and complaint. Nothing moves the doorkeeper. The man spends his life by that door until he is an old, old man. He dies, never having gained admission.

One of the many interpretations of this story is that a relationship of power and hierarchy binds the petitioner, who requests access to institutional resources, and the gatekeeper, who has the power to decide to allow or deny access and thereby affect the course of the petitioner's life. The experience of one person at the gate, whether admitted or denied, multiplied thousands and millions of times becomes the society in which we live, influenced by many different gatekeepers. It is this reading that made the gatekeeping metaphor a vivid image for the process of social change occurring through the mechanism of institutional selection. For interactional sociolinguists concerned with the problem of social inequality, the iterative decision making of employers, welfare officers, educators, and counselors has been seen as a mechanism by which social inequality is created and replicated, and the gatekeeping metaphor aptly describes the problem of patterned institutional discrimination.

In the field of sociolinguistics, institutional gatekeeping has come to mean, broadly, "any situation in which an institutional member is empowered to make decisions affecting others" (Scollon 1981:4), or more specifically, "brief encounters in which two persons meet, usually as strangers, with one of them having authority to make decisions that affect the other's future," that is, "talking to 'The Man'—the person in authority" (Erickson & Shultz 1982:xi). Roberts & Sayers (1998:25) refer to "gatekeepers" as "people who hold certain resources, facilities or opportunities, and who decide, within the constraints of the organization they represent, who should have them—who should be allowed through 'the gate.'"

Discourse analysis has been one method by which the process of institutional selection is viewed at close range, through micro-linguistic analysis of audio- and videotapes of similar gatekeeping encounters. Since the 1970s, gatekeeping has been a fertile area of research. Frederick Erickson drew the term into the field through his study of the verbal and nonverbal behavior of junior college students and their academic counselors during brief, routine face-to-face advising sessions that were audio- and video-taped (Erickson 1975, 1976; Erickson & Shultz 1982). Through discourse analysis, gesture analysis, and video playback with participants, Erickson & Shultz (1982) found that a counselor's interpretation of a student's listener response behavior as well as the degree of social similarity between counselor and student (comembership) influenced the degree to which a counselor acted as an advocate (who represented the student's interests and helped the student navigate the bureaucratic system) or a judge (who represented the institution's interests to the possible detriment of the student). Erickson & Shultz (1982) also found that interactions between counselors and students of different ethnic backgrounds had a higher number of "uncomfortable moments," in which misunderstandings occurred due to differences in interpretation of listener response behavior.

John Gumperz studied interactions between people of different linguistic and ethnic backgrounds as a way to understand patterns of miscommunication and their links to large-scale social discrimination (see, for example, Gumperz [1982a, b]). Some of the patterns of miscommunication in intercultural gatekeeping that Gumperz found were role-played and then recorded for an innovative BBC feature film called *Crosstalk* (Gumperz et al.

1979). In one role play, Anglo British people playing the role of employers chose not to hire a qualified Pakistani applicant because of several communication difficulties. Continuing this line of research, Cook-Gumperz & Gumperz (1997) investigated the use of narratives of personal experience in real-life job interviews. They found that Anglo British interviewers gave specific contextualization cues (including questions such as, "Why are you interested in engine repair when your experience has been in bodywork?") at points in the interview when they hoped to elicit a narrative explanation. Anglo British interviewees recognized the implicit request for an explanatory narrative and produced them accordingly. However, Indian and Pakistani interviewees did not recognize that a narrative was requested and usually responded with a statement of personal preference ("I like engine repair"). Responses such as these led to communicative breakdowns and—in many cases—South Asian applicants did not receive job offers despite levels of prior experience equivalent to those of the Anglo applicants.

Scollon's gatekeeping studies (1981, 1982) focus on the fact that metaphorical gates swing both ways: either to block access or hinder escape. He analyzed the attempts of university administrators to increase "retention" of Alaska Native students, who often resisted efforts to keep them at the university. The source of the resistance was that these attempts were interpreted by students as one of many practices used by university members to change Native students' identities and their relationships with their home communities.

My own research (Johnston 2003, 2004) analyzes the decision-making patterns of U.S. immigration officers, who decide to approve or deny visas to green card applicants based upon the applicant's document file and a face-to-face interview. Using a corpus of 51 interviews, I found that officers often develop a footing toward the applicant of "advocate" or "judge" (both terms used by Erickson & Shultz 1982) based upon their review of the document file, which occurs before the face-to-face meeting. The officer's initial footing sets the tone of the interview and influences how service-oriented or adversarial the officer is toward the applicant throughout the interview.

In addition to these studies, the rich literature on institutional gatekeeping includes analyses of encounters between patients and doctors, students and teachers, and writers and publishers. Within interactional sociolinguistics, however, it has not yet been considered whether the gatekeeping metaphor may be constructively applied within the domain of the family. Social psychology, on the other hand, offers a growing body of research that seeks to define and measure "maternal gatekeeping."

Maternal Gatekeeping in Social Psychology

Maternal gatekeeping is defined by Allen & Hawkins (1999:200) as "beliefs and behaviors employed by mothers that inhibit greater involvement by fathers in family work." The interest in this phenomenon has grown due to studies that have shown that paternal involvement with childcare and housework (referred to below as "work at home") has increased, but not in proportion to women's paid employment outside the home (Hochschild 1989; Lamb 1986). Furthermore, a reduction in work hours for a man does not necessarily translate into increased hours of work at home. As Hochschild (1989) points out, women usually do more, both inside and outside the home, such that they work an extra month per year, which Hochschild terms "the second shift." Why is it that men have not achieved an equal share of family work in dual-earner households? A survey cited in Pleck (1983) indicates that although 40% of fathers say that they would like more time than they currently have with their children, 60–80% of women indicate that they do not want their husbands to be more involved with their children than they are.

There are many complex, interwoven reasons for why men have not achieved an equal share of housework and childcare. One of the possible reasons that many of these studies explore is that mothers may—intentionally or unintentionally—act in ways that inhibit fathers' greater involvement in caregiving and decision making about caregiving. However, though this is often termed "maternal gatekeeping" (e.g., Allen & Hawkins 1999), I refer instead to "parental gatekeeping" because both parents contribute to the interactional pattern in which one makes more decisions or "takes charge" more than the other.

In the literature of social psychology, the term "gatekeeping" can be traced back to the work of Kurt Lewin, who introduced the term in the 1940s. Lewin was a member of the Committee on Food Habits (1940–1947), which had a mandate to develop methods to encourage Americans to consume less-preferred protein sources, such as organ meats (Wansink 2002). Lewin surmised that the behavior of social actors is influenced by a combination of barriers and incentives and that the barriers (gates) to consumption must first be systematically determined and then reduced in order to change the habits of the "gatekeeping" shopper and cook (Wansink 2002). He developed a model of how food items move from farm to table through a series of channels and gates. The gates represented points at which decisions were made by people who were called gatekeepers, such as farmers, grocery managers, shoppers, and cooks. In Lewin's studies, the woman of the household was both shopper and cook, and so he concluded that efforts to change food consumption patterns should target the home-maker as the primary household gatekeeper.

Lewin was aware that the gatekeeping metaphor had application beyond the movement of goods through a system of consumption:

> The constellation of the forces before and after the gate region are decisively different in such a way that the passing or not passing through the whole channel depends to a high degree upon what happens in the gate region. This holds not only for food channels but also for the traveling of a news item through certain commu-nication channels in a group, for movements of goods, and the social locomotion of individuals in many organizations. (Lewin [1948], cited in Gold 1999:268)

As the last phrase "the social locomotion of individuals in many organi-zations" indicates, Lewin connected the phenomenon of gatekeeping to social discrimination, just as Erickson, Gumperz, and many other dis-course analysts concerned with social change would explore almost thirty years later. Lewin continued: "Discrimination against minorities will not be changed as long as the forces are not changed which determine the decisions of the gatekeeper" (Lewin [1948], cited in Gold 1999:268). Lewin's work for the Committee on Food Habits not only offered a metaphor for social discrimination but provided the image of a woman as a household gate-keeper. This image has appeared in later studies of "maternal gatekeeping."

Beitel (1989:19) uses the following definition: "Gatekeeping, or mater-nal moderation of paternal involvement, is proposed as a process by which wives' attitudes and behaviors modify their husbands' involvement in childcare and their assumption of that responsibility on a regular basis." Beitel sought to determine whether maternal moderation of paternal in-volvement with infants exists, can be measured by self-report, and can predict paternal involvement. To answer these questions, Beitel adminis-tered a survey to 244 married, first-time mothers with 3- to 5-month-old babies. The survey attempted to tap the women's attitudes and beliefs about the capabilities, skills, and motivations of their husbands to provide child-care and, secondarily, to relate women's behaviors to the men's assessments of their own competence and degree of involvement. From the survey of mothers, Beitel developed a set of maternal moderation factors that included the value a mother places on paternal involvement, the degree to which a mother believes in innate sex differences with respect to the ability to nurture, the mother's perception of father's competence as caregiver, the degree to which a mother's identity depends on her role as mother, and the standards of childcare expected by the mother. Beitel also administered a self-report survey to the women's husbands in which the fathers rated their own degree of involvement in many areas of childcare and assessed their own competence in the various areas.

Beitel then videotaped fifty-five of the families in their homes for one hour. The families followed a series of tasks, in which responsibility for a task was explicitly given to the father to perform with the baby (such as testing the baby's reflexes), tasks in which mothers and fathers were required to shift responsibility, and ambiguous "free time" segments. In father-designated tasks, in which the father was asked to change the baby's diapers and clothes, a coded scale was used to measure the degree to which mothers engaged with their babies or husbands. Did mothers hold the baby or readjust diaper and clothes after the fathers were finished? Were the mothers' interactions with their husbands neutral, supportive, or intrusive?

The results, determined by regression analysis of variables derived from the self-reports, showed that, in triadic interactions, the degree of a father's involvement was predicted by the mother's "perception of husband's skill." When the father had responsibility for the baby, the mother's "wish to be in charge" (a component of the self-report surveys) provided the best prediction of the degree of paternal interaction with the baby. Also, women who perceived their husbands to be "unmotivated" tended to repeat tasks assigned to fathers, correct what fathers had done (such as adjusting clothes and diapers), and bring tasks to an end. More husbands in this group handed their babies to their wives during pause periods. In addition, significantly more of the reengagements by this group of women resulted in mother-infant exclusive interaction. According to Beitel, "the process of mothers' reengagements seems to reflect perceptions of poor motivation on the part of their spouses and, in some cases, husbands collude in that process" (113).

Belief in innate sex differences also played a significant role. Women who expressed strong belief in survey items such as "mothers are naturally more sensitive to a baby's feelings than fathers are," "mothers are more skillful when it comes to taking care of babies than fathers are," "fathers have to learn what mothers are able to do naturally in terms of childcare," and "men lack the patience to be good caregivers" showed behaviors such as talking to their babies significantly more during father-designated tasks, repeating those tasks, and ending father-designated tasks more often than those who did not hold these beliefs. Beitel concluded that maternal moderation behaviors predicted paternal involvement in direct care. He also found that women were most resistant to "giving up" primary control over aspects of childcare that involved the greatest responsibility, such as nutrition and daycare. Indeed, several of my own examples are drawn from these two aspects of direct care. Beitel speculates that this is because those aspects of childcare are most intimately enmeshed with gender ideology and identity as a mother.

Beitel also considered the behaviors of the fathers and how their behaviors may have affected their wives. For example, according to the surveys, Beitel found that men's self-perceptions sometimes did not correspond with their wives' perceptions. Whereas the women perceived their husbands as unmotivated, the men perceived themselves as unskilled rather than unmotivated. The men's lack of confidence in their own abilities, Beitel concluded, could come across as a lack of motivation to their wives, who might then respond by taking over more childcare work and decision making. Overall, the women placed more emphasis on motivation than skill. They were less concerned with skill if their husbands were willing to put forth the effort.

Allen & Hawkins (1999) also found that gender ideology correlated with maternal gatekeeping. They developed a threefold conceptualization of what constitutes maternal gatekeeping: (1) mothers' "reluctance to relinquish responsibility over family matters by setting rigid standards" (199); (2) mothers' belief in mothering as a primary source of self-esteem and identity confirmation; and (3) mothers' belief in differentiated family roles. A sample of 622 mothers in dual-earner households completed a self-report survey with Likert-scaled items, which was then subjected to cluster analysis. They found that the three dimensions appeared together: mothers tended to score higher on all three dimensions or lower on all three dimensions. Mothers with the highest scores on all three dimensions (about 22% of the survey) were labeled gatekeepers. The gatekeepers seemed to have less equitable divisions of labor in the household and did more domestic labor than "collaborators," who scored lower on the three dimensions. In addition, Allen & Hawkins identified an interactional pattern that they termed a "manager-helper relationship" in which "mothers and fathers may work together in order to maintain distinct spheres of influence in families" (1999:203). In this type of interaction, wives act as managers by "organizing, delegating, planning, scheduling, and overseeing the work done by husbands in order to maintain responsibility for the day-to-day aspects of family work. Their husbands act as helpers by doing what is requested, but by waiting to be asked and requesting explicit directions" (Coltrane 1996, cited in Allen & Hawkins 1999:203). Allen & Hawkins emphasize the collaboration of *both* partners in maintaining the pattern.

Hoffman & Moon (1999) examined personal characteristics and gender role attitudes in relation to supporting father involvement in childcare. Self-report surveys were filled out by 364 women in dual-earner families, who answered questions on self-esteem, trust in their spouse, hostility, gender ideology, and the role of father involvement. The authors found that non-traditional gender role attitudes (beliefs that women and men can care for children equally well, for example), high trust in their spouse, and low hostility toward men predicted the women's support for father involvement. In their study, the education, age, marital status, and other demographic information did not correlate with the respondents' support for father involvement. The authors concluded that a woman's personal characteristics and gender role attitude influence her support for father involvement.

With few exceptions, studies of maternal gatekeeping tend to rely on self-report surveys as primary data for subsequent statistical correlations. Of the three studies reviewed here, Beitel's is notable for including in-home videotaped observation, which was designed to examine the gap between what people say they do and what they actually do (in this case, in an experimental, in-home setting). Beitel's study is notable also for including the father's perspective by administering surveys and observing dyadic and triadic interaction with fathers.

Discourse analysis of interactions between spouses as they negotiate childcare in daily interaction can shed more light on how family members work to position one another as primary decision makers or gatekeepers. But before adopting the discourse of gatekeeping with respect to the family domain, the nuances of the term bear examination. Though these studies state that fathers do play a role in creating patterns of gatekeeping interactions, the fact that gatekeeping in the family has been labeled "maternal" singles out mothers and their words and actions. In fact, gatekeeping in the family is the product of words and actions by *both* fathers and mothers.

The gatekeeping metaphor carries a significant baggage of nuance from its history of use. However, research studies on gatekeeping in the family have not explored the implications of applying the metaphor to the family realm. First, to return to Lewin's use of the term, gatekeeping was something that people did to objects: did they buy sirloin steak or beef liver to cook for dinner? Then the metaphor was expanded to the institutional realm, in which people made decisions about other people. The scope of the metaphor was enlarged from representing the flow of objects through a consumption system to representing the flow of people through a social system. This brought the issue of power and discrimination to the forefront.

Is it useful to talk about gatekeeping within the family? In interactional sociolinguistics, the metaphor highlights relationships of power and inequality among participants, which rings true in encounters between immigration officers and visa applicants or employers and job applicants. However, as much as familial relationships—between partners, or between parents and children—have elements of hierarchy and inequality, they are also complementary and cooperative, and these two tendencies exist in dynamic interaction. Tannen (2001) sees these dynamics as two intersecting continua of connection and control, which she refers to as the connection-control grid (and elsewhere as the intersection of power and solidarity [Tannen 1994]). She notes that "[i]n any family relationship you have to find the right place on the grid—that is, the right position between hierarchy and equality as well as between closeness and distance. Finding that place drives family conversations" (Tannen 2001:69).

However, the gatekeeping metaphor emphasizes hierarchy and distance to the exclusion of equality and closeness. Indeed, it is this aspect that has made it particularly fitting to describe encounters between institutional representatives and those seeking access to institutional resources. The formal, distant relationship that is constructed between two strangers or semi-strangers in an institutional context relies to such an extent on differences in power and authority that the exception to the rule—the collegial feeling of connection that develops through the discovery of social similarities—has been given its own term: "comembership" (Erickson & Shultz 1982).

In addition, though gatekeeping encounters are in fact distributed across time and have important, ongoing intertextual connections (Johnston 2003), most institutional gatekeeping encounters are described as "brief encounters in which two persons meet, usually as strangers" (Erickson & Shultz 1982:xi). However, family relationships and the effects of those relationships generally last throughout one's lifetime, often in spite of distance or even death. Furthermore, institutional gatekeepers rarely have intimate, holistic knowledge of the person in the way that a spouse or a parent has and rely on partial knowledge of the person about whom they are making a decision. Institutional encounters do not create the rich history and intertextuality that is produced through daily interaction among family members.

Gatekeeping in the family domain has generally been employed to mean "someone who keeps someone else from doing something that they want to do." This has two effects. First, the focus is placed not only on power and hierarchy, as mentioned above, but also on one person—the person who is assumed to thwart the other's desires. However, as Goffman (1959) and many sociolinguists, conversation analysts, and linguistic anthropologists have shown, roles and relationships are collaboratively created by all participants in an interaction. It is to convey this sense of collaboration that I use the term "positioning." Scollon (1998:33) summarizes the perspective of scholars in these fields, stating that "any social encounter . . . has as its . . . ongoing highest priority to position the participants in the social encounter in relationship to each other." That is, interactants make claims about themselves and one another, about what sort of people they are, what sort of relationship they have with one another, and what sort of relationship will continue into the future. These claims range from non-agentive and below the level of conscious awareness to highly agentive and purposeful.

Second, the focus on one person—in this case, the mother—is one easy step away from allocating blame. Although I use the term "gatekeeping" in this chapter, I resist any implication of blame as well as the focus on one person. I hope to demonstrate that gatekeeping, in the way I define it, is a collaborative effort by which family members position one person as a primary decision maker in a given domain.

The Discourse of Egalitarian Coparenting

This study examines gatekeeping in one family that participated in the Work and Family Project. Kathy and Sam have one daughter, Kira (aged two years and one month), and Kathy is eight months pregnant with their second child. Kathy and Sam audiotaped themselves over the course of two weeks. After they completed taping, I visited them in their home for one evening to observe them. Later, I shadowed Sam at work and at home for one full day. These home and work visits inform my interpretation of the conversations I transcribed from their tapes, some of which I excerpt in this chapter.

Kathy and Sam both talk and act in ways that show they believe in being equal partners in caring for their daughter, Kira, and their soon-to-be-born baby, Jenny. They have both arranged their work week so that each spends an equal amount of time as Kira's primary caregiver. As Kendall (this volume) notes, one day as Kathy and Sam discuss their finances with a financial counselor, Kathy explains their efforts to make equal time to care for their daughter. (Because this excerpt sets the stage for my analysis, as it does for Kendall's, I repeat it here.)

(1a) Kathy: Well, right now we feel like we have such great balance,
            because she's at a daycare on-site at my work.
            She's only there three days a week.
            He takes off Mondays,
            I take off Fridays,
            um, he's home with her in the mornings,
            I'm home with her in the evenings.
            So we really have a nice balance
            where he's spending just as much time with her as I am.

In describing their schedules, Kathy uses two pairs of phrases that teeter-totter on a verb phrase (take[s] off, [be] home with her): *He takes off Mondays, I take off Fridays; he's home with her in the mornings, I'm home with her in the* evenings. Kathy expresses a sense of balance in the content of her words that is mirrored in the parallelism of her phrases. In the excerpt that follows, Kathy explains why this balance is important:

(1b) Kathy: And: u::m, we— it's important to ME,
            'cause I know that if I were to stay home,
            I would be the, y'know,
            I'd have all the- the time with her,
            which is- is fine for me,
            but it's important for both of us
            to be part of her primary care taking.

Kathy and Sam both demonstrate the importance they attribute to both of them being Kira's primary caregivers through the enthusiasm and patience that mark their one-on-one time with their daughter. Throughout the two weeks of audiotaping, they both show a high degree of competence and caring in the basic tasks of feeding, clothing, entertaining, distracting, and comforting their daughter. Four days a week, Sam begins his day by waking, dressing, and feeding Kira. The following excerpt shows his gentle style of waking up his daughter:

(2) Sam: *<gently>*Ki-Ki::!>
It's morning!
You're out girl.
You're out.
((*short pause*))
<singing> We're GONNA go to school today,
we're GONNA go to school,>
Where's your baba.   ((*baba=bottle*))
You sucked that right down.
There's a little bit left.
((*long pause*))
Mommy put out a Pooh shirt for you somewhere.
I got laundry to get up and down.
<sighs>
Well, maybe I'll go get the laundry first.
<baby-talk voice> We're gonna go to school!
Okay?
Ki-ki?
You're gonna go to school today.>

Sam shows his connection to his daughter by using the family language that he and Kathy both use with Kira and by speaking in soft, gentle tones, often in "baby talk." He calls her by the diminutive "Ki-Ki" and uses words such as "baba" for "bottle." He continually talks to her as he lists his routine tasks, such as bringing the laundry upstairs and dressing her. However, it is important to note that it is Kathy who has chosen the Pooh shirt that Kira will wear to daycare and prepared a lunch for her to take. Nevertheless, throughout the week and during my interviews with Sam, he showed no evidence that he conceived of his role as anything less than that of a primary caregiver—and that he was proud of this role.

Sam demonstrates his role as primary caregiver through talk with others outside the family. One day, for example, when he takes Kira out to a fast food restaurant for lunch, an elderly man strikes up a conversation:

(3)   Man: ((*to Kira*)) Where's your mommy.
        Sam: Mommy's at work today.
        Man: Oh.
→   [So you're the babysitter—]
→   Sam: [Today's- today's Daddy's day.]
        Man: Yeah <*laughs*>
               That's nice you can be around while she's little
        Sam: Yeah, for—
               Well, I take—
               I've been taking Mondays off
               and she's been taking Fridays off.

In this excerpt, the elderly man, perhaps unaccustomed to the sight of a man and a toddler out to lunch in the middle of the day, marks the absence of the presumed primary caregiver by asking where Kira's mother is. He then further supports the traditional arrangement of caregiving by framing Sam in a helper role: *So you're the babysitter*. Speaking at the same time as the man, Sam chooses not to use this word but to frame the time spent with his daughter as *Daddy's day*. This alternative framing adds the nuance that his time with his daughter is special and reserved for him in his role as Daddy. Nowhere in the transcripts of the week does Kathy or Sam ever refer to their time spent with Kira as "babysitting." The use of the term is reserved for anyone else, besides Sam or Kathy, who takes care of their daughter in their absence. This rejection of the term "babysitting" to describe a father's time with his child is more evidence of their participation and belief in the discourse of egalitarian coparenting.

Gatekeeping and Caregiving: Manager-Helper Interactions

Kathy and Sam spend equal time with their daughter and engage in the same types of direct caregiving tasks (such as feeding, dressing, diaper changing, comforting, and so on) with equal competency and connection in their one-on-one time with Kira. However, there is another pattern that co-exists along with the pattern of egalitarian coparenting. When Kathy and Sam interact with one another concerning childcare decisions, or when they both simultaneously engage in caregiving tasks, it is often Kathy who directs, corrects, or criticizes her husband's choices. The pattern exemplifies the manager-helper relationship described by Allen & Hawkins (1999:203). Below, I show examples of Kathy and Sam positioning Kathy as primary decision maker with respect to food and nutrition, Kira's daily routine, and choice of daycare.

Food and Nutrition

In Kathy and Sam's household, Kathy manages the menus. She prepares the lunches, snacks, and drinks that Kira takes to daycare. She remembers when to prepare an extra snack for Kira in case the daycare serves cheese, to which Kira is allergic. As Sam said during the day I shadowed him at work, "I forget these things. Kathy looks after that." Since she often arrives home earlier than Sam, Kathy makes Kira's afternoon snacks as well as the evening meal. She talks about food much more often than Sam and, when she does, she focuses on the nutritional content. She buys and serves foods such as fish, leafy greens, fruits, and vegetables. In addition, Kathy takes pleasure in preparing and eating healthy and delicious food; Sam, however, does not share that pleasure to the same extent. During my day of observation, he characterized their differences by telling me that "I eat to live, and Kathy lives to eat."

In her role of family nutritionist, Kathy emphasizes first and foremost the health aspects of food consumption and secondarily the flavor. During a family dinner, for example, Kathy encourages Kira to eat her vegetables by saying, *Mm! We eat vegetables because they're good for us! And they taste good.* In another dinnertime example, Kira seems to ask for something but Sam has difficulty interpreting her utterances and gestures. He asks her, *Salt? You want salt? Or pepper?* Kathy, perhaps anticipating that her husband might give Kira the salt and pepper shakers, says, *We'll let that go because she doesn't need it.* Here, Kathy frames her child's "need" as a nutritional need, not a flavor need. She also frames herself as a nutritional expert. There are no similar examples over the two weeks of her husband framing one of Kira's food desires in terms of her nutritional needs. Kathy also takes this role of nutritional expert toward her husband, telling him, *You need to drink more water* in order to avoid dehydration. This pattern reflects that found by Margaret Mead (1959), who showed that North American mothers emphasized nutrition while French mothers emphasized flavor and social aspects of food consumption, and Ochs et al.

(1996), who observed similar results in their comparison of North American and Italian mothers.

As Tannen (2001) has shown, suggestions about food consumption within the family are ambiguous and polysemous with regard to connection and control. As a nutritional gatekeeper, Kathy shows she cares about the health of her husband and child by offering and encouraging them to eat highly nutritious foods. On the other hand, she also shows her control over their diets by providing some foods and limiting others. In addition, she directs her husband to buy certain foods and negatively evaluates his food-buying choices, such as when Sam buys popsicles for their daughter, which Kathy says are *just sugar and water* and then directs him to buy those made from one hundred percent juice (I analyze this exchange later in more detail). Kathy not only questions and critiques Sam's choice of what to feed their daughter—and, occasionally, himself—but she also monitors his preparation of food. Although Kathy usually cooks their meals, this evening Sam has returned home late and is heating fried fish pieces and rice for himself as Kathy feeds Kira dinner. Kathy keeps an eye on his cooking:

(4) Kathy: Turn the rice off Daddy.
    Sam: I—<*laughs*>
          I was trying to turn the microwave off, .
    Kathy: I know,
          ((*short pause*))
    Sam: Making mental errors,
          ((*short pause*))
    Kathy: Did you turn the pot off as [well.]
    Sam: [Yes.]
          Yes I did. Thank you for checking on me.
    Kathy: That sounded facetious,
    Sam: Oh no, I was—
          I need it,
          I was trying to express my need for,
          ((*short pause*))
          [You want fish,]
    Kathy: [Facetiousness.]

Sam seems to be juggling a number of tasks, including cooking rice, warming a pot on the stove, and heating fish in the microwave. Kathy tells him to turn the rice off at the same time that Sam seems to be heating the fish in the microwave. Then she asks him if he turned off a pot, to which Sam remarks *Yes, I did. Thank you for checking on me.* This meta-communicative comment suggests that he feels an awareness—and perhaps resentment—of being monitored. Kathy, perhaps sensitive that her remarks have been understood in that way, comments on his delivery (*That sounded facetious*). Sam, still distracted by cooking procedures, plays it straight as he jokingly implies that he needs to be checked on: *Oh no, I was—. . . I need it, I was trying to express my need for. . . .* As he trails off, checking pots and pans, he begins to offer the fish that he has prepared. Kathy, following the lighter note, finishes his lost sentence for him, joking that he was expressing a need for *facetiousness*. The conversation is successfully steered away from potential conflict by humor.

Sam shows he is aware of Kathy's control over and concern for their diets by asking permission to feed something to Kira, or even asking if he himself may drink a can of Coca-Cola (*Can I drink a Coke since I helped clean?*). When he does not ask permission—something Kathy <u>never</u> does— there are examples such as the following, from a dinner conversation, in which Kathy notices that Kira has a glass of Coke:

(5a) Kathy: WAI:T a minute.
Where did you get Coke?
Sam: *<laughs>* Da da.
Kathy: *<baby talk to Kira>* Da da gave you Coke?>
<breath intake> Ha::!>
<baby talk> Mommy says "No:: no:: Co::ke!">
Sam: Just a little bit!
Kathy: Daddy gave you COKE?
Sam: If Mommy can give her pop,
Daddy can give her Coke.
Kathy: Pops are made from juice.
Sam: 'Kay, how bout Hershey's.
Kathy: *<sigh>* Well…
Sam: /??/
Kathy: Pop is for—
Soda is for ve:ry special occasions.
((*ten lines of talk about the term "pop" and about noodles follow*))

Here Kathy contests Sam's decision to give Kira some Coca-Cola to drink. She approximates Kira's level of speech, using words she is sure to under- stand: *Mommy says "No:: no:: Co::ke!"* In response, Sam minimizes his transgression against Kathy's household rule, saying he gave her *just a little bit*. When Kathy repeats, *Daddy gave you COKE?* he tries to justify his decision a second time by claiming equivalency between the two sweet treats each parent provides: pop (juice popsicles) and soda (*If Mommy can give her pop, Daddy can give her Coke.*). Kathy explains that popsicles are made from juice, which implies that they have redeeming nutritional content that soda does not provide. Sam quickly pulls out a low-nutrition card of his own when he reminds Kathy that she gave Kira some Hershey's chocolate. Acknowledging this with a sigh, Kathy drops the nutrition angle and reiterates her household rule: soda is for special occasions. Although Sam seems to undermine Kathy's rule by offering soda to his daughter, he is asked to explain and defend his act. The alternative situation, in which Sam requires Kathy to defend her actions in the childcare domain, did not occur during taping. (However, he *does* require her to defend her actions in the domain of the household budget, which will be shown later in more detail.)

Kathy has another reason for critiquing her husband's choice to give their daughter soda:

(5b) Kathy: You gonna fire her up all night?
                    She's gonna be fired up anyway.
         Kira: <*coughs*> Coke.
         Kathy: [You can stay up with her.]
         Kira: [<*coughs*>]
         Sam: Eat your nu-nus. ((*nu-nus=noodles*))
         Kathy: No more more² Coke.
         Sam: More more nu-nus.

Kathy reminds her husband that a caffeinated drink will stimulate their daughter instead of calming her for bedtime and says if he is *gonna fire her up all night*, then he can also *stay up with her*. She repeats her rule about no Coke at dinner by telling Kira directly that she will not receive any more Coke (*No more more Coke*). Sam seems to support her by repeating the family term *more more* and encouraging Kira to eat her noodles as an alternative to Coke.

The manager-helper interaction in the domain of food preparation may have evolved from a real difference in cooking skill and the different emphasis each partner puts upon skillfully prepared food. This is reflected in

---

2. Reduplication is a common practice in this family's "familylect." "Nu-nus" refers to "noodles" and "more more" means "more."

the "popcorn fight," a conflict analyzed in detail by Tannen (2001, this volume). Kathy has begun to prepare popcorn for an evening snack when Sam, who needs a brief respite from a crying Kira, suggests they switch tasks. Kathy resists relinquishing the popcorn, saying, *But you always burn it.* Sam immediately responds, *No I don't! I never burn it. I make it perfect.* When Kathy insists that he is *going to ruin it,* the gauntlet is thrown on the kitchen floor. Sam, asserting that he'll get it *just right,* overcomes Kathy's tenacious resistance and takes over the task. *Fine,* Kathy finally acquiesces, *but if it starts smoking, you have to take it off the oven. Remember last time you burned it? That's what happened.* The end result: he burns it. The popcorn is thrown out. Would Kathy monitor and control food preparation so much if Sam did not burn the popcorn or forget to bring Kira's snack to daycare? We may not know the answer, but the methodology of this study reveals examples of discourse and actions that may lie behind self-reported survey data of other studies.

Kira's Daily Routine

Just as Kathy manages the household's food, she manages Kira's daily routine. The following example shows how Kathy is able to control her daughter's nightly bath routine, in spite of an alternative suggestion by her husband: she indirectly overrules Sam's inclination to let Kira watch a video before taking her nightly bath. Kathy has finished eating dinner before her husband and is moving on with the evening routine, which involves giving Kira a bath and preparing her for bedtime. Kathy has already told Kira that she cannot watch a video for children starring the baby monster Elmo from the television program *Sesame Street.* Kira begins to insist instead on "*cease,*" her pronunciation of "Dr. Seuss," which refers to her collection of videos and computer games featuring the popular children's characters by Theodore Geisel:

(6a)   Kira: Cease, cease, cease.
      Kathy: Let's take our bathy, okay.
      Sam: You wanna take a bathy?
      Kira: Cease!
      Kathy: Did you cut her nails?
      Sam: ((*to Kira*)) Girl.
           ((*to Kathy*)) I put clothes in the wash.
      Kira: Cease cease cease cease.

```
       Sam:  Okay.
  →           You can go put it in.
       Kira:  Cease cease.
       Sam:  You know where it is.
              You know where it is.
       Kira:  <urgent, feet pounding> Cease cease!>
  →   Kathy:  Let's go take our bathy.]
  →    Sam:  [You know where the video is, right.]
       Kathy:  [Yes. Yes she does. Okay.]
       Sam:  [She's on a track,]
  →           Better to let her put Seuss in and then give her her bath.
       Kathy:  Mm.
       Sam:  She'll probably be interested in it two minutes.
```

Kathy and Sam seem to be following the same routine when they both let Kira know that it is time for her bath. Kathy asks Sam if he has cut Kira's nails (if not, presumably Kathy would have to make preparations to incorporate this task into the bath routine). Sam does not directly say no but instead substitutes a task that he did complete (*I put clothes in the wash*), as if to say either that he was too busy with the wash to cut her nails or that he performed one task of use to the household despite not completing another.

Then, in response to Kira's growing insistence, Sam gives her permission to put in the video, at the same time that Kathy repeats, *Let's go take our bathy*. Sam explains that, since Kira is so focused on her desire to watch the video (*on a track*), it is *better to let her* watch the video for a short time. The unstated implication is that she will escalate her insistence to a tantrum (already her feet are pounding) if she does not get her way. And, given the attention span of a toddler, Sam says that *she'll probably be interested in it two minutes* and then be ready to take her bath. Kathy listens to her husband's decision with a noncommittal *Mm*. She then understands from her daughter's actions that she wants to play a Seuss computer game, not watch a video:

```
  (6b)   Kathy:  Ahh, what happened.
                 Oh, you wanna play Seuss on the computer.
                 You know what—
         Sam:  O:::h.
  →    Kathy:  Let's get our bathy first, okay.
```

Kira: Cease, cease, cease, cease.
→ Kathy: Let's get our bathy and then Seuss.
→ Who can we take to the bathtub.
Kira: Abows. Abows.
Kathy: Bubbles? Okay.
((*Kathy and Kira walk into the bathroom; Sam finishes eating dinner and starts pushing in chairs.*))
Kathy: That'll be FUN in the tub, won't it.
You never tried to play soccer in the tub.
Kira: Cease cease.
Kathy: Let's see what happens.
TUBBY:::!
Need some water?
Kira: Yes.
((*Kathy turns on the faucet*))

Kathy is not persuaded to let Kira watch a video or play on the computer and remains on task to get her into the bath. In an attempt to redirect and distract her daughter, Kathy promises Seuss after the bath and asks her daughter what she would like to have in the bathtub. Kira replies *abows* (bubbles) and walks with her mother into the bathroom. Despite the last reminder of *cease* from Kira, Kathy keeps directing Kira's attention toward the bath, greets the bathtub with a cheery *TUBBY:::!* and asks if they need water. Kira, finally on board with the bath program, replies with a clear *yes*. The bath continues without distraction.

In this way, Kathy, without directly disagreeing with her husband's suggestion about how to conduct the evening activities, smoothly continues with her plan for getting their daughter bathed and ready for bed. During the week of taping, it seemed that Kathy's plans for her daughter's diet and daily routines took precedence; the reverse situation, in which Sam overruled (or attempted to overrule) Kathy's caregiving decisions, did *not* occur. This absence of challenge by Sam to Kathy's decision making is as important as Kathy's direct and indirect challenges to Sam's decision making. The cumulative effect of the interactive strategies of both spouses contributes to creating and maintaining Kathy's position as the primary decision maker concerning their daughter. This can be seen as a type of parental gatekeeping, in the sense that Kathy's choices seem to outweigh Sam's with respect to decisions of day-to-day childcare.

Kira's Daycare

In addition to making decisions over Kira's daily routine, such as meals and bathtime, Kathy is in charge of daycare options for the near and long term. Kira currently attends a daycare center provided by Kathy's employer. Sam's company does not provide daycare facilities. During the day I shadowed him at work, Sam told me that even if his company instituted a daycare, Kathy "would not let" Kira attend because his company is located near a sewage treatment plant. His choice of words—that Kathy would not let Kira attend—frames the choice as principally hers. This follows the pattern described by Hochschild (1997), in which she noted that a mother can either provide childcare herself or outsource care: in both cases, the realm of childcare is framed as the mother's.

Gatekeeping and the Household Budget

There is another pattern of gatekeeping in this family. With respect to the household budget, it is Sam who often critiques Kathy's spending and Kathy who defends her choices. Sam judges his partner's fiscal responsibility much as Kathy judges Sam's nutritional choices. One sore point is the telephone bill; Sam thinks that Kathy makes too much use of telephone services like "star sixty-nine," which calls back the last person who called:

(7)	Kathy:	Your mom called and didn't leave a message.
		I star sixty-nined her.
→	Sam:	You don't need to do that.
	Kathy:	I know.
→	Sam:	'Cause it's fifty cents every time you do that.
	Kathy:	I know.
→	Sam:	You do that a hundred times,
→		it's the same as paying a mortgage late.
	Kathy:	/??/
→	Sam:	A penny saved is a penny earned.
→		Jenny's gonna need all the pennies we have. ((*Jenny is the unborn baby*))

After Kathy mentioned that she *star sixty-nined* Sam's mother, Sam responds with a lecture. He tells her that it is unnecessary (*You don't need to do that*); reminds her of the cost (*it's fifty cents every time you do that*); extrapolates the cost (*You do that a hundred times, it's the same as paying a mortgage late*); quotes an old saw (*A penny saved is a penny earned*); and appeals to her desire to provide for their soon-to-be-born daughter (*Jenny's gonna need all the pennies we have*).

This may seem like a disproportionate reaction to a fifty-cent phone call, but "Kathy's spending" has become a mutually recognized topic of discussion and something that Sam monitors and judges, much as Kathy monitors and judges his cooking and nutritional choices. Kathy's spending encompasses more than telephone bills. In the session she scheduled with a financial counselor, she tells the (female) counselor that she often uses shopping as a way to get out of the house and that *being at work keeps me out of the stores*. In the same conversation, she says, *I guess I feel like I'm not willing to look like a pauper . . . when you work somewhat hard, it— you know, I shouldn't have to go to Goodwill*. Then she acknowledges *Sam's telling me I have Mercedes taste, and I want Mercedes things, but I make Geo money, and that's probably true*. Kathy spends money on different things from Sam, such as more expensive food and clothing (Sam is proud that he still wears some clothing from high school, for example). These differences frame a conversation that the couple have later at home, when they discuss the counseling session. Sam, who views himself as frugal, suggests a somewhat tongue-in-cheek solution to their finances: *Kathy stops spending money and I keep doing whatever I want*. Sam's monitoring and critiquing of Kathy's spending choices are met with the same kind of defensive reaction from Kathy (e.g., *Don't blame me*, from a conversation in which they argue about who bears responsibility for what they agree is a less-than-ideal financial situation) as when Kathy criticizes Sam's food preparation ("*I never burn the popcorn!*").

These overlapping issues of nutrition, childcare, and spending come together one afternoon when Sam offers to make a run to the grocery store. In the following example, Kathy asks Sam to buy juice popsicles, one of their daughter's favorite snacks.

(8)   Kathy: Could you bring me some—
            Sam: Pop and medic—
→ Kathy: The Dole pops,
                the Dole juice ones.
→   Make sure it's a hundred percent juice.
            Sam: Okay.

Kathy: Make sure they're the skinny ones.

        Sam: Okay.

             Like the ones that I got before? the size.

→ Kathy: Yeah but I think you always get the cheapest brand,

             which is all sugar and water.

        Sam: It's the same thing. .

→   Okay, splurge for my princess.

In this excerpt, Kathy explicitly reminds Sam to make sure of the brand, the ingredients, and the size of Kira's juice popsicles. In requesting a specific brand name item she wants Sam to buy at the store, Kathy exhibits the classic type of consumer gatekeeping behavior that was first defined by Lewin, in which a homemaker directs and controls the flow of consumer goods into the household. She is also a nutritional gatekeeper, in that she monitors the nutritional intake of her daughter (*Make sure it's a hundred percent juice*) and explicitly criticizes her husband's nutritional choices for their daughter by buying popsicles that are *all sugar and water*. In addition to the nutritional and consumer gatekeeping that is evident, references to their different money styles are woven in. Kathy shows her preference for paying more for food with higher nutritional content. She highlights their differences in spending habits by noting that Sam *always get[s] the cheapest brand*. As noted earlier, Sam is a self-described "eat to live" person who rarely discriminates among food choices, and here he insists that the different types of popsicles are *the same thing*. Then, in a move that simultaneously acquiesces to his wife's request and shows his care for his daughter, he agrees to buy the expensive brand by reframing the purchase as a *splurge* for Kira. His use of the endearment *princess* reframes what earlier may have seemed an unnecessary expense as a treat for his daughter.

Implications

Kathy and Sam both talk in ways that exemplify the discourse of egalitarian coparenting. For example, they do not refer to Sam's time with Kira as "babysitting," they discuss in positive terms the arrangements they have made to spend equal time with their daughter, and they refer to themselves and one another as primary caregivers and indeed act as such. At the same time, Kathy makes most of the decisions that affect both daily and long-term care for their daughter, such as choosing her daycare facility, preparing her meals, and organizing her routines. A pattern emerges of a manager-helper interaction, such as that described by Allen & Hawkins (1999), in which Kathy monitors, changes, and critiques her husband's choices, especially concerning nutrition and food preparation (though, as the popcorn incident shows, this is perhaps with good reason). Beitel (1989) found that women most commonly moderated paternal involvement in childcare in areas that require planning and responsibility, such as organizing the child's environment. Kathy exemplifies the manager-helper interactional patterns in these areas: she decides what clothes Kira should wear (and Sam dresses her), plans what food Kira should eat (and Sam feeds her), and chooses the type of daycare (and Sam drives her there in the mornings). In each case, Sam carries out a decision that Kathy has made.

Sam's behavior contributes to Kathy's pattern of decision making and delegation. During taping, Sam never changed or critiqued Kathy's choices with respect to taking care of their daughter. This absence of challenge is as important as Kathy's challenges to Sam's decisions (such as giving Kira soda or suggesting that she play a video game before taking her bath) because both contribute to Kathy's decisions carrying the day. His responses to her monitoring (such as *I never burn the popcorn!* and *Thank you for checking on me*) are defensive and/or humorously facetious: both strategies respond to the pattern without renegotiating it. In a different domain, the household budget, Sam does critique and attempt to change Kathy's choices, such as her phone use and personal shopping. Her response, though often defensive (*Don't blame me*), also includes making an appointment for the two of them to meet with a financial counselor in order to gain knowledge that they both could use to better manage their money. The examples drawn from their day-to-day conversations show how both spouses position themselves and one another as a type of gatekeeper in different domains: Kathy in childcare and nutrition and Sam in money management.

Studies of maternal gatekeeping in social psychology have relied upon self-reported data as the basis for statistical correlations between maternal attitudes and gatekeeping behaviors, such as monitoring and critiquing paternal involvement. For example, Hoffman & Moon (1999) and Beitel (1989) have shown that self-reported belief in egalitarian gender roles does not co-occur with gatekeeping behavior, while belief in "traditional" gender roles does. However, the examples drawn from the conversations of Kathy and Sam during actual interactions over two weeks of their life show that this is not necessarily the case in practice: expressing the principles of egalitarian coparenting can occur with instances of gatekeeping. The co-existence of these two patterns might be lost in a self-report survey or overlooked in a one-time, in-home observation. These findings show the importance of micro-linguistic analysis of multiple conversations occurring over time in order to study a phenomenon as complex as gatekeeping in the family.

In her study of dual-career couples with children, Hochschild (1989:20) found many couples who "*wanted* to share and imagined that they did"— and yet somehow the women ended up taking on the majority of work at home. Hochschild called the mistaken belief that they shared the work, when they actually didn't, a "family myth." Rather than casting the co-occurrence of egalitarian coparenting *and* parental gatekeeping as inconsistent or as a "family myth," I believe it is a starting point for addressing questions that may tell us much more about family dynamics. What needs does each pattern fulfill? Who benefits from each pattern? I believe that two seemingly contradictory patterns can co-exist and simultaneously fulfill family members' co-existing needs for connection and control. It might be that Kathy wants to have both the satisfaction of an egalitarian role division as well as the satisfaction of taking the lead with respect to daily and long-term childcare decisions. She can honor both a wish to share primary caregiving with her highly involved husband—which fulfills a need for connection to both her husband and her daughter—and also feel that she has a special commitment to nutrition and education choices for her daughter—which fulfills a need for control as well as her sense of obligation as a mother. And, indeed, Kira gets the best of both worlds: a highly involved, caring father and a mother who is satisfied that she is applying the best of her knowledge toward raising a healthy, happy child. Perhaps it is the existence of these two co-existing patterns that strikes the right balance for this family.

All family members influence other family members in various ways and contribute to defining one another's roles and positions within the family. The use of discourse analysis to study gatekeeping in the family bridges the gap between the literature on family gatekeeping in sociology and social psychology and the literature on institutional gatekeeping in interactional sociolinguistics. Studies of maternal gatekeeping have primarily focused upon the mother (with the notable exception of Beitel [1989], who administered surveys to fathers and videotaped in-home observations). Using the epistemology and methodology of interactional sociolinguistics, which holds that interactions are created and affected by all parties to the interaction, I have shown how Sam contributes to the interactional patterns just as much as Kathy does. Both parents' discourse contributes to positioning mother as "parental gatekeeper"—a term I suggested—and father as financial gatekeeper.

This study also brings the consideration of gatekeeping in the family domain into the field of interactional sociolinguistics. Though the metaphor has been expanded from its use in the 1940s, when it was used by Lewin to represent the flow of consumer goods, I believe we can use the metaphor, with care, to describe how family members position one another as primary decision makers and watchdogs in different domains. We cannot ignore the influence of household partners in inhibiting or encouraging positions of primary decision making with respect to taking care of one another, doing housework, budgeting, preparing meals, and everything else that families do together in daily life. It may be helpful for families to see how their words and actions affect one another—not to blame one another, but to understand the patterns of interaction that make them who they uniquely are as a family.

References

Allen, Sarah M., and Alan J. Hawkins. 1999. Maternal gatekeeping: Mother's beliefs and behaviors that inhibit greater father involvement in family work. Journal of Marriage and the Family 61(1).199–212.

Beitel, Ashley Howard. 1989. Toward a reconceptualization of paternal involvement in infancy: The role of maternal gatekeeping. Champaign and Urbana: University of Illinois at Urbana-Champaign dissertation.

Coltrane, Scott. 1996. Family man. New York: Oxford University Press.

Cook-Gumperz, Jenny, and John J. Gumperz. 1997. Narrative explanations: Accounting for past experience in interviews. Journal of Narrative and Life History 7(1–4).291–298.

Erickson, Frederick. 1975. Gatekeeping and the melting pot: Interaction in counseling encounters. Harvard Educational Review 45(1).44–70.

Erickson, Frederick. 1976. Gatekeeping encounters: A social selection process. Anthropology and the public interest: Fieldwork and theory, ed. P. R. Sanday, 44–70. New York: Academic Press.

Erickson, Frederick, and Jeffrey Shultz. 1982. The counselor as gatekeeper: Social interaction in interviews. New York: Academic Press.

Goffman, Erving. 1959. The presentation of self in everyday life. New York: Anchor Books.

Gold, Martin, ed. 1999. The complete social scientist: A Kurt Lewin reader. Washington, D.C.: American Psychological Association.

Gumperz, John J. 1982a. Discourse strategies. Cambridge: Cambridge University Press.

Gumperz, John J., ed. 1982b. Language and social identity. Cambridge: Cambridge University Press.

Gumperz, John, T. Jupp, and Celia Roberts. 1979. Crosstalk: A study of cross-cultural communication. London: National Center for Industrial Language Training in association with the BBC.

Hochschild, Arlie Russell, with Anne Machung. 1989. The second shift. New York: Avon.

Hochschild, Arlie Russell. 1997. The time bind: When work becomes home and home becomes work. New York: Metropolitan Books.

Hoffman, Charles D., and Michelle Moon. 1999. Women's characteristics and gender role attitudes: Support for father involvement with children. Journal of Genetic Psychology 160(4).411–418.

Johnston, Alexandra Marie. 2003. A mediated discourse analysis of immigration gatekeeping interviews. Washington, D.C.: Georgetown University dissertation.

Johnston, Alexandra Marie. 2004. Files, forms and fonts: Mediational means and identity negotiation in immigration interviews. Discourse and technology: Multimodal discourse analysis. Georgetown University Round Table on Languages and Linguistics 2002, ed. Philip LeVine and Ron Scollon, 116–127. Washington, D.C.: Georgetown University Press.

Kafka, Franz. 1993[1914]. Collected stories. Trans. by Willa Muir and Edwin Muir. New York: Knopf.

Lamb, Michael, ed. 1986. The father's role: Applied perspectives. New York: Wiley.

Lewin, Kurt. 1948. Group decision and social change. Readings in social psychology, ed. T. M. Newcomb and E. L. Hartley, 330–341. New York: Henry Holt.

Mead, Margaret. 1959. Four families. [Film with commentary by Margaret Mead; 60 min., sound, black and white]. National Film Board of Canada.

Ochs, Elinor, Clotilde Pontecorvo, and Alessandra Fasulo. 1996. Socializing taste. Ethnos 61(1–2).7–46.

Pleck, Joseph 1983. Husbands' paid work and family roles: Current research issues. Research in the interweave of social roles, vol. 3: Families and jobs, ed. Helena Lopata and Joseph Pleck, 231–233. Greenwich, Conn.: JAI Press.

Roberts, Celia, and Pete Sayers. 1998. Keeping the gate: How judgments are made in interethnic interviews. The sociolinguistics reader, vol. 1: Multilingualism and variation, ed. Peter Trudgill and Jenny Cheshire, 25–43. London: Arnold.

Scollon, Ron. 1981. Human knowledge and the institution's knowledge. Final report on National Institute of Education Grant No. G-80-0185: Communication Patterns and Retention in a Public University, 1–26. Fairbanks, Alaska: Center for Cross-Cultural Studies, University of Alaska.

Scollon, Ron. 1982. Gatekeeping: Access or retention? Southwest Educational Development Laboratory, Working Papers in Sociolinguistics, no. 96.

Scollon, Ron. 1998. Mediated discourse as social interaction: A study of news discourse. New York: Longman.

Tannen, Deborah. 1994. The relativity of linguistic strategies: Rethinking power and solidarity in gender and dominance. Gender and discourse, 19–52. New York and Oxford: Oxford University Press.

Tannen, Deborah. 2001. I only say this because I love you. New York: Random House.

Wansink, Brian. 2002. Changing eating habits on the home front: Lost lessons from World War II research. Journal of Public Policy and Marketing 21(1).90–99.

CYNTHIA GORDON
DEBORAH TANNEN
ALIZA SACKNOVITZ

eight

A Working Father: One Man's Talk
about Parenting at Work

L ike so many gendered terms and phrases, the ubiquitous collocation
"working mother" has no parallel in "working father."[1] For one thing,
fathers are presumed to work. For another, as Hochschild (1989) and
Maddock & Parkin (1994) observe, women's identity as mothers is more
salient in the workplace than men's identity as fathers. Whether it be cause
or effect, Kendall (1999) suggests that based on gendered ways of interacting, women might be more likely to talk about family at work, while
Tannen (1994a) finds this pattern borne out in her observations and tape
recordings of interactions among employees at several large corporations.
The couples with young children who recorded their conversations at
home and at work as participants in the Work and Family Project all expressed and enacted a commitment to sharing childcare responsibilities.
However, as Kendall (this volume) and Johnston (this volume) discovered and demonstrate, this did not mean that the couples constructed
breadwinner and primary caregiver identities in equal measure, although

1. We are grateful to Shari Kendall for extensive comments on an earlier draft of this
chapter. We thank, too, the Sloan Foundation for funding the project, as well as Neil and his
coworkers for generously allowing us to listen in on our work lives.

the three fathers in families with small children did a significant amount of primary caregiving. This pattern raises the question: to what extent does their participation in caregiving affect fathers' construction of their parental identities in the context of their professional lives? In the present chapter, we address this question by examining one father's talk about parenting at work. Our analysis provides insight into what it means to be a working father and how this compares to prior work focusing on working mothers.

Tannen (1994a) is one of many discourse analysts who observe that social talk is vital in the workplace in that it establishes a friendly working environment, opens lines of communication for work-related issues, and facilitates the flow of information. Talk about family is a common type of social talk at work. Tannen (1994a) and Kendall (1999) have identified family as one topic of talk at work that not only builds solidarity among coworkers but also enacts gender-related, or sex-class linked (Goffman 1977, Tannen 1994a), interactional patterns in terms of both who participates in family-related social talk at work and in what ways.

Kendall (1999, 2006) conducted a case study in which one woman tape-recorded herself at home and at work over the course of a week. She found that the women and men with whom this woman spoke during this period all talked about family but tended to do so differently. The female employees whose discourse about family she captured tended to strengthen their association with their family-related position (usually mother) by talking about topics that pertained to themselves as individuals. In Kendall's terms, they engaged in *individualized* talk about family. To do so, the women often voiced themselves as parents using "constructed dialogue" (Tannen 2007[1989]). In contrast, the male employee whose discourse Kendall considers in detail tended to engage in *generalized* talk about family, that is, to talk about family in more general terms, weakening the association between himself and his family role (father). For example, when the woman whose discourse Kendall focuses on tells her male coworker that her daughter frequently forgets to feed her pet guinea pig, the man replies not by offering similarly individualized information about his own family, but instead by generalizing the topic to "kids" by observing, "I think that's the way kids are, at that age." Thus Kendall's work demonstrates that not all family-related workplace discourse has the same implications for the construction of gender-related family identities and, in particular, for the types of identities interlocutors create in relation to traditional caregiving and breadwinning identities (see Kendall, this volume, for an in-depth discussion of these identities).

Building on and complementing Kendall's study as well as other work focusing on the discourse of working mothers and fathers, our analysis provides an in-depth look at one father's talk about family at work. We explore how Neil, the man whose discourse we examine, interactionally creates and draws upon his identity as a parent while at work and how being a parent "interpenetrates" (to borrow a term from Kendall) the sphere of his work. Our study draws on the theoretical and methodological framework of Goffman's (1974, 1981) notions of *alignment* and *footing* as well as Davies & Harré's (1999) related concept of *positioning*. These conceptual frameworks assume that interactants shift their alignments (or positions or stances) vis-à-vis one another from moment to moment and that such alignments are linguistically constructed.

Our analysis demonstrates that a father's identity as a parent becomes a resource for sociability with his coworkers in that he builds rapport with and provides support for colleagues who are also parents. We find as well that his parental responsibilities at times interfere with his work-related responsibilities but that he linguistically minimizes their perceived potential impact on his work performance. Finally, through talking about his family at work, he positions himself as a father, specifically as one-half of a parenting team, as well as a parenting expert. Our study also illustrates that, in drawing on his parental identity as a resource for talk, Neil speaks in ways linked with women as well as those linked with men.

Specifically, we show how this father, Neil, talks about his family in ways that highlight his position as a father, similar to how the women in Kendall's study talked in ways that highlighted their positions as mothers. However, whereas the women in Kendall's study used language to construct "primary caregiver" positions, Neil linguistically constructs his role in the family as one-half of (and sometimes the more competent half of) a parenting team. We also show that Neil frames talk about family in ways typically associated with men, for example, by creating interactional asymmetry by positioning himself as a judge (see Tannen 1990; Kendall 1999) and by talking about his family in generalized terms (Kendall 1999), in addition to using language in ways that are sex-class linked with women, such as participating in symmetrical rituals like mutual self-disclosure (see Tannen 1990) and talking about family in highly personal terms (Tannen 1994a; Kendall 1999, 2006). In this way, we capture how one man's talk about family at work relates to gender-related patterns of talk and explore how one father who assumes significant childrearing responsibilities at home talks about his parenting at work. We show how this talk creates connections between Neil and his coworkers, between what is happening at work and at home, and between his identities as a worker and as a father.

In what follows, we first review prior research on workplace social talk, focusing in particular on research considering family talk at work and language and gender in the workplace. In the next section, we introduce Neil and his family and provide a brief sketch of the environment in which he works. In the main section of this chapter, we present excerpts of Neil's self-audiotaped discourse in order to understand how his family talk interpenetrates the sphere of his work; how his identity as a father serves as a conversational resource; and how he discursively manages the interference it constitutes. The linguistic strategies by which he accomplishes these interactive goals include narrative, constructed dialogue, pronoun use, the giving and gathering of details, and parallelism. We conclude by discussing how our findings provide insight into what it means to be a working father and how this compares and contrasts to prior work focusing on working mothers.

Theoretical Background: Social Talk, Gender,
and Alignments at Work

When individuals talk, at work and elsewhere, they constantly negotiate what Goffman (1981) calls *footings* or *alignments* or what Davies & Harré (1999) call *positionings*. According to Goffman, *footing* is "the alignment we take up to ourselves and the others present as expressed in the way we manage the production or reception of an utterance" (128). *Positioning,* as defined by Davies & Harré, refers to "the discursive process whereby people are located in conversations as observably and subjectively coherent participants in jointly produced story lines" (37), where "story lines" are roughly comparable to Goffman's notion of "frames"—that is, culturally recognizable networks of actions, assumptions, or relationships. The notions of footing, alignment, and positioning can all be conceived as ways that interlocutors negotiate relationships vis-à-vis one another moment-by-moment in talk, and how individuals construct identities in all types of interactions, including workplace interaction. Among the ways that footings and alignments are negotiated in a workplace context are the participation in and exchange of talk on social topics–discourse generally characterized as "small talk."

Holmes (2003), in the context of a study examining the discourse of workers with intellectual disabilities, observes that the most fundamental function of workplace small talk is to construct, maintain, and reinforce positive social relationships or solidarity between coworkers—in other words, to "do collegiality." Holmes (2000) emphasizes that small talk is also a resource for "doing power"—for instance, Holmes, Stubbe & Vine (1999) illustrate how senior participants generally "manage" office small talk. In addition, small talk marks interactional boundaries and is used to fill "gaps" between planned work-related activities with "valuable, relationship-maintaining social interaction" (Holmes 2000:48).

Tannen (1994a), in a study of women and men talking at work, demonstrates that during the workday in offices, talk shifts continually between work and social topics. Social talk, which can include conversation about a speaker's personal life, banter about politics, and discussion about topics as diverse as clothes, haircuts, public figures, and sports, "establishes the friendly working environment that is the necessary backdrop to getting work done" (64). In other words, it serves as "the grease that keeps the gears running in an office" (65), keeping the lines of communication open and creating a comfortable working environment. Coupland (2003) similarly argues that sociality should not be marginalized as a "small" concern but should be treated as a necessary element of institutional success at any level. As a result of the large role played by small talk at work, as these and other researchers have observed, social talk is so necessary that those unable to effectively participate due to intellectual disabilities (Holmes 2003), or to the gender-related nature of conversations (Tannen 1994a), may have difficulty navigating the workplace—and getting their work done.

Kirby (2000) examines the negotiation of work-family boundaries as well as conflicts that surround talk about family at work based on self-reports from employees and their supervisors in an organizational branch of the U.S. government. Supervisors in her study reported that social talk about family was an important element in getting to know the employees but also noted that a coworker's personality and the relationship between coworkers influenced whether or not one initiated social talk about family. Kirby found, moreover, that workers were more likely to talk about family with coworkers who faced similar life issues and with coworkers who were considered friends. Kirby's self-report data, then, support the observational studies cited that find social talk about family to be a means of creating solidarity and negotiating working relationships on the job.

Tannen (1994a) identifies gender differences in family-related talk at work. Based on observation as well as audiotapes of workplace interaction, Tannen found that the women in her study tended to discuss their personal lives or events in the lives of people who were close to them while the men more often favored topics such as sports and politics. In addition, Tannen found that gender patterns she identified in her earlier work on conversational discourse (Tannen 1990) are borne out in the context of the workplace: women often frame their topics through symmetrical rituals such as mutual self-disclosure, whereas men often frame their topics through oppositional rituals such as teasing or good-natured argument. This suggests that even when men and women talk about the same general topic in the same general context (e.g., talking about family in the workplace), they often do so differently.

In a study presenting close analysis of two instances of small talk at work, Tannen (1999) compares the ways women and men use small talk to create solidarity while reinforcing status hierarchies. In the conversation among women, a mail clerk is complimented on her clothes by three women who range in rank from manager to temporary worker. At the same time that the complimenting ritual is a kind of "rapport talk," it reinforces hierarchy insofar as it is initiated by the highest-ranking woman, is reinforced by the two lower-ranking office workers, and positions the mail clerk as the object of inspection. The small-talk conversation between two men that Tannen examines also negotiates solidarity and hierarchy, but by very different conversational means. It begins when a subordinate offers a ritual complaint about his computer to his superior, who responds with a literal offer to fix it and a humorous self-presentation as an expert, "Mr. Computer." The resulting tension is mediated by a second stage in which the superior shares details of a stomach ailment in which he positions himself as a man who needs no help, even when sick, especially not from a woman. Thus solidarity was created among the women by a complimenting ritual that reinforced hierarchy off the record. Between the men the initial complaining ritual was reframed as a literal offer of help that placed on the record and then exaggerated (in Goffman's term, "guyed") the status hierarchy that distinguished the men, followed by another complaining ritual in which solidarity was established between the men in opposition to hypothetical women who make illness worse by trying to help.

In perhaps the most comprehensive study of one working mother's language use, Kendall (1999) explores how a management-level woman,

Elaine, linguistically creates positions through the language she uses at work and at home. Kendall examines how Elaine and her coworkers engage in or avoid engaging in social talk about their families at work. In response to earlier studies which found that women's identities as mothers have gender-related social and professional implications, Kendall finds that though Elaine mentions family to almost everyone in her division, she does so in different ways. For example, in a conversation with her (female) boss, Elaine only mentions family incidentally. In conversations with people in her division who have children at home, family surfaces as a ratified primary topic of talk. Yet even in these conversations, talk about family does not play out the same way. Specifically, talk about family seems to be related to the interlocutors' genders.

Kendall finds that when Elaine speaks with lower ranking female colleagues, they both speak about their families in *individualized* ways from the position of mothers, creating rapport by exchanging matching stories. For example, when Elaine's coworker Rebecca describes some problems she had with her son at a baseball game she attended with both her children, Elaine responds by relating a description of her daughter's behavior at a Cincinnati Reds baseball game. In addition to describing matching events, both women use constructed dialogue to animate themselves in the mother role, further bringing it into focus. However, when Elaine initiates similar conversations with a male colleague, Richard, he responds asymmetrically: he positions himself as judge of her actions as a parent and talks about his own family only in *generalized* terms. For instance, when Elaine describes how she encourages her daughter to do chores, Richard responds by evaluating her parenting: "Well, that's good. You're doing the right things." When Elaine explains that her daughter wants a dog, Richard replies that "Every kid does," rather than talking about his own children. Kendall suggests that through these strategies Richard avoids framing his statements as his own personal experience and, in so doing, creates an identity asymmetrical to Elaine's: whereas her talk foregrounds her identity as a mother, his talk backgrounds his identity as a father. Another way of understanding this conversational move is that his personal experience as a parent becomes a resource for reinforcing hierarchy rather than establishing solidarity.

In sum, Goffman's notions of footing and Davies & Harré's concept of positioning provide a theoretical and methodological framework for exploring workplace interaction, including gendered patterns in social talk. The studies cited are just a few that identify linguistic strategies that work toward creating alignments and (gendered) identities. They also demonstrate that alignments are collaboratively constructed moment by moment in interaction.

A Father at Work and at Home

The discourse analyzed in this chapter was gathered as part of the larger study that provides data for the collective chapters in this book. We analyze the discourse of one working father, Neil. Neil and his wife Clara both work full-time, and both play major roles in caring for their son Jason. (They are also the same age: 43.) Each carried a digital audiotape recorder over the course of one week, taping throughout the day. Neil is a vice president of finance administration for a non-profit organization, while Clara is a high-ranking employee (equivalent to vice president) in a government agency. Jason is 4 years 10 months old. He attends "junior kindergarten" and is involved in many after-school activities that require a parent to drive him from place to place. During the taping period, Jason was sick, adding further complexity to the logistics of work and family. Neil stayed home with Jason on Wednesday, while Clara stayed home with him on Friday. (On Thursday he went to school.) Thus Neil recorded four days of workplace interaction. The research team member who accompanied Neil to work after taping was completed, Philip LeVine, noted that Neil's office is relaxed, friendly, and characterized by casual dress. Neil has family photos in his office, and he talks about his family a great deal while at work. The family sphere interpenetrates his work sphere, and it serves as a resource for sociability as well as for supporting coworkers. Talk about family also allows Neil to present himself as a father and as a member of a parenting team.

A Father's Talk about Family at Work

Parenting as a Resource for Sociability

Like Elaine, the woman in Kendall's study, Neil draws on his identity as a parent as a resource for being sociable and creating solidarity with coworkers. In this section, we demonstrate that talk about family at work becomes a resource by which Neil constructs alignments with his coworkers that reinforce solidarity with them and also create his identity as a father. Neil engages in conversation about family as part of ritual "troubles talk" (Jefferson 1988) with another coworker who is also a parent, but he also spontaneously brings up the topic of his parenting when coworkers inquire about his project-related audiotaping. Other coworkers also use Neil's family as a resource for engaging in small talk with Neil.

In our first set of examples, Neil talks with his coworker Marianne, a married mother of two, and aligns himself with her by positioning himself as a fellow parent. Though Neil is higher-ranking (by one level) than Marianne, the two create solidarity in this interaction by telling matching parenting stories about dealing with sick children. This is a particularly interesting interaction in that it shows a man and a woman engaging in "troubles talk," a ritual exchange of matching problems for the purpose of building solidarity that has previously been observed to be more common among women than among men (e.g., Tannen 1990). The conversation takes place on Monday, the first day of taping. Neil and Marianne have been talking about a meeting when Neil inquires about Marianne's children. Note that it is Neil who brings up the topic of family, and the topic of Marianne's family in particular. He does so in a way that makes clear he knows about the health problems Marianne's children have been experiencing, so his question takes the form of an expression of concern about a known condition. (Neil's son Jason has not yet become sick.) As the conversation unfolds, and Marianne continues to talk about her children's struggles with health problems, Neil responds with backchannels that assess her talk as serious and express empathy with and admiration for her handling of the challenges she faces as a parent. (We present the conversation as divided into five excerpts, each of which followed the preceding one in context; therefore they are identified by letters designating them as subdivisions of excerpt 1.)

(1a) →   Neil: How are the kids by the way,
      →   are they [better.]
           Marianne: [Better.]
                      They're actually /??/
           Neil: That's good,
                 [that's good.]
           Marianne: [/But/] Sammy now has a . piece of equipment /????/
           Neil: Really?
                 For the asthma?

By asking, *are they better* Neil frames his inquiry as a specific follow-up to an assumed prior conversation in which he was informed that Marianne's children were sick. This invites Marianne to talk about her family in individualized terms (which she does throughout the conversation). It also indexes the prior conversation and thus Neil and Marianne's ongoing relationship. Furthermore, when Marianne refers to a *piece of equipment* Neil's response makes clear that he is familiar with her son Sammy's health condition (*For the asthma?*). Neil's query is a demonstration of solidarity insofar as it places on record not only his concern for Marianne's personal life but also that he shares background knowledge about it. In other words, he assumes the footing of a friend who is both interested in and familiar with his colleague's home situation.

As the conversation continues, Marianne provides more details about her children's health problems, and Neil continues to align himself not only as an interested and informed friend but also as a compassionate person by expressing sympathy and asking questions. Other coworkers join the conversation, and they also create supportive alignments with Marianne.

(1b)   Marianne: Yeah asthma,
              he's got asthma bad that's why he's [got this] nebulizer →
→   Neil: [Oh gosh.]
       Marianne: that you know,
              kinda blows smoke in his face and →
              <*laughing*> for ten- ten minutes ev- three times a day →
              you gotta chase him around!>
→   Neil: <*groans*>
       Woman: <*sarcastically*> That's gotta be easy.>
→   Neil: Oh man.
              ((*short pause*))
→   <*whispering*> Gosh!>
       Marianne: The pink eye's gone.
              The bronchitis is gone.
→   Neil: Jee::z.
       Man: Two outta [three,]
       Neil: [That's—]
       Man: not bad /??/
→   Neil: <*sighs*>
       Woman: I don't know how you do it Marianne.

Neil provides supportive backchannels that express empathy for Marianne (he groans and sighs and says, *Oh man, Gosh,* and *Jeez*). This type of supportive backchannelling has been shown by Pritchard (1993) and others to build rapport during troubles talk, by supporting the speaker and his or her turn at talk (see also Gordon, this volume). In producing these backchannel signals Neil aligns with Marianne through responding to her storytelling, though in this segment he does not talk about his own family experiences. (Note that the two other coworkers present likewise supportively align with Marianne without sharing any personal information of their own.)

As the conversation continues, Neil further aligns with Marianne by positioning himself as a father who has experienced challenges similar to those Marianne has just described. Specifically, he individualizes the talk by explaining how he and Clara deal with the difficult task of giving Jason medication when he is sick.

(1c) →	Neil:	Well I remember—
	Marianne:	I joke I'm not a- I'm not a- a mother,
		I'm a pharmacist.
		[*<laughs>*]
	Woman:	[*<laughs>*]
	Man:	[*<laughs>*]
→	Neil:	[*<laughs>*]
→		Well the- they kid- the medicines they make for kids →
→		just taste so bad,
→		I remember . we used to mix Jason's like,
→		if he had um you know uh some sort of infection,
→		we put the Amoxicillin in with like →
→		the sweetest juice drink we could find,
→		and hope [that he] would drink it,
	Man:	[*<chuckles>*]
→	Neil:	'cause you couldn't give it to him.

Marianne's response to Neil's query about her children's health has evolved into a catalogue of childhood illnesses (asthma, pink eye, bronchitis). She sums up this segment of discourse with a humorous remark exaggerating the many medications she administers (*I'm not a- a mother, I'm a pharmacist*). Neil builds on this humor by addressing the issue of medicines for children. First he makes a general statement (*the medicines they make for kids just taste so bad*), but then he quickly personalizes the discussion by describing how he and Clara try to improve the taste of medicine they give Jason. Thus he ratifies and builds on Marianne's discourse but also matches troubles as a means of building rapport. It is interesting to note that Clara is not mentioned directly in Neil's comment, but she is invoked by his use of the plural pronoun "we," by which he also positions himself as a member of a parenting team. This contrasts with Marianne's use, here and in other excerpts, of the singular first person pronoun, even though she is married.

The next excerpt, continuous with 1c, shows that Marianne and Neil have had different experiences with giving their children medication. Despite this difference, however, they use this topic of talk as an occasion to display similarity and thus reinforce solidarity. Although Marianne cannot claim that her children also dislike Amoxicillin (her children like it), she expresses similarity rather than difference by offering an account of one of her children disliking other medicines.

(1d)	Marianne:	Oh really?
	Neil:	[Uh h—]
	Marianne:	[My] kids love that stuff!
	Neil:	Really?
	Marianne:	Oh yeah.
→	Neil:	Oh gosh,
→		he would NOT- not drink that,
→		so we- we'd mix it in with like . y'know cherry soda →
→		and we'd add like a spoonful of sugar into that,
→		/to/ stir it up,
→		I mean,
	Marianne:	Yeah,
→	Neil:	['cause he could taste it.]
	Marianne:	[/? ? ? ? ?/]
		Sometimes Dee had to take the steroids that →
		/they'd have her/ take,
		they were the worst tasting things,
		and I tried EVerything,

By mentioning that her daughter Dee dislikes the taste of steroids, Marianne's contribution to the conversation continues the tapestry that she and Neil are jointly weaving. She is, for one thing, continuing the matching troubles talk. She also builds on and ratifies Neil's topic of bad-tasting medicine, which was in itself a ratification and building-on of her topic of mother as pharmacist. The structure of the talk reinforces the creation of solidarity as well, as her talk overlaps Neil's in what Tannen (1994b) would characterize as a "cooperative overlap."

The final lines from this interchange that we examine are shown in excerpt 1e. Here Neil ratifies Marianne's comment (*Oh yeah*) then continues recounting his experiences with Jason. This time he talks about wasting medication, and again, Marianne responds by matching and then building on Neil's account.

```
(1e)          Neil: Oh yeah.
                    Yeah he would taste it in his juice and he would like- →
                    he wouldn't drink it,
                    he'd spit it out,
                    he'd run over to the- get a trash →
       →            <laughing> [can and spit it out.>]
       → Marianne:            [And then of course] →
       →            you'd run out,
       →            and then you've gotta go back →
       →            and get another prescription →
       →            because you've run out [prematurely,]
             Neil:                          [Yeah.]
         Marianne: and then they wonder why you- you know →
                    "Are you double dosing?"
                    "No!
       →            [My daughter spilled it all over the floor!"]
             Neil: [<laughs>]
         Marianne: <laughs>
             Neil: Yeah th- [those pink stains don't come out of the- →]
         Marianne:          [/? ? ? ?/]
             Neil: They don't come out of the sheets →
       →            or whatever [he- he] spills it on.
         Marianne:             [<laughs>]
             Neil: Oh gosh.
          ((a coworker walks by and reminds them of an upcoming meeting))
```

Throughout excerpt 1e, Neil and Marianne mutually create an alignment of solidarity with one another by evaluating, ratifying, and building on the other's talk. Thus Neil laughs and says *Oh yeah* to acknowledge Marianne's comment on her daughter's dislike of the taste of steroids before continuing with his account of getting Jason to take bad-tasting medicine. Note too the use of repetition: Marianne uses the word "spilled" (*My daughter spilled it all over the floor*) and Neil incorporates the same word when he adds a comment about the problem of medicine staining sheets (*They don't come out of the sheets or whatever he spills it on*). Laughter, repetition, and overlapping talk—all of which characterize this interchange—are conversational strategies that have been shown to create solidarity and what Tannen (2007[1989]) calls *conversational involvement*. Throughout this conversation with Marianne, Neil draws on his father identity—largely indistinguishable, in this discourse, from a mother identity—and uses it as a resource for building solidarity at work by comparing notes with another working parent. (Reciprocally, Marianne does the same.) Note, however, that although Marianne presents herself as the primary caregiver in her family, or the person ultimately responsible for managing childcare, by using the first person singular pronoun "I" (even though she is married), Neil constructs his family role as part of a parenting team by using the plural pronoun "we." We will return to this later in this section.

The way this excerpt closes is another type of evidence of the interpenetration of work and family spheres. As Marianne and Neil engage in this exchange of details about their children's health, another coworker calls their attention to an upcoming meeting. This is external evidence of what readers may have been thinking while reading our analysis thus far: haven't these employees got work to do? As the research cited earlier confirms, small talk like this plays a big role in greasing the wheels of communication, wheels whose smooth turning facilitates getting work done in an efficient manner. But the fact that another worker interrupts the exchange to remind the participants of the meeting also indicates that the business of the business is perceived to take priority over social talk.

Excerpts 1a–e, then, which took place on Monday, Neil's first day of taping at work, show Neil drawing on his parental identity in engaging in small talk focused on Marianne's experiences as a mother of sick children. In the following excerpts, 2a–c, we again see Neil spontaneously bringing up the topic of his family and his parenting to socialize with coworkers. These excerpts come from a conversation that took place on Thursday. The previous day, Wednesday, Neil stayed home from work because his son Jason was sick. (This in itself is evidence of the egalitarian coparenting that Neil and Clara espouse and enact. A common complaint of mothers—and one we observed in the discourse of the mother in another family [see Kendall, this volume]—is that when a child is sick, it is always the mother rather than the father who has to miss work to stay home with the child.)

Excerpt 2a is an exchange that takes place after Neil and a female coworker have been talking about a work-related task. The coworker switches into a small-talk frame by asking Neil about the tape recording he is doing for this study. In his reply, Neil introduces the topic of family, reframing the topic as parenting rather than taping. He talks about his personal experiences with his own family in particular:

(2a)   Woman: How's it going,
                      being wired.
           Neil: Okay.
                      You know I actually [have to check—]
    Woman: [Are you used to-] totally →
                      used to it now?
           Neil: Uh,
                      pretty much.
    Woman: Yeah I'm sure.
           Neil: Yeah.
                      It was weird . yesterday,
                      because um .
    Woman: It's a pretty fancy little . ((re: the digital tape recorder))
           Neil: Yeah it's really,
                      it's actually,
                      it's really neat.
                      Um,
                      it was kinda weird yesterday,
→   I had it off a lot yesterday →
→   'cause I was HOME with Jason,
→   and he was sleepin' a lot,
→   or just sittin' there kinda vegged out,
→   cause he's . just had a real high- →
                      y'know high temperature,
→   so.
    Woman: O:h.

The coworker's backchannel response, a drawn-out "Oh," is a display of sympathy and solidarity similar to Neil's use of backchannels to show sympathy and understanding in his conversation with Marianne, although the sympathy seems directed at Jason's experience of having a high temperature rather than at Neil's experience as the parent of a sick child. Nonetheless, her backchannel is evidence that Neil's reframing of the conversation from the topic of taping to that of fathering a sick child is cooperatively taken up.

Neil continues by tying his talk about his sick son to the query about taping for the project:

(2b)   Neil: Um,
                 <laughing> it wasn't a whole lot of interaction going on.>
         Woman: Oh great!
         Neil: They heard y'know probably, ((they = researchers))
                 a couple episodes of Scooby Doo,
                 and [things like that /were ??/]
         Woman: [Great. And how I pity] the poor graduate student,
                 who is gonna sit and listen to these HOURS.

After a brief discussion about the study and about Deborah Tannen, whom Neil identifies as associated with the study, Neil again shifts the conversation to the day he spent at home with his sick son. He positions himself not as a father who is inconvenienced by having to spend a day at home with a sick child but rather as one who takes advantage of the day at home to read a book.

(2c)   ((several minutes of discussion about the project precedes))
         Neil: I spent like most of my day reading that,
                 so I got through like about a third of the book yesterday,
                 just sittin' around the house.
                 So.
    →   That's the one good thing →
    →   about having a kid who's home sick,
    →   you know.
    →   THEY're not doin' anything,
    →   so you're just kinda sittin' there like,
                 "Okay,
                 well I'll catch up on my <laughing> reading,"
                 [or somethin' like that.>]
         Woman: [Yeah that's true,]

it's kinda like a quiet day you didn't count on.

Neil: Yeah.

Neil's description of his day at home becomes the basis for conversational solidarity: his coworker indicates that she understands his point by overlapping his discourse with *Yeah that's true* and paraphrasing his point (*it's kinda like a quiet day you didn't count on*). The repetition leads to a conversational coda as Neil ratifies her contribution by repeating the word "Yeah."

Thus in excerpts 2a–c, we see that Neil talks about his son spontaneously, positioning himself as a parent and engaging his coworker in social talk where they can display shared understanding. It is worth noting that Neil's talk about his family is personalized and individualized: he reframes a query about taping to address his experience as a father. He does not, however, turn the talk into a troubles talk ritual but rather emphasizes the positive aspect of having had to stay home with Jason: the opportunity to catch up on reading. (He was reading the book *Bobos in Paradise.*) Interestingly, Neil does not depict himself as a parent needing to attend to other aspects of caring for a child and family, for example, doing laundry or other household chores. Thus Neil positions himself as a caregiver, but the caregiving role he takes up differs from the traditional, female caregiving role.[2]

About 30 minutes after excerpts 2a–c, Neil again receives a casual query from a coworker about taping that occasions social talk about family. Excerpts 3a–b occur in the moments before a staff meeting. Here too, Neil responds to a question about taping by talking about his day at home with Jason. When the coworker inquires about Jason's health, Neil elaborates, animating his account of his interaction with Jason with constructed dialogue, thus creating a vivid father-son scene and focusing attention on his identity as a father. (At least one other female coworker is present for this conversation, though her only contribution to this portion is laughter.)

(3a)   Woman: How's the taping going.

           Neil: Okay.

                 I didn't tape a lot yesterday →

   →   'cause I was home with Jason so,

   →   y'know two guys sittin' there →

   →   watchin' Scooby Doo cartoons all day,

2. The authors thank Shari Kendall for this observation.

→   it just <*chuckles*>
→ Woman: Is he sick?
    Neil: Yeah.
       He had a real- he had a—.
       I guess it was Tuesday . night,
       he was just really hot,
       /and/ his face was all red,
       he was just kinda sittin' there like this you know s- and so,
       he actuall—
→   I said, "Jason you wanna go to bed?"
→   And he's like, "No:."
       And this was about seven thirty →
       and about ten minutes later →
       I turned around again and he was out of it.
       [<*laughs*>]
   Woman: [<*laughs*>]
  Woman2: [<*laughs*>]
    Neil: U:m he stayed home yesterday,
       but he went to school today.
       He was a lot better so.
       ((*talk turns to a coworker who is sick*))

The scene Neil constructs is a poignant one that emphasizes his position not only as a parent but as a father of a son. He describes himself and Jason as *two guys sittin' there watchin' Scooby Doo cartoons all day.* The phrase "two guys" foregrounds his and Jason's shared gender and backgrounds the difference in their ages and relative status in the family. The shared male context is also indirectly signaled by Neil's dropping the final "g" in "sittin'" and "watchin'"—a linguistic form well documented to be more common in the speech of boys and men than of girls and women (e.g., Lakoff 1975; Wardhaugh 2002). It is significant in this interchange, as in the previous one, that Neil's introducing the topic of parenting, and personalizing it, is entirely self-selected; he could easily have responded to the queries about his taping without such reference. The solidarity-building effect of this story is manifested by shared laughter.

  Whereas the previous examples show Neil reframing queries about taping to talk about family, there are other instances in which a coworker introduces the topic of family by inquiring into Jason's health. In asking specifically about Jason, Neil's coworkers show that they know details—

not only his name but also the fact that he was ill—as Neil did in the interaction with Marianne discussed earlier. Neil is about to leave the office Thursday evening when the following conversation occurs:

(4)　　　Man: You off /???/
　　　　　Neil: Yep.
　→　　　Man: So how is Jason,
　→　　　　　　I was thinking about him.
　　　　　Neil: He went to school today so.
　　　　　Man: Oh he did?
　　　　　Neil: Yeah.
　→　　　　　　Clara took him to school so.
　　　　　Man: /? ?/ ((*Neil is shuffling papers, hard to hear*))
　　　　　Neil: Uh nope.
　　　　　　　　She said he was fine.
　　　　　Man: /Nice./
　　　　　　　　((*short pause*))
　　　　　　　　Amazing how . quickly kids get over stuff.
　　　　　　　　((*short pause*))
　　　　　Neil: Oh I know.
　　　　　　　　[He-]
　　　　　Man: [/?/] just gets up and ? ?/ the next day they're fine.
　　　　　Neil: Yeah we're layin' around dead,
　　　　　　　　moaning, [crying.]
　　　　　Man:　　　　[/?/]
　　　　　　　　((*short pause*))
　　　　　Neil: U:m.
　　　　　　　　((*short pause, shuffling through papers*))
　　　　　　　　But he's doing okay,
　→　　　　　　so I'm going to get him at school.
　　　　　　　　((*talk turns briefly to a work-related topic, then Neil leaves*))

This conversation is interesting in that it shows a male coworker inquiring about Neil's family in a very specific way, which invites Neil to talk about his family from an individualized perspective (which he does). The coworker's comment, *I was thinking about him*, not only draws on shared knowledge about Jason's health but puts on record an expression of concern. In response to Neil's reply that Jason recovered from his illness and went to school that day, the coworker makes a general observation about how quickly children recover from illness, and Neil responds with a matching evaluation. This interchange provides a nice comparison to the personalized talk about family that Kendall found among women in her study in that Neil, a man, is talking about his family with a male coworker in an individualized way. This exchange also shows two men collaboratively interweaving individualized and generalized stretches of social talk about family; however, although Neil talks about family from both individualized and generalized perspectives, his coworker speaks only from a generalized perspective. Neil returns the conversation to the personal when he explains that he will pick Jason up from school. He also positions himself as a member of a parenting team by referring to Clara (*she said he was fine*). He constructs parallelism between Clara and himself by noting that Clara dropped Jason off at school and he (Neil) will pick him up. Most importantly, this excerpt shows that others in the office enable and encourage Neil to draw on his identity as a father as a resource for social talk.

In summary, excerpts 1–4 have shown Neil using his identity as a parent and his parenting experiences as resources for social talk at work by contributing to matching troubles talk with Marianne, by spontaneously reframing queries about his tape recording for our project to replies about parenting, and by responding to a coworker's specific inquiries about his son's health. We have seen in this section that Neil talks to both male and female coworkers about his family, and he does so through engaging in troubles talk and talking about family in personalized as well as generalized terms. We have also seen that Neil positions himself as a primary caregiver (though not necessarily as someone who has responsibility for maintaining a household), as well as a member of a parenting team. An interesting aspect of these examples is the cumulative impression made by the range of specific inquiries into coworkers' children's health addressed to each other by so many different employees. Although we cannot prove but can only speculate, we surmise from the accumulated examples that asking coworkers about their children's health problems is an office-wide conversational ritual, a practice that has become part of the organization's "companylect" (to coin a term). The fact that the organization is a non-profit could also be a factor in the prevalence of this type of talk. As Holmes (2000:38) points out, the extent to which social talk is "tolerated, encouraged or obligatory is one distinguishing feature of different organisational cultures"—talk about children's health could be a further distinguishing ritual of the social talk of Neil's workplace.

The Interpenetration of Parenting and Work Spheres

In the previous section, we saw the topics of family and of parenting as resources for social talk at work. A pattern we observed in the discourse of all the families who participated in the study is the inseparability of the home and work spheres, the constant interpenetration of each of these spheres within the other. As part of this pattern, Neil and Clara communicate with each other about Jason throughout the day; telephone calls between them, in which Neil seems to be keeping track of the home sphere, as well as references to those phone calls, occur repeatedly while Neil is at work. By talking about these calls, Neil positions himself not only as a parent but as a member of a parenting team.

This pattern is seen in the following social-talk interaction with Sally, a young (mid-twenties) employee who is not married and has no children. Prior to the exchange, both Neil and Sally have said that they are not as committed to exercising at the gym as they should be. This shared sentiment, an admission of fault you might say, creates a symmetrical alignment, particularly significant in that Sally ranks lower than Neil. At the beginning of the following excerpt, Neil says he might be able to go to the gym that day, but whether or not he can depends on his parental responsibilities, notification of which will come in the form of a telephone call from Clara.

(5) → Neil: I still might go today if I don't have to →
    →   pick my kid up from s- from school I might go today,
    →   'cause I know I won't be able to go tomorrow,
    →   and um <*smacks lips*> I'll know →
    →   if Clara calls me within the hour,
    →   I'll know whether I have to <*chuckling*> go or not,>
    →   to pick him up,
    →   but I thought, "Well I ran Saturday and Sunday,"
    →   so I don't think I'll run but I wanna lift weights,
    →   and it's like, "Oh gosh,
    →   I don't wanna go over there at six o'CLOCK →
    →   and lift weights y'know and get home late,"
    →   so,
         Sally: Mhm.
         Neil: it is tougher but,
             ((*talks about a former roommate who exercised regularly*))

Several aspects of this small-talk example illustrate interesting ways that Neil draws on his parental identity. Whereas their shared interest, and negligence, in going to the gym provides a resource for rapport between Neil and Sally, he alone is limited by family obligations. Referring to Jason as "my kid" contrasts with the level of rapport that was evident in conversations with coworkers who spontaneously referred to Neil's child by name. Most significantly for our purposes in this section, this example illustrates the complexity of everyday work/family/personal activity logistics: throughout the day, Neil expects to field calls from Clara pertaining to the home sphere, and these calls influence how his day unfolds. These calls, and the integration of the information they convey into his activities, provide a resource for Neil to position himself as a parent and as a coparent. We will see, however, that he also distinguishes himself from Clara in regard to his parenting style.

The following example shows an interchange with a male coworker in which Neil refers to differences between his and Clara's parenting approaches. The interaction takes place on Friday; it follows a phone call between Clara and Neil. Clara had the day off work, and she kept Jason home from school that day, as Neil had done on Wednesday. In the phone call Clara complained that Jason was not behaving well. This provides Neil the occasion to relate a humorous remark he made to Clara. The coworker walked into Neil's office shortly after the telephone call ended; Neil was eating lunch in his office:

(6a) → Man: How's Jason feeling.
       Neil: Oh he's a lot better.
       Man: Oh good.
           [/??/]
       Neil: [In fact, Clara-] Clara kept him home today because,
           he went to school yesterday →
           but she kept him home today 'cause she's off work,
       Man: Oh /good./
       Neil: and she just told me he just threw a temper tantrum.
   →   I was like,
   →   "Well you should have taken him →
   →   to <chuckling> school.">
       Man: Yeah.
           "Take him now."
           <laughs>

Neil: Really.

Mm.

He won't go now.

As we have seen in previous examples, the coworker knows that Neil's son has been sick (probably because of Neil's absence from work on Wednesday), and he knows Jason's name. In his reply, Neil draws on his just-completed phone call as a resource. It is interesting that in his account of his response to Clara's complaint that Jason threw a tantrum, Neil portrays himself much as Kendall observed a male coworker responding to Elaine's complaint about her child: rather than expressing sympathy or understanding for Clara's experience, he positions himself as a judge of her parenting ("*Well you should have taken him to school*"). There is no reason to believe Neil is seriously critiquing Clara's parenting, however. It seems likely that he provides this judgment as a humorous rather than serious response to Clara, and he repeats his joke as a way to involve his coworker in the humor. Still, it contrasts with other conversations where Neil evidences conversational patterns that are sex-class linked with women, such as where he exchanges matching stories with Marianne.

As this excerpt proceeds, Neil's humorous account of his conversation with Clara does provide a resource for him to position himself as a parenting expert and to characterize Clara as an overindulgent parent:

(6b)   Man: Oh.

Poor little guy.

Maybe he just doesn't feel that well and—

→ Neil: Oh he knows he doesn't have to nap →

→   when he's home with his mother.

Man: Oh okay.

Neil: She's trying to make him nap.

Man: It's a political issue.

Neil: Yes,

very much so.

((*short pause*))

Man: I guess everything /is/.

((*short pause, coworker leaves, Neil eats his lunch*))

It is clear that this conversation is successful in its primary purpose, to establish sociable talk and hence rapport between the interlocutors. Neil's coworker's expression of sympathy for Jason (the *poor little guy* may be throwing a tantrum because he doesn't feel well) is reframed by Neil as evidence of Jason's manipulating Clara (*She's trying to make him nap* but *he knows he doesn't have to nap when he's home with his mother*). This brief exchange becomes a resource for on-the-spot humor as the coworker quips, *It's a political issue*, Neil agrees (*Very much so*), and the coworker constructs a coda to the interchange (*I guess everything is*).

Although these examples and other types of evidence attest to the interpenetration of work and home spheres, they do not indicate that this interpenetration is troublesome. In other examples, in contrast, Neil directly discusses potential or real conflicts between the demands of these two spheres. He does so in a way, however, that makes clear that Clara too faces these demands, thus indicating that he is a co-caregiver, not a primary caregiver in the traditional sense.[3] In the following example, Neil groups himself and Marianne, the mother we saw in excerpt 1, into the category of "working parent." He does this by commenting to another coworker that both he and Marianne are responsible for picking up their children after school and thus may be unable to attend a work event, a going-away party for a coworker who is leaving the organization. This conversation, like the one above, occurred on Friday. The coworker Neil is talking to, Diane, is not married and has no children. They have been discussing the option of having the going-away party at Diane's house. Neil then explains that he may or may not be able to attend the party for family reasons, and he mentions an occasion where Clara had to leave work early to pick up Jason when Neil was attending another work-related social gathering (a going-away party for another employee, Jenny):

(7a)   Neil: <*sighs*>
                Well it- it <*sighs*>
                I think that's probably a good option,
                to . have it at your house, ((*"it"* = *going-away party*))
                y'know if people can go they can go,
                if they can't they can't,
                it's- it's tough—
                I like having 'em here,
    →   it was tough to be around . um the thing for Jenny,

3. We thank Shari Kendall for calling this to our attention.

→	because Clara was- had to work late that night,
→	she ended up having to leave to go pick up Jason,
→	and y'know that's MY situation →
→	of having to pick up the kids,
→	as is . y'know Marianne's in that situation too,
→	she's got two of 'em,
→	so .
Diane:	Well kids would be invited.

Diane's remark that *kids would be invited* shows that she misses Neil's point: it is having to pick Jason up at school that would make it "tough" for him to attend the party, not the problem of taking care of Jason once he's been picked up. Neil specifically includes Marianne as in the same "tough" situation of being responsible for picking up children and therefore potentially unable to attend the party. In mentioning Clara and a prior instance where Clara had to sacrifice work time to pick up Jason, Neil positions himself and Clara as individuals struggling together to balance the demands of work and family. This account, along with his inclusion of Marianne in his remarks, serves to create parallelism between the working mother and working father experience, but note too that he represents himself, but not Marianne, as sharing caregiving responsibility. A possible further layer of meaning may be related to relative rank. Diane is Neil's status equal; like Neil she is a vice president. Marianne's rank is lower. Thus Neil may be standing up for Marianne, explaining to Diane why she too may not be able to attend the work-related event.

The interaction continues as shown in excerpt 7b: Neil comments that Diane's solution of inviting children to the party does not solve his dilemma because of the distances between locations. He thus continues to highlight how parenting can interfere with work and again uses both himself and Marianne as examples, though again, Neil references his status as coparent by talking about Clara's role in Jason's care.

(7b)	Neil: Yeah.
	But . for ME,
	I wouldn't want to go all the way out to—
	I'd have to leave early to go all the way out to F County →
	to pick up Jason,
	and then try to drive through traffic back up →

to your place y'know,

it's- unless y'know- so if Clara couldn't pick him up, .

→   I would be stuck.

And like I said,

Marianne's got the two kids,

she's gotta pick up by a certain time,

um . so you just might have smaller attendance,

but if it's- y'know if you think for office morale it's- . →

it's good,

that's great.

((intervening talk about the party))

Neil: Okay,

I'll- I'm comfortable with y'know doing the party at your house,

I don't know if I'll be able to make it,

→   hopefully I will,

→   but if—

→   The twentieth,

→   I probably will,

→   Clara is out of town part of next week I think.

→   So she should be around on the twentieth.

She's all nervous,

y'know about this . whole election,

((talk continues about the U.S. presidential election, which took place during the week of taping))

These interchanges between Neil and Diane about planning a work-related party show that Neil's family responsibilities at times impinge on his work. They make things "tough" and can cause him to be "stuck," though this is often contingent on Clara's schedule (*so if Clara couldn't pick him up, . I would be stuck*). They also thus illustrate that Neil and Clara both have to make sacrifices at work to attend to their son's needs and that their ability to attend work events depends on coordination between their schedules. Overall, these excerpts show how work and family become intertwined during the workday as Neil deals with issues at home through phone calls and plans the logistics of his personal activities (going to the gym) as well as work-related ones (a going-away party). At the same time, these examples illustrate how Neil positions himself as a responsible parent and equal partner in a parenting team.

Sunderland (2000) observes that parenting books often present fathers as "bumbling assistants" or "baby entertainers." Kendall (1999, 2003) demonstrates that the father whose discourse she analyzed at home in her study operated during dinner within a single frame, "playmate," whereas the mother self-positioned as the primary caregiver, that is, the manager of caregiving with ultimate responsibility, by operating in numerous frames including Head Chef, Civilizer, Social Secretary, and so on. Johnston (this volume), examining the discourse of another family in our study, observes that despite the couple's very real sharing of childcare responsibilities, the mother frequently critiqued the father's parenting behavior, whereas the father never critiqued the mother's. With these and other studies as backdrop, we find it significant that Neil, in his talk about parenting at work, positions himself not only as a competent coparent but also as a parenting expert, equal to or even superior to Clara in this regard. This self-positioning is of particular interest because it provides a comparison to other studies looking at how fathers position themselves or are positioned by others in different contexts.

Excerpt 8 shows Neil presenting himself as a competent coparent in conversation with a female coworker, Brigit. Neil arrives in the office on Thursday (the fourth day of taping and the day after the one he spent at home caring for Jason) and asks Brigit how another coworker is feeling since she too was out the day before due to illness. After discussing the coworker's health, Brigit initiates troubles talk by saying that she and her husband Carl are also not feeling well. (Brigit does not have children.) Neil responds with matching troubles talk by saying that his son is also ill. In doing so he presents himself as a member of a parenting team:

(8)   Brigit: But u:h I don't know whatever she had,
                   I don't think I have the same- I don't feel well.
        Neil: Well I /didn't/ but I just think it /was/ →
              just because lack of sleep. [*<chuckles>*]
        Brigit: [Yeah.]
               Now Carl is gettin' something.
        Neil: Jason's sick.
              Well I don't know if he's home today.
              He- he was like—

Tuesday night,
→ I came home and Clara was like, "He's hot to the touch,"
→ and he was.
His face was really ho:t,
and . yesterday he was kind of like that,
and last night . he was doin' a little better but . still →
<*trailing off*> he- his fever was goin' up, so.>
Brigit: Oh wo:w.
So Clara is staying home /today/?
→ Neil: Well she- he wasn't up when I left,
→ she's gonna check him,
→ if he was really warm,
→ yeah she was gonna stay home.
→ Tomorrow she's off tomorrow,
→ it's a hol:iday for them,
((*short pause*))
Brigit: Yeah . . . I'm gonna try and make as much of this day →
as I can.
Neil: <*half-chuckling*>Me too.
Check my schedule first.>

In this exchange, Clara is identified as the parent who was at home first and therefore discovered that Jason was *hot to the touch*, but Neil indicates that he confirmed her opinion (*and he was*). Thus Neil has raised the topic of Jason's health in connection with the troubles-talk theme: a coworker is sick; Brigit and her husband are not feeling well; Neil himself isn't feeling well, but he attributes this not to illness but to *lack of sleep*; and Neil's son is ill—or might be, depending on how Clara finds him when he wakes up. Thus Neil's position as part of a parenting team provides a resource for sociable talk. In another conversation, however, Neil discusses the same event with another coworker and self-positions as the wiser parent.

The following interaction takes place between Neil and Liz, another vice president of the organization. This interaction also occurs Thursday and similarly serves to position Neil as a caregiver father. Note, furthermore, that Neil positions himself as a parenting expert and critiques Clara's parenting:

(9a)   Liz: Hi.
Neil: Good morning.
Liz: How's Jason.

Neil: <sighs>

I don't know he was still asleep →

<chuckling> when I left this morning,>

so Clara is staying home with him.

Least I think she is. <laughs>

She was gonna stay home with him if he was sick,

→   he was still kinda ho:t last night when we put him to bed,

→   his cheeks were y'know, <chuckling>all> re:d,

→   and →

Liz: Mhm.

→ Neil: um . Clara was reading to him and- →

and I was really exhausted,

→   and he's like, y'know, he's like, I hear him in bed,

→   <high pitched> "Daddy I'm still hot,">

→   so I go in there,

→   well she's got like →

→   <chuckling> these long . sleeved . pajamas> on him,

→   and long-sleeved pants,

→   I'm like, <inhales> "Clara,"

→   I said, "the other night he- I went in there →

→   to check on him →

→   and he had <chuckling> taken his shirt off> →

→   'cause he was so hot."

And um . so, he had a good night's sleep I think,

but she was gonna see if he was hot this morning →

she was gonna keep him home another day.

But he just has a bit of a fe:ver.

As before, we see that Neil positions himself as part of a parenting team, for example by saying "we" (i.e., Clara and Neil) put him to bed. Though it was Clara who reads to Jason before bedtime, Neil is the one Jason calls for when he is uncomfortable (*he's like, I hear him in bed, "Daddy I'm still hot."*). Neil then positions himself as the more competent parent, as he implies that the reason Jason was hot is that Clara put him to bed wearing too-warm pajamas (*these long-sleeved pajamas* and *long-sleeved [sic] pants*). He then uses constructed dialogue to animate his exasperated comments to Clara, further implying criticism of her choice of bedclothes for Jason (*"Clara," I said, "the other night I went in there to check on him and he had taken his shirt off 'cause he was so hot"*). This is similar to Neil's use of constructed dialogue in excerpt 6a, where he voices criticism (albeit humorously) of Clara for allowing Jason to stay home from school. Both of these instances of constructed dialogue show Neil taking an "expert" stance as he evaluates his wife's parenting.

As the conversation continues, Liz asks about a relatively new way of taking children's temperature (in the ear). She thus maintains social talk but shifts the talk to a more generalized topic. However, she soon adds a comment about her personal life by talking about putting drops in her dog Sneaker's ears.

(9b)   Liz: Don't they have . easy ways →
              of taking kids' temperature now,
              like don't you stick something in his ear or somethin'.
        Neil: Well yeah,
              but . he hated that when he was little.
              [I mean can you- y'know can you-] can you imagine like →
        Liz: [Oh, so, yeah.]
        Neil: with a one-and-a-half- or two-year-old trying to say →
              "Well, this won't hurt,"
              then <chuckling> sticking something in their ear.>
              'Cause you have to keep them still for like . five seconds →
              or so when they [do that.]
→   Liz: [(? ?)] do that with Sneaker →
→   'cause we have to put drops in his <laughing> ears.>
              [<laughs>] →
        Neil: [<chuckling> Oh God!>]
        Liz: <laughs>
        Neil: Yeah,
              so I don't know,
              I- I've gotta call her →
              and see if she stayed home or not with him,
→   my guess is she probably did because . sh- she's →
→   much more apt to keep him at ho:me.
→   I was like- yesterday I was like,
→   "Hey, if he starts feelin' better,
→   I'm takin' him in to school,"
→   but he uh . he didn't. <chuckles>
→   So we went to the ma:ll,
→   we went to <chuckling> Starbucks,

$\rightarrow$ went to the bank,
$\rightarrow$ went to the grocery store.>
  Liz: / ? ? / $\rightarrow$
  Neil: <*very quietly*> [It was kinda fun].>
  Liz: [/? ? /] /??/ kids.
  ((*another coworker joins the conversation, topic shifts*))

In this part of the interaction, Neil contrasts his parenting style with Clara's, depicting her as more (perhaps excessively) protective (*she's much more apt to keep him at ho:me*). He also, by the same token, positions himself as a knowledgeable coparent: He knows Clara's parenting style and predicts that she probably kept Jason home from school. (In fact, she didn't. Jason went to school on Thursday, though Clara kept him home with her on Friday.) By contrasting his own parenting behavior (the day he kept Jason out of school they didn't stay home but *went to Starbucks, went to the bank, went to the grocery store*), Neil positions himself as a coparent, one whose parenting choices are different from but as valid as (if not more valid than) those of his parenting partner, the child's mother.

The excerpts in this section illustrate that Neil's talk about his family at work is not just a resource for socializing with coworkers but also a resource for presenting himself as an equal member of a parenting team, a father who is a competent caregiver, perhaps even a more competent one than the child's mother. In the next section, we consider what Neil's workplace talk about family adds to our understanding of what it means to be a working father.

Discussion

In this chapter, we have explored the concept "working father" by examining one father's talk about family at work. We identified three patterns that characterize these conversations—patterns that often co-exist in individual conversations. First, Neil's talk about his family and his parenting serves as a resource for socializing with his coworkers, both women and men, and those with and without children of their own. In some instances, Neil draws on his parenting experience in order to establish solidarity with a coworker whose children have been sick. In others, he spontaneously talks about his family, reframing queries about audiotaping (as part of his participation in this project) into talk about the day he spent at home with his sick son. In yet other instances, his coworkers raise the topic of family by inquiring about his child's health. In these varied contexts, Neil sometimes engages in troubles talk, personalizing his talk about family, and at other times talks generally about parenting. These patterns combine ways of talking about family that Kendall (1999) found characterized the discourse of the mothers in her study about family at work (talking about family in individualized terms) with ways of talking that have been linked to the discourse of working fathers (talking about the family in more generalized terms).

Second, Neil's workplace talk about family provides insight into the interpenetration of the spheres of workplace and home. Neil both engages in and talks about frequent family-related telephone calls during the work day. These phone calls also serve as a resource for sociable talk, in addition to facilitating logistical planning regarding Neil's son and providing him with information about his parental responsibilities, such as whether or not he will have to pick Jason up from school. The family-related conversations also make clear that family responsibilities sometimes impinge on work-related responsibilities as well as personal needs. A conversation with a coworker about finding time to exercise also addresses the difficulty of integrating work, parenting, and other activities. We see the intrusion of parenting into the domain of work in an extended conversation in which Neil discusses the logistics of attending a work-related party with another vice president, Diane. On one hand, he explains that he won't be able to attend the party if he has to pick Jason up after school; on the other, he draws on this situation to explain to Diane, his peer, why a lower-ranking employee, Marianne, also might be unable to attend. These findings build on Kendall's study of how a mother's conversations about family at work shed light on the "interpenetration of (gendered) spheres." However, although Neil's workplace discourse about family positions him as a father who has primary caretaking responsibilities, he does not present himself as ultimately and solely responsible for Jason's care, as his coworker Marianne does with regard to her children.

Finally, Neil's talk about family at work creates his parental identity. He positions himself as an equal member of a parenting team, a parenting expert, and at times even the more competent member of this team. These findings provide an interesting point of comparison with earlier studies that found fathers being assigned identities of "bumbling assistant" and "baby entertainer" in parenting texts (Sunderland 2000) or assuming a single "playmate" identity in dinner table conversation (Kendall 1999).

Neil draws on this identity and on how he and Clara, his coparent, approach parenting differently as a source of humor.

The four couples who took part in the larger study from which this chapter's analysis is drawn are at the leading edge of a cultural revolution in their determination to share childrearing responsibilities. Our examination of one father's talk about family at work provides unique and rare documentation of how this new social phenomenon may play out in everyday discourse. Our findings thus provide further insights into the functions of discourse about family in the work sphere. We have examined the role played by Neil's talk about family in his interactions with coworkers and demonstrated that the discourse analysis of his workplace conversation provides a window on how work and family are intertwined and sometimes conflict. We suggested that Neil's talk about family at work serves the same basic functions as women's talk about family at work: it provides a resource for socializing with coworkers and for creating a (competent) parental identity. In prior research (Tannen 1994a) women were observed to discuss their families at work more than men. However, as dual-income parents continue to espouse egalitarian caregiver ideologies and workplace cultures transform over time, this pattern may change, and Neil and his coworkers may be a harbinger of that change. In any case, this study, in focusing on one working father and his discourse about family at work, suggests that this avenue merits further exploration.

In addressing the question of why Neil talks about his family frequently and in the individualized way Kendall observed in the discourse of women at work, we need to consider not only his role in sharing parenting but also the character of his workplace as well as other linguistic strategies he uses in talking about family. Neil works at a non-profit organization that is characterized by an informal atmosphere. Perhaps equally significant, more than half of his coworkers are women, and a woman holds the top position. (Of 46 employees, 28 were women, including two of the four vice presidents and the president herself.) As Kendall (1999) points out, not all talk about family at work has the same implications for the construction of gender-related family identities. Neil does not use individualized family talk to construct what might be thought of as a traditional primary caregiver identity. Instead, he positions himself as part of a parenting team where he shares childcare responsibilities. Through this strategy, Neil minimizes the perceived possible (negative) impact his family responsibilities might have on his commitment to his career yet still displays an identity as an involved, competent parent.

Though many more studies of fathers' talk at work will be needed to contextualize our findings, this study adds to our relatively limited but evolving understanding of what it means to be a working father. These findings, however, say nothing about the potential consequences of women's and men's engaging in talk about family at the workplace. Kendall, for example, building on a study by Glass & Camarigg (1992), observes that a woman's workplace talk about family can impede her advancement, if it contributes to constructing for her the identity of "a mother who works" in contrast to the identity "professional with children," which characterized the women in Kendall's study who were destined for promotion. Similarly, Williams (2000) notes that the "cult of domesticity" marks women who are mothers in a way that men who are fathers are not affected. For example, she notes that when a man has a family photograph on his desk, it is taken to imply, "He's a solid family man, conscious of his responsibilities," whereas when a woman has a family photograph on her desk, others may conclude, "Her family will always come before her career" (Williams 2000:247). These types of assumptions and expectations clearly link to broader sociocultural beliefs about women and men and are not necessarily linked to how individual men or women talk. Nonetheless, talking about family at work can have different consequences for women and men in terms of constructing a worker identity (e.g., committed versus non-committed), whether or not they participate in this type of talk in much the same way. The design of our study provides no information on whether or not the frequency with which Neil's family surfaced as a topic of talk at work negatively affected his advancement, but our strong impression is that it did not, that it served as a resource to integrate him into the social fabric of the organization in which he worked. In the spirit of Williams's observation, Neil positions himself as a "solid family [person], conscious of his responsibilities," a gendered identity not typically socioculturally available to working mothers, regardless of how they speak. If this is true, it would arguably enhance Neil's opportunities for advancement as well as likeability. This, however, we must stress again, is simply an impression, not a research finding.[4]

In sum, our study provides an illuminating glimpse of one father's family-related workplace discourse that in some ways differs from and in other ways coordinates with previously identified gendered patterns of interac-

4. In September 2004, 3 years and 10 months after these conversations took place, Neil still held the same position in the same organization.

tion as well as previous findings regarding how mothers and fathers talk about family at work. It remains for future work to continue to explore how both women and men, mothers and fathers, use language to navigate and negotiate the everyday interpenetration of work and family.

References

Coupland, Justine. 2003. Small talk: Social functions. Research on Language and Social Interaction 36(1).1–6.

Davies, Bronwyn, and Rom Harré. 1999. Positioning and personhood. Positioning theory, ed. Rom Harré and Luk van Langenhove, 32–52. Oxford and Malden, Mass.: Blackwell.

Glass, Jennifer, and Valerie Camarigg. 1992. Gender, parenthood, and job-family compatibility. American Journal of Sociology 98.131–151.

Goffman, Erving. 1974. Frame analysis. New York: Harper & Row.

Goffman, Erving. 1977. The arrangement between the sexes. Theory and Society 4(3).301–331.

Goffman, Erving. 1981. Footing. Forms of talk, 124–159. Philadelphia: University of Pennsylvania Press.

Hochschild, Arlie Russell, with Anne Machung. 1989. The second shift: Working parents and the revolution at home. New York: Avon Books.

Holmes, Janet. 2000. Doing collegiality and keeping control at work: Small talk in government departments. Small talk, ed. Justine Coupland, 32–61. Harlow, England: Longman.

Holmes, Janet. 2003. Small talk at work: Potential problems for workers with an intellectual disability. Research in Language and Social Interaction 36(1).65–84.

Holmes, Janet, Maria Stubbe, and Bernadette Vine. 1999. Constructing professional identity: "Doing power" in policy units. Talk, work and institutional order: Discourse in medical, mediation and management settings, ed. Srikant Sarangi and Celia Roberts, 351–388. Berlin: Mouton de Gruyter.

Jefferson, Gail. 1988. On the sequential organization of troubles-talk in ordinary conversation. Social Problems 35(4).418–441.

Kendall, Shari. 1999. The interpenetration of (gendered) spheres: An interactional sociolinguistic analysis of a mother at work and at home. Washington, D.C.: Georgetown University dissertation.

Kendall, Shari. 2003. Creating gendered demeanors of authority at work and at home. The handbook of language and gender, ed. Janet Holmes & Miriam Meyerhoff, 600–623. Oxford: Blackwell.

Kendall, Shari. 2006. Positioning the female voice within work and family. Speaking out: the female voice in public context, ed. Judith Baxter, 179–197. London: Palgrave Macmillan.

Kirby, Erika L. 2000. Communicating organizational tension: Balancing work and family. Lincoln, Nebraska: University of Nebraska dissertation.

Lakoff, Robin. 1975. Language and woman's place. New York: Harper & Row.

Maddock, Su, and Di Parkin. 1994. Gender cultures: How they affect men and women at work. Women and management: Current research issues, ed. Marilyn J. Davidson and Ronald J. Burke, 29–41. London: Paul Chapman Publishing Ltd.

Pritchard, C. Ruth. 1993. Supportive devices in language and paralanguage in the achievement of affiliation in troubles talk. Australian Review of Applied Linguistics 16(1).57–70.

Sunderland, Jane. 2000. Baby entertainer, bumbling assistant and line manager: Discourses of fatherhood in parentcraft texts. Discourse & Society 11(2).249–274.

Tannen, Deborah. 2007 [1989]. Talking voices: Repetition, dialogue, and imagery in conversational discourse. Cambridge: Cambridge University Press.

Tannen, Deborah. 1990. You just don't understand: Women and men in conversation. New York: Ballantine Books.

Tannen, Deborah. 1994a. Talking from 9 to 5: Women and men at work. New York: Quill.

Tannen, Deborah. 1994b. The relativity of linguistic strategies: Rethinking power and solidarity in gender and dominance. Gender and discourse, 19–52. New York and Oxford: Oxford University Press.

Tannen, Deborah. 1999. The display of (gendered) identities in talk at work. Reinventing identities: The gendered self in discourse, ed. Mary Bucholtz, A. C. Liang, and Laurel A. Sutton, 221–240. New York and Oxford: Oxford University Press.

Wardhaugh, Ronald. 2002. An introduction to sociolinguistics, fourth edition. Malden, Mass.: Blackwell.

Williams, Joan. 2000. Unbending gender: Why family and work conflict and what to do about it. New York and Oxford: Oxford University Press.

part III

Family Values and Beliefs

CYNTHIA GORDON

nine

"Al Gore's our guy": Linguistically Constructing a Family Political Identity

Researchers have suggested that family discourse can work toward socializing children into the political beliefs of their parents, thereby "reproducing" political values and behaviors across generations of the same family (e.g., Liebes & Ribak 1991, 1992; Liebes et al. 1991; Ribak 1997).[1] Other work illustrates how parents socialize children into behaviors and beliefs appropriate to and reflective of the family, as well as the wider culture, through dinner table interaction (e.g., Blum-Kulka 1997; Ochs & Taylor 1992; Ochs, Taylor, Rudolph & Smith 1992). Pontecorvo & Fasulo (1999), also examining family mealtime interaction, emphasize that all family members use language to socialize one another at any given interactional moment. This paper brings together an understanding of socialization as multi-directional and the idea that political identity is (or can

1. I am grateful to the Sloan Foundation for funding this study and to Clara, Neil, and Jason for their participation. I thank Deborah Tannen for her comments on earlier versions of this chapter, including one presented at the Annual Conference of the American Association for Applied Linguistics (2003). I also thank Teun van Dijk and one anonymous reviewer for their helpful remarks on a version of this chapter that was published in *Discourse & Society* 15(4) 2004. Finally, I thank Shari Kendall for her thoughtful comments, which have shaped the current version.

be) part of a family's identity to illustrate how members of one family work moment by moment to produce, negotiate, and socialize one another into the political aspect of their shared family identity. In doing so, it draws on and extends past work that demonstrates how individuals use language to construct identities in interaction (e.g., Schiffrin 1996, 2000, 2002; Adelswärd & Nilholm 2000; Petraki 2002).

Specifically, I consider how members of one white middle-class American family, which consists of a mother (Clara), a father (Neil), and one child (Jason, age 4 years 10 months), linguistically construct the political aspect of their shared family identity as Democrats and supporters of Al Gore (the Democratic Party's 2000 presidential candidate). To do so, I analyze excerpts of audiotaped conversations the parents recorded over the course of the week of the 2000 presidential election as part of their participation in the Work and Family project. The election was one (if not the) major event that shaped the family's interactions that week. Because it occurred on their second day of taping and the winner remained undetermined during the course of the taping period,[2] the election and the presidential candidates were an ongoing topic of discussion. Politics was also a frequent topic of talk because the election was particularly important to this family: the workplaces of both parents would be greatly affected by its outcome (the husband is a vice president of a non-profit organization while the wife is an assistant director of a government agency).

2. The election for President of the United States in 2000 was one of the closest elections in U.S. history, and a victor was not identified for some time after the election. The candidates of the two major political parties were then Governor of Texas George W. Bush (Republican) and then Vice President Al Gore (Democrat). This is the election story, as described by wordIQ.com (http://www.wordiq.com/definition/U.S._presidential_election,_2000):

> The election took over a month to resolve, highlighted by two premature declarations of a "winner" on election night and an extremely close result in the state of Florida. Florida's 25 electoral votes ultimately decided the election by a razor thin margin of actual votes, and was certified only after numerous court challenges and recounts. Al Gore publicly conceded the election after the Supreme Court, in the case Bush v. Gore, voted 7-2 to declare the recount procedure in process unconstitutional because it was not being carried out statewide and 5-4 to ban further recounts using other procedures. Gore strongly disagreed with the court's decision, but decided that "for the sake of our unity of the people and the strength of our democracy, I offer my concession." He had previously made a concession phone call to Bush the night of the election, but quickly retracted it after learning just how close the election was. Following the election, a subsequent recount conducted by various U.S. news media organizations indicated that Bush would have won using some of the recount methods (including the one favored by Gore at the time of the Supreme Court decision) but that Gore would have won if other methods were adopted.

The transcriber who initially transcribed the family's election-day morning conversation noted in the transcript that "[b]oth Neil and Clara are noticeably vigorous in their support for Al Gore. They reach a tone that would be common at the Democratic National Convention."[3] However, while listening to the entirety of Clara's tapes and transcribing many of the family's recorded interactions, it became apparent to me that the identity of "Democrat and supporter of Al Gore" "belonged" not just to Clara and Neil but to the whole family. This included Jason, who was not old enough at the time of taping to have "real" political opinions. However, all family members, including Jason, started and participated in conversations about the election. For example, Jason asked his parents questions about the candidates when the family was watching election updates on television, and they responded to these queries.

The analysis that follows demonstrates how all members of this family co-construct the political component of the family's identity, while simultaneously socializing one another into it. It draws on research in linguistics such as by Schiffrin (1996, 2000, 2002) and Adelswärd & Nilholm (2000) that suggests that individuals use language to create alignments that work toward constructing particular identities. However, whereas the work of these scholars focuses on the construction of the identities of individual interlocutors, I examine the creation of one aspect of family members' shared identity. The analysis also builds on past work that shows how parents socialize their children through interaction, as well as on prior studies that suggest that parents' discourse can work to reproduce political outlook in children by illustrating how Jason is socialized through interaction with his parents into the notion that the family identity includes being Democrats and supporting Gore. In addition, I demonstrate how Jason is a key participant in the co-construction of the family's political identity, as well as in the co-socialization of all family members into this shared identity.

I identify four major strategies this family uses throughout their week taping to create alignments that together construct their shared family identity while also socializing members into this identity. They (1) use referring terms for the candidates that create closeness to Gore and distance from Bush, (2) repeatedly discuss Bush's 1976 drunk driving arrest, (3) negatively assess Bush and those associated with him, and (4) refer to family members as

3. I thank John Damaso for making this observation.

Democrats. Members of this family create alignments toward the political candidates and toward each other in enacting these strategies through their use of referring terms, intertextual and intratextual repetition, laughter, storytelling, and what Tannen (2007 [1989]) calls "constructed dialogue."

I first briefly review prior work in two areas: socialization (in particular, political socialization) and identity construction, both as they have been studied in the context of family. Second, I provide more background on the family whose discourse I analyze here. I then demonstrate how the four previously mentioned strategies work toward constructing the political aspect of this family's shared identity, discuss the linguistic features family members use in enacting these strategies, and show that all family members play a role in this process. I also illustrate how the identity of "Democrats and supporters of Al Gore" serves as a resource family members use to realign and create harmony in the course of an argument: in other words, I demonstrate that the shared family identity serves as a cohesive device. Finally, I discuss implications of these data for studies of political socialization and identity construction in the context of family.

Theoretical Background

Socialization in Families

A great deal of work has examined socialization, which, in Pontecorvo & Fasulo's (1999:315) terms, consists of "a set of practices for cultural reproduction," as it occurs in the context of family. For example, Blum-Kulka (1997), Ochs and her colleagues (Ochs & Taylor 1992; Ochs, Smith & Taylor 1996; Ochs, Pontecorvo & Fasulo 1996; Pontecorvo & Fasulo 1997, 1999) and Tulviste et al. (2002) suggest that family socialization practices and interactional patterns vary as a function of culture. In these studies, the distribution and form of conversational moves such as issuing directives and telling stories are shown to work toward re-instantiating the family hierarchy and toward teaching children values and beliefs of the family (in other words, they work toward creating a family identity), while also exhibiting larger cultural patterns (e.g., of the family's ethnic, national, and/or socioeconomic group).

For example, in her study of Israeli and Jewish-American family discourse, Blum-Kulka (1997) finds differences in the dinner table narrative practices of these two groups, noting for instance that in Jewish-American families, children are expected to (and do) participate more. She shows that parents socialize their children into these cultural patterns of story-telling; for example, Jewish-American parents select their children as tell-ers more often whereas Israeli parents take up a larger portion of narrative space in their families. One way of interpreting such patterns is as parents socializing children into both family norms or a family identity and into the norms or identity of the larger cultural group.

In another analysis of family mealtime discourse, Ochs, Smith & Taylor (1996) examine problem-solving in the dinner table discourse of American families, finding that joint problem-solving through narrative works toward constructing and negotiating family beliefs and values, as well as toward structuring and restructuring the family as a social unit. They note that co-narrative practices empower individuals to socialize one another, thus implying that all family members are subject to socialization. Like-wise, in a related study, Pontecorvo & Fasulo (1999) suggest that family conversation is in fact a process of *mutual apprenticeship*, that is to say, both parents and children are socialized into their family roles in interac-tion moment by moment.

Though past work in the area of political socialization has considered the family to be of great importance, few studies have examined how family members socialize one another into political beliefs in actual interaction, instead relying primarily on interview and survey data. Though it is not agreed upon to what extent parents are able to reproduce their political opinions in their children (e.g., see Connell 1972), prior work does sug-gest that the family is one important context where political learning takes place. For example, Jennings & Niemi (1968), considering interviews with American high school seniors and their parents, find that partisan attach-ment is often reproduced across generations, while opinions about par-ticular issues (e.g., prayer in public schools) are less frequently shared. This implies that family interaction socializes children into partisanship, though the study does not examine how this occurs. More recently, Whyte (1999), considering political socialization in Northern Ireland, identifies the family as one of several major mechanisms affecting adolescents' political out-look, though she does not analyze actual family interaction.

One body of work that has specifically considered socialization into political outlook in the family setting and confirms that the family is one mechanism for political socialization analyzes interviews with family mem-bers both quantitatively and qualitatively (Liebes & Ribak 1991, 1992; Liebes et al. 1991; Ribak 1997). This research has examined data drawn from 400 interviews with Israeli adolescents and their parents about the Arab-Israeli conflict. In a quantitative analysis of these interviews, Liebes & Ribak (1992) find that political outlook can be reproduced across generations of the same family, though the success of such reproduction depends on a number of factors, such as parents' education. For instance, they found that approximately two-thirds of the time, if a highly educated parent advocated relinquishing territory to maintain peace, the child felt the same or similarly. In contrast, among lower-educated parents, only those advocating military action were able to reproduce their outlook in the next generation. Taking a qualitative approach by analyzing excerpts of one family's interview, Liebes & Ribak (1991) and Ribak (1997) emphasize that political socialization is in fact a process of negotiation as parents and children agree and disagree, and align and realign, during talk about politics. These two articles highlight the point that adolescent children judge their parents' opinions rather than merely absorbing them, while also considering the impact of television viewing on family communication about politics and the political socialization of adolescents. Like Pontecorvo & Fasulo (1999) and Ochs, Smith & Taylor (1996), Ribak (1997) and Liebes & Ribak (1991) suggest that parents and children mutually influence or socialize one another through talk.

It is worth noting that though prior work on political socialization primarily focuses on adolescent children, it has been suggested that the process begins at an early age. Stacey (1978) notes that studies have shown that a "fairly solid world picture" of politics, for example, who "friends" and "enemies" are at home and abroad, has developed by age twelve. He also notes that by the age of twelve, nearly two-thirds of children in Britain and the United States have developed political party preferences. Schwartz (1975:229), in a study where American preschoolers were interviewed about politics, suggests that much political learning takes place between the ages of three and six, and perhaps earlier. She found, for example, that the preschool children in her study evidenced a strong preference for the American flag and recognized the President as someone important. Considering these types of findings, Ichilov (1990) suggests that political socialization should be viewed as a lifelong process.

In sum, past work on socialization in the family context has focused on how parents socialize children into a particular culture and view of the world, and several researchers have suggested that socialization is best understood as multi-directional. Prior work has also shown that language is used to construct and negotiate family members' (shared and unshared) beliefs and behaviors across a range of domains, from culturally appropriate storytelling and reception behaviors to political outlook. Where political outlook is concerned, prior studies identify family discourse as an important means by which socialization occurs, though little work has examined how this actually occurs. My analysis builds on this body of work on socialization by examining how it occurs moment by moment in interaction. In doing so, it also illustrates how family members actively co-construct a shared identity.

Identity Construction in Families

Just as socialization, political or otherwise, is an ongoing process that involves multiple mutually influencing interlocutors, identity too is interactionally co-constructed. So Ochs (1993:296) argues that "at any given actual moment," interactants are "actively constructing their social identities rather than passively living out some cultural prescription of social identity." She suggests that identities are created as individuals perform socially meaningful acts (e.g., interrupting, making a request) and by verbally displaying certain stances, or "socially recognized" points of view or attitudes (288).

Taking a similar social constructivist approach but focusing on alignments rather than acts and stances, Schiffrin (1996) considers how two women create "portraits" of themselves as mothers in audiotaped sociolinguistic interviews. Both narrators talk about experiences wherein they represent relationships between themselves and younger women in their families who depart from family norms. Schiffrin shows how in narrating these experiences, the women construct their maternal identities by creating alignments between themselves as story world figures and other figures in the story as well as between themselves as tellers and their narrative audience.

Schiffrin (2000) focuses on maternal identity as it is tied to the identity of "daughter." Considering how one Holocaust survivor portrays her relationship with her mother in a videotaped life story interview, Schiffrin focuses the role of referring terms and constructed dialogue in creating a picture of this relationship as fraught with ambivalence and indirectness. Similarly, Schiffrin (2002) explores how the same Holocaust survivor represents her relationship with her mother and with her friends in a life story interview. Schiffrin's work shows that identity is constructed or displayed through linguistic strategies that create alignments between a storyteller and other individuals in his or her life (e.g., friends and family members) and between a storyteller and his or her co-interlocutor. These linguistic strategies include syntax, speech acts, constructed dialogue, repetition, and referring terms. Similarly, my analysis indicates that several of these strategies, in particular referring terms and repetition, work toward constructing one aspect of a shared family identity.

In another study of identity from a constructivist viewpoint, Petraki (2002) examines the discourse and social identities that family members produce during storytelling. She considers a relatively unstructured interview with one Cypriot-Australian woman and two of her daughters (which was part of a larger study about women in Cypriot-Australian and Greek-Australian families) where the husband was also present. Petraki examines the contribution of the father and daughters during the course of the mother's turn at storytelling in exploring two aspects of identity. First, she considers how the participants create discourse identities such as "story elicitor" and "story contributor" (building on Ochs & Taylor 1992). Second, she examines how and when the interlocutors co-construct social identities (e.g., "unwilling suitor," "happy daughter") in the stories and in the telling. For example, she found that when the mother constructed an "unwilling suitor" identity for her husband in the story of their courtship, the father took on a "teasing husband" identity in the ongoing interaction.

As Schiffrin and Petraki explore family identities as they are created in interview storytelling situations, so Erickson (1990) examines dinner table conversation. He analyzes excerpts from one dinner conversation of one Italian-American family, focusing on the interactional organization of discourse coherence strategies. He identifies four types of participation structures, finding that the general family structure, and thus the identities, or family roles, of particular family members, manifests through these participation structures. For example, in a storytelling episode about bikes and biking accidents, the family hierarchy was re-created and displayed, as the father's story was the most prominent (it was longest, was singly told, and occurred in the most serious key). In contrast, the two oldest brothers in the family collaboratively told a less weighty bike accident story, while the youngest daughter's attempt to tell a bike accident was entirely ignored. Erickson's study thus suggests that patterns of storytelling and reception re-instantiate the family hierarchy, or, in other words, individuals' identities (e.g., father, daughter) and the relationship between them within the confines of the family.

Other work shows that the identities of family members are constructed in non-narrative discourse. Aronsson (1998), in her study of "identity-in-interaction," demonstrates how a father in a family therapy session allocates turns at talk in the session, and in doing this, constructs a "co-therapist" identity. Taking a similar approach, Adelswärd & Nilholm (2000) consider the family identities of "mother" and "child" in their case study analysis of one teacher-parent-pupil conference at a school for children with learning difficulties in Sweden. In this case, the child, Cindy, has Down syndrome. They focus on how the child's identity as a child and pupil is constructed and how this is directly related to the kinds of identities that are created for the child's teacher and her mother. Adelswärd & Nilholm find that the mother often works as a "communicative broker helping her daughter to present herself in situ, i.e., as a participant in the interaction at hand" (559). For example, Cindy's mother elaborates and interprets Cindy's turns. (Note that these could be thought of in terms of Ochs's [1993] discussion of social acts and stances.) The authors suggest that "the focus of some of these sequences involved management of Cindy's identity, while others appeared to be more concerned with presentation of the mother-child relationship" (559). For instance, the mother reformulates some of the child's conversational contributions so as to make them coherent. In addition, she jokes with Cindy to display a close mother-daughter relationship. This also works toward constructing a "fun mother" identity for the mother and toward displaying Cindy's competence by showing that she understands playful mocking.

Though a fair amount of work has considered the identities of individuals within their families, less work has considered how families construct a shared family identity. Past work has shown that shared family identities are both real and meaningful, however. For example, Byers (1997) examines the role of family stories in communicating a family culture and maintaining a family identity. Analyzing broad, open-ended interviews of 100 participants ranging in age from 20 to 56 years of age, she finds that people believe family stories are told to define who the family is and what it values, as well as to maintain the family. These findings indicate that families not only have a sense of what might be called "familyness" but also that language (in this case, storytelling) plays a pivotal role in maintaining and expressing this familyness.

Ochs et al. (1992), focusing on the socialization of children, also suggest that language is a means by which families create their sense of familyness. The authors identify family storytelling as an opportunity for family members to "affirm their own shared beliefs and values and to contrast them with those of 'others' outside the co-present family group" (38). Similarly, Blum-Kulka (1997:280) notes that talk not only serves to construct cultural and personal identities but familial identities as well, though she does not examine this in detail.

Portions of Varenne's (1992) analysis of the distribution of power in one family consider the "American" aspect of one family's identity. He argues that the family's "Americanness" is created through everyday conversation, for example, by family members talking about topics linked to broader institutions in the United States (e.g., talk of a child doing his homework is linked to U.S. educational institutions). Furthermore, Varenne identifies patterns of interaction as creating Americanness. For instance, he suggests that the child-centeredness of the family's everyday conversations and activities is an American cultural phenomenon.

Summarizing, prior work on identity construction in the context of family has focused on how individual family identities (e.g., mother, father) and the relationships between them (e.g., mother-daughter) are constructed, whereas less work has considered shared family identity. Past research has established that interaction is a means by which individuals construct their identities as individuals within a family and that the analysis of conversation as it unfolds moment by moment reveals how particular linguistic strategies and conversational moves produce alignments and identities. My analysis builds on the work of Schiffrin (1996, 2000, 2002) in particular by identifying specific linguistic devices that work toward constructing an identity. However, whereas Schiffrin considers the identity of individuals within families, my focus is a shared group identity. In addition, whereas work to date on identity construction in the family has relied primarily on data from interviews (e.g., Schiffrin) and family mealtime conversations (e.g., Ochs and her colleagues), the analysis that follows considers family interactions across a range of contexts.

The Family

I analyze here excerpts of conversation involving members of the family consisting of Clara, Neil, and their son Jason (age 4 years 10 months). Clara and Neil audiotaped their own interactions for 7 days as part of their participation in the larger study. I was the research team member who shadowed Clara after taping was complete. Although family political identities were not the focus of the larger study, the tapes of this particular family provide an opportunity to examine how family political identities are created in and across conversations.

As I mentioned, because the family taped during the week of the 2000 presidential election, and because both adults' places of work would be affected by its outcome, the topic of the election surfaced frequently during the taping period. Neil is a vice president of a nonprofit environmental organization whose goals are typically compatible with the environmental policies of Democrats. Clara is a high-ranking government employee whose direct superior is a presidential appointee. From having talked to Clara and Neil and having listened to many of their recorded interactions, it is evident that they believed that their respective workplaces would be negatively affected if George W. Bush were to be elected President. Thus it is perhaps not surprising that they construct a family identity as Democrats and supporters of Gore in and across interactions during their taping week.

Conversations about the election and the candidates occurred during a number of different activities, for example, while watching television (the family watched election news frequently), driving in the car, talking on the telephone with family friends, and talking at the polls. I consider excerpts from the family's election-related conversations in which at least two family members are present.

Creating a Family Political Identity

This family uses four major strategies throughout their taping week to create alignments that together construct and display their shared family identity as Democrats and supporters of Al Gore. These strategies include: (1) using referring terms for the presidential candidates that create closeness to Gore and distance from Bush; (2) repeatedly making references to news that came out just days before the election that in 1976 George W. Bush was arrested for drunk driving; (3) assessing Bush, and people associated with him, negatively; and (4) the parents explicitly positioning themselves and their son as a Democrat in his presence. I discuss each of these strategies in turn and consider how particular linguistic devices, specifically, referring terms, repetition, laughter, storytelling, and constructed dialogue, create alignments in the political conversations where these strategies surface. Finally, I illustrate how the family identity serves as a cohesive device in this family.

Throughout the week of taping, Gore and Bush were referred to quite differently by members of this family. Table 9.1 shows all referring terms family members used for the candidates in family conversations. The names in parentheses are those family members who used these noun phrases during the week of taping.

Table 9.1 shows a number of patterns that create the family's pro-Gore and anti-Bush stance. First, note that noun phrases that refer to Bush use the demonstrative "that." This demonstrative is used to point to a "distant" referent and can connote "emotive rejection" (Quirk & Greenbaum 1973:107). In contrast, noun phrases that refer to Gore include first-person plural pronouns that encompass all family members and create a close relationship with Gore, as in "*our* guy," "*our* President," and "the guy *we* like." Second, Gore is aligned with the family as a "friend" of both Neil and Jackie (Clara's boss and good friend), while Bush is distanced from the family as someone that "Daddy doesn't like." Third, Gore is described as someone who is "cool," whereas Bush is dubbed an "alcoholic" who drives while intoxicated (this will be discussed in greater detail in the next section). Each of these patterns in referring term usage works toward creating a positive alignment toward Gore while rejecting Bush.

Excerpt 1 shows how several of these referring terms are used in one conversation. This interaction occurred Tuesday (Election Day) morning, and it shows referring terms being used by Neil and Clara to create the family identity while also collaboratively socializing Jason (and each other) into it. Here Jason talks about a mock-presidential election that was going

Table 9.1. Ways of referring to the presidential candidates

Ways of referring to George W. Bush	*Ways of referring to Al Gore*
• W (Neil, Clara, Jason)	• Al (Neil, Clara, Jason)
• GW (Clara)	• Gore (Neil, Clara, Jason)
• Bush (Neil, Clara, Jason)	• Al Gore (Neil, Clara, Jason)
• George Bush (Neil, Clara, Jason)	• a cool guy (Neil)
• that W guy (Neil)	• our President (Jason)
• the W guy (Neil, Jason)	• our guy (Neil)
• the man that Daddy doesn't like (Clara)	• the guy we like (Neil)
• the other guy that's tryin' to be President (Neil)	• Daddy's friend (Clara, Neil)
	• my friend (Neil)
• that alcoholic car-driving man (Neil)	• Jackie's friend (Clara, Neil)
• some alcoholic drunk driver (Clara)	((*Jackie = Clara's good friend and boss*))

to take place at his Montessori school that day. In addition to voting for President, the children were going to vote for their favorite ice cream flavor. Note that this is the conversation where Neil and Clara were described as reaching "a tone that would be common at the Democratic National Convention."

(1) Tuesday (Election Day) morning at home

   1   Jason: So they—
   2   And we're also voting for President at my school too.
   3   Neil: *<exaggerated surprise>* For President?>
   4   [Or just ice cream?]
   5   Jason: [/They're/ talking] about the President.
   6 → Neil: *<louder>* Oh well you tell 'em you're votin' for Al Gore.>
   7 → Jason: [Yea:h!]
   8 → Clara: [Yea:h!]
   9 → Neil: Not that [W guy.]
  10   Clara: [/That's the one./]
  11 →   Not W!
  12 → Neil: Say no W.
  13 → Clara: No [W!]
  14 → Neil: [We] want Al.
  15 → Clara: *<louder>* We want Al.>
  16   Jason: Who's Al?
  17   Neil: Al Gore.
  18 →   He's a cool guy [that we—]
  19 → Clara: [He's Daddy's] friend.
  20 → Neil: That's right.
  21 →   He's my friend.
  22 →   He's gonna be President.
  23 → Clara: We hope.
  24 → Neil: We hope.
  25 → Clara: He's Jackie's friend too.
  26   Neil: *<sniffs>*
  27 →   That's right,
  28 →   Jackie knows him.
  29   Clara: ((*to Jason*)) /??? shoes ?/

In this excerpt, Clara and Neil use a number of the referring terms that were shown in table 9.1 to construct their alignment with Gore, who is portrayed as a family friend (lines 19, 21, 25), and against Bush, who is referred to as *that W guy* (line 9). In addition, Clara and Neil jointly encourage Jason to vote for Al Gore and to reject Bush. In doing so, they repeat one another, for example, when Neil says, *Not that W guy* (line 9), Clara agrees, *Not W* (line 11). Reciprocally, when Clara says of Gore, *He's Daddy's friend* (line 19), Neil echoes, *He's my friend* (line 21). This repetition works toward creating a supportive alignment between the participants (following Tannen 2007 [1989]). The use of *we* rather than *I* also works toward constructing a shared family alignment, as family members speak for the whole family rather than for themselves as individuals (e.g., *We hope*, lines 23 and 24). Jason and Clara's simultaneous *Yeahs* (lines 7 and 8), which respond to Neil's suggestion that Jason tell everyone he will vote for Gore (line 6), also evidences a shared alignment. This segment shows the parents socializing Jason and one another in that they collaboratively (re)create and (re)produce the family identity.

Two of the referring terms highlighted in excerpt 1 resurface approximately ten minutes later in a conversation occurring as Neil drives Jason to school. These again show a positive stance toward Gore. Neil and Jason have been discussing the ice cream election at Jason's school when Neil begins talking about the mock presidential voting that will also take place:

(2) Neil driving Jason to school

1		Neil:	Well if you vote for . if you vote for President,
2	→		tell 'em you want AL GORE,
3	→		Daddy's friend and Jackie's friend.
4			/S- the- s—/
5		Jason:	/?/ what'd you just say?
6	→	Neil:	AL GORE.
7			((*short pause*))
8	→		Say,
9	→		<*chanting*> We like Al.
10	→		We like Al.>
11			((*short pause, Neil turns on the radio to news talk radio*))

In this excerpt, referring terms used for Al Gore are intertextually repeated as Neil once more identifies Gore as someone who is a friend of both him and Jackie. Again, here we see Jason being socialized into the belief that people in the family (and close to the family) support Gore. As a member of the family, Jason is encouraged to vote for Gore (line 2, *tell 'em you want*

AL GORE). Furthermore, in addition to repeating referring terms that create closeness with Gore, Neil encourages Jason to chant, *We like Al* (lines 9–10) rather than *I like Al*. Though this encouragement is likely intended primarily to be humorous, Neil's use of *we* again aligns Jason with his parents, as well as family friend Jackie and possibly the Democratic Party, as someone who supports Gore.

Table 9.1 and excerpts 1 and 2 illustrate that across family interactions where the presidential candidates are referred to and their proper names are not used, referring terms used create alignments of approval and closeness with Gore and rejection of Bush. Schiffrin (2000, 2002) shows that referring terms are pivotal to how one narrator constructs her relationship with her mother in a life-story telling. This section thus builds on that work by showing how referring terms, and the repetition of these terms, work toward constructing this family's political identity. It extends Schiffrin's work in that it illustrates how these linguistic devices work toward constructing the shared identity of a group.

Repeated Discussion of Bush's 1976 Drunk-driving Arrest

The second strategy this family uses to construct and display their family identity as Democrats and supporters of Gore is repeatedly discussing George W. Bush's 1976 arrest for drunk driving, news of which came out a few days before the election. In Jason's presence, Neil and Clara discussed how "unfortunate" it was that the information about the drunk-driving arrest did not get picked up by the media earlier (though it is not clear from the tapes whether Jason was or was not listening to their conversation). However, on Election Day, Neil was at the polls talking to a friend and fellow Democrat (Ellen) who was working there when Clara showed up with Jason to vote. The conversation shown in excerpt 3 ensued between Clara, Jason, Neil, and Ellen. Here Clara prompts Jason to talk about the mock election held at his school. Note that this is reminiscent of patterns of interactions between mothers, fathers, and children identified by Ochs & Taylor (1992) in that the mother prompts the child to tell the father about something that happened during the child's day. It is also reminiscent of Schieffelin's (1986, 1990) work on language socialization of Kaluli children, which shows that Kaluli mothers create triadic interactions by prompting their very young children to repeat utterances to other family members. In the excerpt that follows, Clara prompts Jason to tell about the mock presidential election at his school, and Neil, Clara, Ellen, and a voter passing by react to Jason's explanation about why Bush won:

(3) At the polls

1	Clara:	They- they voted in his school.
2		Jason,
3		tell Daddy who won the election in your school.
4	Jason:	U:m George Bush.
5	Neil:	*<with exaggerated horror>* [OH no!]*>*
6	Jason:	[He-]
7 →		He was [um . um .] drinking alcohol and →
8	Neil:	[*<laughs>*]
9 →	Jason:	[/then they were/ driving.]
10	Neil:	[*<laughs>*]
11	Clara:	[*<laughs>*]
12	Ellen:	[*<laughs>*]
13	Neil:	*<laughing>* Wow!
14		Boy they've got these ki- these kids up to →
15		[/last-minute reports!/>]
16	Voter:	[And that's why he won?]
17	Clara:	[*<laughs>*]
18	Ellen:	[*<laughs>*]

Here, all the adults respond positively to Jason's utterance about Bush drinking alcohol and driving. Their shared laughter creates affiliation between them (following Ellis 1997). This includes Ellen, who, like Jason's parents, shows appreciation for his utterance. In Goodwin & Goodwin's (1992:157) terms, all interlocutors assess Jason's utterance through laughter, participating in the "evaluative loading" of Jason's talk while creating matching "affective displays."

It is not clear from the tapes where Jason got the idea that Bush got elected in his school's mock election because he was arrested for drunk driving, but in excerpt 3 Clara knows Jason will say this and prompts him to do so. We know this because later in a tape-recorded interaction Clara explains to Jackie (her boss and friend) that while at the polls, she prompted Jason several times to repeat his explanation that Bush was elected "because he drinks alcohol and drives."

It is later that same day when Clara tells Jackie, on the telephone, the story about Jason identifying Bush's drunk driving as the reason for his winning the school election. During her conversation, Neil appreciatively chuckles in the background, and Jason is also present. John is Jackie's husband. Only Clara's side of the conversation was captured by the recorder. In excerpt 4, Clara describes how Jason first told her that Bush got elected because he drinks and drives (note that the original conversation was not captured on tape, though Clara's prompting of Jason to say this at the polls to Ellen and Neil was). In the excerpt, when Clara re-creates Jason's utterance as constructed dialogue, she rephrases it, giving it more fluency and "punch" than what was likely actually said.

(4) Clara on the phone with Jackie

1	Clara:	Did John tell you what I- when I called earlier,
2		you were having family hour,
3		*<laughing>* did I t- did I tell- →
4		did he tell you what I told him?>
5		About- at Jason's school,
6		they had- they had two elections today,
7		one was for their favorite ice cream,
8		*<chuckling>* vanilla or chocolate,>
9		*<laughing>* and the other one was- →
10		the other one was for President.>
11		And Bush won apparently,
12		at Jason's school,
13		and I said to Jason,
14		*<laughing>* I said- I know,>
15		I said to Jason,
16		"Why did- why did he win?"
17 →		And he said,
18 →		*<laughing>* "Because he drinks alcohol and drives!">
19	Neil:	*<laughs>*
20	Clara:	*<laughs>*

Clara continues to tell Jackie about her visit to the polls (with Neil and Jason as overhearers), describing how she "set up" Jason to say that Bush got elected *because he drinks alcohol and drives* in front of Neil and Ellen (which was shown in excerpt 3). She also tells of how she set up Jason to say it again in line at the polls (an event which was not recorded), for which she says she received annoyed looks from people who she *thinks were Republicans.* Clara's telling of this story and her obvious appreciation of

Jason's behavior at the polls projects the family identity to Jackie. Simultaneously, alignments are created between all co-present family members. Neil shows alignment with Clara and her story by laughing at the appropriate moment (line 19), while Clara creates an alignment with Jason by appreciatively laughing about his utterance at the polls. Furthermore, she contributes to the construction of Jason's identity as a Democrat and Gore supporter by telling this story about him in his presence (following Miller et al. 1990).

Clara also tells this story to one other friend in a telephone conversation the next day, and Neil tells it one day at work. The repeated retellings of this story serve as what Tannen (2007 [1989]) calls "savoring repetition." In addition, Clara's "setting up" of Jason at the polls to say Bush won the election because *he drinks alcohol and drives* and her and Neil's retelling of the story, which includes the constructed dialogue of their son, allows Clara and Neil to share the family identity with friends and coworkers (and the researchers) while clearly including their child. This fits into Byers's (1997) finding that stories are told to define what a family values, and Ochs et al.'s (1992) observation that stories work to affirm shared family beliefs, though the stories told here are not dinnertime narratives. The repeated reference to Bush's drunk driving by Jason and his parents and the repetition of the story where Jason says Bush got elected because he drinks and drives also work to position the family within a larger group —the Democratic Party and/or people who do not like George W. Bush.

Negative Assessment of Bush and the People He Is Associated With

A third strategy that constructs the shared family identity of being Democrats and supporters of Gore and socializes the family into this identity is their characterizing Bush and the people he is associated with negatively, which creates a socially meaningful *stance* (Ochs 1993) indicative of a non-Republican identity. In other words, family members collaboratively assess Bush negatively, asserting the moral superiority of their family (following Ochs et al. 1992). In this way, the family creates an identity through contrasting the in-group with "others." This strategy is discussed by van Dijk (1987) (though not in the context of family) in his examination of the discursive strategies by which white people in Amsterdam create positive self-presentation and negative other-presentation in their talk about "foreigners." He found that in everyday interaction majority group members reproduce opinions about others through differentiating themselves from those others.

In a number of interactions during their week of taping, Clara, Neil, and Jason create a contrast between what Bush does or values and what the family does or values. For example, in one telephone conversation with Jackie (with Neil also present in the room with Clara), Clara describes Bush as someone who looks like "an old drunk frat boy." This serves to depict Bush as someone who drinks excessively and indirectly references his arrest for drunk driving. In another conversation with Jackie on the phone with both Neil and Jason as overhearers, Clara refers to Bush as "stupid."

In one interesting case, a negative portrayal of Bush emerges in a non-election-related conversation that creates Bush as someone who does not value what the family is implied to value: treating others well. In this conversation, shown in excerpt 5, the family is watching television just prior to leaving the house to go to Starbuck's one evening. At the time of taping, the family was planning on having a backyard deck built, and Jason brought up this topic, asking about the deck-builders (*they* in line 1):

(5) Talking about the deck-builder

1	Jason:	Are they gonna build the deck?
2	Clara:	We're gonna see about it.
3		Because the last time they came,
4		they didn't come back.
5		So I called,
6		and I talked to Joey, ((*Joey = the company manager*))
7		who was very nice to me last time.
8		And this time he was a little SNIPPY,
9		so I'm not sure we're gonna [go with Joey or not.]
10	Jason:	[What's "snippy."]
11	Clara:	"Snippy" is—
12 →	Neil:	W was snippy [/yesterday./]
13 →	Clara:	[<*chuckling*> Yeah,]
14 →		W is snippy.>
15		Um,
16		it's when you get som- kind of IRRITATED
17		with somebody,
18		and you don't treat them quite right.
19	Jason:	Oh.

Note that although this conversation at first is about the deck, and the deck-builder, Clara's use of "snippy" indirectly references the election in that it was a word Gore reportedly used in the telephone conversation he had with Bush in which he retracted his concession of the election.[4] Thus, when Jason asks the meaning of the word "snippy," Neil uses this as an opportunity to criticize Bush, and Clara enforces the validity of this assessment through repetition. She expands to explain that when someone is snippy they *don't treat (other people) quite right* (line 18), thereby implying that Bush also *doesn't treat (other people) quite right,* whereas members of the family do.

At times, Bush and the people he is associated with are characterized negatively not just in terms of overall cultural beliefs (e.g., the fact that drinking excessively is generally not acceptable and that people should "treat other people right"), but also in direct opposition to what might be identified as the family's core beliefs. For example, members of this family demonstrate strong support for the environment in a number of their recorded interactions (recall also that Neil works for an environmental organization, and note that all family members are vegetarians). Thus, in one interaction occurring while watching television when Neil tells Jason that George W. Bush doesn't care about "rivers and trees as much as Al Gore does," he constructs Bush in opposition to the "good" things that the family believes in. As the conversation continues, Jason says that at his school Bush won the election, and Neil explains that people are allowed to vote for whomever they want, and that they can vote for President once they turn eighteen. At that point, Jason says, "When I grow up, I'm gonna put W in jail," and Neil chuckles appreciatively, saying, "No, we don't do that." In this case, Neil speaks negatively about Bush, portraying him as anti-environment, and Jason tries to participate by showing his own alignment against Bush. Perhaps trying to top what his father has said (thereby enacting a gendered interactional pattern identified by Tannen [1990], among others), he takes it a bit too far.

Like excerpt 5, excerpt 6 occurs in front of the television set, which is showing election news. On the first day of taping, Jason and Clara were

4. I initially did not recognize the intertextual "source" of Clara's use of "snippy." However, several years after the family taped, I read the book *The Bush Dyslexicon*, by Mark Crispin Miller, and was interested to learn that on November 9, 2000, the very day when Neil and Clara agreed that Bush was "snippy" in conversation with Jason, a *New York Times* article reported that when Gore telephoned Bush and retracted his concession of the election, Bush replied with an "incredulous tone" and Gore reportedly responded, "You don't have to be snippy about it." I emailed the family asking if their use of "snippy" was inspired by the reported use of the term by Gore when talking to Bush as reported in the *New York Times*; Clara responded that they had "seen the news reports of the Bush/Gore exchange on television" and that she recalled that their use of "snippy" in fact related to that report.

watching television when Clara pointed out Bush, who was giving a speech, to Jason. In this interaction it is Clara who indicates that Bush is associated with people who are "bad."

(6) Clara and Jason watching TV

1	Clara:	That's the man that Daddy doesn't like.
2	Jason:	Who.
3		Where.
4	Clara:	That guy.
5		Bu- GW.
6		*<coughs>*
7	Jason:	/Is that the guy?/
8	Clara:	That's the one.
9	Jason:	Oh . . how come they're all clapping about him.
10	Clara:	Um,
11 →		I guess some people like him,
12 →		but- but I think—*<sighs>*
13 →		I think it's the hunters,
14 →		and the pe- the other people who don't know any better.

Here we see Clara using the phrase *the man that Daddy doesn't like* to refer to Bush. This serves as an intertextual tie to the conversation on Election Day morning (shown in excerpt 1) where she describes Gore as *Daddy's friend*, reinforcing the family identity across interactions. In addition, a contrast is co-constructed by Jason and Clara between "us" and "them," as the people who are clapping for Bush on television are referred to as *hunters* and *other people who don't know any better*. It is important to note that elsewhere in the tapes, Clara likens hunters to "murderers" and "thieves" in conversation with Jason; thus the word "hunters" has negative connotations in this family, in particular for Clara (LeVine, this volume, discusses this at some length). Thus, seeing Bush on television and Jason's subsequent questions allow Clara the opportunity to talk about Bush and work toward constructing the political aspect of the family's identity by associating Bush with people who are in opposition with the family's belief system. This again is reminiscent not only of van Dijk (1987) but also Ochs et al. (1992).

In sum, through characterizing Bush and those who vote for him negatively, this family takes a stance against Bush that contributes to the construction of their family identity as Democrats and Gore supporters. Though it is Clara and Neil who participate most in portraying Bush in a negative light, this activity is also dependent on Jason's participation, as his parents frequently explain Bush's shortcomings to their son. Additionally, in one interaction not shown in this analysis, Jason explicitly asks if Bush is "mean," while in another he asks about the "bad things" Bush has done. Thus, all family members create and re-create the family identity by participating in negatively evaluating Bush and those who are associated with him, while also reaffirming their own shared beliefs as a family.

Positioning Family Members as Democrats

A final strategy the family uses to create their identity as Democrats and supporters of Al Gore is the parents' positioning Jason as a Democrat and themselves as Democrats in his presence. In excerpt 7, members of the family are at the polls, talking to each other and Neil's friend Ellen when Neil asks Jason about what kind of ice cream he voted for at school in the favorite ice cream flavor voting:

(7) At the polls

1	Neil:	Well did you- what did you pick?
2		What kind of ice cream [did you vote on?]
3	Jason:	[U:::m] vanilla [and] chocolate.
4	Neil:	[Van—]
5		You picked BOTH of them?!
6	Clara:	Ye:s.
7		[/He had-/] strawberry was the odd man out.
8	Neil:	[Oh.]
9 →		Well see he's a good Democrat,
10 →		he votes several times.
11		[<laughs>]
12	Clara:	[<laughs>]
13	Ellen:	[<laughs>]

((8 lines elided: talking about ice cream))

22	Neil:	Who–and who did you vote for →
23 ·		in the election for President.
24		((short pause))
25 →	Jason:	Gore.
26	Ellen:	<chuckles>
27	Clara:	<laughs>

28	Ellen:	See,
29 →		you're raising a Democrat.
30		[Me too.]
31	Neil:	[Jeez.]
32	Clara:	[<*laughs*>]
33	Ellen:	((*to a voter*)) Hi.
34	Neil:	((*joking, to a voter*)) They've got him brainwashed already.

Here, Neil explains Jason's voting for two "candidates" in the ice cream election at his school by positioning his son as *a good Democrat*, humorously implying that Jason would vote several times for a Democratic candidate in the presidential election if he could. Jason supports this positioning by saying that he voted for Gore in the school presidential election. Interestingly, Ellen joins in describing Jason as a Democrat, thus displaying awareness of the family identity and her support of it. She also creates an alignment of sameness as she says she is also *raising a Democrat: me too.*

Though this is the only interaction where Jason is explicitly positioned as a Democrat, elsewhere in the tapes, Neil tells numerous people at work about how he woke up at a quarter to five in the morning to put up signs for the Democrats, while Clara laments to Jackie on the telephone about the great number of campaign signs in her neighborhood for Republican candidates. As shown previously, people who reacted negatively to Jason saying that Bush got elected because he *drinks alcohol and drives* in line at the polls were identified by Clara as being Republicans. Taken together, these interactions align family members, including Jason, as members of the Democratic Party and distance the family not only from George W. Bush but also from other members of the Republican Party.

Political Identity and Family Cohesion

I have thus far shown how the family's use of referring terms for the candidates, repeated discussion of Bush's 1976 arrest for drunk driving, negative comments about Bush and the people who are associated with him, and identification with the Democratic Party work toward creating their political identity. In this section, I give one example that shows how this identity works as a cohesive device in this family. Specifically, I demonstrate how it works to bring about family harmony in the course of an argument.

Excerpt 8 illustrates how the identity as supporters of Gore binds Clara, Neil, and Jason together. Prior to the start of this excerpt, in which the family is driving to a party, Neil and Clara began arguing about who does more household chores (see Tannen [2006] for an analysis of this extended argument). The argument progressed to Clara saying she was tense because if Bush were elected, her place of work would be dramatically affected. She also worried aloud that Neil would not provide the support that she would need if a Republican were to take the White House. Jason, silent throughout the argument and seemingly on the verge of tears when he does speak, offers a solution: that Clara do some things to help Neil and Neil do some things to help Clara.

(8) During an argument

1	Jason:	Mom,
2	Clara:	What, Jason?
3	Jason:	How about you guys pick, u:m . um . um see what,
4		you guys want,
5		um . um,
6		like, i:f Daddy wants YOU to do something,
7		and you want HIM to do something,
8		you can both do it, okay?
9	Clara:	<sing-song> [That's a GREAT idea,] Jason!>
10	Neil:	[That's a good idea, Jason.]
11	Clara:	<chuckles>
12	Neil:	Hey Jason?
13	Clara:	<sing-song> Jason has the PERFECT idea!>
14	Neil:	Hey Jason?
15	Jason:	Hm?
16	Neil:	I'll tell you what I'll do,
17		I'll try to support your Mommy,
18		okay?
19	Clara:	Yea:h.
20 →	Neil:	Even if that . →
21 →		alcoholic [car-driving man becomes the President,]
22	Clara:	[<laughs>]
23		[<laughs>]
24	Jason:	[<laughs>]
25	Neil:	[<laughing> okay?>]
26 →		[[If W becomes the President, okay?]]

27	Clara:	[[<laughs>]]
28	Jason:	[[<laughs>]]
29	Neil:	<chuckles>
30	Jason:	[<laughs>]
31	Clara:	[<laughs>]
32 →	Neil:	If it's Al Gore,
33 →		we'll just have one big party,
34		okay?
35	Jason:	[<laughs>]
36	Clara:	[<laughs>]

This excerpt shows that the family's shared political identity is indeed shared, and that it functions as a type of "glue" that pulls the family back together in the course of an argument. Note that all family members laugh when Neil draws on what Becker (1995) would call "prior text" in referring to Bush as "that alcoholic car-driving man." This phrase intertextually reformulates Jason's utterance at the polls (*He was drinking alcohol and then they were driving*) and the constructed dialogue attributed to Jason in Clara's narrative about the results of Jason's school election (*He drinks alcohol and drives*). Though Neil directs his comments to Jason, Clara is an intended overhearer. Furthermore, Neil suggests that a Gore victory would be a reason for the family (*we*, line 33) to have a party. The simultaneous laughter that follows Neil's comments works toward aligning interactants with one another. Though the argument resurfaces later that day when Jason is not present, the shared laughter in this conversation creates affiliation between the participants. In doing so, it references prior family interactions where shared opinions were expressed and humor was present (i.e., where Jason said at the polls that Bush won the election because he drinks alcohol and drives). Mention of Bush in this way works to momentarily realign family members during a heated disagreement between parents.

Discussion

Throughout their week of taping, Neil and Clara frequently talk about the election to each other and explain the election and describe the candidates to Jason. Jason too sometimes starts conversations about the election, for example, by asking questions while the family is watching updates on television or listening to news radio. Though many of the conversations show the parents socializing Jason into their political views, Jason also shows himself to be an active participant in the family's discourse on politics.

My analysis illustrates how all family members co-construct the political aspect of their shared identity: a family identity, like the identities of individual interlocutors, is created moment by moment in interaction through the use of specific linguistic devices. Thus this study builds on and adds to past work examining how individuals construct their identities as family members (e.g., Schiffrin 1996, 2000, 2002; Petraki 2002). In addition, in highlighting Jason's active role in this process and taking the perspective advocated by Ochs, Smith & Taylor (1996), Pontecorvo & Fasulo (1999), and others that socialization is multi-directional, my analysis builds on prior work in the area of socialization in general and political socialization in the family context in particular (e.g., Liebes & Ribak 1991).

First, this study shows that use of referring terms, repetition, narratives (the "drinking alcohol and driving" story), constructed dialogue, and laughter work to create alignments or stances in interaction that create an aspect of one family's identity. My analysis illustrates how a group identity may be constructed through many of the same linguistic means as individual identities, while also showing how every family member participates in constructing this identity. All family members use referring terms for the candidates that show positive alignment with Gore and rejection of Bush. Clara and Neil participate in creating the family political identity by taking on the alignment of "explainers" to Jason, while Jason typically participates by asking questions and responding to his parents' prompting. Clara and Neil also tell the story about Jason at the polls to other people, something Jason does not do. All family members laugh at appropriate moments in discussions about Bush. Though each family member participates in different ways, they together succeed in constructing a shared family political identity through their individual interactional contributions.

Second, the analysis highlights how in collaboratively constructing the shared family identity, family members simultaneously—and necessarily—socialize one another and themselves into it by employing linguistic practices that accomplish "cultural reproduction" (Pontecorvo & Fasulo 1999:315). In this way, it adds to the work of Liebes and her colleagues, who considered interview data, and to Ribak's (1997) and Liebes & Ribak's (1991) suggestion that children are active participants in socialization and also can influence the views of their parents. Furthermore, whereas these prior studies and many others have considered how adolescents are socialized into the political outlook of their parents, this analysis has focused on a much younger child. In fact, Liebes et al. (1991:248) suggest that parental impact on political socialization reaches its maximum before the age of twelve, and Schwartz (1975) suggests that much political learning takes place between the ages of three and six. Though identity construction is the primary focus of my analysis, my findings support the suggestion that socialization into political outlook begins when children are quite young and indicate that even young children participate in constructing and socializing others into this aspect of the family's identity.

Third, because this analysis illustrates how a family's *shared identity* is constructed, it contributes to a topic that has received less attention than the construction of individual family identities such as "mother" and "father." Whereas prior studies have effectively illustrated how individuals create their identities in their families in interviews (Schiffrin 1996, 2000, 2002), and in family dinner table conversation (Erickson 1990; Ochs & Taylor 1992), this study focuses on the construction of family members' shared identity. It illustrates how linguistic devices and conversational moves (such as prompting) contribute to this construction, thus drawing on and extending past work in this area.

Fourth, this chapter adds to the relatively few prior studies that view language as a means by which families create a culture or identity (e.g., Varenne 1992; Blum-Kulka 1997). These prior studies focus primarily on ethnic or national identity. My analysis builds on this body of work in exploring an identity that is political, while also analyzing specific linguistic devices the family uses to create this identity. This study additionally shows how interactions with outsiders to the family (e.g., family friends Ellen and Jackie) contribute to creating the family's identity. Conversations with individuals outside the family provide family members the opportunity to reaffirm the family identity amongst themselves and to publicly exhibit a coherent family political identity that includes even the family's youngest member.

Hamilton (1996), in her study of the identity of an Alzheimer's patient as it is constructed interactionally, notes that identities are perhaps best understood not as they are constructed in individual interactions (which she refers to as *intratextually*), but as they are constructed across interactions involving the same interlocutors (*intertextually*). Thus my analysis not only moves outside of the family dinner table and interview setting to consider family discourse and the construction of identity, but it also takes an intertextual perspective. In drawing excerpts from a number of interactions occurring across the course of six days, this study has shown how disparate interactions are related through the use of repeated referring terms (e.g., "W" to refer to George W. Bush, "Daddy's friend" to refer to Al Gore) as well as repeated topics (Bush's drunk-driving arrest) and themes (e.g., "bad" people who support Bush). In these conversations, linguistic devices creating alignments appear and reappear, including referring terms, repetition, storytelling, constructed dialogue, and laughter. Though in isolation each interaction that touches on the election puts forth a piece of the family's political views, when taken together, they paint a clearer "portrait" of the shared political identity that members of this family collaboratively construct.

References

Adelswärd, Viveka, and Claes Nilholm. 2000. Who is Cindy? Aspects of identity work in a teacher-parent-pupil talk at a special school. Text 20(4).545–568.
Aronsson, Karin. 1998. Identity-in-interaction as social choreography. Research on Language and Social Interaction 31(1).75–89.
Becker, A. L. 1995 [1982]. Beyond translation: Esthetics and language description. Reprinted in Beyond translation: Essays towards a modern philology, 297–315. Ann Arbor: University of Michigan Press.
Becker, A. L. 1995 [1984]. Biography of a sentence: A Burmese proverb. Reprinted in Beyond translation: Essays towards a modern philology, 185–210. Ann Arbor: University of Michigan Press.
Blum-Kulka, Shoshana. 1997. Dinner talk: Cultural patterns of sociability and socialization in family discourse. Mahwah, N.J.: Erlbaum.
Byers, Lori A. 1997. Telling the stories of our lives: Relational maintenance as illustrated through family communication. Athens, Ohio: Ohio University dissertation.
Connell, R. W. 1972. Political socialization in the American family: The evidence re-examined. Public Opinion Quarterly 36(3).323–333.
Ellis, Yvette. 1997. Laughing together: Laughter as a feature of affiliation in French conversation. Language Studies 7.147–161.
Erickson, Frederick. 1990. The social construction of discourse coherence in a family dinner table conversation. Conversational organization and its development, ed. Bruce Dorval, 207–238. Norwood, N.J.: Ablex.
Goodwin, Charles, and Marjorie Harness Goodwin. 1992. Assessments and the construction of context. Rethinking context: Language as an interactive phenomenon, ed. Alessandro Duranti and Charles Goodwin, 147–189. Cambridge: Cambridge University Press.
Hamilton, Heidi E. 1996. Intratextuality, intertextuality, and the construction of identity as patient in Alzheimer's disease. Text 16(1).61–90.
Ichilov, Orit. 1990. Introduction. Political socialization, citizenship education, and democracy, ed. Orit Ichilov, 1–8. New York: Teachers College Press.

Jennings, M. Kent, and Richard G. Niemi. 1968. The transmission of political values from parent to child. American Political Science Review 62.169–184.

Liebes, Tamar, and Rivka Ribak. 1991. A mother's battle against TV news: A case study of political socialization. Discourse & Society 2(2).203–222.

Liebes, Tamar, and Rivka Ribak. 1992. The contribution of family culture to political participation, political outlook, and its reproduction. Communication Research 19(5).618–641.

Liebes, Tamar, Elihu Katz, and Rivka Ribak. 1991. Ideological reproduction. Political Behavior 13(3).237–252.

Miller, Mark Crispin. 2001. The Bush dyslexicon: Observations of a national disorder. New York: W. W. Norton & Company.

Miller, Peggy J., Randolph Potts, Heidi Fung, and Judith Mintz. 1990. Narrative practices and the social construction of self in childhood. American Ethnologist 17.297–311.

Ochs, Elinor. 1993. Constructing social identity: A language socialization perspective. Research on Language and Social Interaction 26(3).287–306.

Ochs, Elinor, and Carolyn Taylor. 1992. Mothers' role in the everyday reconstruction of "Father knows best." Locating power: Proceedings of the Second Berkeley Women and Language Conference, ed. Kira Hall, Mary Bucholtz, and Birch Moonwomon, 447–462. Berkeley: Berkeley Woman and Language Group.

Ochs, Elinor, Clotilde Pontecorvo, and Alessandra Fasulo. 1996. Socializing taste. Ethnos 61(1/2).7–46.

Ochs, Elinor, Ruth Smith, and Carolyn Taylor. 1996. Detective stories at dinnertime: Problem-solving through co-narration. The matrix of language: Contemporary linguistic anthropology, ed. Donald Brenneis and Ronald K. S. Macaulay, 39–55. Boulder, Colo.: Westview Press.

Ochs, Elinor, Carolyn Taylor, Dina Rudolph, and Ruth Smith. 1992. Storytelling as a theory-building activity. Discourse Processes 15(1).37–72.

Petraki, Eleni. 2002. The play of identities in Cypriot-Australian family storytelling. Narrative Inquiry 11(2).335–362.

Pontecorvo, Clotilde, and Alessandra Fasulo. 1997. Learning to argue in family shared discourse: The reconstruction of past events. Discourse, tools, and reasoning: Essays on situated cognition, ed. Lauren B. Resnick, Roger Saljo, Clotilde Pontecorvo, and Barbara Burge, 406–442. Berlin: Springer.

Pontecorvo, Clotilde, and Alessandra Fasulo. 1999. Planning a typical Italian meal: A family reflection on culture. Culture & Psychology 5(3).313–335.

Quirk, Randolph, and Sidney Greenbaum. 1973. A concise grammar of contemporary English. Fort Worth, Ind.: Harcourt Brace Jovanovich College Publishers.

Ribak, Rivka. 1997. Socialization as and through conversation: Political discourse in Israeli families. Comparative Education Review 41(1).71–96.

Schieffelin, Bambi B. 1986. Teasing and shaming in Kaluli children's interactions. Language socialization across cultures, ed. Bambi B. Schieffelin and Elinor Ochs, 165–181. Cambridge: Cambridge University Press.

Schieffelin, Bambi B. 1990. The give and take of everyday life: Language socialization of Kaluli children. Cambridge: Cambridge University Press.

Schiffrin, Deborah. 1996. Narrative as self-portrait: Sociolinguistic constructions of identity. Language in Society 25.167–203.

Schiffrin, Deborah. 2000. Mother/daughter discourse in a Holocaust oral history: "Because then you admit that you're guilty." Narrative Inquiry 10(1).1–44.

Schiffrin, Deborah. 2002. Mother and friends in a Holocaust life story. Language in Society 31.309–353.

Schwartz, Sandra Kenyon. 1975. Preschoolers and politics. New directions in political socialization, ed. David C. Schwartz and Sandra Kenyon Schwartz, 229–253. New York: The Free Press.

Stacey, Barrie. 1978. Political socialization in western society: An analysis from a life-span perspective. New York: St. Martin's Press.

Tannen, Deborah. 2007 [1989]. Talking voices: Repetition, dialogue, and imagery in conversational discourse. Cambridge: Cambridge University Press.

Tannen, Deborah. 1990. You just don't understand: Women and men in conversation. New York: Ballantine Books.

Tannen, Deborah. 2006. Intertextuality in interaction. Reframing family arguments in public and private. Text & Talk 26(4/5).597–617.

Tulviste, Tiia, Luule Mizera, Boel de Geer, and Marja-Terttu Tryggvason. 2002. Regulatory comments as tools of family socialization: A comparison of Estonian, Swedish and Finnish mealtime interaction. Language in Society 31(5).655–678.

van Dijk, Teun A. 1987. Communicating racism: Ethnic prejudice in thought and talk. Newbury Park, Beverly Hills, London, and New Delhi: Sage.

Varenne, Hervé. 1992. Ambiguous harmony: Family talk in America. Norwood, N.J.: Ablex.

Whyte, Jean. 1999. Political socialization in a divided society: The case of Northern Ireland. Roots of civic identity: International perspectives on community service and activism in youth, ed. Miranda Yeats and James Youniss, 157–177. Cambridge: Cambridge University Press.

PHILIP LEVINE

ten

Sharing Common Ground: The Role of Place
Reference in Parent-Child Conversation

I t is difficult to imagine a facet of experience with a greater influence on human conduct than occupying a place in the world.[1] Though conscious reflection on the impact of surroundings might be infrequent and fleeting, the fact is that we are never without place. In one respect we are always "watching where we are going"—evaluating our physical surroundings as we negotiate our encounters with people, other creatures, and objects. The effect of place is so much a part of experience, in fact, that it is easy to overlook its importance. In spite of the ever-present need to respond to surroundings, or perhaps because of it, there may be nothing more easily taken for granted.

This study examines how place reference contributes to creating interpersonal connections and understandings of family identity in talk between members of one family who participated in the Work and Family Project.

1. I would like to thank Deborah Tannen for numerous helpful comments on earlier drafts of this chapter. I would also like to thank Anne Kelly Knowles for comments on the original and revised drafts. The ideas for this chapter were first developed during her seminar in cultural geography. Finally, my thanks to Neil for his kindness and patience during the observation phase of this project and for his thoughtful replies to questions throughout. Any errors or omissions are my own.

In what follows I look at a few moments of interaction between a 4-year-10-month-old boy and his parents when awareness of surroundings surfaces as a topic in speech. These are brief verbal exchanges of the most ordinary kind: questions about and observations of material surroundings. Despite their commonplace nature, they provide evidence for at least three ways place reference establishes interpersonal connection and creates ties of commonality binding family members together. First, talk has navigational and interactional functions: there is an impulse to orient oneself to surroundings, expressed as a desire to verify that perceptions are shared by others. Second, place reference is a reminder that all activity is situated somewhere and that people, their activities, and the material surroundings in which actions unfold are interconnected and value-laden. Finally, place and talk are mutually constitutive. Place is a resource for talk, providing the context and the content for conversational exchange. In turn, talk about place holds specific locales up for contemplation and imbues them with the thoughts, attitudes, and experiences that make them meaningful.

Linguistics, Geography, and Place

Place as a factor affecting the use of language has been a central concern in sociolinguistic analysis from its outset. Variation studies evaluate linguistic alternations within and among different locales. Macrosociolinguistic analysis often focuses on whole regions: the issues of multilingualism, language contact and conflict, or the legislation and implementation of policy regarding language and nationality. Closer to the approach taken in this paper are studies in which place plays a role in conversational style (e.g., Tannen 1981) or serves as the context for the study of narrative (e.g., Johnstone 1990; Finnegan 1998). This study also links in a general way to the concept of "setting" as it is articulated in the ethnography of communication (e.g., Gumperz & Hymes 1972; Saville-Troike 1989).

The approaches to linguistic analysis mentioned above generally conceive of place in static terms, where spatial boundaries describe an area within which linguistic phenomena tend to occur. This is not to say that the influence of place has been overlooked. The fundamentally emplaced nature of all interaction is implicit in much linguistic research as well as in research that has had an influence on interactional sociolinguistics. The sizeable body of literature on deictic terms of place reflects this. A number of studies make the connection between features of the material environment and its impact on discourse more explicit. For example, Erickson (1982) includes a discussion of how objects (food, dishes, etc.) are taken up by family members as a topical resource in dinner table conversation. Streeck (1996) examines a negotiation between two businessmen in which products (cookies and their packaging) are taken up as symbolic tools, developing in the unfolding interaction as integral components of the communicative process. A related current of research has been undertaken recently in which the material features of context are seen as central to social action. Scollon & Scollon's (2003) "geosemiotics" analyzes signs in place, how they are taken up in human action, and how the resulting meanings can only be understood as an outcome of where and when these actions and signs are placed within the material world. In a similar vein, de Saint-Georges (2004) investigates how talk about place transforms largely unnoticed features of the physical environment into resources for "motivated action." Objects are thus situated in place and constitutive of the built environment.

This chapter shares with the aforementioned studies an interest in how discourse is linked to immediate physical surroundings. It differs in its focus on the values reflected by talk about place. My aim is to combine the methods of interactional sociolinguistics with the conception of place developed within the field of humanistic geography. One of the founders of this field, Yi-Fu Tuan (1977:4), defines place as "an organized world of meaning" where human needs are satisfied and where direct experiences and thoughtful reflection lend places their particular value. "Places" differ from "spaces" by virtue of the direct engagement of the senses, which leads to emotional attachment, or what Tuan calls "topophilia," "the affective bond between people and place or setting" (1974:4; see also Sime 1995). A closely related concept explored within geography and anthropology is "sense of place," roughly defined as the particular character of surroundings that comes to be known through repeated contact: "a lively awareness of the familiar environment, a ritual repetition, a sense of fellowship based on a shared experience" (Jackson 1994:159; see also Relph 1976; Feld & Basso 1996).

Both geographers and linguists have taken note of the important relationship that exists between language and place. In an overview of the field of cultural geography, Peter Jackson (1989:169) argues that "[a] revitalized cultural geography will need to explore the way that language reflects and reinforces social boundaries, constituted in space and time." In "Language and the Making of Place," Tuan (1991:684) notes that despite a central focus on how places are made, geographers have neglected "the explicit approval of the crucial role of language, even though without speech humans cannot even begin to formulate ideas, discuss them, and translate them into action that culminates in a built place."

In an article comparing conceptions of place in the fields of variationist sociolinguistics and geography, Barbara Johnstone (2004) considers how sociolinguists might incorporate the kinds of questions geographers have raised about the human dimension of place. She comments that within the phenomenological perspective associated with humanistic geography, "speakers are seen as constructing place as they experience physical and social space, and different speakers may orient to place, linguistically, in very different ways and for very different purposes" (66).

The link between language and places as sites of meaning is treated explicitly in the work of linguistic anthropologist Keith Basso (1983, 1996). His analysis of Western Apache narrative demonstrates how storytelling regulates social behavior by calling to mind morally charged events played out within specific sites. Basso's work touches on an attribute that has been observed in a variety of disciplines: the tendency of places to become associated with the actions carried out within them. It is a quality the philosopher Edward Casey (1996) refers to as "gathering." Places gather by fixing together a particular, recognizable assembly of physical properties and by embracing "experiencing bodies"—sensing persons—as part of their character. Gathering is most keenly experienced as the release of a unique set of memories, sentiments, and sensations when returning to a familiar locale.

The link between place and activity has also been observed by sociologists. For example, Erving Goffman, in "The Neglected Situation,"[2] calls for a more principled investigation of the conditioning effects of material settings on speech behavior, a notion echoed in the following comment made by Adam Kendon (1977:180) in connection with the relationship between place and action: "Activity is always located. A person doing something always does it somewhere and [their] doing always entails a relationship to the space which has in it objects or people with which the doing is concerned."

In the excerpts of conversation between one child and his mother and father that I discuss below, the "doing" is taking stock of the social land-

---

2. It might be noted that three of Goffman's books, *Behavior in Public Places, Relations in Public*, and *Asylums*, all deal with actions determined by the places in which they occur.

scape, evaluating the people and activities unfolding before the inquisitive eyes of the child.

A more direct mapping of connections between place and language within linguistic anthropology sees the phonology of a given language as shaped by features of the perceived landscape. Gell (1995), for example, argues that the forest habitat of the Umeda in Papua New Guinea privileges the auditory sense to such a degree that the phonological inventory of the language mirrors sounds in the physical environment. This questioning of the arbitrary relationship between sound and meaning has also been advanced by Weiner (1991) whose ethnography of the Foi of Papua New Guinea is based on the relationship between space and language. Oppositions exist throughout the Foi language (open vs. closed, past vs. present), reflecting an iconic relationship that can be tied to all manner of Foi expression, including poetry and the organization of living space.

Psychological studies reveal that environment has pervasive effects on social development, well-being, and mental performance. In a study of recovering hospital patients, Ulrich (1984) showed that a view of natural settings from the windows of hospital rooms contributed to quicker recovery than was the case for patients in rooms with views of adjacent buildings (see also Jasnoski 1992). Environmental psychologists Proshansky et al. (1995:88) challenge the assumption that the formation of self-identity is solely an outcome of social contact. They propose the notion of "place-identity," in which "the subjective sense of self is defined and expressed not simply by one's relationship to other people, but also by one's relationships to the various physical settings that define and structure day-to-day life."

An interesting extension of place-identity is Maria Cattell's (1999) analysis of complaint discourse among the elderly in western Kenya and the neighborhood of Olney in Philadelphia. Here she touches on a merging of place and identity in conditions where longstanding relationships to surroundings undergo radical change, leading to what she calls a "person-environment dissonance . . . the sense of unease that follows from being in an environment which has changed so much that one feels like a stranger" (299). The residents of Olney complained about shop signs in languages other than English, a decline in neighborhood cleanliness, and "behavior that impinged on physical space and privacy" (309). Through complaint, Olney residents "provided each other with comfort and sympathy, a sense of shared memory and identity" (312).

Within the paradigm of conversational analysis, Schegloff (1972) looks at "locational formulations" demonstrating that place reference is conditioned by such factors as where speakers are located relative to one another, how they are situated vis-à-vis the places being referenced, and what assumptions speakers can make about a given region, topic, or activity under discussion. In an experimental study, Schober (1995) demonstrates that speakers tend to adopt the perspective of their addressee when describing locations, possibly as a way to "minimize effort" for their partner. Similar studies based on cognitive models of language focus on the range of spatial distinctions languages make (e.g., Talmy 1983). Linde & Labov (1975) analyze the description of apartment layouts as a method for evaluating links between conceptualization of space and its syntactic representation. The authors comment that description of apartments is ideal for their study because "people are extremely interested in talking about their apartments" (925). Labov & Linde's observation is notable because it states most directly what is suggested by all of the studies I have cited. In ways that are varied and often quite subtle, surroundings matter. Places shape our early psychological development and our ongoing states of mind; they determine turns in physical movement just as they do turns of phrase. As I looked at the transcripts in this study I saw the effects of place on how talk took shape. I found that in several instances, talk about place established "common ground": shared perceptions of surroundings that anchor parent and child to the physical world and provide a context for the communication of values.

In what follows, I examine three excerpts from a single family—Neil, Clara, and their son Jason—to demonstrate how common ground is established through talk about place. Two of the excerpts are from conversations that occur on a day when Jason is ill. On that day, Neil and Jason make food, watch television, and run errands. In the third excerpt, Jason and Clara have a kind of debate over behavior associated with a neighbor whose home plays a significant role in Jason's talk with his father. Although there is no place reference in this third excerpt, it shows how the values associated with place develop from previous interactions. In these interchanges, talk is implicitly or explicitly affected by where the talk takes place. Moreover, the content of the talk is often about surroundings: objects in the immediate environment, people and landmarks observed from cars, recollections of interactions that revolve around where the interactions took place. Talk about place provides a way for family members to share common ground by establishing a common perspective with other family members as they move through time and space.

Talk about Place in Parent-Child Interaction

Conversation and the Impulse for Orientation

A sense of an unmarked, normative place in which "home" is situated—
a sense of neighborhood—is important for families. The following segment illustrates how talk about place addresses a desire to make sense of
the complex and often changing contours of the neighborhood environment. In this excerpt Neil and Jason are standing in the driveway but have
not yet entered Neil's car. Jason has just expressed interest in visiting his
friend Kenneth. Neil reminds Jason that he is sick and needs to recover
before he visits friends. Jason then notices some activity across the street:

(1) 1 Neil: Better feel better . toMOrrow.
    2   I want you to go to DANCE class tomorrow.
    3 Jason: Hey what's THAT guy doing there.
    4 Neil: There that's called the Merry Maids.
    5   They clean the house for- for Patty and Fred over there.

The spontaneous quality of Jason's comments suggests that reference to
place grows out of a desire to orient oneself to new conditions in the environment. Neil's comments (1–2), *Better feel better . toMOrrow/I want
you to go to DANCE class tomorrow,* reference future activity and reflect
his ongoing concern with Jason's illness. They are the kind of remarks Neil
has been making throughout the day, as he checks on the state of his son's
health, gives him medication, and suggests different meal options. I include Neil's turns to show that Jason's response (3), *Hey what's THAT guy
doing there,* has no connection to them. Something in the environment
has seized Jason's attention.

Jason's use of the exclamation *Hey* and emphasis on *THAT* indicate sur-
prise and perhaps mild alarm in response to a disturbance of expectations
about the who and where of his neighborhood. Jason explicitly references
the local environment while looking to his father for help in explaining
the unfamiliar, evidence of Jason's interest in and concern about the activities and people surrounding home. Jason's question may be as much
an inquiry into the nature of the Merry Maids' activity (the duties they
perform as professional house cleaners) as it is a territorial response to the
appearance of strangers. Neil's response confirms the inextricable tie between events and the place in which they unfold. To mention the Merry

Maids almost demands some mention of the actions conditioned by the social relationships and physical contours connected to their appearance in this scene.

Jason's question regarding the Merry Maids also reflects what Proshansky et al. (1995:96) call the "recognition function" of place-identity, "the affirmation of the belief that the properties of his or her day-to-day physical world are unchanging." This may be one of the primary functions of talk about place: it serves to check impressions about the world against the impressions of others by prompting affirmation (or challenge) from our interlocutors. To talk about place is to make public a point of view. In this case it prompts a response by Neil calculated to restore normalcy to the scene by connecting the unknown to the known. Further, Neil's use of simple present (line 5, *They clean the house for- for Patty and Fred over there*) serves to situate the cleaners' actions and presence in the neighborhood as general, habitual.

Not to be overlooked in all of this is the location of Neil and Jason as this exchange unfolds. Jason has just emerged from the familiarity and enclosed security of home to the less known and more ambiguously delimited world of neighborhood. There is a parallel social transition, from the closeness of family to a less certain world of public and private, foreign and familiar that characterizes relationship to neighbors.

A Neighborhood Inventory

Neil and Jason address this transition from inside to outside by taking a kind of inventory of the neighbors and their homes. This serves to situate their family within the larger social landscape of the visible neighborhood, as I illustrate in the following excerpt, a continuation of the one just discussed. Neil and Jason are still standing in the driveway just prior to entering Neil's car, looking across to the homes on the opposite side of the street. Jason initiates the interchange by indicating the house next to the one they've just been discussing:

(2) 6 Jason: And that's a bad guy house?
     7 Neil: Well he's a hunter.
     8 Jason: Oh hunter.
     9 Neil: Yeah Hunter Guy.
     10 Jason: Oh.

11		Does he live next to um . ?
12	Neil:	Patty and Fred?
13		Yep he [lives] next to Patty and Fred and Zack.
14	Jason:	[Uh huh]
15		And . and
16		Who's that over there?
17		No I mean next=
18	Neil:	=And then [that's where]
19	Jason:	[to Kenneth's] house.
20	Neil:	Next to Kenneth's /house/
21		That's where Amy lives.

A neighborhood inventory begins with Jason's question (6), *And that's a bad guy house?* Neil confirms that Jason has properly identified the neighbor in question but offers another label: He's a "hunter" (7). Jason's response (8), *Oh hunter,* and Neil's follow up (9), *Yeah Hunter Guy,* form the focal point for the rest of the segment. The two collaborate on the naming of this troubling figure, combining Jason's *bad guy* (6) with Neil's *hunter* (7) to form *Hunter Guy* (9).

Through this kind of talk Neil and Jason provide spatial emplacement for their family within the neighborhood; in addition, Jason's inquiries provide an opportunity to assert a family profile, a shared identity that can be affirmed by contrast or comparison to others within the neighborhood. The exchange involving the hunter demonstrates this. And when Jason asks, *Does he live next to um . ?* (11), Neil completes his turn (12), *Patty and Fred?* and adds a third name (13), *Yep he lives next to Patty and Fred and Zack,* effectively filling out the household by including Jason's counterpart, Patty and Fred's son Zack. A parity is thus achieved, with the house directly opposite Neil and Jason mirroring them in physical placement as well as family composition.

Jason's next question (16), *Who's that over there?* is followed by Neil's identification of another home and neighbor (in this case Jason's babysitter), *That's where Amy lives* (21). The words Jason and his father apply to this scene thus accomplish the interactional goal of confirming a shared perspective, evident in the use of back channels ([14] *Uh huh*) and affirmations of Jason's perceptions (e.g., Neil's response [13] *Yep*).

Jason's questions could be construed in total as an attempt to address a situation in which expectations are disrupted by the appearance of something unfamiliar. Neil's answer (4), *There that's called the Merry Maids,* responds to the concern by identifying the strangers as house cleaners. Note that Neil links his turn to Jason's with the deictic *there* and then follows up with an explanation that connects purpose (house cleaning) with the home and occupants familiar to Jason: *They clean the house for-for Patty and Fred.* This brief segment demonstrates how father and son take note of and co-construct a layout for the neighborhood in order to address concerns about how the familiar world outside home is configured. Jason's impulse for orientation prompts an exchange in which language fixes landscape, and where father and son confirm their place within a freshly mapped network of place and person.

Place, Person, and Activity

The neighborhood inventory is notable for the fact that apart from the Merry Maids, the people Jason and Neil refer to are not actually visible at the time of speaking. In a sense, the homes serve as extensions of their occupants, allowing Jason to speak of a "who" (16) while looking at a "that."

Just as place and person merge, so too does activity become linked to the people and places where actions are carried out. Jason's first comment (3), *Hey what's THAT guy doing there,* reflects a concern with what is appropriate according to location. (He could have simply asked, "Who's that?" or "Who's over there?") Neil's response ([4–5] *There that's called the Merry Maids/They clean the house for- for Patty and Fred over there*) responds to this concern by identifying the Merry Maids according to their site-specific role. Jason's follow up question (6), *And that's a bad guy house?* prompts a response specifying the activity (hunting) that makes the neighbor "bad."[3]

The next interchange demonstrates how talk about place, person, and actions combines and accumulates to invest places with meaning. I begin with an excerpt that provides some explanation for Jason's focus on the Hunter Guy's house. Jason's characterization of the neighbor as *a bad guy* is linked to a conversation with his mother, Clara. Jason had kicked Clara during a temper tantrum. Now he wants a present and protests when his

---

3. During playback, Neil explained that it was his intention to discourage Jason from reflexively equating hunting with poor character. See note 6.

mother tells him presents aren't for boys who misbehave. Although Clara makes her disapproval clear to Jason, she conducts this exchange in a humorous key:

(3) 1 Clara: [*<high pitched>* There aren't] very many people →
     2   who would give a
     3   temper-tantrum-[thrower a present.>]
     4 Jason: [That's because] um he- he wants to get it .
     5   when he wants to,
     6   so then—
     7 Clara: Oh. *<high-pitched>* So- so that way—
     8   Well that's- that's an interesting thing,
     9   because /that way/ you'll be teaching that little boy→
    10   that no matter what he does,
    11   he can get a present!
    12 Jason: Yes.
    13 Clara: *<high-pitched>* He can be a bank-robber,
    14   [or a] KILLER,
    15 Jason: [No:.]
    16 Clara: [or a HUNTER,]
    17 Jason: [*<laughing>* No::.]
    18 Clara: [and you'll just] give him [nice presents!>]
    19 Jason: [No:!]   [No:!]
    20 Clara: [He—]
    21 Jason: [I'm not] gonna give him a present→
    22   if he's a killer or a hunter,
    23   [or a /robber—/]
    24 Clara: [What if he's] a mommy-kicker?
    25 Jason: *<laughs>* Yes.
    26 Clara: *<laughs loudly>* I don't think so!

When Clara suggests that most people would not reward temper-tantrum-throwers with presents (1–3), Jason replies with an amusingly tautological response: *he wants to get it/when he wants to* (4–5) whether he kicks his mother or not. Clara challenges this position by restating Jason's argument to expose its illogic (*because that way you'll be teaching that little boy that no matter what he does,/ he can get a present!*). When Jason replies affirmatively (12), Clara responds with a list of "bad" types: bank robbers, killers, and hunters—who would also be deserving of presents according to Jason's reasoning.[4] Clara has set up a context for judgment in which Jason is forced to consider his own behavior alongside wrongdoers of the worst kind.

There is nothing sharply accusatory in Clara's approach to this topic. The light-hearted nature of this exchange is evident in Jason and Clara's laughter (17, 25–6), playful overlap (14–21, 23–4), and Clara's use of high pitch (13–18). In addition, all of the wrongdoers are referred to in the third person by Clara and Jason, as if they were both considering a hypothetical situation unconnected to the event that precipitated their exchange. This humorous detachment is further emphasized through Clara's ironic meta-comment (8), *Well that's- that's an interesting thing*, as if to voice a stance that takes Jason's proposition seriously. This detachment and sense of play engages Jason as a willing participant in a debate over right and wrong in which his own behavior is subtly implicated.

The connection between this conversation and the exchange between Jason and Neil is the issue of hunters and how they are to be judged. In contrast to Neil, Clara portrays hunters as "bad guys" using a variety of devices to lump them in the same category with robbers and killers. This is achieved in part through the use of a list structure (13–14, 16). The list is evaluative (Tannen 2007 [1989]; Schiffrin 1994), each noun phrase (*a bank robber, a KILLER, a HUNTER*) providing another example of a type who (ironically) can be rewarded "no matter what he does." Note that "hunter" in the phrase *or a HUNTER* (16) is spoken with emphatic stress, is syntactically parallel to the phrase *or a KILLER* (14), and punctuates the list. The use of repetition, high pitch, and targeted emphasis contributes to a sense that hunters are as bad as robbers and killers.

Perhaps most importantly, Jason acknowledges the inclusion of hunters in Clara's trio of wrongdoers. He demonstrates his disapproval of bank robbers, killers, and hunters by responding with an emphatic *No!* when Clara asks if they deserve presents (13–19) and by following Clara's list with the pronouncement, *I'm not gonna give him a present if he's a killer or a hunter, or a robber* (21–23). Jason now enthusiastically declares a position aligned with Clara's in which hunters, killers, and robbers are all undeserving of reward.

4. This exchange should be read in light of Clara's attitude about hunters. In correspondence with one editor of this volume, Clara wrote that she is "a long time animal rights activist." Clara, Neil, and Jason are vegetarians.

In light of the negative assessment of hunters, it is no wonder that Jason has come to see the occupant of the house across the street as "a bad guy." In the following segment, Jason's reference to the hunter guy demonstrates how values connected to these categories are supported through report of his own actions. Below I return to the exchange between Neil and Jason, just as they finish their inventory (6–23) of the neighborhood:

(4) 21   Neil: That's where Amy lives.
      22   Jason: Oh yeah.
      23   I thought she lives next to him . too.
      24   We didn't go to the hunter's house for
      25   [trick or treating.]
      26   Neil: [For Halloween?]
      27   No.
      28   That's good.

After the brief mention of the *bad guy house* (6) that begins the neighborhood inventory, Jason comes full circle, now announcing to his father that he skipped the "hunter's house" on Halloween[5] (24–25). Jason's report recalls a scene in which the "bad guy house" comes forward as an extension of its occupant—a "bad house" to be avoided. Neil displays support for Jason's recollected action, in part by helping him to complete his sentence (26), *For Halloween?*, and through straightforward endorsement of his action (27–28), *No./ That's good.*[6] Reinforcement of family identity occurs through prior discourse about the hunter (of the kind discussed above in Jason's exchange with Clara), prior actions carried out in direct connection to the house, and Jason's verbal report of his experience there.

It would be difficult to measure the extent to which these factors—person, place, and activity—bear on the sense of place Jason develops as an outcome of these utterances. Homes can enclose and seclude, but they are also sites of social contact, where, in Jason's case, playmates (Kenneth) and babysitters (Amy) live. Homes are private realms with public

5. Halloween is an American holiday during which children, often accompanied by their parents, dress in costume and walk from house to house to collect candy from their neighbors.
6. Neil's comments, *No./ That's good,* are spoken under his breath. My first impression was that Neil spoke quietly to avoid making a spectacle of his dislike for the neighbor. During playback, however, Neil explained that his muted response was meant to acknowledge what Jason saw as a commendable action, without giving the impression that he viewed the neighbor in starkly negative light.

margins. Homes protect from intrusion and conceal private behavior. Yet we see our neighbors come and go; we evaluate them in part by the exterior face their homes project. Homes are extensions of the identities of their inhabitants. Who has not looked at their neighbor with curiosity, knowing they have made a transition from the private to the public and wondered about the world behind the walls from which they have emerged?

Jason's break into talk about the neighborhood expresses this kind of apprehension in a double sense: first in using this pause to register perceptions about surroundings in which he has a personal investment but also to express mild alarm. Jason looks to his father for help in settling what appears to be a disruption of what is known and familiar and in doing so initiates an exchange in which the visible surroundings undergo meaningful changes, new characters appear on the scene, the placement of known figures is reestablished, and a "bad guy house" becomes a "hunter's house."

The Place-talk Dialectic

In this section I discuss how the features of the physical landscape serve as a resource for talk and how talk in turn has its own influence on the particular contours of place. On one side of this mutually influential relationship between place and talk is "the seemingly magical idea that mere words can call places into being" (Tuan 1991:691). While on the one hand places trigger reflection, it is also true that a verbal response to particularities of a vast and fluid stream of impressions is what transforms space into place.

The following brief exchange between Neil and Jason provides an example of how impressions of place make their impression on talk and how, in turn, talk calls attention to place. This excerpt takes place not long after Neil and Jason's discussion of the neighborhood. Now they are in the car on the way to do errands. Neil mentions the plans they have once they reach their destination when Jason makes the following remark:

(5) 1 Jason: I saw a man gardening over there.
     2 Neil: Me too.
     3   ((*short pause*))
     4 Jason: Daddy.
     5 Neil: What.

6	Jason:	Um . /these people/
7		um . um back over there on the hill?
8		They have a um a- a um . um
9		water ground?
10		And they make put /they dig it/?
11		And- and they make it water come insi:de.
12		Water goes in the um ground.
13		Goes in the ground.
14		It goes on the dirt too.

Jason begins this set of turns by calling attention to people and how they interact with the landscape. His statement (1), *I saw a man gardening over there*, recalls his earlier interest in the figures appearing in his neighborhood and touches on the three related topics discussed in the previous section: person (*a man*), activity (*gardening*), and place (*over there*). Most importantly, this brief statement brings into consciousness a scene that has seized Jason's attention. It suspends a loosely organized combination of impressions, crafts them into language, and transforms them into a particular kind of place.

This period of interaction is also a case of place shaping a particular kind of talk. One factor bearing on this exchange that distinguishes it from the excerpts already discussed is that it takes place in a car. Jason's use of the past tense (*I saw*) reflects the influence of movement on his impressions. In addition to the scene that captures Jason's attention, the context of the car conditions his utterances, producing an ever-flowing series of new scenes.

Neil's response (2), *Me too*, acknowledges Jason's observation, although without a comment or follow-up question, the topic appears to vanish. Jason persists, however, this time with a summons *Daddy* (4), and a brief narrative-like account, beginning with *these people* and the place referent *hill* (6–7). He specifies location by referencing distance with the adverbial phrase *back there* and uses the locative prepositional phrase *on the hill* to place the figures in a particular orientation within the landscape. Despite the dysfluencies in this stretch of talk (e.g., *um . um* and *water ground*), Jason constructs a fairly elaborate picture, notable for his continued attention to place and action. What immediately emerges is a picture of human interaction with elemental materials and surfaces: *ground, hill, dirt,* and *water* (7–14). The mini-narrative follows a logic of cause and effect: people situated *on the hill* manipulate the earth (*they make put- /they dig it/*). His comments could be construed as fundamental to the concerns of geographers in that his focus is on how the landscape is altered by human practices. What distinguishes this segment is the overlap of form and content. While Jason speaks of the manipulation of landscape, he simultaneously shapes his surroundings into a distinct place through manipulation of language.

All of the preceding discussion touches on this dialectic. Neil and Jason's neighborhood inventory takes the particular form it does due to their physical orientation with respect to it. In turn, all of their talk feeds back into the impressions developed about place as an outcome of emergent talk.

Conclusion

Conversation could be seen as a way to navigate space: to make sense of, integrate with, or adapt to the landscape and its role in our ongoing experiences. As A. L. Becker writes: "Successful interaction with the environment—nowadays we would say context—is mediated for humans . . . by language" (1995:302). I began this chapter with a sample of conversation between a father and son to demonstrate how talk about place reflects an impulse for orientation: the desire to situate oneself within a physical and social landscape. With the help of his father, Jason locates his place vis-à-vis the homes of familiar people. I also suggested that this talk served an interactional function by confirming that perceptions and meanings connected to place are shared. As father and son review the layout of the visible neighborhood, they strengthen interpersonal bonds through the mediation of place.

I followed with a discussion of how linguistic processes assign value to place, suggesting that language calls to mind the links among people, place, and activity. Jason's curiosity about the "bad guy house" prompts his father to craft a more balanced image of the neighbor. In contrast to Neil's stance toward the neighbor who hunts, Clara engages Jason in a debate that positions hunters in a starkly negative light. Jason's own actions come into play in conversation: he seeks approval when he reports skipping the hunter's house during Halloween. Conversations about the neighbor, his house, and Jason's actions in connection to it combine to produce an emotionally charged locale.

I concluded by looking briefly at how place and talk stand in a mutually constitutive relationship. Places take on significance and bear lasting traces of the talk that goes on within them and about them and are also a resource for talk, providing the medium through which interlocutors share perceptions.

Jason's curiosity about place hints at a potentially rich area for research in family interaction. I noted in the introduction that we are always "in place." In *The Poetics of Space* (1964), Gaston Bachelard argues that home is the reference point for all future understandings of place, a model on which to conceive of and gauge relationships to place throughout the sensing person's life. The home is more than a familiar shelter and comes to represent "our first universe, a real cosmos in every sense of the word" (4). Bachelard insists on the primacy of the home as the locale that shapes our conceptions of place beyond the actual dwelling in which we first begin to understand and interact with the external environment. Moreover, the home not only is imbued with a particular set of memories and associations but also establishes a blueprint for the imagination itself. Jason's comments on the threshold of home, then, go beyond simple identification of a trouble spot in the neighborhood. They represent contact with a vital transition away from the social and spatial comforts home provides.

The interest Jason takes in his surroundings provides support for the notion that development of identity is not simply a matter of social contact but is also a response to environment. Jason situates himself and his family spatially with reference to places of social significance, and he signals his appreciation of the values permeating this social-spatial layout by reporting his own practices within the neighborhood. I have tried to show that contact with physical surroundings feeds into talk in ways that reveal and shape values, attitudes, and beliefs about the people who occupy those places and the activities carried out within them.

While this study has been anchored by the issue of place and its expression in ordinary conversation, it is important to note that these segments are examples of a particular kind of talk between parents and children. They are exchanges in which knowledge is transferred, where interchanges are crafted to package a particular kind of family identity. For Jason and Neil, this takes the form of question and answer sequences about the world outside of home and their family's place within that social landscape. In Jason's discussion with his mother, lessons about proper conduct are linked to activities known to be associated with a particular neighbor, the hunter. And so in these examples we have evidence that parent-child talk is where connections from the physical world to world view first begin to take form.

References

Bachelard, Gaston. 1964. The poetics of space. New York: Orion Press.

Basso, Keith H. 1983. "Stalking with stories": Names, places, and moral narratives among the Western Apache. Text, play, and story: The construction and reconstruction of self and society, ed. Edward M. Bruner, 19–55. Washington, D.C.: American Ethnological Society.

Basso, Keith H. 1996. Wisdom sits in places: Notes on a Western Apache landscape. Senses of place, ed. Stephen Feld and Keith H. Basso, 53–90. Santa Fe: School of American Research Press.

Becker, Alton L. 1995. Beyond translation: Essays toward a modern philology. Ann Arbor: University of Michigan Press.

Cattell, Maria G. 1999. Elders' complaints: Discourses on old age and social change in rural Kenya and urban Philadelphia. Language and communication in old age, ed. Heidi E. Hamilton, 295–232. New York and London: Garland Publishing.

Casey, Edward. 1996. How to get from space to place in a fairly short stretch of time: Phenomenological prolegomena. Senses of place, ed. Stephen Feld and Keith Basso, 13–52. Santa Fe: School of American Research Press.

de Saint-Georges, Ingrid. 2004. Materiality in discourse: The influence of space and layout in making meaning. Discourse and technology: Multimodal discourse analysis, ed. Philip LeVine and Ron Scollon, 71–87. Washington, D.C.: Georgetown University Press.

Erickson, Frederick. 1982. Money tree, lasagna bush, salt and pepper: Social construction of topical cohesion in a conversation among Italian-Americans. Analyzing discourse: Text and talk. Georgetown University Roundtable on Languages and Linguistics 1981, ed. Deborah Tannen, 43–70. Washington, D.C.: Georgetown University Press.

Feld, Steven, and Keith H. Basso, eds. 1996. Senses of place. Santa Fe: School of American Research Press.

Finnegan, Ruth. 1998. Tales of the city: A study of narrative and urban life. Cambridge: Cambridge University Press.

Gell, Alfred. 1995. The language of the forest: Landscape and phonological iconism in Umeda. The anthropology of landscape: Perspectives on place and space, ed. Eric Hirsch and Michael O'Hanlon, 232–253. Oxford: Clarendon Press.

Goffman, Erving. 1961. Asylums: Essays on the social situation of mental patients and other inmates. New York: Anchor Books.

Goffman, Erving. 1963. Behavior in public places: Notes on the social organization of gatherings. New York: The Free Press.

Goffman, Erving. 1964. The neglected situation. American Anthropologist 6(6, part 2).133–136.

Goffman, Erving. 1971. Relations in public: Microstudies of the public order. New York: Basic Books.

Gumperz, John J., and Dell Hymes. 1972. Directions in sociolinguistics: The ethnography of communication. New York: Holt, Rinehart & Winston.

Jackson, John Brinckerhoff. 1994. A sense of place, a sense of time. New Haven: Yale University Press.

Jackson, Peter. 1989. Maps of meaning. London and New York: Routledge.

Jasnoski, Mary Banks. 1992. The physical environment affects quality of life based upon environmental sensitivity. Journal of Applied Developmental Psychology 13.139–142.

Johnstone, Barbara. 1990. Stories, community and place. Bloomington: Indiana University Press.

Johnstone, Barbara. 2004. Place, globalization, and linguistic variation. Sociolinguistic variation: Critical reflections, ed. Carmen Fought, 65–83. New York and Oxford: Oxford University Press.

Kendon, Adam. 1977. Studies in the behavior of social interaction. Bloomington: Indiana University Press.

Linde, Charlotte, and William Labov. 1975. Spatial networks as a site for the study of language and thought. Language 51(4).924–939.

Proshansky, Harold M., Abbe K. Fabian, and Robert Kaminoff. 1995. Place-identity: Physical world socialization of the self. Giving places meaning, ed. Linda Groat, 87–113. San Diego: Academic Press.

Relph, Edward. 1976. Place and placelessness. London: Pion Limited.

Saville-Troike, Muriel. 1989. The ethnography of communication: An introduction, 2nd edition. Oxford: Blackwell.

Schegloff, Emanuel A. 1972. Notes on a conversational practice: Formulating place. Studies in social interaction, ed. David Sudnow, 75–119. New York: The Free Press.

Schiffrin, Deborah. 1994. Approaches to discourse. Oxford: Blackwell.

Schober, Michael F. 1995. Speakers, addressees, and frames of reference: Whose effort is minimized in conversations about locations? Discourse Processes 20.219–247.

Scollon, Ron, and Suzie Wong Scollon. 2003. Discourses in place: Language in the material world. London and New York: Routledge.

Sime, J. D. 1995. Creating places or designing spaces? Giving places meaning, ed. Linda Groat, 27–41. San Diego: Academic Press.

Streeck, Jürgen. 1996. How to do things with things. Human Studies 19.365–384.

Talmy, Leonard. 1983. How language structures space. Spatial orientation: Theory, research and application, ed. Herbert L. Pick, Jr. and Linda P. Acredols, 225–282. New York: Plenum Press.

Tannen, Deborah. 1981. New York Jewish conversational style. International Journal of the Sociology of Language 30.133–149.

Tannen, Deborah. 2007 [1989]. Talking voices: Repetition, dialogue, and imagery in conversational discourse. Cambridge: Cambridge University Press.

Tuan, Yi-Fu. 1974. Topophilia: A study of environmental perception, attitudes and values. New York: Columbia University Press.

Tuan, Yi-Fu. 1977. Space and place: The perspective of experience. Minneapolis and London: University of Minnesota Press.

Tuan, Yi-Fu. 1991. Language and the making of place: A narrative-descriptive approach. Annals of the Association of American Geographers 80.684–696.

Ulrich, Roger S. 1984. View through a window may influence recovery from surgery. Science New Series 224.420–421.

Weiner, James F. 1991. The empty place: Poetry, space and being among the Foi of Papua New Guinea. Bloomington and Indianapolis: Indiana University Press.

ALLA V. TOVARES

eleven

Family Members Interacting
While Watching TV

This study investigates the relationship between the public and the private in family discourse by focusing on family members interacting
while watching television.[1] Television viewing is a key site where the public and the private intersect: family members watch and react to the public medium of television in the privacy of their own homes. Tannen
(2001) looks at family as a small community of speech with its own
history of talk. Family interactions prompted by television programs
are just one type of family talk that is dialogic (Bakhtin 1981) and intertextual (Kristeva 1986). Adopting a dialogic approach [Bakhtin 1981,
1984, 1986, 1990] to the analysis of family interactions prompted by

1. An earlier version of this chapter was presented at the 2002 annual meeting of Georgetown University Round Table on Languages and Linguistics (GURT), Washington, D.C.,
March 7, 2002. I am indebted to Deborah Tannen for her detailed and insightful comments
on earlier drafts of this chapter. I am also grateful to Shari Kendall and Cynthia Gordon for
their thoughtful and careful reading of an earlier version of this chapter. I would also like to
thank Cynthia Gordon, who helped me identify several examples for this analysis.

television programs, I demonstrate how by intertextual repetition of words and phrases from television texts family members express their own feelings, educate their children, and identify shared values and interests.

Many studies on "televiewing" are based on self-reports, such as surveys, interviews, and questionnaires (e.g., Austin et al. 1990; Buerkel-Rothfuss et al. 1982; Kubey & Csikszentmihalyi 1990). One shortcoming of such methodologies is that participants might indicate what programs they believe they should watch instead of what they actually watch. In this study the use of portable digital audio tape (DAT) recorders by participants in the Work and Family Project allowed for capturing viewers' interactions in the absence of a researcher. This work contributes to the study of the television viewing experience and to research on family communication by proposing a methodology that focuses on the detailed analysis of family members' immediate responses to television programs, commercials, and news. It also adds to our understanding of intertextuality and the relationship between the public and the private by showing how public/private intertextual repetition occurs moment by moment in family discourse.

I begin with an overview of work on the relationship between the public and the private and the role of television in everyday family interaction. Then I demonstrate how the notions of dialogicality, involvement, answerability, and the linguistic strategy of repetition allow for the analysis of the complex relationship between the public and the private in family interactions when family members are at home with the TV set turned on. I continue by demonstrating the complexity of what is ordinarily described as "watching television." I show that family members' responses to television programs occur in the midst of other family activities. Therefore, conversations prompted by television programs are not isolated interactions; rather they are woven into the polyphony of diverse family interactions. Finally, I argue that by intertextual repetition of phrases from television programs, family members express their own feelings, educate their children, and identify and reinforce shared values. I conclude by suggesting that linguistic analysis of intertextual repetition of television texts in family interaction shows how a dialogic unity of the public and the private is achieved moment by moment in discourse and that television is a type of social mirror that reflects and refracts individual lives.

The Public and the Private: A Dialogic Approach

The Public and Private

This analysis of interactions among family members while watching television draws on the interdisciplinary body of research on the relationship between the public and the private in society. My understanding of the public and the private stems from the work of Erving Goffman (1959). Goffman, using the metaphor of theatrical performance, identifies front and backstage regions, where the front region correlates with the public and backstage with the private. The author observes that while access to the frontstage is open to everybody, access to the backstage is limited. However, he emphasizes that the distinction is fluid: in most situations there is no clear-cut division between front and backstage. Depending on the circumstances, a frontstage region may become a backstage region, and a backstage region may become a frontstage region. For instance, a children's playground, which is a frontstage region, can become an extension of the backstage if mothers demonstrate home-like behavior in terms of more relaxed manners and more casual dress. On the other hand, a household, which is a backstage region, can become a frontstage region when there are visitors in the house. In this paper, I build on and add to Goffman's discussion of the front and backstage regions by showing that even in the absence of visitors, television brings the public into the privacy of the household, thus changing how we understand the public and the private and the relationship between them.

A number of researchers challenge the dichotomy between the public and the private by demonstrating that they are inextricably intertwined. Habermas (1989) stresses the "mutual infiltration" between public and private spheres. Bourdieu (1996) argues that the traditional opposition between the public and the private only serves to mask the extent to which the public is present in the private. He emphasizes that the public is inevitably present in the private; for example, family discourse is shaped by ideas, principles, or beliefs acquired through political and judicial constructions.

In her comparative study of language ideologies in the Unites States and Eastern Europe, Gal (2005) maintains that the ideology of public/private divides people, places, moralities, and linguistic practices into opposed categories (24). She employs the semiotic concept of fractal recursions to analyze the relationship between the public and the private. Gal understands fractal recursions as repetitions of the same co-constitutive contrasts, such as "public" and "private," "right" and "left," and others in different contexts. She goes on to suggest that every repetition results in "a change in perspective by those making the comparison" (27). According to Gal, the boundaries between the contrastive elements can be redrawn any time. For example, what is considered "public" in one context may be perceived as "private" in another. Thus Gal, along with Bourdieu, Goffman, Habermas, and other researchers, stresses the dynamic nature of the relationship between the public and the private.

Related to the notions of the public and the private are Bakhtin's concepts of the "self" and the "other." The relationship between the "self" and the "other" is one of the key themes in Bakhtin's philosophical thought. For Bakhtin a human identity is "unfinalizable," that is, it is always under construction, never finished. "As long as a person is alive he [she] lives by the fact that he [she] is not yet finalized, that he [she] has not yet uttered his [her] ultimate word" (1984:59). According to Bakhtin, only through dialogue can people question, refute, or accept any "finalized" perception of "self." In a number of works, Bakhtin (1979, 1984, 2000) draws on the metaphor of a social mirror: we see ourselves through the eyes of others; our perception of "self" is inevitably influenced by the ideas, tastes, etc. of others. As Clark & Holquist (1984:79) point out, for Bakhtin the concept of the mirror is not that of a passively reflecting glass but rather a refraction of the views and words of others that influences the perception of the "self." As social beings we can only see ourselves as we are seen by others.

My understanding of Bakhtin's concept of "mirror" as reflecting and refracting everyday life is indeed intertextual. In *Sobranie sochinenij* (*Selected Works*) of Bakhtin (1996), I came across his short essay *Chelovek u zerkala* (*Person in Front of the Mirror*). In the commentary to this essay, Sergey Bocharov, one of the editors of the volume and a Bakhtin scholar, writes that Bakhtin's concept of "mirror" is often discussed in relation to that of Lacan's. Bocharov cites American scholars Clark & Holquist (1984), who state, "[a]s opposed to Lacan, Bakhtin conceives the mirror stage as coterminous with consciousness; it is endless as long as we are in the process of creating ourselves, because the mirror we use to see ourselves is not a passively reflecting looking glass but rather the actively refracting optic of other persons" (1996:499, Clark & Holquist: 79). Thus, I first came across Clark & Holquist's discussion of Bakhtin's concept of "mirror" in Bocharov's commentary in Russian. Elaborating on Clark & Holquist,

I argue that in our age of omnipresent mass media, television can be seen as a type of social mirror that both reflects the lives of the viewers and transforms or "refracts" their lives as well.

My analysis of audiotaped family interactions adds to the ongoing theoretical discussion of the relationship between the public and the private by demonstrating how the notion of dialogicality helps us understand the interplay between the two. By zeroing in on dialogic repetition of television texts in family interactions, I suggest that the private is a refraction of the public in family discourse. I argue that family members are not passively repeating words and phrases from television texts; rather they are actively involved in shaping those public words and phrases into the context of family interactions.

Television Viewing and Everyday Family Interaction

Because of its pervasiveness, television viewing is a key site for research on the relationship between the public and the private in family discourse. Marshall & Werndly (2002:54) view television as a "domestic medium" since television viewing is part of the everyday life of the viewers. It would be hard to find an American household that does not have a TV set. According to the A. C. Nielsen Co. (1998), 98% of U.S. households have at least one television set and many households have more than one TV. In addition to the pervasiveness of television sets, Americans keep the set turned on many hours per day. A. C. Nielsen Co. reports that in the average U.S. home the television set is on seven hours and twelve minutes per day. However, such a finding should not be taken as a measure of how much television is actually being watched. Even if family members are sitting in the living room with the TV set turned on, they may not be watching TV. Rather, family members may be spending time together, relaxing after a day's work, or eating dinner, among a variety of other possible activities.

Fiske (1989:57), comparing a family viewer to an isolated spectator in a movie theater, finds that "the family viewer does not always give the screen such concentrated attention, but watches more sporadically in between or while reading the paper, eating, or holding snatches of conversation." Hobson (1982) finds that women with young children are "half-watching/half-listening" to television programs while taking care of their children. Thus, depending on the context in which television programs are watched, the viewers can demonstrate different levels of involvement with the program.

Goffman (1963:43) refers to involvement as "the capacity of an individual to give, or withhold from giving, his [or her] concerted attention to some activity at hand—a solitary task, a conversation, a collaborative work effort." Goffman further subdivides involvement into *main* involvement, which absorbs the major part of someone's attention, and *side* involvement, which a person can carry on without disrupting his or her main involvement. Thus, while for viewers in the theater the spectacle is their main involvement, televiewing in the home easily shifts from main to side involvement and back again.

In a related view, Scollon (1998) understands televiewing as "polyfocal," that is, viewers may be engaged in a variety of activities while the television set is turned on. According to Scollon (1998:116), watching television is "much more than focal attention to the screen for the purpose of making an interpretation of what is being projected there." He further suggests that it is important to analyze what kind of action is taking place when family members get together in front of the television set. Scollon proposes Mediated Discourse Analysis (MDA) with mediated action as the unit of analysis as an approach to investigate media discourse as social interaction. Following Wertsch (1991), Scollon argues that people carry out actions with cultural tools or mediational means, similar to what Tannen (this volume) refers to as "resources." For instance, family members can use television texts as one of the mediational means in interaction with one another. Following Kristeva (1986), Bakhtin (1981), Wertsch (1991), and others, Scollon suggests that television texts as mediational means are polyvocal because they "incorporate the voices of other texts" (252). He also points out that one of the ways that Bakhtin's concept of polyvocality reached Western audiences was through Boris Uspensky (1973) whose work Goffman (1974) cited in *Frame Analysis*. My understanding of television texts and public texts in general as resources in family interaction derives from Scollon's notion of mediational means.

Another area of research on the television viewing experience centers on the effects of television on family communication. Although some studies report that television suppresses family interaction (Maccoby 1951; Steiner 1963), others demonstrate that television does not necessarily impede family conversations or other forms of family interactions (Bryce & Leichter 1983; Lull 1980; Messaris 1983). Lull (1980) even finds that reference to television themes facilitates children's entering adults' interactions. Barrios (1988), in his study of televiewing in Venezuelan families, concluded that TV viewing both enhances and disrupts family communication since TV viewing can be used both to introduce topics of interactions and to avoid communication.

Ellis (1992) finds that in most Western countries televiewing has become a normal, integral, and ever-present part of everyday domestic life. Bryce & Leichter (1983) note that as television increasingly becomes a part of daily family life, shared cultural knowledge is increasingly television related; and verbal references to television are expected to become more implicit, more embedded, in family interactions. Hobson (1982:125) compares the knowledge that television viewers acquire about a program to "a form of cultural capital which excludes those who do not watch the programs."

Meinhof & Smith (2000:3) demonstrate a complex intertextual relationship between television texts and everyday life, which "enables us to think of media discourse as being qualitatively continuous with the experience of everyday life." Not only are televiewers influenced by television, but the content of television programs incorporates contemporary elements of viewers' family lives. Ellis (1992) finds that in many TV programs the familial and the domestic are used as points of reference, thus confirming the normalcy of domestic life for the viewing audience.

Analyzing viewers' responses to the British soap opera *Crossroads*, Hobson (1982) challenges the stereotypical notion that women watch soap operas just to escape from their everyday lives and argues that soap operas often provide "a way of understanding and coping with problems which are recognized as 'shared' by other women, both in the programme and in 'real life'" (131). Bachmair (2000) compares contemporary televiewing to a self-service buffet from which viewers select what to integrate into the text of their everyday lives, and by such an individualized process they produce new meanings. He calls this type of relationship between the media and their audiences hermeneutic to highlight the audiences' active involvement in the production of meaning.

Hall (1980) suggests that there is a dynamic interrelationship between media and audience. A body of work on the television viewing experience (e.g., Fiske 1989; Hobson 1982; Livingstone 1999; Schroeder 1994) develops this idea by emphasizing the active role of the audience in the meaning making process. Hobson (1982) and other researchers view television as a form of popular art that both reflects and is reflected in everyday life. In his short article *Art and Answerability* Bakhtin (1990:1) writes that art and everyday life "gain unity only in the individual person who integrates them into his [or her] own unity." For Bakhtin answerability represents the mutual responsibility of art and life to influence each other. Thus he sees art and life in a dialogic relationship where art can be seen as the public and human life as the private. Bakhtin's notions of dialogicality and answerability allow us to see the interpenetration of the public and the private within interactions in which family members engage in meaning making within the privacy of the home through the use of public television texts.

Intertextual Repetition as a Linguistic Approach to the Study of the Public and the Private in Family Discourse

In what follows, drawing upon the theoretical model of the prepatterned or dialogic nature of language, I focus on repetition as a linguistic strategy. Elaborating on Bakhtin's (1981, 1986) notion of dialogicality, Kristeva's concept of intertextuality, and Tannen's 2007 [1989] work on repetition, I approach the question of how family members incorporate public television texts in private family interaction.

For Bakhtin, dialogicality is essential for language production. Bakhtin finds that any idea is distributed among many, often conflicting, voices. Thus dialogicality lies at the heart of his understanding of the nature of discourse. According to Bakhtin, there are no neutral words that belong to no one. Every word is saturated with the intentions of other members of the verbal community. Bakhtin (1981:293) argues that "the word in language is half someone else's. It becomes 'one's own' only when the speaker populates it with his [*sic*] own intention, his own accent, when he appropriates the word, adapting it to his own semantic and expressive intention." Elaborating on Bakhtin's idea of dialogicality (1984, 1986), Kristeva introduces the concept of "intertexuality," extending the dialogic principle from words and utterances to the relationship between different texts. In her words, "any text is constructed as a mosaic of quotations; any text is the absorption and transformation of another" (Kristeva 1986:37).

Repetition has emerged as a primary linguistic means for the intertextual incorporation of one text into another. Tannen 2007 ([1989]:95) argues that repetition is pervasive in both literary texts and spoken discourse. She finds that repetition points to a delicate balance "between the individual and the social, the fixed and the free, the ordered and the chaotic." She maintains that prepatterning enables the individual to speak through the group and the group to speak through the individual. Even though people talk about their personal experiences and express their personal opinions, their choice of what to say and their understanding of the appropriateness of their choices are influenced by previous interactions. Tannen points to Becker's (Ms.:4) observation that what might be perceived as "apparently free conversation is a replay of remembered texts —from TV news, radio talk, the New York Times . . ." (44). In her work on repetition, Tannen views dialogicality as the tension between novelty and fixity and states that such a tension constitutes creativity. Thus for Tannen meaning making is a dialogic construction where the old and the new, the social and the individual are in a dialectic and dialogic relationship.

In the following pages, I use the dialogic principle to bring together research on the public and the private, television viewing, and family discourse. My goal is to demonstrate how linguistic analysis of the repetition of words and phrases from television programs in family interaction sheds light on the interrelationship between the public and the private in family discourse.

Intertextual Repetition of Television Texts in Family Talk: The Dialogic Unity of the Public and the Private

I consider here examples from all four families that participated in the Work and Family Project. Each family had at least one television set. The number of hours the television set was on during the week of recordings varied from family to family. However, I noticed that in the three families with small children the TV was on more often than in the family with older children. Listening to the recordings and reading the transcripts I was intrigued by how often family members would make references to television programs in their daily interactions with family and friends. They would discuss television programs while watching television, immediately after watching a program, and several days after a program aired. Elsewhere (Tovares 2006), I explore how family and friends discuss the television show *Who Wants to Marry a Multimillionaire?* days and even weeks after the show aired. In this chapter, to discuss how public/private intertextual repetition occurs moment by moment, I focus my analysis on the interactions that occur when family members are watching television.

Family Televiewing as a Polyfocal and Polyvocal Activity

In what follows I demonstrate that watching television in a familial context often occurs simultaneously with other activities. With their TV set turned on, family members eat, talk to each other, call friends (often in reaction to TV programs), look through family pictures or shopping catalogues, clean the house, read to each other, as well as respond to TV texts. Consequently, analysis of participants' verbal responses to TV texts in isolation from other interactions that happen at the same time and place would not reflect the whole complexity of the television viewing situation.

The following example shows how in one family, interaction about a television program occurs in the midst of other actions. This example comes from the family of Clara, Neil, and their son Jason. It is worth mentioning that Clara and Neil have a keen interest in politics, are strong supporters of the Democratic Party, and taped during the week of the 2000 U.S. presidential election (see Gordon, this volume). Moreover, since Clara's boss is a political appointee, her job will be strongly affected by the election results. Thus, it is not surprising that the election very often was Clara's and Neil's main involvement, in Goffman's sense, both at home and at work. At work they spent a lot of time discussing the election with their coworkers, and at home they were following TV reports and calling their friends and coworkers to discuss the latest news.

In the following example, Jason is already in bed, while Clara and Neil and their two dogs are in the living room with the TV tuned to election news. Since the interactions were audio-taped, I rely on participants' verbal cues that mark the shift of their main involvement. Clara and Neil are involved in different actions simultaneously. As they are looking through and commenting on family pictures, Clara talks to the dogs and comments on a Senator's remarks on TV. Some of these actions become their main involvement for some time before being taken over by another main involvement.

(1) 1 Neil: ((*referring to someone on TV*)) Here's a crook.
     2 Clara: Yeah.
     3   ((*short pause*))
     4 Clara: ((*to dog*)) <high-pitched> You stay right there buddy.
     5   You stay right there,
     6   you little hoppin' dog.>
     7   ((*short pause*))

8   <quietly> Let's hear about Senator /???/> ((re: someone on TV))

9   ((short pause))

10 Neil: I guess all they're gonna talk about (("they" = TV reporters))

11   /??/ the presidential election.

12 Clara: Here's my little outdoor boy. ((referring to Jason, in a photo))

13   <chuckles>

14 Neil: Oh that was the only picture we got.

15 Clara: Well no, there's a whole bunch.

Judging from her verbal reactions, Clara's main involvement in the excerpt above changes from TV news (line 2, *Yeah*), to paying attention to the dog (lines 4-6, *You stay right there buddy, You stay right there, you little hoppin' dog*), then back to the TV news (line 8, *Let's hear about Senator / ???/*), and finally to the family photographs (line 12, *Here's my little outdoor boy*). Such swift changes of involvement demonstrate the polyfocal (Scollon 1998) nature of participants' actions when they are sitting in front of a TV set. As we consider the examples that follow, knowledge of the range of activities the participants are involved in while watching TV promotes a better understanding of how repetition of the phrases from television texts relates to their other activities. I also suggest that watching television is not only polyfocal but polyvocal as well. Voices of television anchors, characters in TV programs, and those of present family members, that is, public and private voices, enter the family's home at the same time. Thus when family members react to television texts, they add their voices to an already polyvocal speech situation.

Public Voices in Private Settings

In this section, I demonstrate how by intertextual repetition of phrases from television programs, family members express their own feelings and opinions, educate their children, and identify shared values. As discussed earlier, in a number of works, Bakhtin (1990, 2000) addresses the metaphor of a social mirror: we see ourselves through the eyes of others; our perception of "self" is inevitably influenced by the ideas, tastes, etc. of others. In this part of my analysis, I argue that television plays the role of "the other," the mirror that reflects and refracts participants' lives. Specifically, family members respond to television in relation to their own families and friends and to their own lives. Thus being a public medium, television prompts private responses in which the public is dialogically connected with the private.

Public Text, Private Feelings

The following example comes from the family of Greg and Nora and demonstrates how Greg uses a television text in his interaction with his wife Nora. As the interchange occurs, Nora is cleaning the kitchen. The movie *Sliding Doors*, which is about how missing a subway train impacts one woman's life, is playing on the TV. Greg comes in and together they are looking through the pantry and compiling a shopping list. Meanwhile the male protagonist in the movie tells the female protagonist (who is pregnant) that he loves her. After a short pause Greg says to Nora:

(2) 1 Greg: I love you.
    2 Nora: And I love you too. ((*sounds of kissing*))
    3 Greg: You are not pregnant. You are not barefoot.
    4 Nora: <*in a smiley voice*> But here I am at the sink.>

In the interaction above, Greg's words, *I love you*, are prompted by the TV text. Specifically, he repeats the words of the male protagonist with almost the same intonation. According to Bakhtin's (1984) classification, Greg's *I love you* is passive double-voiced discourse, where the initial discourse is reproduced literally but with a new intention. In this case, Greg uses repetition of the public text to express his feelings to his wife and to introduce a note of humor. Judging from the sounds of kissing, Nora accepts Greg's words not as a simple repetition of someone else's words but as an expression of his feelings.

As I mentioned earlier, knowledge of the broader context in which televiewing occurs facilitates understanding of how repetition of the phrases from television texts is linked to other activities the participants are involved in while watching TV. For instance, the fact that Nora is in the kitchen cleaning helps us see more vividly the connection between the public and the private in Greg's utterances. In line 3, Greg's words (*You are not pregnant. You are not barefoot.*) represent an intertwined combination of different voices. On the one hand, Greg produces the intertextual connection between the current context and the context of the movie on TV where the female protagonist is pregnant. On the other hand, he connects the fact that in real life his wife is in the kitchen cleaning to the common stereotypical expression "barefoot, pregnant and in the kitchen." Greg's words are what Bakhtin (1984:199) calls "discourse with a sideward glance at someone else's word." By negating the stereotypical expression, Greg creates what Bakhtin identifies as a hybrid construction where a single speaker within one utterance mixes "two utterances, two speech manners, two styles, two languages, two semantic and axiological belief systems" (1981:304–305). Such creative juxtaposition of several different public voices allows Greg to express his own feelings and views, thus fusing the public and the private in a dialogic unity. In this dialogic unity Greg's and Nora's voices interplay with the TV text, traditional notions of women's and men's roles, and each other's voices.

Public Text, Private Teaching and Expertise

Another example illustrates how a mother uses television texts to educate her child about health and, in so doing, establishes her authority as the family expert on hygiene and health. The excerpts that follow come from the family of Neil, Clara, and their son Jason and occurred two days apart. In the first interaction, in excerpt 3, Clara, Neil, and Jason are in the living room. The TV is on and the family members switch channels back and forth from a hockey game to election news. Neil draws his wife's and son's attention to a TV commercial about registering an on-line business. In the commercial one woman gets an idea for her on-line business after catching another person using her toothbrush. The commercial ends with the statement that "it does not matter how you got the idea for your on-line business, but it does matter where you register the name." The part of the TV commercial where one woman used the other woman's toothbrush sparks the following family interaction about using other people's toothbrushes:

(3) *Day 1*

1	Neil:	Have you seen this commercial?
2	Jason:	Huh?
3	Neil:	((*echoing the woman's voice in the commercial*))
4		"Is that my toothbrush." <*chuckles*>
5 →	Clara:	Ew.
6	Jason:	<*chuckles*>

7		Neil:	<chuckles>
8		Jason:	How come she said, "Is that my toothbrush?"
9		Neil:	Because the girl . was using her toothbrush.
10	→	Clara:	And you never use somebody else's toothbrush. It's icky.
11		Neil:	Yes you can. You can do that.
12	→	Clara:	No you CAN'T.
13	→		You can catch Hepatitis C doing that.
14		Neil:	((to Jason)) Mine or Mommy's.
15			If you've never had- you don't have yours.
16	→	Clara:	((to Jason)) No you can't!
17	→		I'll always make sure you have a toothbrush,
18	→		buddy.

From the very beginning of their interaction, Clara and Neil react differently to the events portrayed in the commercial. Neil chuckles when he repeats the phrase from the commercial, *"Is that my toothbrush"* (line 4), thus showing that he finds the situation funny. In contrast, Clara utters *Ew* (line 5) in disgust and immediately insists that Jason never use somebody else's toothbrush. She uses this situation to educate Jason about possible dangers of sharing toothbrushes such as the risk of contracting Hepatitis C.[2] Clara disagrees with Neil when he says that Jason could use his mother's or father's toothbrush if he does not have his. Bringing the television text about sharing a toothbrush into a private family interaction makes it evident that Neil and Clara have somewhat different beliefs concerning this aspect of personal hygiene.

Two days later, while Neil is at work and Clara stays home with Jason, who is sick, another TV text gives Clara a chance to repeat her point of view. It is early afternoon and Jason and Clara are in the living room watching a TV cartoon. The main character of the cartoon is on a treasure hunt for "the golden toothbrush." It turns out that a Cyclops is the owner of the golden toothbrush and does not want to give it up. When the main character asks if he can just borrow the golden toothbrush, the Cyclops finds the idea of borrowing a toothbrush disgusting. In line 2, Jason asks about something written appearing onscreen:

2. In fact, Clara is not alone in thinking that Hepatitis C can be transmitted through sharing toothbrushes. Several recent studies find that in rare cases Hepatitis C may be spread through toothbrushes and other common household items (e.g., Lock et al. 2002).

(4) *Day 3*

1	Clara:	Uh! The golden toothbrush? ((*re: TV show*))
2	Jason:	Mom, what did it say?
3	Clara:	It says "This way to the golden toothbrush."
4	Jason:	Yeah.
5	Clara:	Eh. <*laughs*> ((*at TV show*))
6	Jason:	<*laughs*> What did THAT say.
7	Clara:	It said, "See it, don't miss it, the golden toothbrush,
8		you're getting [real close—"]
9	Jason:	[What's it] SAY.
10	Clara:	It says, "You're getting real close →
11		to the world-famous golden toothbrush, this way!"
12	Jason:	What does that- [what does that say.]
13	Clara:	[I can't read it] from here, it's too little.
14		((*short pause, a Cyclops comes on the cartoon*))
15		A Cyclops is somebody with ONE EYE in the middle,
16		it's a make-believe thing. ((*short pause*)) Mm.

((*Meanwhile in the cartoon the main character grabs the golden toothbrush and refuses to give it back to the Cyclops.*))

TV Dialogue:

17	Cyclops:	I admire this commitment for dental hygienic excellence,
18		but I am not going to give up that toothbrush →
19		without a fight.
20		I /??/ 24 karat gold, and the bristles are VERY deep
21		for DEEP cleaning and a satisfying gum massage.
22		You come back here with that toothbrush!
23	Main character:	But I need to borrow it.
24 →	Cyclops:	BORROW it? That's DISGUSTING!
25	Jason:	[Ha.]
26	Clara:	[Ah!]
27 →		See! I told you you don't use other people's toothbrushes.

The text of the cartoon, especially the character's line that it's disgusting to share a toothbrush, *Borrow it? That's disgusting!* (line 24), provides Clara an intertextual connection with her utterance about sharing the toothbrush that she used two days before. Thus, when she states, *See! I told you you*

don't use other people's toothbrushes (line 27), she refers to that prior interaction. Specifically, she draws on the TV text to support her view in
contrast to Neil's. This example demonstrates how the television texts
became a part of this family's history of talk. In excerpts 3 and 4 above
Clara uses the public text of television to educate her son and at the same
time to position herself as the family expert on hygiene and health. In both
interactions, Clara uses the television text in relation to her own family;
that is, she is blending the public and the private to create meaning that is
relevant to her and her family members.

In many interactions family members relate television texts to their
private lives, thus providing a dialogic connection between the public
and the private. Chafe (1994), in his work on consciousness, notes that
while people are trying to construct a larger model of the world, they
cannot avoid centering it around *the self.* Consequently, it is not surprising that family members repeat words and phrases from television that
are relevant to their lives. In the next section I further demonstrate how
family members integrate television texts and family interaction into a
dialogic unity.

Public Text, Private Concerns

The following example comes from the family of Sam, Kathy, and their
daughter Kira. At the time of the recording Sam and Kathy were expecting
their second child. A lot of family interactions were centered on pregnancy,
including ones prompted by television texts. In the following example,
Kathy relates extraneous bits of news discourse to her pregnancy and
health. It is Monday evening. Kira is already in bed. Kathy and Sam are in
the family room. The TV is on and tuned to the local news. The news coverage swiftly moves from the story about a planned truckers' protest against
the rising cost of fuel and how this protest will affect the traffic in the area
to a report about bacterial meningitis. The news makes Kathy concerned
that the timing of the expected traffic disturbance may coincide with the
time when she has an appointment with her midwife. Then, when she hears
on the news about bacterial meningitis, she again establishes the connection between the television text and her own life. (In a number of interactions with her midwife, family, and friends, Kathy indicates that she tries
to stay healthy to avoid taking any medication that might affect her unborn child.)

(5) 1   ((*TV news story about truckers continues,*
    2   *newswoman describes how this will affect traffic*))
    3 Sam: [There you go.]
    4 Kathy: [That's time] to go to the midwife.
    5   ((*short pause, news story about bacterial meningitis*))
    6 Sam: Why don't the truckers BUY a refinery.
    7   ((*short pause, news story about meningitis continues*))
    8 Kathy: Did you have contact with somebody with meningitis?
    9 Sam: How would I know.

In lines 1 and 2 the news story about possible traffic disruptions because of a truckers' demonstration triggers Kathy's concern about her prospective visit with a midwife. While Sam is still discussing the situation about the truckers, the news moves to the story about bacterial meningitis. In line 8, *Did you have contact with somebody with meningitis?* Kathy picks up the word "meningitis" from the news report to see if this deadly bacterium might be endangering her own family. By incorporating the texts of different news stories into the context of her own life, Kathy provides a dialogic connection between the public and the private where the public becomes an integral part of the private.

Of interest in the example above is Kathy's concern about germs and health. Recall how Clara in excerpt 3 uses television texts to warn Jason that sharing toothbrushes can lead to contracting Hepatitis C. In one of the following examples, Janet and her mother watch and react to a program about "real natural baby food." These common worries of the three mothers with small children point to general parenting fears and concerns in the United States about germs and health. Several recent books on parenting (e.g., Furedi 2002; Stearns 2003) stress the growing parental anxiety over children's well-being that is reflected in and created by the literature on parenting and the media. In *Paranoid Parenting*, Furedi suggests that numerous and often contradictory kinds of childrearing advice create anxiety among parents, including concern about their children's health. He notes:

Health scares affecting children are a particularly invidious source of anxiety to parents. It only takes one speculative study on a potential new risk to set off another parental panic. According to a recent survey of 1,600 parents of young children in the journal *Pediatrics*, 25 percent worried that routine vaccination could weaken their infants' immune systems. Such fears, completely unsupported by scientific evidence, are the product of ill-informed gossip transmitted through the media. (12)

Furthermore, Furedi reports that even scientific studies send conflicting messages to parents by overriding previous studies or claming them to be inaccurate. Stearns suggests that in the twentieth-century, germ theory fueled parental anxiety. According to Stearns, in the middle decades of the last century "recurrent reports of polio epidemics, carried by germs in turn associated with public contact and dirt, helped keep parental anxieties at fever pitch" (30). He further argues that even with the steady decline of children's mortality as the result of rapid improvements in children's healthcare, parental anxieties over children's health have not subsided; moreover, new information about new potential dangers for children keeps parental anxiety at high levels. Therefore, when Clara, Kathy, and Janet repeat words and phrases about germs and health from television programs in their private interactions with family and friends, they reflect and co-construct the anxiety of American parenting.

The dialogic repetition of the television texts in family interactions connects family members with the world outside of their circle of family and friends. Tannen (2007 [1989]:97) finds that "repetition is a resource by which conversationalists together create a discourse, a relationship, and a world." In the interactions above, family members, by repeating words and phrases from television texts in their private family interactions, relate the small world of their families to the larger outside world, thus fusing the public and the private into a dialogic unity. In this sense, television plays the role of a social mirror that reflects and refracts private lives.

Public Text, Private Intergenerational Talk

Such reflection and refraction of the public in the private are demonstrated in the following excerpts from the family of Janet, Steve, and their daughter Natalie (age two years eleven months), where family members are actively incorporating texts of television shows into the context of their own lives. Janet and Steve, like Kathy and Sam, are expecting their second baby. Thus it is not surprising that a number of family interactions in Janet and Steve's family are also centered around pregnancy and delivery.

The excerpts below were recorded one Monday afternoon when Janet and Natalie were visiting Janet's mother Laura, or "Boo-Boo," as Natalie calls her grandmother. When Natalie and Janet arrived at Laura's house, Janet suggested watching *A Baby Story* on TV. *A Baby Story* is a show on The Learning Channel (TLC) that follows expectant couples through all the events of pregnancy, labor, and bringing the baby home. While watching *A Baby Story*, Laura and Janet use television images and interactions of the expectant couple with doctors, family, and friends to educate Natalie about pregnancy, babies, and baby food. They also connect television stories to the fact that Janet is expecting a child, and in doing so they are preparing Natalie for the arrival of her baby brother and including her in the conversation. Thus Laura and Janet integrate the public and the private in their interactions with Natalie. In the following excerpt Laura uses the TV show to teach Natalie about a sonogram machine. The expectant couple on TV is at the doctor's office where, with the help of the sonogram, they can look at their unborn baby.

(6) 1 Natalie: They're gonna have a baby! ((*re: a couple on TV*))
    2 Laura: They're gonna have a baby, just like .
    3 Natalie: Mommy.
    4 Laura: Mommy and . there's the baby machine!
    5   Called the sonogram.((*re: TV*))
    6   ((*short pause*))
    7   They're gonna look at the baby through the screen.
    8   We saw you,
    9   you know what you did?
    10   Here's what you did when you were in Mommy's tummy.
    11   Watch me.
    12   "Hi!"
    13   You waved to us.
    14   "Hi!"
    15   "I'm gonna come out and meet you soon!"

When in line 1 Natalie says about the TV couple, *They're gonna have a baby*, Laura immediately provides a link to the pregnancy of her own daughter, Natalie's mother, *They're gonna have a baby, just like . Mommy* (lines 2 and 4). Then Laura draws Natalie's attention to *the baby machine* (lines 4 and 5) and explains that the sonogram allows a couple to look at the unborn baby through the screen (line 7). Laura also uses the text of the television program to tell Natalie an animated story about the time when Natalie herself was *in Mommy's tummy* (lines 8–15), thus connecting the

TV story with that of their own family. Laura's story also serves to entertain Natalie, as well as to help her see her unborn baby brother as a person.

Similarly, in the excerpt below, Laura picks up on the text of another segment of *A Baby Story* to talk to Natalie about her baby brother. Through active involvement with the TV text Laura exposes Natalie to the world outside her immediate family by showing similarities between experiences of her family and those of the family depicted on the TV show. In the show a male relative of an expectant couple says that the newborn is "the first male grandchild in the family, and he's actually the first male baby in a long time on this side of the family. So everybody is really thrilled."

(7) 1 Laura: ((*to Natalie*)) Just like your brother, ((*re: A Baby Story*))
    2   gonna be the first male in the family.

By repeating the words from the show, Laura incorporates the TV text into the context of her family. In other words, she makes someone else's discourse hers. In Bakhtin's (1981:293) words, she "populates it with [her] own intention, [her] own accent . . . adapting it to [her] own semantic and expressive intention," linking her family events to those portrayed on the public medium of television.

In the next excerpt Laura uses the TV text to continue her conversation with Natalie about babies by explaining how and what babies eat. A woman on the show is teaching expectant mothers how to make "real natural baby food." She starts with bananas and comments that she will *mash them first*. When Natalie suggests carrots for the baby food, Laura, echoing the TV text, says that it is important to *mash them*.

(8) 1 Natalie: There's some carrots for the baby!
    2 Janet: Yeah.
    3 Laura: They've got to mash them up though.
    4 Natalie: Why they have to mash them up?
    5 Janet: Because babies don't have teeth!
    6 Laura: They can't chew,
    7   they can just go like this, ((*makes smacking sounds*))
    8   like that.

Of interest in this excerpt is that Janet aligns with her mother in teaching Natalie about why babies cannot eat solid food. The two women are building on each other's utterances: *Because babies don't have teeth* (Janet); *They can't chew* (Laura). However, as we will see in the next two excerpts, Janet and Laura do not display such harmony in all the interactions prompted by television.

The final two excerpts show how television texts can reveal intergenerational differences in the values and attitudes of family members. The beginning of another segment of *A Baby Story* about belly dancing for pregnant women as a way of alleviating back pain makes both Janet and Laura laugh. However, as the program progresses, Janet finds the idea of pregnant women belly dancing more acceptable, while Laura, uncomfortable with the idea, continues insisting that it is rather odd. Janet even tells Natalie that her grandmother *is not very open-minded* to new ideas. The excerpt below shows Janet's and Laura's first reactions to the content of the show.

(9) 1 Janet: Belly dancing?
     2 Laura: Oh,
     3   oh my God.
     4 Janet: <*ironically*> This ought to be good.>
     5   DELPHINA?! ((*re: belly-dancing instructor's name*))
     6 Laura: Oh my God.
     7 Janet: DELPHINA,
     8   the instructor!
     9   Oh my <*laughing*> God.>
    10 Laura: I'm telling you,
    11   this is .
    12 Janet: <*laughing*> DELPHINA!>
    13   <*laughs*>
    14 Laura: La-La land.

Both women are initially intrigued and puzzled by the idea of belly dancing for pregnant women. They also find the name of the instructor funny. Janet laughs and repeats the name "Delphina" three times in appreciation of the humor of the situation. Tannen (2007 [1989]:64) identifies such a function of repetition as "savoring" repetition. While Tannen discusses an interaction where friends repeat one another's words to savor humor, in the excerpt above the source of savoring repetition is a public text of a television program. Bringing the words from the television program into their interaction, Janet and Laura align together as critics of something they see on the TV program.

In addition, Laura's phrase, *I'm telling you, this is . La-La land* (lines 10, 11, and 14), frames not only the name of the instructor but the entire situation of belly dancing for pregnant women as something so strange and unusual that it could only happen in a fantasy world, or as she puts it, *La-La land* (line 14). While in the excerpts discussed above, examples 6, 7, and 8, Laura emphasizes similarities between the families depicted on the TV show and her own family, in example 9, she projects the normalcy of her family against the backdrop of the "bizarre" actions of people that appear on television. Bringing the words from the television program into their interaction, Janet and Laura (or Boo-Boo, as Natalie addresses her grandmother) align together as critics of something they see on the TV program.

In the next excerpt, occurring a few minutes later, Janet and Laura display different alignments. With the television still being tuned to the program about belly dancing, Janet complains to her mother that her back is "killing" her and admits that she might be ready to belly dance herself if that relieves her back pain. In the excerpt that follows, while Laura insists that belly dancing for pregnant women is bizarre, Janet suggests that belly dancing itself is not bizarre:

(10) 1 Laura: Oh my God in Heaven.
      2   This is too . bizarre.
      3   Ranks only second to the body mold.
      4 Janet: Now there's nothing wrong with dancing Boo-Boo!
      5   I think what's [bizarre is her—]
      6 Laura: [Belly dancing?]
      7 Janet: Huh?
      8 Laura: Belly dancing?
      9 Janet: What's the trouble?
     10 Laura: It's bizarre.
     11 Janet: It's <*laughing*> bizarre.>
     12   <*ironically*> Boo-Boo,
     13   always open to new <*laughing*> ideas.>>
     14 Laura: That's [/right./]
     15 Natalie: [She will] go . /higher/, ((*playing with a doll*))
     16   she went up there for her nap.
     17 Laura: ((*to Natalie*)) Oh,
     18   that was a good idea for her to have a little nap.
     19   But she [/????/]
     20 Janet: [I think the only thing that's] . bizarre,

21		is that woman's name,
22		Delphina.
23	Laura:	Oh, ((*re: something on TV*))
24		lovely.
25	Janet:	Never heard of that in my life.
26	Laura:	/Plastic girl./
		((*short pause, TV still on*))
27	Natalie:	((*to Laura*)) What were you telling Mommy.
28	Laura:	I was telling Mommy that I thought that was
29		very strange to learn a belly dance.
		((*short pause*))
30	Janet:	<*yawning*> Boo-Boo's not very open-minded.>

Here, even though Laura and Janet, prompted by the television show, both talk about belly dancing, they demonstrate different attitudes toward it. Laura finds belly dancing to be *too . bizarre* and suggests that it *Ranks only second to the body mold* (lines 2 and 3), a plaster cast of a pregnant woman's torso. In contrast, Janet states that for her belly dancing is just a type of dancing when she tells her mother, *Now there's nothing wrong with dancing Boo-Boo!* (line 4).

Janet makes ironic comments about her mother not being open to new ideas (lines 13, 30), and in doing so she positions Laura as someone from an older and less progressive generation. Such positioning is intensified by Janet's use of the address term "Boo-Boo," the nickname Natalie uses to refer to Laura, her grandmother. Janet's use of this name highlights Laura's age by indexing her status as a grandparent. What is interesting about the last two excerpts is that the intertextual repetition of the bits from the same television show in family interaction both evokes the moments of harmony between Laura and Janet and reveals their differences. In excerpt 9 the two women make fun of the show. In contrast, excerpt 10 reveals intergenerational differences in Laura's and Janet's attitudes toward belly dancing during pregnancy. Such active incorporation of television texts into family interaction ties together the public and the private into an ever-evolving dialogue.

Conclusion

By focusing on a specific type of intertextual repetition, I have demonstrated how the public and the private are intertwined moment by moment in family interaction. Considering the relationship between the public and the private as essentially dialogic helps demonstrate that family discourse is not private per se; rather it is a complex combination of the public and the private. By incorporating elements of television texts into their discourse, family members blend the public and the private into a dialogic unity. I have argued that television viewing is a key site for studying the interrelationship between the public and the private and that television texts can be understood as *the other* or a social mirror (Bakhtin 2000) that links family members with the world that lies outside their circle of family and friends.

Family members do not merely repeat words and phrases from TV texts in their daily interaction; rather they saturate, or in Bakhtin's (1981:293) words "populate," the words of others with new intentions. In doing so, they relate public texts to their own families and friends. My analysis demonstrates how by intertextual repetition of television texts in family settings, family members educate their children, express their thoughts and feelings, and discuss their differences in attitudes and values. In this way television texts become part of the history of family talk in which family members add their voices to already polyvocal television texts.

A detailed analysis of family interaction while watching television shows that family members are often involved in many different activities simultaneously, and watching television is only one of those shifting involvements. Therefore, to gain a better understanding of how television texts are integrated into family discourse, the complexity of what ordinarily can be identified as "watching television" should be considered not only in linguistic research but in research on the television viewing experience as well. Even more, research on the television viewing experience can benefit from adopting the linguistic methodology of detailed analysis of participants' immediate reactions to television texts to gain a more naturalistic perspective on audience reactions to television programs rather than relying on often unreliable self-reports.

Finally, the present work has implications for the study of the dialogic nature of language. Building on the works of Bakhtin (1981, 1986), Kristeva (1984, 1986), and Tannen (2007 [1989]) and focusing on a specific type of public/private intertextual repetition, I argue that repetition is essential for language production and understanding. Specifically, I demonstrate that by repetition of television texts in family settings, family members not only use public texts as a resource for private interactions but by adding their voices to the ongoing dialogue, they show that creativity of language does not simply equate with arranging new words in a grammatical order but rather is achieved through active engagement with the words of others.

References

Austin, Erica Weintraub, Donald Roberts, and Clifford I. Nass. 1990. Influences of family communication on children's television-interpretation processes. Communication Research 17(4).545–564.

Bachmair, Ben. 2000. Creator spiritus: Virtual texts in everyday life. Intertextuality and the media, ed. Ulrike H. Meinhof and Jonathan Smith, 115–131. Manchester and New York: Manchester University Press.

Bakhtin, Mikhail. 1979. Estetika slovesnogo tvorchstva [The aesthetics of verbal creative work]. Moskva: Iskusstvo.

Bakhtin, Mikhail. 1981. The dialogic imagination. Austin: University of Texas Press.

Bakhtin, Mikhail. 1984. Problems of Dostoevsky's poetics, ed. and trans. Caryl Emerson, with an introduction by Wayne C. Booth. Minneapolis: University of Minnesota Press.

Bakhtin, Mikhail. 1986. Speech genres and other late essays. Austin: University of Texas Press.

Bakhtin, Mikhail. 1990. Art and answerability: Early philosophical essays, ed. Michael Holquist and Vadim Liapunov; translated and notes by Vadim Liapunov; supplement translated by Kenneth Brostrom. Austin: University of Texas Press.

Bakhtin, Mikhail. 1996. Sobranie sochinenij. Tom 5. Sergey G. Bocharov, and Luidmile A. Gogotishvili (redaktory). [M. M. Bakhtin. Collection of works, vol. 5, ed. Sergey G. Bocharov and Luidmile A. Gogotishvili.] Moskva: Russkie slovari.

Bakhtin, Mikhail. 2000. Chelovek u zerkala [Person in front of the mirror]. Avtor i geroy: K filosofskim osnovam gumanitarnyh nauk, 240. Sankt Petersburg: Azbuka.

Barrios, Leoncio. 1988. Television, telenovelas, and family life in Venezuela. World families watch television, ed. James Lull, 49–79. Newbury Park, Calif.: Sage Publications.

Becker, A. L. Ms. Correspondences: An essay on iconicity and philology.

Bourdieu, Pierre. 1996. On the family as a realized category. Theory, Culture & Society 13(3).19–26.

Bryce, Jennifer, and Hope Leichter. 1983. The family and TV: Forms of mediation. Journal of Family Issues 4(2).309–328.

Buerkel-Rothfuss, Nancy, Bradley Greenberg, Charles Atkin, and Kimberly Neuendorf. 1982. Learning about the family from television. Journal of Communication 32(3).191–201.

Chafe, Wallace. 1994. Discourse, consciousness, and time (selections). Chicago: University of Chicago.

Clark, Katerina, and Michael Holquist. 1984. Mikhail Bakhtin. Cambridge, Mass.: Belknap Press of Harvard University Press.

Ellis, John. 1992. Visible fictions: Cinema, television, video. London and New York: Routledge.

Fiske, John. 1989. Television culture. London and New York: Routledge.

Furedi, Frank. 2002. Paranoid parenting: Why ignoring the experts may be best for your child. Chicago: Chicago Review Press.

Gal, Susan. 2005. Language ideologies compared: Metaphors of public/private. Journal of Linguistic Anthropology 15(1):23–37.

Goffman, Erving. 1959. The presentation of self in everyday life. Garden City, N.Y.: Doubleday.

Goffman, Erving. 1963. Behavior in public places: Notes on the social organization of gatherings. New York: The Free Press.

Goffman, Erving. 1974. Frame analysis: An essay on the organization of experience. New York: Harper Colophon.

Habermas, Jurgen. 1989. The structural transformation of the public sphere: An inquiry into a category of bourgeois society, trans. Thomas Burger. Cambridge, Mass.: MIT Press.

Hall, Stuart. 1980. Encoding/decoding. Culture, media, language, ed. Stuart Hall, Dorothy Hobson, Andrew Lowe, and Paul Willis, 128–138. London: Hutchinson.

Hobson, Dorothy. 1982. Crossroads: The drama of a soap opera. London: Methuen.

Kristeva, Julia. 1984. Revolution in poetic language. New York: Columbia University Press.

Kristeva, Julia. 1986. The Kristeva reader, ed. Toril Moi. New York: Columbia University Press.

Kubey, Robert, and Mihaly Csikszentmihalyi. 1990. Television and the quality of life: How viewing shapes everyday experience. Hillsdale, N.J.: Lawrence Erlbaum Associates.

Livingstone, Sonia. 1999. Mediated knowledge: Recognition of the familiar, discovery of the new. Television and common knowledge, ed. Jostein Gripsrud, 91–107. London and New York: Routledge.

Lock, Guntram, Martin Dirscherl, Florian Obermeier, Cornelia M. Gelbmann, Claus Hellerbrand, Antje Knoell, Juergen Schoelmerich, and Wolfgang Jilg. 2002. Hepatitis C—transmission by toothbrushes: A myth or a real possibility? Abstract 217. Digestive Disease Week. April 19–22, 2002. San Francisco.

Lull, James. 1980. The social uses of television. Human Communication Research 6(spring).197–209.

Maccoby, Eleanor. 1951. Television: Its impact on school children. Public Opinion Quarterly 15(fall).421–444.

Marshall, Jill, and Angela Werndly. 2002. The language of television. London and New York: Routledge.

Meinhof, Ulrike H., and Jonathan Smith. 2000. The media and their audience: Intertextuality as paradigm. Intertextuality and the media, ed. Ulrike H. Meinhof and Jonathan Smith, 1–17. Manchester and New York: Manchester University Press.

Messaris, Paul. 1983. Family conversations about TV. Journal of Family Issues 4(2).293–308.

Schroeder, Kim Christian. 1994. Audience semiotics, interpretive communities and the "ethnographic turn" in the media research. Media, Culture and Society 16.337–347.

Scollon, Ron. 1998. Mediated discourse as social interaction. A study of news discourse. London and New York: Longman.

Stearns, Peter N. 2003. Anxious parents: A history of modern childrearing in America. New York and London: New York University Press.

Steiner, Gary. 1963. The people look at television. New York: Knopf.

Tannen, Deborah. 2007 [1989]. Talking voices: Repetition, dialogue, and imagery in conversational discourse. Cambridge: Cambridge University Press.

Tannen, Deborah. 2001. I only say this because I love you: How the way we talk can make or break family relationships throughout our lives. New York: Random House.

Tovares, Alla V. 2006. Public medium, private talk: Gossip about a TV show as "quotidian hermeneutics." Text & Talk 26(4/5).463–491.

Uspensky, Boris. 1973. A poetics of composition. Berkeley: University of California Press.

Wertsch, James. 1991. Voices of the mind: A sociocultural approach to mediated action. Cambridge, Mass: Harvard University Press.

Index

accounting for behavior, 72, 77, 85,
  95–96, 97, 105
A. C. Nielsen Co., 287
Adelswärd, Viveka, 72, 74, 98, 234,
  235, 241
adolescents, political socialization of,
  237, 238, 258
advice giving, 34n.1, 104, 107, 116–18,
  119
advocates, gatekeeping and, 167, 168
affection
  expressions of, 36
  for pets, 64, 66, 67
  teasing and, 59
  ventriloquizing and, 64
affective displays, 248
affective stances, 72, 73, 93, 99, 105
affiliation, 248, 257
agentivity, 74
Ainsworth-Vaughn, Nancy, 7
Alaska Natives, 168
Alfred P. Sloan Foundation, 9

alignment, 5, 6, 111–12
  identity construction and, 72, 73–
  80, 239–40
  maternal identity construction and,
  84–98, 105, 239
  paternal identity construction and,
  104, 107, 116, 119–20
  political identity construction and,
  235–36, 243, 244, 245–46, 247,
  250, 252, 255, 257, 258, 260
  television viewing and, 302, 303–4
  workplace social talk and, 197, 198,
  202–3, 204, 205, 207–8, 215
Allen, Sarah M., 169, 172–73, 179, 189
ambiguity, 50n.2
  power/solidarity and, 5, 14, 28–32,
  34, 36–40, 46–47
answerability, 19, 284, 289–90
anthropology, 265
  linguistic, 5, 8, 27, 267
anxiety, parental, 299–300
Apache narratives, 266

apologies, 65, 66–67, 77
appreciation, 80, 98
arguments
    political identity as cohesive device
        in, 255–57
    power/connection maneuvers and,
        41–45
    ventriloquizing and, 50, 51, 67, 140–
        41,
Arluke, Arnold, 50, 51, 61
Aronsson, Karin, 241
Art and Answerability (Bakhtin), 289
assessment
    maternal identity construction and,
        80, 85, 88–95, 97, 98–99, 105
    paternal identity construction and,
        107–12
    political identity construction and,
        243, 250–54, 255
    as social act, 79–80
assessment activity, 80, 89–90, 93, 109
attitudes
    identity construction and, 239
    intergenerational differences in, 303,
        304–5
authority, 9

Baatombu (people), 55
Baby Story, A (television series), 301,
    302, 303
baby-talk register, 39, 49, 51, 53–54,
    57, 58–59, 60, 63
Bachelard, Gaston, 279
Bachmair, Ben, 289
backchannels, 203, 205, 209–10, 271
backstage regions, 285
Bakhtin, M. M., 126
    answerability, 19, 289–90
    dialogicality, 8, 19, 283, 290
    discourse, 126, 294, 295, 302,
        306
    hybrid construction, 295
    "ideological becoming," 126
    polyvocality, 15, 19, 55, 68, 288
    "self" and "other," 286, 293

social mirror, 286, 293, 306
    "ventriloquate," 54–55
Barrios, Leoncio, 288–89
Basso, Keith, 265, 266
Bateson, Gregory, 5, 6, 59, 105
Bavelas, Janet Beavin, 29
Baxter, Judith, 126
Beauvoir, Simone de, 128
Becker, A. L., 5, 257, 278, 291
"Before the Law" (Kafka), 166
Beitel, Ashley Howard, 170–72, 173,
    189, 190
beliefs
    family identity and, 4–5, 8, 17–19,
        242
    political identity construction and,
        250, 252, 253, 254
    socialization in families and, 236,
        237
Benin, 55
Bentham, Jeremy, 89
Bilger, Burkhard, 50, 51
Billig, Michael, 126
blame, 77, 83, 96, 97, 166, 175
Blum-Kulka, Shoshana, 4, 5, 8, 27,
    29n.2, 32, 103–4, 105–6, 233, 236–
    37, 242, 259
Bocharov, Sergey, 286
Boston Women's Health Book
    Collective, 79
Bourdieu, Pierre, 285, 286
Bradley, Greg (pseudonym), 14
    background of, 13
    paternal identity construction and,
        15–16, 106–19
    pets as interactional resource and,
        64–67
    television viewing and, 294–95
Bradley, Susan (pseudonym), 13, 106–
    19
Brady Bunch, The (television series),
    130n.5
breadwinner role, 8, 16, 123–63, 196
Bredmar, Margareta, 146
Brody, Jill, 54n.4

complaints, buffering of, 64–66, 67
complimenting rituals, 200
compromise, 42
concern, expression of, 107–12, 119
conflict, 29, 65
    homecomings and, 36
    parent-child, 105, 108
    pets as deflection resource, 51, 57,
        66–67
    work-family, 116, 137–43
connection, 5–6, 14–15, 17, 27–48,
        190
    and control, 5, 6, 15, 17, 28, 38, 40,
        41–42, 46, 105–6, 115, 174, 180,
        190
    detail sharing/solicitation and, 78
    direction giving and, 34–36
    fathers and, 106–20, 198
    homecomings and, 36–40
    multidimensional model of, 30–31
    Tannen's concept of, 105, 174, 180
    "telling your day" ritual and, 32–34,
        78
    unidimensional view of, 29–30
connection-control grid, 174
connection maneuvers. See power and
    connection maneuvers
Connell, R. W., 237
constructed dialogue, 86, 90–91, 118,
        142, 150
    assessment and, 80
    identity construction and, 73, 240
    mother-daughter relationship and,
        239
    pets and, 52
    political identity construction and,
        236, 243, 249, 257, 258, 260
    workplace social talk and, 196, 201,
        211–12, 222–23
constructivism, 7, 71–72, 73, 98, 239,
        240
consumer gatekeeping, 169–70, 188,
        191
context, 127, 265, 278
contextualization cues, 50, 168

control, 17, 28, 38, 190
    and connection, 5, 6, 15, 17, 28, 38,
        40, 41–42, 46, 105–6, 115, 174,
        180, 190
    fathers and, 6, 106–20
    Tannen's concept of, 105, 174, 180
control acts, 32
control maneuvers, 29, 40 (see also
        power and connection
        maneuvers)
conversational involvement, 91, 208
conversational rituals, 214
conversational style, place and, 264
Cook-Gumperz, Jenny, 168
Coontz, Stephanie, 7, 123, 130
cooperative overlap, 207
co-parenting. See egalitarian co-
        parenting
Cosby Show, The (television series),
        130n.5
Coulthard, Malcolm, 113
Coupland, Justine, 199
criticism, 40
    buffering of, 51, 57, 58–59, 63–64, 67
Crossroads (soap opera), 289
Crosstalk (film), 167–68
"crying literal meaning," 35
cult of domesticity, 228
cultural geography. See humanistic
        geography
cultural knowledge, 289
cultural reproduction, 258
culture
    socialization and, 8, 236–37, 238
    speaking through intermediaries
        and, 55–57

daily routines, gatekeeping and, 183–
        85
Damaso, John, 235n.3
Dambrot, Faye H., 130n.5
daughters
    fathers and, 104–20
    mothers and, 34n.5, 73–74, 78, 79,
        86, 87–88, 97, 239, 241

Davies, Bronwyn, 5, 76, 125, 126, 127n.3, 197, 198, 201
daycare, 155, 186, 189
De Beauvoir, Simone, 128
decision makers, gatekeeping and, 17, 165–93
deictic terms, 264, 272
Democratic Party, family identification with, 18, 234, 235, 236, 243, 247, 250, 253, 254–55, 292
de Geer, Boel, 8, 236
de Saint-Georges, Ingrid, 265
detail sharing/solicitation
  fathers and, 107, 116–18, 119
  mothers and, 77–79, 81, 84, 85–88, 97, 98–99, 105
dialogicality, 8, 19, 283–84, 287, 290, 291
dialogic interaction, television viewing and, 8, 18–19, 283–309
dialogic unity, 19, 284, 295, 298, 300, 306
Diane Rehm Show, The (radio program), 10
dinner. *See* mealtime interactions
Dinner Talk (Blum-Kulka), 29n.2
direct imperatives, 114
direction giving, 34–36
directives, giving of, 107, 112–15, 116, 118, 119, 236
direct reported speech. *See* constructed dialogue
discourse analysis, 4, 5, 6, 7, 124n.2, 227
"Discourse and the Novel" (Bakhtin), 54
discourse planes, 96
discourses
  and discourse, 124n.2
  on fatherhood, 124, 131
  identities and, 125–28, 196
  of parenting, 17, 124, 129, 131, 138, 142

of work and family, 125, 132, 135–36, 138, 143, 144–45, 148, 151, 153, 154–55, 157, 165, 188
  See also family discourse; feminism
discourse strategies, 5
  as ambiguous and polysemous, 50n.2, 180
  baby-talk register and, 51, 53–54, 57, 58–59, 60, 63
  family interaction and, 28, 34
  gendered identity construction and, 7, 240, 242, 258, 259, 260
  gendered parental identity and, 7, 15–16, 73
  ventriloquizing and, 15, 40, 50, 52–64, 91
  workplace social talk and, 198, 201–2
discrimination, 167–68, 170, 174
discursive strategies. *See* discourse strategies
distance, 30, 174
  referring terms and, 235, 243, 244
division of labor, 129–30, 145, 172
dogs. *See* pets
domesticity, cult of, 228
domestic work, 129-30, 133, 134, 169, 172 (*see also* caregiving)
Donna Reed Show, The (television series), 130n.5
Douglas, Susan J., 155
Downs, Barbara, 155
Drew, Paul, 7
dual-income families
  gendered identities and, 4, 7, 16–17, 123–63
  housework and, 129–30, 133, 134, 169, 172

Echols, Alice, 129
Edley, Nigel, 131–32, 133
egalitarian co-parenting, 129–33, 138–43, 208–9, 227
  gatekeeping and, 17, 165–66, 175–78, 188, 189–90

egalitarian frames, 112
egalitarianism
    childcare and, 124, 129–33, 138–43,
        165, 175–78, 188, 189–90, 208–9,
        227
    dual-income families and, 16, 138–
        54
    family, 174
    multidimensional model of, 30
    parent-child, 105, 106, 108
elections. *See* political identity
Ellis, John, 289
Ellis, Yvette, 248, 289
Emerson, Caryl, 54
emotive rejection, 244
employment. *See* work/workplace
environmentalism, 243
environmental psychology, 267
equality. *See* egalitarianism
Erickson, Frederick, 4, 5, 167, 168, 170,
    174–75, 240, 259, 265
Ervin-Tripp, Susan, 5, 32, 33, 113
esteem, 32
ethnicity, 167
ethnography of communication, 5,
    264
evaluative loading, 248
Evans, Carol, 155–56

Fabian, Abbe K., 267, 270
Fairclough, Norman, 126
familiarity, 31–32
families
    beliefs and values of, 4–5, 8, 17–19,
        236, 237, 242, 250, 252, 253, 254
    budgets and, 186–88, 189
    cohesive devices for, 243, 255–57
    dinner time and. *See* mealtime
        interactions
    dual-income, 4, 7, 16–17, 123–63,
        169
    gatekeeping in, 17, 165–93
    identity construction in, 239–42
    naturally occurring interactions in,
        3, 4, 104

pets and, 15, 49–69
political identity and, 8, 18, 233–62
power/connection maneuvers in,
    14–15, 27–48
socialization in, 236–39, 258
television viewing and, 283–309
traditional, 130
work and, 6–8, 16–17, 123–63, 208
workplace social talk about, 196–
    229
See also children; egalitarian co-
    parenting; fathers; mothers
family discourse
    dynamics of, 4, 14–15, 20
    and family values/beliefs, 8, 17–19
    framing and, 5, 6, 14, 20, 105–6
    maternal identity construction and,
        80–99, 103, 105, 106
    paternal identity construction and,
        104–20
    pets as interactional resource in, 15,
        49–69
    public and private in, 285, 287, 291–
        307
    socialization and, 239
    television viewing and, 283, 284,
        287, 288–89, 290–91
    themes of, 4–8
family identity, 4, 6, 8, 18–19
    pets and, 15, 51, 57, 61, 67, 68
    place and, 18, 263, 275, 279
    politics and, 18, 233–62
familylect, 36, 182n.2
family myths, 190
familyness, 20, 241–42
family stories, 241–42
family therapy, 29
Family Ties (television series), 130n.5
family values, 4–5, 8, 17–19, 236, 237,
    242, 250
Fasulo, Alessandra, 4, 8, 27, 233, 236,
    237, 238, 258
Father Knows Best (television series),
    130
"father knows best" dynamic, 33, 34, 78

Han, Wenjui, 157
Hanks, William F., 127
Happy Days (television series), 130n.5
Harré, Rom, 5, 76, 125, 126, 127n.3, 197, 198, 201
Hasselbach, Ingo, 126
Haviland, John, 55
Hawkins, Alan J., 169, 172–73, 179, 189
Hays, Sharon, 124, 134, 135
Henwood, Karen L., 34n.5, 78, 79
Heritage, John, 7
hidden dialogue, 54
hierarchy, 28–31, 46, 105
  family identity construction and, 240
  family members' places in, 33, 35–36
  gatekeeping and, 166–67, 174, 175
  inequality and, 174
  multidimensional model of, 30
  socialization and, 236
  workplace social talk and, 200, 201, 215
high pitch, 274
Himsel, Amy J., 130
hints, as directives, 113
Hirsh-Pasek, Kathy, 57
Hobson, Dorothy, 287, 289
Hochschild, Arlie, 129, 169, 186, 190, 195
Hoffman, Charles D., 173, 189
Holmes, Janet, 199, 214
Holquist, Michael, 54, 286–87
Holt, Elizabeth, 79, 80, 98
home, place and, 275–76, 279
homecomings, 36–40
household budgets, 182, 186–88, 189
household gatekeepers, 170
housework, 129-30, 133, 134, 169, 172
  (*see also* caregiving)
"how was your day" routine, 34n.5 (*see also* "telling your day" ritual)
humanistic geography, 18, 265–66
humor, 257
  pets as interactional source of, 15, 51, 57–63, 65, 67

workplace social talk about, 205–6, 217, 218
  See also laughter
hybrid construction, 295
Hymes, Dell, 5, 264

Ichilov, Orit, 238
ideational structure, 96
identity
  as "child," 74, 241
  construction of, 4, 71–101, 103–20, 234, 239–42
  discourses and, 125–28, 196
  as "father," 6, 14–17, 103–20, 124, 196, 197, 202–3, 208, 214, 221–27
  language and, 75–76
  moral, 126
  as "mother," 5, 6, 7, 14–16, 71–101, 103, 105, 106, 124, 172, 195, 239, 241
  narratives and, 71–72, 73, 74, 96–97, 99, 103, 239, 240, 258
  place and, 279
  political, 8, 18, 233–62
  positioning and, 125–26, 153–54
  sociocultural knowledge and, 75–79, 83, 106
  women and, 7, 14, 16, 72, 124, 144–45, 148–49, 158, 195
  work-related, 16, 124, 125, 144–45, 148–49, 154, 156
  See also family identity; gendered identity; social identity construction
identity displays, 73
ideological becoming, 126, 157–58
ideological dilemmas, 126, 128
ideology,
  of egalitarian role-sharing, 16, 129, 139, 140, 144, 158, 227
  gender and, 84, 172, 173
  of intensive mothering, 124, 134–35, 153
  language, 285
  of the workplace, 135

identity and, 75–76
institutional, 7
narrative, 71–72, 73, 74
phonology and, 267
place and, 18, 264–68, 278
See also sociolinguistics
"Language and the Making of Place"
(Tuan), 265–66
laughter, 90, 208, 212, 274
political identity construction and,
236, 243, 248, 257, 258, 260
See also humor
Lazar, Michelle M., 16, 132, 133
Learning Channel, The, 301
Leave It to Beaver (television series),
130
Leichter, Hope, 288, 289
LeVine, Philip, 10, 13, 14, 34, 202
place's role, 8, 18, 263–81
Levinson, Steven C., 75, 91–92
Lewin, Kurt, 169–70, 174, 188, 191
Liebes, Tamar, 8, 233, 237, 238, 258–59
Linde, Charlotte, 268
Linell, Per, 146
linguistic anthropology, 5, 8, 27, 175,
266–67
linguistics. *See* language;
sociolinguistics
list structure, 274
locational formulations, 268
Lull, James, 288
Lundberg, Shelly, 156
Lyman, Stanford M., 77

Maccoby, Eleanor, 288
Maddock, Su, 195
main involvement, 288, 292–93
Malcuzynski, M.-Pierette, 54
manager-helper relationship, 173,
178–86, 189
Marinova, Diana, 6, 13, 15–16, 103–20
Marsh, Nora (pseudonym), 14
background of, 13
connection/control and, 106, 112,
118

pets as interactional resources and,
15, 64–67
television viewing and, 294–95
Marshall, Jill, 287
masculinity types, 132
Mason, Sylvia, 82
matching stories, 201, 203, 206–7, 214,
217, 221–22
maternal moderation behaviors, 170,
171, 172, 189
maternity leave, 155
McElhinny, Bonnie S., 7
MDA. *See* Mediated Discourse
Analysis
Mead, Margaret, 179
mealtime interactions, 4
child socialization and, 8, 105–6,
233, 236–37
family identity construction and,
103, 240, 259
"father knows best" dynamic and, 78
problem-solving and, 237
mediated action, 50, 288
mediated discourse, 53
Mediated Discourse Analysis, 288
mediational means, 50, 288
Meinhof, Ulrike H., 289
men
details and, 77–78, 84
"how was your day" routine and,
34n.5 (*see also* "telling your day"
ritual)
identity and, 7, 14
masculinity types and, 132
sociocultural expectations for, 7, 228
workplace social talk and, 200, 201
See also fathers; gendered identity
Messaris, Paul, 288
metamessages, 6, 35, 59
Mexico, 55
Millar, Frank E., 29
Miller, Mark Crispin, 252n.4
Miller, Peggy J., 250
Millett, Kate, 128
Mintz, Judith, 250

misbehaving children, 77, 81–98
  accounting for, 85, 95–96, 97, 105
Mitchell, Robert W., 57
Mizera, Luule, 8, 236
"mommy" wage gap, 156
Moon, Michelle, 173, 189
mothers, 4
  anxiety and, 299–300
  authority and, 9
  blame issues and, 77, 83, 96, 97, 175
  breadwinner role and, 8, 16, 134,
    135, 145, 151, 154
  caregiving and, 8, 17, 124–25, 129–
    31, 133, 135, 136, 138–43, 154,
    155, 165–66, 169–73, 179–86,
    188–90, 197, 287
  cult of domesticity and, 228
  daughters and, 34n.5, 73–74, 78, 79,
    86, 87–88, 97, 239, 241
  details and, 77–79, 81, 84, 85–88, 97,
    98–99, 105
  in family hierarchy, 33, 34
  as gatekeepers, 17, 165, 166, 169–73,
    179–86, 188–90
  Generation X cohort of, 155–56
  guilt and, 97
  homecomings and, 36–40
  identity as, 5, 6, 7, 14–16, 71–101,
    103, 105, 106, 124, 172, 195, 239,
    241
  "intensive," 124, 125, 134–35, 136,
    138, 142, 143, 148, 153, 154
  lifetime earnings and, 156
  outside employment and, 7, 16–17,
    123–63
  as parenting experts, 39, 179, 295–98
  part-time employment and, 155,
    156–57
  power/connection maneuvers and,
    5, 31–36
  professional identity and, 16, 124,
    125, 144–45, 148–49, 154, 156
  role sharing by, 125, 129, 134, 135–
    36, 140–44
  self-portraits of, 71, 98, 103, 239

sociocultural expectations for, 72,
    76–79, 96, 97, 98, 228
  "stay-at-home," 155, 156
  television viewing by, 287, 295–98
  "telling your day" ritual and, 32–34,
    78, 87–88, 247
  workplace social talk and, 196, 200–
    201, 227, 228
motivated action, 265
mutual self-disclosure, 197, 200

narratives
  gatekeeping and, 168
  identity construction and, 71–72,
    73, 74, 96–97, 99, 103, 239, 240,
    258
  place and, 264, 266
  political identity construction and,
    236, 243, 250, 260
  problem-solving and, 237
  social behavior regulation and, 266
  socialization and, 8, 236, 237, 239,
    241–42
  story contributors/elicitors and, 240
  story lines and, 127n.3, 198
  story worlds and, 72, 73, 74, 75, 96–
    97, 99, 239
  "telling your day" ritual and, 32–34,
    78
Neeley-Mason, Janet (pseudonym), 13
  background of, 11–12
  maternal identity construction and,
    15, 72–73, 80–97
  parental anxiety and, 299, 300
  power/connection maneuvers and,
    14, 34–36, 46
  television viewing and, 299, 300–305
  work-family issues and, 16, 124,
    137, 140–44, 148–53, 157
Neeley-Mason, Natalie (pseudonym),
    34, 137, 142–43
  background of, 11–12
  maternal identity construction and,
    72, 81–97
  television viewing and, 300–303

Neeley-Mason, Steve (pseudonym),
    13, 300
  background of, 11–12
  power/connection maneuvers and,
    14, 34–36, 46
  wife's identity construction and, 72,
    80–96
  work-family issues and, 137, 140–
    43, 148–53
"Neglected Situation, The" (Goffman),
    266
neighborhoods, 270–72, 275–76, 278
"new man," 132, 133
New Our Bodies, Ourselves, The
    (Boston Women's Health Book
    Collective), 79
New York Times, 252n.4
New York Times Magazine, 155
Nielsen, Mark R., 7, 123
Niemi, Richard G., 237
Nilholm, Claes, 72, 74, 98, 234, 235, 241
nondeferent orders, 32
nonverbal third parties, 50, 52–55, 58–
    64 (see also ventriloquizing)
Norris, Sigrid, 14
nutrition. See food and nutrition

O'Connor, Mary Catherine, 5, 32, 33
Ochs, Elinor, 4, 5, 179–80, 241
  children's language acquisition, 8, 27
  family narrative practices, 32-34, 87-
    88, 103-104, 240, 247, 259
  "father knows best" dynamic, 33, 34,
    78
  identity construction, 5, 7, 71, 72, 74–
    76, 78, 80, 98, 103, 104, 105, 106,
    127, 239, 240, 241, 242, 250, 259
  indexing, 127
  "parental panopticon"/
    "panopticon-like role," 88–89, 95,
    97
  shared family beliefs, 233, 241-242,
    250, 252
  socialization practices, 4, 8, 27, 179–
    80, 233, 236, 237, 238, 253, 258

"telling your day" ritual, 32–33,
    34n.5, 87–88, 103, 247
oppositional rituals, 200
other-presentation, 250–51
overlapping talk, 207, 208, 211, 274

Papua New Guinea, 267
paralinguistic features, 38–39
parallelism, 214, 219
Paranoid Parenting (Furedi), 299–300
parental panopticon, 89, 95, 97
Parentcenter.com, 131
parents
  anxiety and, 299–300
  gatekeeping and, 165, 169, 185, 190,
    191
  legal responsibilities of, 77
  place-related talk and, 264, 266–67,
    268–79
  political socialization and, 233–38,
    243–60
  sociocultural expectations for, 72,
    76–79, 96, 97, 98, 228
  work interpenetration and, 215–20,
    226, 229
  See also fathers; mothers
Parkin, Di, 195
participation frameworks, 96
passive double-voiced discourse, 294
paternity leave, 155
Patterson, Susan, 131, 133
Paugh, Amy L., 4, 8
performative theory of gender, 126
person-environment dissonance, 267
Peterson, Kathy (pseudonym), 12, 13–
    14
  gatekeeping and, 17, 165–66, 175–91
  parental anxiety and, 299, 300
  power/connection maneuvers and,
    14, 36–45, 46
  television viewing and, 298–99
  ventriloquizing and, 52–53
  work-family issues and, 16, 124,
    136–40, 143, 144–48, 153, 154,
    157–58

"self," 286, 293, 298
self-identity, 74, 267
self-interested gain, 135
self-portraits (mothers/women), 71,
    98, 103, 239
self-presentation, 250–51
sense of place, 18, 265, 275
sequencing, 155, 156
setting, 264
"sex-class linked" language, 76, 90, 95,
    127, 197
    maternal identity construction and,
        15, 78, 79, 81, 83, 84, 86, 88
    workplace social talk and, 196, 197,
        217
Shaffer, Margaret A., 140
shared identities. *See* family identity
Shepherd, Clara (pseudonym), 14
    background of, 12–13
    husband's workplace social talk and,
        202, 205, 206, 208, 214–26
    parental anxiety and, 299, 300
    pets as interactional resource and,
        15, 58–64, 66
    place-related talk and, 268, 272–74,
        278, 279
    political identity construction and,
        18, 234, 242–58
    television viewing and, 292–93, 295–
        98, 299
Shultz, Jeffrey, 167, 168, 174–75
siblings, 33
Sime, J. D., 265
Sinclair, John, 113
Singapore, 132–33
Sliding Doors (film), 294
small talk. *See* social talk
Smith, Jonathan, 289
Smith, Kristin, 155
Smith, Ruth, 4, 27, 233, 237, 238, 241–
    42, 250, 253, 258
soap operas, 289
sociability, 17, 197, 202–14, 225–26,
    227
sociability frames, 16, 105–6

social action, 265
social acts
    assessment and, 79–80
    maternal identity construction and,
        72–73, 97–99, 105
    paternal identity construction and,
        104, 107, 119
    as "sex-class linked" behavior, 78, 88
social identity construction, 7, 71–76,
    80, 96, 98, 153, 239–41
socialization
    children and, 8, 29n.2, 103–4, 105–
        6, 233, 236–37, 241–42, 258
    families and, 236–39, 258
    family values and, 8, 236, 237, 242
    politics and, 18, 233–39, 243–60
    television and, 8, 238
socializing frames, 104, 105–6, 107–8,
    115, 117, 119
social mirror, 284, 286–87, 293, 300,
    306
social psychology, 17, 165, 166, 169–
    73, 189
social talk, workplace and, 8, 17, 19,
    195–230
    constructed dialogue in, 196, 201,
        211–12, 222–23
    father's, 8, 17, 19, 195–230
    about family, 196–229
    footing in, 197, 198, 201, 204
    framing and, 197, 204
    generalized, 196, 197, 201, 214, 224,
        226
    hierarchy in, 199, 200, 201, 215
    about humor, 205–6, 217, 218
    individualized/personalized, 196,
        201, 204, 205, 211, 213–14, 226,
        227
    mothers and, 196, 200–201, 227, 228
    positioning, and, 197, 198, 201, 203,
        205, 206, 210, 211, 214, 215, 216,
        217, 220, 221, 225, 227
    rapport and, 197, 200, 201, 205, 206,
        216, 217
    "sex-class linked," 196, 197, 217

solidarity and, 199–204, 206–8, 211, 212, 225
sociocultural expectations
for fathers, 228
gender-based, 7, 76–79, 127
for mothers, 72, 76–79, 96, 97, 98, 228
sociocultural knowledge, 75–79, 83, 106
sociolinguistics, 7, 8, 9, 27, 167, 264–68
gatekeeping studies and, 17, 165, 166–69, 174, 190–91
identity and, 73, 75, 98–99, 103
interactional, 5, 6, 165, 166–69, 174, 190–91, 264, 265
place and, 18, 264–68, 278
variationist, 266
solidarity, 4, 5–6, 14–15, 174
ambiguity and polysemy of, 5, 14, 28–32, 34, 36–40, 46–47
arguments and, 41–45
mother-daughter, 73
multidimensional model of, 30–31
paternal identity construction and, 15–16
pets' role in establishing, 63, 67
and power, 4, 5, 14, 15, 27n.1, 28–31, 38, 46–47, 174
workplace social talk and, 199–204, 206–8, 211, 212, 225
solidarity maneuvers. See power and connection maneuvers
"speaking for another" strategy, 53
"speaking through intermediaries" strategy, 55–57
speech acts, 73, 240
Stacey, Barrie, 238
stance, 5, 60, 81–82, 127
affective, 72, 73, 93, 99, 105
gendered/"sex-class linked," 95, 97
identity construction and, 72, 73, 74–76, 239, 241
maternal, 96, 98–99, 105
parental, 90, 95, 97, 104, 107, 116, 119

political identity construction and, 250, 253, 258
status, 29, 30, 34, 200
stay-at-home mothers, 155, 156
Stearns, Peter N., 299, 300
Steinem, Gloria, 128
Steiner, Gary, 288
story contributors, 240
story elicitors, 240
story lines, 127n.3, 198
storytelling. See narratives
story worlds, 72, 73, 74, 75, 96–97, 99, 239
Streeck, Jürgen, 265
stress, 36
Stubbe, Maria, 199
Sunderland, Jane, 16, 130–31, 133, 134, 221, 226
Supreme Court, U.S., 234n.2
Sylvan, Jason (pseudonym), 292
background of, 12–13
father's workplace social talk and, 202, 203, 205, 206, 207, 208, 210, 211–19, 222–26
pets as interactional resource and, 58–61
place-related talk and, 268–79
political identity construction and, 18, 234, 235, 242, 244–58
television viewing and, 295–98, 299
Sylvan, Neil (pseudonym), 14
background of, 12–13
pets as interactional resource and, 15, 58, 61, 63–64
place-related talk and, 268–72, 276–79
political identity construction and, 18, 234–35, 242–58
television viewing and, 292–93, 295–98
workplace social talk and, 17, 197–98, 202–28
symmetrical rituals, 197, 200
sympathy, 80, 98
syntax, 73, 240

Waite, Linda J., 7, 123
Waldfogel, Jane, 156, 157
Waletzky, Joshua, 149
Wallat, Cynthia, 5, 28, 63
Wansink, Brian, 169–70
Wardhaugh, Ronald, 212
warnings, issuing of, 107, 115–16, 118, 119
Watts, Richard J., 5, 28
Weiner, James F., 267
Werndly, Angela, 287
Wertsch, James V., 50, 288
West, Candace, 7,
Wetherell, Margaret, 131–32, 133
Who Wants to Marry a Multimillionaire? (television series), 291
Whyte, Jean, 237
Williams, Joan, 128–29, 155, 156, 157, 228
Wills, Dorothy David, 66
Woollett, Anne, 129
women
   authority and, 9
   cult of domesticity and, 228
   details and, 77–79, 81, 84, 85–88, 97, 98–99, 105
   friendships and, 33
   housework and, 129–30, 133, 169
   "how was your day" routine and, 34n.5 (*see also* "telling your day" ritual)

identity and, 7, 14, 16, 72, 124, 144–45, 148–49, 158, 195
   "mommy wage gap" and, 156
   self-portraits and, 71, 98, 103, 239
   sociocultural expectations for, 7, 72, 76–79, 96, 97, 98, 228
   television viewing by, 287, 289
   troubles talk and, 203
   in workforce, 7, 16–17, 123–63, 195
   workplace social talk and, 196, 200–201, 227, 228
   See also mothers
women's movement. *See* feminism
Work and Family Project, overview of, 9–14
work/workplace
   egalitarian vs. traditional views of, 130–34, 143, 144–55
   family and, 6–8, 16–17, 123–63, 208
   father's social talk at, 8, 17, 19, 195–230
   parenting interpenetration with, 215–20, 226, 229
   part-time, 155, 156–57
   sequencing, 155, 156
Wortham, Stanton, 74

You Just Don't Understand (Tannen), 34n.5

zero pronouns, 74